L. Rev.
The Law Review Experience in American Legal Education:
A Personal Memoir

L. Rev.
The Law Review Experience in American Legal Education:
A Personal Memoir

By
Roy S. Gutterman

Academica Press, LLC
Bethesda

Library of Congress Cataloging-in-Publication Data

Gutterman, Roy S.
    L. rev. : the law review experience in American legal education : a
personal memoir / Roy S. Gutterman.
    p. cm.
    Includes bibliographical references and index.
    ISBN 1-930901-52-6
    1. Gutterman, Roy S. 2. Periodical editors—Untied States—
Biography. 3. Syracuse law review. I. Title: Law review experience in
American legal education. II. Title

PN4874.G88 A3 2002
070,5'1—dc21

20020908851

Editorial Inquiries:
Academica Press, LLC
7831 Woodmont Avenue, #381
Bethesda, MD 20814
Website: www.academicapress.com
To order: (202) 388-1800

Dedication

To Bob and Karen.

Table of Contents

Acknowledgements

This book just sort of happened. I did not join the Syracuse Law Review with the goal of writing a book. I did not seek the position of Editor-in-Chief to write a book. This started as a sporadic journal and a mechanism to help me plan for and cope with a torrent of difficult challenges and conflicts facing me as editor.

Upon graduation, a slight sabbatical from the working world gave me the time to collect my thoughts, reflect on my experiences and put it all in writing.

I owe a debt of gratitude to my fellow members of the Syracuse Law Review, who bestowed the honor of editor to me for Volume 50.

I wish to thank two wonderful friends and former journalism professors from the S.I. Newhouse School of Public Communications at Syracuse University: Lynne Flocke, who offered motivation, insight and criticism during the early drafts; and Joel Kaplan, who advised and counseled me on the writing and publishing process.

I wish to thank Dr. Robert West and his staff at Academica Press and Ginger McNally for their keen editing and wise decision to publish this book.

I also wish to thank several friends who provided insight, advice, commentary and support during various stages of this process: Ian Davies, Rachel Kaufman; Michael T. Maroney; Stephen J. Jones; and Sara N. Scheideman.

Finally, my parents, Robert and Karen Gutterman who supported me in every way possible.

L. Rev.

The sun cast a shadow over the piles of papers, books and Coke cans on my desk as it gently slid behind the now-verdant Onondaga Hills. This was a familiar scene from my cluttered desk in my private corner office in Winifred MacNaughton Hall—that is when the sun was actually visible; after all this was Syracuse, New York. For some odd reason, the sun frequently appeared through the gray clouds as the daylight dwindled. As it reappeared just in time to set, it almost seemed to be a few miles away from my westward window.

The picturesque vista, coupled with the silence of an empty office at the end of the day made for a tranquil setting, which was a polar opposite to the days in the office.

The year had just about wound down and now I was catching up for my last batch of finals. The chaos of the spring semester had caught up with me. After my second semester at the helm of the Syracuse Law Review, I had to make up for lost time and learn a semester's worth material for three classes in about 10 days—Securities Regulation, Estates, Decedents and Trusts and Federal Income Tax. I had all of my pass-fail credits saved up. I planned to apply enough of the seven credits to two of the classes, it was just a matter of which two.

Classes ended a few days earlier but the law review office hours continued during the pre-exam reading period. We needed to utilize as much of the human capital as possible in the waning days. We still had several articles that needed serious editing. There were two entire articles and 10 percent of a third outstanding—our "dedicated" authors failed to meet their deadlines—two of them by about five months, the other by nine months. One of our delinquent authors, the one who was nine months overdue, was kind enough to submit two partial drafts. By finals I was only waiting on 10 percent of that article.

I had holed myself up in my office all day. With my door to the outer office partially ajar, I spent a portion of my day fielding and answering questions from the staff, which was a non-stop daily occurrence. Several of the senior editors were already gone. Some were exiled elsewhere preparing for their last finals. Some were just never there all year and certainly would not appear to chip in to the effort now that finals were imminent.

My tax materials were strewn across piles of files, partially-edited articles and a colorful array of yellow and pink Post-its with various notes, addresses, messages and reminders.

The pile was high with my casebook, the rules supplement, my outline, my friend's master outline and two hornbooks, which I hoped would provide me with the requisite knowledge because I was gambling on tax. This was the class I would take for a grade this semester. I hedged my bets because the professor proclaimed that he would institute a B+ curve for this class because he liked us so much. Most upper class professors grade on a C and B curves, depending on the professor's disposition.

Tax was an urgent issue in my life right now, and I intended to make the most of my moment of solitude. I was wrestling with what seemed like the arduous task of determining how to calculate the capital gains tax along with a gross income problem. Then the telephone broke the silence. The phone was always ringing at inopportune moments, usually when I was busy or otherwise occupied. I gave my usual business-like greeting—"Syracuse Law Review," this slightly more welcoming than the way I answered my phone at the old newspaper, a curt "Gutterman," which was once described to me as an uninviting bark.

The caller was one of our authors, Professor Harrison, calling to find out about the status of our first book, Syracuse Law Review 50:1. She was curious about when she would receive her precious article reprints. In the past week, the other two authors in our first book had made similar inquiries. I was lucky to dodge their calls and reply with messages to their respective voice mails. But Professor Harrison was lucky, I was in the office studying.

"Hi. How are you? This is Professor Harrison, I wanted to know what the status of the book is?" she said.

"We just received our first box of books three days ago. You should be receiving your reprints any day now," I told her.

"When do you think I'll be getting my reprints?"

"Soon. They're mailed from the printer in Nebraska."

"How are things going?"

"We're behind schedule and finals start in a few days and I don't know a damn thing about my three classes. At least I know what I'll be doing after the bar exam."

"What happened? When we first signed the contract in the fall you said you wanted to get the book to the printer in October and now we're just getting it back. That's pretty late, what happened?"

"Chaos, that's what happened. Pure, uncontrollable chaos. First, we had difficulty signing authors. Then, once we signed authors, one of our articles was absolutely nuts and needed extensive work because it cited the most obscure texts you could think of, like a Hungarian law treatise. Then, the article kept freezing our computers. Then, we lost a senior editor because I had to prosecute him for plagiarizing his note that was supposed to go in our first book. Then, we had a team fall behind and our computers did not always work. Now, it's finals time and the staff is evaporating while the work still exists. Plus, it's our fiftieth anniversary and we had all kinds of stuff to deal with there. That's just the executive summary. It was a crazy year."

"Oh my. I'm sorry that I asked. I'm sorry you had to go through all that. It sounds awful," she said.

"Well, I asked for it, nobody held a gun to my head," I replied.

I did ask for it. I took the affirmative steps to join the Syracuse Law Review. I took the affirmative steps to seek the position of Editor-in-Chief. I was encouraged by classmates and senior board editors on law review during my second year to run for the top position. But I was equally fueled by my own interest in writing and editing as well as my own ambition and desire to lead.

I had editorial and management experience that nobody else on law review had: several years as a reporter at a large daily newspaper and a few as an editor at my award-winning campus daily paper. I had subtly built up the confidence and support of classmates on law review and the senior editors for whom I worked as a 2L on staff. Unlike many of my classmates I enjoyed the work on law review: the fact-checking, cite-checking, editing, writing, and "Bluebooking," the painstaking rules of legal citation.

With the staff's support at election time, the desire to lead and a vision, I had a plan: publish interesting articles by solid law professors and lawyers; and publish them on time in our four issues, including the dense Survey of New York Law. Simple professionalism would get our books out well before graduation, I thought. The staff of 80 second and third-year law students could even have a little fun and bask in the celebration of the law review's 50th Anniversary.

I thought I knew what I was stepping into. Even if things got out of control, I thought my background, work ethic and common sense would be able to counter and overcome anything that came at me or the law review.

But could I live up to my own vision and ambition? Could I actually lead a group of the best students at this law school to publish the law review on time and do it professionally while having fun? Could I repair the morale without compromising the publication's integrity? Could I actually execute any of the elaborate and intricate plans ranging from intensive orientation to a gala banquet? Could the books get out before graduation? What would it all lead to, the perfect job after graduation?

This year would be the consummate test of my own mettle.

Just about a year earlier, during my second year, I was nominated, then elected for a job with responsibilities that would linger well past graduation and the bar exam.

After delivering a smooth, yet convincing election speech, and deftly handling 40 minutes of public questioning with confident and sometimes humorous responses, I was elected by an overwhelming majority of the law review staff. Then, my staff was elected. As I left the building that sunny Friday afternoon, an out-going senior editor approached me, saying, "You should go celebrate because you are now at the top. Now, you will have it all."

Those words reverberated in my head that night. Late that night, actually, early the next morning, at around 2 a.m., I was jarred awake by one of the worst stomachaches I ever experienced. It was a hard dull pain. It was not a burning or an outright stomach cramp. Just hard dull pain, like I ate a bag full of rusty nails embedded in a concrete matrix that stuck somewhere inside my belly without moving. I left the bed and just sat in a chair, staring into the darkness unable to focus on anything but the pain and the colossal job ahead of me. The pain subsided, along with the slight panic, as the sun rose. But the self-doubt and personal reassessment would frequently return. Then, the adrenaline pumped. I was in charge. The success or failure of the Syracuse Law Review rested on my shoulders.

This book is a memoir of my year as Editor-in-Chief of the Syracuse Law Review. This book chronicles the crazy year I experienced as a third-year law student as the publisher of a 1,300-page scholarly law journal. The events, conversations and characters are real. Most of the names and biographical data of the people depicted here have been changed or modified. No matter how strange these stories appear, they are accurate accounts of real conversations, real events and real personal dilemmas.

There are several well-known memoirs about law school life as well as the perpetual flood of "How-to-Succeed-In-Law-School" books. There have been movies and even a spin-off television series about the trials and tribulations of the law school experience. Many of these documentaries, set at the top law schools, touch on the law review experience.[1] As entertaining and idyllic as some of these documentaries are, the law review experience is treated peripherally, lost in a cacophony of discussions about first-year pressures, legal scholarship, law school politics and academic accolades exclusively bestowed upon students at only the very top law schools.

Law review editors are second and third year law students, charged with the honor and responsibility of selecting articles, editing them and publishing them with the goal of honing their legal research and writing skills while chronicling, critiquing and exploring legal issues. Law review articles are intended to educate, inform, prompt and influence readers: lawyers, law students, politicians and judges.

Despite the lofty and important goals and responsibilities held by law review editors, law review membership is shrouded in mystery. The mystique of law review is perpetuated by the absence of any honest, practical or reflective depiction of how a law review operates and the daily barrage of tensions, frustrations and impediments law review editors face.

Every year a steady stream of law review articles about legal education and law reviews flows into academia. These articles frequently discuss such topics as the most-cited law review articles, which law review is the most prestigious, the impact of specialized law reviews, the tensions between law professors and student editors or the abominable impact of footnotes on legal writing. To date, no legal scholarship comes close to addressing the grueling and often thankless job that thousands of law students perform every year.

Like the law itself, this book follows the precedent and models set by those documentaries from earlier years. But like any legitimate

---

[1] *See* SCOTT TUROW, ONE L 160-62, 210, 213, 218-19 (Warner Books 1977); CAMERON STRACHER, DOUBLE BILLING (1998); JOEL SELIGMAN, THE HIGH CITADEL: THE INFLUENCE OF HARVARD LAW SCHOOL 182-85 (1978); MARTIN MAYER, THE LAWYERS 110 (1967); RICHARD D. KAHLENBERG, BROKEN CONTRACT 45-46, 60-61 (1996); ELEANOR KERLOW, POISONED IVY: HOW EGOS, IDEOLOGY, AND POWER POLITICS ALMOST RUINED HARVARD LAW SCHOOL (1994).

application of the law, this book is clearly distinguishable from those earlier works for structural and topical reasons.

First, because this story is set in Syracuse, a solid, respectable law school, not a prestigious top-tier law school, this book should appeal to a broader audience. Second, the law review or law journal experience is one shared by students at law schools across the country. And, even though law review staff members compose a sliver of every law school class, membership has been expanded through writing competitions and specialized journals. Thus, the experiences and inquiries of a year on law review transcend the legal community. These experiences—glories and failures—are shared by law review members and editors at every law school, every day, since law reviews emerged as an integral part of the law school education in the late 1800s.[2] Because these experiences are universal in the world of law reviews, this book is titled by another widespread commonality shared by most law reviews: the *Bluebook: A Uniform System of Citation* abbreviation.[3] There are between 300 to 500 student-edited law reviews, journals and specialized publications, and the vast majority share the same *Bluebook* abbreviation: *L. Rev.*[4]

Practically every law student enters law school with the goal of "making law review," with little, if any, understanding or knowledge of the subsequent duties and responsibilities. Law review is an honor society, social club and legal publishing house wrapped into one entity. At practically every law school, members of a law review sit at the top of the class and earn their way on to the staff because of those grades earned during the first year of law school. The other members of the law review, the write-ons, make their way on through a writing competition.[5] The Syracuse Law Review, like the majority of the law reviews published, invites the members in the top 10 percent of the class at the end of the first year. The other members of the law review were the top

---

[2] Robert A. Emery, *The Albany Law School: the Only Surviving Copy*, 89 LAW LIBR. J. 463 (1997); Michael I. Swygert & Jon W. Bruce, *The Historical Origins, Founding, and Early Development of Student-Edited Law Reviews*, 36 HASTINGS L.J. 739 (1985).
[3] (THE) BLUEBOOK: A UNIFORM SYSTEM OF CITATION (17th ed. 1999)
[4] *Id.* (Periodicals, T.13); Michael L. Closen & Robert J. Dzielak, *The History and Influence of the Law Review Institution*, 30 AKRON L. REV. 15, 38 (1996).
[5] LAWRENCE M. FRIEDMAN, A HISTORY OF AMERICAN LAW 693 (2nd ed. 1985).

scorers in a closed-universe writing competition that takes place at the conclusion of the first year of law school.

Making law review is not easy. Top grades rarely come without hours and hours of studying while write-on competitions sometimes span a week, with candidates preparing a complicated research memo or essay and a detailed editing project.

The honor of making law review entitles a law school's allegedly elite students to perform detail-oriented fact and citation checking that could render even the most energetic student editor catatonic. Student editors choose the articles from piles of unsolicited submissions, then edit and check them for style, spelling and conformity with the rules of the *Bluebook.* The honor of making law review allows a student to smooth-out and proofread articles sometimes written with no apparent care for accuracy, spelling, grammar or style. The honor allows student editors to read pages upon pages of judicial opinions, news articles or other law review articles to make sure a footnote stands for the proposition the author says it does.

The honor of law review, for many, is also the key that opens doors to the best law firms, the most prestigious clerkships and a world of opportunity.[6] The legal community actively seeks out law review members because of the luster conferred by membership and the skills membership develops: strong legal writing; precise footnoting; management and negotiation skills; and an impressive sounding title for the law firm's bio or firm listing.

Inside the law school, law review members attain a degree of status. They are frequently recognized as the ones who will get the best jobs at the best places. Some professors single them out for the toughest questions in class. They are met with jealousy, contempt and a even subtle admiration for a devotion that generates hours of volunteer work each week, all that on top of class work and other commitments. At most law schools, administrators and alumni promote their law review editors to the legal community as the best and brightest their school has to offer.

Law review, as an institution is a huge part of legal education and law school culture. Yet, there is a noted void about what transpires once a student "makes law review" and how these vital institutions operate.[7]

---

[6] EDWARD LAZARUS, CLOSED CHAMBERS: THE RISE, FALL AND FUTURE OF THE MODERN SUPREME COURT 19 (1999).
[7] James W. Harper, *Why Student-Run Law Reviews?*, 82 MINN. L. REV. 1261, 1274-75 (1998); Jordan H. Leibman & James P. White, *How The Student-Edited*

The Law Review Experience in American Legal Education
A Personal Memoir

This book steps up to fill that void. This is *L. Rev.*

The Election Day Jag
Friday, March 26, 1999

My palms clammed up a little. My heart rate accelerated. Then the role took over. Today, for the first time in a couple of years, a ball bounced my way: I was elected Editor-in-Chief of the Syracuse Law Review. The election represented a tremendous honor. It was an accomplishment, a validation and a symbol of irony.

The competition was stiff. I had two opponents today. Competition was nearly a lot stiffer. A handful of worthy candidates declined their nominations over the past few weeks. One said she did not want the headaches. One said he did not want to waste his time. And, one other was bitter about his law school experience and just did not enjoy law review enough to get involved for his third year.

My name came up first on the nominations list early on in the two-week application period. People had been talking to me about running for editor as far back as the middle of the fall semester and for the last month; the campaign had reached somewhat of a fever pitch. I had a couple of friends assisting me as de facto campaign whips. My friend, Cody, had been talking me up around the law review and had introduced me to a third-year friend of his who could deliver a handful of votes from third-year law review members who were not involved in the operations. Hardly a day had gone by in the months leading up to this when someone did not mention the election to me. I felt as though I was setting myself up for another law school disappointment. I knew of at least two classmates who declined to run for a position for fear of coming up short.

The campaign had to have been subtle, yet decisive. I did not want to come off as too eager, but I also wanted the word to be out there. Before long, I started keeping track of possible votes, doing almost a daily straw poll with Cody and Sara, my girlfriend and fellow law review member. Both provided helpful advice and insightful feedback, and likely helped attract votes prior to the Election Day. Cody enjoyed the excitement and often raised the topic for discussion, even when I did not

---

Law Journals Make Their Publication Decisions, 39 J. LEGAL EDUC. 387 (1989).

want to talk about it. Sara, loyal, devoted and supportive, lent a voice of reason to my thinking.

But election day was the big day. The staff election was scheduled for 1 p.m. and was predicted to last several hours. Somehow I made it to my two classes today, but had difficulty paying attention. I also had difficulty falling asleep the night before. I was excited, nervous and pumped up. One friend, Edith, a 3L who sat next to me in labor law and who also worked at the Syracuse campus newspaper, *The Daily Orange*, years ago before I got there, was amazed that I could make it to class. She said, "If I were in your shoes, I'd go shopping. I could not make it to class."

It was exciting. I was on the cusp of one of those monumental, life altering events. If my fellow law review members, those with the best grades, had the confidence to elect me, the doors to the legal community shuttered by my first-semester grades would swing open. If it worked out, this election might salvage my law school education while giving me instant standing and status among my classmates. I would make my mark on the law school and the legal community. I would be able to lead a scholarly publication: write, edit, manage, publish; many of the reasons I left newspaper journalism for law school in the first place. If it worked out, I might also be able to exorcise the demons of coming up one vote short in a popularity contest for the top job at my college newspaper, a career and a lifetime ago.

I had a lot riding on this election, maybe too much. But I was ready. I decided a long time ago that if I wanted to win big, I had to be prepared to lose big. And, this was judgment day.

I wore one of my dark charcoal suits, a starched white shirt and one of my favorite bright red ties. I did not write a formal speech, but for weeks had been working on talking points and thoughts to describe myself and my ideas for running the law review. I spent the morning sipping warm water with a slice of lemon to counter the lingering effects of an old cold.

The meeting took place in one of the classrooms where the rows of seats were arranged in a semi-circle, in a pit-like amphitheater. There was pizza, soda and beer. I could not touch food, but did open a soda. My classmates devoured the pizza and beer.

The alphabetical order of the five-minute speeches fell in my favor. The other candidates were Willie, a mild-mannered, soft-spoken, almost timid guy who spoke first, followed by Donna, a beefy, gregarious woman.

Willie spoke from his prepared outline from far back behind the large control-panel table. His positioning put him far from the crowd and he appeared nervous and uncomfortable addressing the group. As he spoke of building a sense of community and inspiring the staff, his voice occasionally stuttered and cracked. He said that he had editorial and management experience because he had worked for a small start-up Internet company for two years.

Meanwhile, some people in the group were finishing their pizza. A few people even popped open sodas and beers in the middle of his speech, breaking his rhythm. It was somewhat rude, but he was not commanding the crowd. Sara later said, "A minute into his speech, I knew you would win."

Also from behind the table, Donna spoke about community and some of her credentials as a restaurant manager. Her speech was almost as bland as Willie's, but at least she was more vocal. She smiled a lot, too. Both got polite applause. But as they spoke, I just got more excited.

Finally, as Donna returned to her seat, my turn came. Before Kevin, the managing editor and master of ceremony, had fully introduced me, I was up, buttoning my suit jacket and walking down to the pit. I had already decided not to stand far back. Instead, I pulled a trick out of the Elizabeth Dole playbook and remained close to the group.

"I did not prepare a speech and my voice is still recovering from a month-long lingering cough, so I will stand here, rather than behind the table," I said.

"I would like to address two areas for you. First, I know many of you, but many of you I don't know, so I must tell you about my experience and myself. Second, I want to talk to you about my vision and goals for the law review.

"First, I stand before you today with more than a decade of experience in the editorial and publishing world. I graduated from Syracuse in 1993 and spent four years in various editorial capacities at the Daily Orange, where I was news editor and a member of the board of directors. I managed a staff of about 40 reporters, three assistant editors and engaged in long-range planning and inter-departmental coordination. At the DO, we broke some news, put out a daily newspaper and won some awards.

"After graduating in 1993, I went to work for the Cleveland Plain Dealer, the biggest newspaper in Ohio and at the time the 17th-largest paper in the country. It was a good job and I covered news, government, courts, crime and general assignments. I did a lot of investigatory work, used a lot of public records, court files and property records. I covered everything from politicians and government-types to a dog falling through the ice and drowning in Lake Erie.

"But I'd like to talk to you prospectively about some of my ideas and goals for the law review. First, I am disheartened that more of my classmates' names are not on this board. This publication is important to all of us and is a visible example of what we do here. This puts the Syracuse name out there more than anything else and is a reflection on all of the school and us. There is no reason why everyone cannot contribute and be part of this. And, there is no reason why everyone should not contribute to putting out a quality editorial and scholarly publication.

"This will begin by streamlining the F&A (Form and Accuracy) process. I think we learned a lot this week with the take home assignments. I believe this process must be more efficient and accountable. I would like to entertain changing the process to make each team member responsible for portions of articles, similar to the take home assignments—where the staff member is responsible for everything in that portion: form, accuracy, citations, Shepardizing, grammar and spelling. This will give people a clear idea of what is expected of them and encourage accountability and efficiency. And, if there is a problem, we can pinpoint it early."

As I spoke, I stood usually, with my right hand in my pocket and my left hand at my side or in the air. I delivered this speech without stammering and continually looked around the room. When I made a specific point directed toward someone, I glanced right into their eyes. Sometimes, a point would garner a nod of approval. I looked over to Sara a couple times. After more than a year and a half together, she knew many of the newspaper stories and all the bio-material and had heard all about my plans for the law review over the course of the past few months. Still, she smiled at me every time our eyes connected.

I continued, "This process will start on Day One with orientation. Our objectives, responsibilities and duties will be clearly described on our first meeting. Many of the problems we encountered this year developed because things got off slowly or people were not informed. If we start the process running, things will be smooth and efficient. And there is no reason why everyone on staff should not be proud of the product and enjoy the working experience.

"I would also like to expand our website. I would like to work with our computer editor and the school's computer tech people to put abstracts or briefs or synopses of our articles online as well as other information. The benefits of this are innumerable. We want to get the Syracuse name out there, and this is one of the best ways. More and more researchers are using the web. I think we could generate more citations and more interest in our product this way.

"Finally, I would like to meet with our library staff and workout some kind of arrangement or accounting system so no law review member has to take out dozens of books for our articles.

"I want everyone on staff to contribute and feel welcome to contribute. My overall goal is to put out a quality editorial product. That is a goal we should all share. Thank you."

As I concluded and returned to my seat, there was solid applause. I was in such a zone that I could not really gauge it, but it sounded pretty good.

Then, the mandated 30-minute question-and-answer period began. All three of us stood in the pit as our classmates and staff mates peppered us with questions including what other activities we planned for the upcoming year and how we would handle certain problems. Given my experience as an interviewer, I had anticipated some of these questions. I was prepared and the answers seemed to roll off naturally. Cody later told me my presence was "amazing, unflappable."

Dealing with difficult questions in a public setting was also nothing new for me or anybody else in the room. After all, many professors still employed the Socratic method of teaching law through questioning. Although I frequently handled professors' questions adeptly, there were really few consequences of a wrong answer in a classroom setting. The stakes seemed so much higher at today's venue, and I felt like I was working the crowd with direct, honest answers and bits of snappy, if not wry, humor.

When one 2L asked what other activities or responsibilities each of us had planned for the next year I answered, "Besides going to class, I will have nothing else to do. My plate is clear."

There were questions about handling sanctions, disciplining delinquent staff members, handling disputes between editors and dealing difficult authors and editing.   The managing editor began as a moderator, but for some questions I kind of took over acknowledging the questioners.

On a question about handling disputes with belligerent or uncooperative staff members, I answered, "If I may read between the lines of your question, I believe you are asking about professionalism. I am professional. I have professional experience and that's how I handle myself and I would expect the same from the rest of the staff."

A few questions followed up on points we each made during our respective speeches. Oddly, both Willie and Donna referred to and appropriated comments I made in my speech.

On a sanctions question, I answered: "I believe deadlines and office hours are vital and crucial. But also there is really only one deadline that matters. All the other deadlines are there to help the note writer. They are important, but people have other commitments, too—midterms, papers, other activities. And there should be flexibility along with professionalism. Memos and notice should be used. If people are persistent or delinquent they should be sanctioned. It's professional, and I think the staff is mature enough to realize that. But when it gets to sanctions they, too, should be treated professionally, not humiliated or berated. Professionalism is the key and people should respect that."

My best answer followed a long-intricate question by a senior board editor named Benedict. His question, more an exercise in hearing his own voice, involved my ability to "make tough decisions in the face of professors, judges, authors or lawyers who try to bully or intimidate you into doing something. Could you make a decision without being intimidated?"

Willie, with his soft-spoken delivery, said he would not be intimidated. Donna said she has no problems making tough or unpopular decisions.

Then, I answered, "I have no problem making tough decisions. I've done it before and do not shy away from it. And, as far as being intimidated, someone once threatened to shoot me for a story I wrote, so I'm not too worried about a lawyer or author trying to intimidate me."

The answer, delivered with my usual deadpan tone, generated loud laughter and a smattering of applause. He inadvertently lobbed up softball, and I hit it out of the ballpark.

By the time the 30 minutes expired, I felt wiped out. I was sweating, but they could not see me sweat. It was a performance, almost like a politician. I had to answer tough questions directly but not in a way that would alienate anyone. No lies, no hesitation; smooth but not slick. For the first time in my life, I truly appreciated the thrill that attracts people to politics and public speaking. It was tremendously exciting. But did they feel the same way about me?

The three of us exited the room and waited outside in the hallway as the nearly 80 staff members—classmates—deliberated before determining the fate of the law review for the year. After about three long minutes, Kevin, the managing editor, came out to inform Donna that she had the lowest number of votes. The run off was between Willie and me. The bylaws mandated whittling down the competition to two candidates regardless of the first round tally.

A minute later Kevin came out, extended his hand and said, "Congratulations Roy. You are the next Editor-in-Chief of the Syracuse Law Review."

He escorted us into the room again. This time there was rousing applause and handshakes. It was an awe-inspiring moment of adulation, or as close to adulation as you can get in law school. Some people stood up to shake my hand as I strolled down to my seat in the second row. I also applauded back. I did not know what else to do. This was the culmination of my first successful campaign. This was also the beginning of the exciting adventure of publishing the Syracuse Law Review.

I returned to my seat, next to Sara. I felt like everyone was watching us. They were. She grinned at me. As I leaned over to kiss her, she stuck out her hand and gave me a warm handshake. We had been a couple for a while now. I should have done it anyway but felt weird with such an audience. Cody slapped me on the back.

For the next three hours, candidates for the remaining 20 or so positions gave their stump speeches and battled the question-and-answer sessions.

After the event, Sara and I went out for a special dinner at the Lemon Grass, a fancy downtown Thai restaurant. We went there on our first date more than a year and a half earlier. The food was excellent. But that night I had one of the worst stomach aches to date—an unyielding dull pain. The pain lasted for hours and kept me awake for most of the night. I hoped it was not an omen.

L.Rev.

Saved by a Bearded Man in a Sundress
Friday, April 16, 1999

Every spring, the law review held its annual banquet. It was sort of like a debutante ball and awards ceremony. The new editor and staff were introduced and the notes selected for publication were announced. This year a local country club hosted the event. The ballroom's picture window overlooked a scenic view of the local green hills, the Syracuse city skyline and Onondaga Lake.

In his brief speech prior to my speech, the Dean, partially preempted the content of my speech when he pointed out that this year would be the 50th Anniversary of the law review. He told the audience of close to 80 that he had pulled volume one from the shelves and looked through it. Referring to the foreword from Volume 1, the Dean quoted his predecessor from 50 years ago, "In his introduction, Dean Andrews wrote of his hopes and expectations for the new journal which he saw as 'a creditable addition to the field' that would 'contribute something to legal scholarship.'" The Dean agreed with this mission statement, then joked that the articles in 1949 only had two or three footnotes per page instead of five or more.

Then, he dispensed with some platitudes: "The law review is very important to the law school. The tradition of publishing is very important, especially the tradition of turning 50."

This was much of which I planned to cover in my own speech. Comedians hate following someone who performed similar material that the audience loved. The last thing I wanted was to look unoriginal or hackneyed here in my first public appearance as Editor-in-Chief.

But luck was on my side that night. I barely touched my meal, fearing an inflammation of my chronic, stress-induced stomach problems. After the meal, I visited the men's room to check my hair and wash my face. I did not want to give my first speech with food all over my face, either. As I passed by the other banquet room, I spied a man wearing a sundress over his clothes. He had a full beard, too. Could my eyesight be so bad after two years of law school reading that I mistook an ugly woman, possibly an escapee from a circus sideshow, for a man in a dress? No, it was a man. Yes, he had a beard and he wore a sundress, another editor confirmed as we left the men's room. I was astonished and confused, but somewhat delighted.

And, he saved my speech. After my predecessor, Connor, recited some of my bio and introduced me, I unfolded my one-page speech, placed it squarely before me and clutched the right side of the lectern. There was also polite applause.

Extemporizing my first lines, to prove that I was not going to follow the Dean's speech completely, I opened with a slightly bizarre anecdote, if not a funny story:

> *Thank you. The Dean was not the only one to pull volume one. Last week, I looked through the first book.* [dramatic pause] *Not many people know this but J. Edgar Hoover, director of the FBI, wrote for us in our premiere edition. I'm not sure if this is related, and I have not been drinking tonight, but when I walked by the other banquet room there was a guy with a beard wearing a dress, a floral print sundress.* [dramatic pause] *I'm not making this up and I'm not quite sure what that is about, but I think Mr. Hoover would definitely have been interested in that.*

The anecdote hit home. There was a lot of laughter and even a few roars. Most people, I think, did not know that I was serious, or at least what to make of my bizarre anecdote. It did not hurt that I whispered to Cody, who sat next to me at my table, to make sure I got a big laugh with the first joke. The hour-long open bar did not hurt, either.

After the laughter subsided, I moved into the original text of my speech:

> Ten years ago this week I first set foot on the Syracuse University campus. I was visiting to see if this university would be right for me to spend four years as an undergrad.
>
> Well, 10 years later ... I am back in Syracuse at the law school. It seems odd, but after holding a career as a reporter at a large newspaper in the Midwest, I am back here as a student. Some days feel like a home-coming. Sometimes it feels like a macabre do-over. I also owe this staff a debt of gratitude because as I stand here now, my 10th high school reunion is underway in New Jersey and you are sparing me a potentially painful trip down memory lane.
>
> But we are here tonight on the cusp of a larger, more important anniversary. This coming year will be the 50th year of publication for the Syracuse Law Review.

Anniversaries are popular events. Some are meaningless commercial fabrications designed to underwrite the greeting card and jewelry business. I mean, what in the world is a cotton anniversary?

Fifty, however, is golden, a precious metal, signifying opulence, malleability and value. The pharaohs constructed glorious adornments with gold; rulers minted their likenesses on gold coins and our country backed its currency in gold for decades.

For us, the fiftieth anniversary is a milestone of durability and tradition. This is what our class inherits. Furthermore, we inherit this publication on the eve of a new millenium in an age of tremendous and nearly instantaneous change in every aspect of our lives, especially the law.

Our task will be to continue the tradition of publishing a respectable, visible, interesting, independent and scholarly law review. This tradition will continue and expand. One such way will be with our website which I hope to include tools for our staff as well as a more expansive representation of our work that will help get the Syracuse name out there in cyberspace. As I have mentioned previously, one such way will be to include abstracts of our upcoming articles and other useful information, as well as an easier way to access the online materials.

But our primary task is publishing a quality law review, which is an important task. The legal community relies on law reviews—lawyers, judges, scholars, people in jail. They rely on timely and accurate information. We must ensure that information is accurate. It is important for our readers and it is important for us. Our names and the name of the law school appear on the publication.

Our task will not be an easy task, but nothing worthwhile is easy. We have a well-qualified and talented staff which I am sure will rise to the task. We will work hard, but we will have a good time too.

There is a place for everyone on this staff. My classmates who bypassed the election for editorial positions, I want your contributions. There will be many opportunities to exploit your talents.

Likewise, there will be many opportunities for pride, for the alumni, the law school administration and most importantly, for us, the members of the law review.

To our 3L staff, I enjoyed working and learning with you and assure you that you leave this publication in competent hands.

I look forward to working with you as we shepherd the law review into its 50th year and the new millenium.

Applause followed. It was nice. I even surprised myself. Beforehand, I was not sure whether I would be able to get out some of the rhetoric about the Gold Standard and history of gold uses. I enjoyed the speaking engagement, but I was relieved when the evening was over. I was also hungry because I did not eat my dinner.

On top of my introduction as editor, my note was selected for publication. It was announced first, which meant it had lead article status. Interestingly enough, Sara's note was chosen second. We were both proud about that.

There was plenty of handshaking and congratulations to go around. One professor came up to me after the event and said he enjoyed my speech. "Your speech was great. You should go into politics," he said. I was surprised by the compliment and graciously thanked him and thanked him for coming.

Politics may never be a future career choice. But I also doubt that there will be many opportunities in life to say I was saved by a bearded man in a dress.

Welcome to the Party
Friday, April 16, 1999

At the first transition meeting with my predecessor, Connor said, "Dude, you will wear many hats and deal with things that are *sui generis* that I cannot even begin to predict. Good luck." Connor and I scheduled a handful of meetings where he began passing the torch and filling me in about the nuances and tensions of his job.

Connor was earnest and his wishes for luck were genuine. His prophecy would likely prove quite accurate. This was corroborated even before beginning my term as Editor-in-Chief for Syracuse Law Review, Volume 50, 1999-2000. Because of low morale on law review, there was a scarcity of volunteers to run for several positions. If I wanted to doubt myself, I could say that there was even a dearth of viable challengers for my position. I would refrain from dwelling on that. But we were unable to attract candidates for one of the Lead Article slots, the editors who sift through piles of submissions to make selections; we had two or three slots for Associate Notes and Comments and Executive Editors, the editors who grade the summer write-on competition and work with the 2Ls on staff during the note-writing process. On top of all that, there were no women elected to any of the top senior positions, besides the business editor, who handled the money and subscriptions.

I convinced a woman who carried some solid academic weight to go for Lead Articles only to have her back out two weeks later because of an impending personal crisis. The slots were filled during a brief supplemental election.

The first order of business was putting together the write-on competition. Nick, the Notes and Comments Editor, had a solid idea for one of the closed-universe hypothetical problems and I offered another. This entailed writing a problem and researching the case law for the competition. As a closed-universe problem, we provided all the case law and research necessary to write the competition memo. No outside research would be necessary or permitted.

Roughly one-third of the law review staff writes-on. The write-on members are the top scorers in a writing competition that takes place at the end of the first year. Because people have to read the memos from the competition, it was somewhat important to make the hypothetical and the cases interesting. It was also important that the material did not duplicate subjects covered in first year classes. Even though the first-year curriculum is the same for every student, certain professors stress certain cases and concepts more than others. As such, one problem focused on a family law matter and the other was a First Amendment and libel issue with Internet jurisdiction mixed in.

As Editor, I felt I needed play a role in grading the competition because this was tantamount to picking the staff. I could also set the deadlines and lead by example. When Connor learned of my plan to participate in the grading, he said, "Dude, I wouldn't do that, you'll get burned out. Reading all those essays is awful. I heard stories."

Staff morale was another reason I felt I had to participate in the grading. The Associate Notes and Comments editors, the six editors who work with 2Ls during the note-writing process, received no academic credit for their work. All other 3L editors received one academic credit hour for the additional work. All law review members earned two academic credits.

Some of the AN&Cs complained that this credit disparity short-changed them. I agreed, but there was little anybody could do at this point in the year. A couple were irritated, especially Cody, who frequently threatened to quit his position even before he began working. I promised the editors that I would do everything possible to try to get them the one credit and establish parity between them and the rest of the senior editors.

One of my first official acts entailed meeting with the Dean about the issue and presenting a four-page report and proposal. It was apparent that this would be an exercise in futility. "The faculty frowns on giving additional credit to such positions because it has nothing to do with a class," he matter-of-factly recited. "You could petition the academic standards committee, but they won't like it, too much. They just shot down the moot court on a similar request."

"I would like to follow this proposal through to the academic standards committee. I owe it to these editors," I said. He said he would submit the report to the committee, but I never heard back.

Like any business, publication or organization, the law review was organized in a logical hierarchy. Most law reviews have the same staff structure, although sometimes, the names and responsibilities differ.

For us, with roughly 80 members the staff was organized as the senior board comprised of elected third-year staff members; the associate members who were third-year members who did not seek editorial positions and the editorial staff, the new second-year members who ranked in the top 10 percent of their class after the first year and those who had the high scorers in the write-on competition that took place just after finals.

The senior board included: the Editor-in-Chief; the Managing Editor, who handled internal staff matters and scheduling; the Notes and Comments editor who administered the write-on competition and the note writing process; the Form & Accuracy editor who served as a copy editor and *Bluebook* specialist; Articles Editors, two editors who choose the articles, dealt with authors and solicited authors for the annual Survey of New York Law; Business Editor who maintained the subscription list and handled all the money that came in; Technical Editor handled the computerized layout of the book, office computer matters and the website.

The senior board also included the six Executive Editors. Each Executive Editor managed a team of six to eight 2L staff members. These were the editors who really held the keys to smooth operations. They had the most hands-on control of the quality of the editing. They could spot problems with articles or staff members and process the articles at a fast pace.

The remaining elected staff members were the Associate Notes and Comments editors.

A Little Information Can be Dangerous
Monday, April 26, 1999

It was standing room only in the large lecture room. There were students lined up two or three deep against the back wall. Every seat was taken and there were students sitting on the floor in the isles. This was the law review informational meeting for the first year students.

Mike, the managing editor, Nick, the notes and comments editor, and I coordinated the meeting with the editors of the other journals: the Syracuse International Law & Commerce Journal and the Syracuse Journal of Law & Technology. This was where we laid out the information about our journals and how to get on to the journals. We explained the "grade on" and "write on" procedures: those who rank in the top 10 percent would be invited as would those with the highest scores in the write on competition. Nick provided the obligatory warning about cheating and collaborating, "You cannot collaborate. If you cheat, we will find out and you will face academic disciplinary charges. Anyway, it is not in your best interest to work with someone else on this because it is a competition."

I brought a copy of the book to use as a prop as I stood front and center in the middle of the room and said, "Making law review can make or break your legal career." There were a couple of gasps.

"I know this sounds a little dramatic, but I am telling you this so you take the write on competition seriously. The work you do on law review is the same kind of work you will be doing in your summer clerkships and your first year jobs. That means that accuracy counts. That means that one or two typos will knock you out. You have to take this seriously."

It may have been melodramatic maybe even a bit self-aggrandizing. But the message was intended to be honest and sincere. It would not take much more than a misspelled word to make the difference between writing onto law review and missing the cut. It made little sense to spend several days right after finals and before starting a summer job to do a half-ass job.

Nick, pragmatic, and almost sage-like, said, "You may think you have the grades after your first semester, but that's no guarantee you'll grade on. Lots can happen between the spring and fall. If you want to make it on, cover your backs and do the write-on competition."

As it was, it did not take much to ensure that a student would not grade-on. One or two Bs instead of As was enough to knock a student out of the top 10 percent. Every year, there were always a couple students who came up a fraction of a grade point short of grading on because of one grade or one erratic professor. Law professors have a propensity to be capricious when it comes to grading exams so I wanted people to take the competition seriously. It might be their only chance. They owed it to themselves.

Writing On and Writing Off
Thursday, May 20, 1999

The write-on packet consisted of about 130 pages of cases, the directions, the Bluebook editing exercise and the honor code contract. Every entrant had to sign the honor code contract vouching that the academic standards of the university and the College of Law would be upheld. It certified that the work was the student's own and that there was no cheating.

By the end of the registration period 164 students signed up and paid $17 for the packet. The fee offset the costs of printing and various mailing expenses. An anonymous number was assigned based on the time and order the student signed up. That would be the only source of identification until after all the essays were graded and ranked. When I picked up the list in Support Services, the law school's copy center and mail room, three people were there signing up as the office closed. The third, a girl, was vacillating and then decided not to sign up because she did not have the money. I told her a supplemental sign-up list would be there for the next two days. Robert, the mild-mannered manager of the support services office, assured me that he would be able to copy and collate the packets in time. He also recommended printing up at least 10 extras to accommodate stragglers.

A few people sought me out personally to see if they could pick up their packets earlier. I made only one exception, and that was for a guy who had booked his flight home a month earlier. Everyone else, including a guy who was friends with a graduating 3L and a guy who wanted to pick it up early so he could go see *Star Wars—The Phantom Menace*, picked up their packets at 4 p.m. this afternoon on the fourth floor. I had just completed a 24-hour take-home exam for constitutional legal history, which took me 19, allowing me only about three hours of sleep. This guy would need a better excuse than that to shake me.

Traditionally, the write-on packets were available on the last day of finals. The write-on competition muted, if not crushed, the relief and celebration of completing the first year of law school. The message is clear: "Congratulations, you're done with your first year, but here's this week-long assignment that could make or break your legal education." Many students burned out from a year of the bizarre world of legal education were not too eager to sacrifice the only week of vacation before starting summer clerkships or jobs for the competition. Some, who knew they would not have the grades, knew what they had to do.

Write-on competitions vary from law review to law review. Some require a detailed essay with Bluebook citations and an extensive editing, proofreading and Bluebook exercise. One prestigious law journal's Bluebook exam takes four hours, plus the candidates have to write a memo analyzing the strengths and weaknesses of three articles. Other journals simply require submission of a paper written in first-year research and writing classes. Most law reviews employ a system similar to ours, a hypothetical question in a closed-universe with all the research supplied, plus completion of an editing exercise. Candidates had eight days.

Restrained chaos consumed the fourth floor lounge. We set up tables and divided the packets into piles based on the sign-up numbers. Each recipient needed to present his or her ID and receipt. The mob scene surrounding the tables resembled the pits at the New York Stock Exchange. In many ways, the consequences of the write-on competition were just as dramatic as the stock market. For the student who put the time and effort into the memo, placing in the competition and making law review could be the difference between getting a decent job and driving an ice cream truck. There was no way to downplay the importance of this organization. Law review membership is integral just to compete for the jobs at reputable law firms or clerkships with judges.

Some of the students were nervous; others were giddy as they picked up the packets. The obvious euphoria of the last day of the first year of law school certainly factored into the jubilation. Many cringed when they opened the packet and counted the 132 pages. On its face, the cases, which were arranged only in alphabetical order, seemed like a lot of material to handle. But eight days is also a lot of time. Several of the cases overlapped and some were inconsequential, included simply as smokescreens.

This was an event with potentially monumental repercussions. Some people realized, others did not. It was exciting just being part of it, because I knew how crucial the write-on competition was to my own law school experience. At about 5:45, 15 minutes before the end of the pick up period, a guy came up and wanted to buy the packet right then and there. Just as Robert predicted, we had walk-up requests. We had printed several extra copies, just for this scenario, and accepted his check.

By the end of the day, all but about 10 of the 166 people who bought the packet picked them up. This was going to be the only opportunity. That night, Sara and I attended a law school end-of-the-year party at a downtown bar. This was the first law school social event we attended besides a charity auction, the Libel Show, a law school talent/gridiron show and the Barristers' Ball, a.k.a., the Law School Prom. At this point, to celebrate the end of another difficult semester, we each decided to have a beer. This was an opportunity to talk with people and socialize. It was an opportunity to relax and go out. Neither one of us was particularly social, preferring to socialize with a handful of friends and avoid the weekly law school parties at local bars.

The bar was loud, crowded and smoky. After about 10 minutes at the bar, Simone', a 1L I had never met, approached me. Simone', a member of the student senate, said she helped organize this party. Then, she said, "I couldn't come to the school to pick up the packet. Benedict, who is on law review, told me it would be okay to pick it up later."

Since the day we first approached the 1L class, we were adamant about the deadlines and procedures. Furthermore, Benedict gave her directions that he did not have the authority to give as a graduating editor.

"Today was the only day you could pick up the packets," I said.

"But Benedict told me it would be okay," she answered.

"The directions were very specific and we were clear with the deadlines," I said.

"I can't believe you," she yelled. "I CANNOT believe that you will not let me have the packet. Picking it up late would not give me any advantage. It would be to my detriment. Anyway, I am part of the student senate, I organized this party. You are not being fair."

"Look, if you missed a deadline with a court for filing a document, you would be in a lot of trouble," I said. "We were quite explicit from the beginning."

"I should be allowed a little leeway because I'm part of the Student Senate and was here organizing this party," she said, flanked by her friends, she began screaming at me while her eyes welled up.

"I'm sorry, I cannot make exceptions for everyone," I said. She walked away, still crying. Meanwhile, her friends glared at me for the next 40 minutes.

When I met up with Connor, about 20 minutes later, I bought him a beer and probed him on his thoughts on this latest unanticipated problem. "She gets no advantage by picking it up late," he said, shrugging his shoulders. I agreed, but was still torn about the deadline issue. How many more exceptions would we have to grant, though? I thought it might be unreasonable to not give it to her because she did pay the $17. Sara moderated by reminding me that our evidence professor cut us a break with an extra credit assignment that we both missed because we misread the directions. "He didn't have to give us a second chance with that, maybe you should give her a second chance," she said. "It's not really that big a deal."

Yes, it really was not that big a deal. About a half-hour later, I went back to Simone' and told her that if she wants her packet to meet me in the office at 9 a.m. the next day. She was ecstatic and hugged me. "Just be there at nine and turn it in on time because I cannot change that deadline," I said.

Lending a Helping Hand
Friday, May 21, 1999

I was in the office by 8:15 to deal with a wealth of paper work. I also wanted to be there well before Simone's newly extended deadline.

Right on the hour, Simone and her friend arrived. I handed over the packets and said, "The deadline for this is still Friday by 4."

A handful of the other no-shows picked up their packets, but about five people never showed up.

When I spoke with Nick, the notes and comments editor, later in the day, I clearly caught him at a bad time. His baby was crying in the background and he seemed really irritated by my ad hoc decision to allow distributions beyond the deadline. "You're the editor, you can do whatever you want," he said. He was not happy with my decision.

Nick was a no-nonsense guy. A year or two older than me, Nick had a family, a masters degree and a number of professional experiences behind him, including work in newspapers and public relations. Aside from his realistic and professional outlook, he also knew his law well. He was one of the only classmates I encountered who successfully argued a point of law with a law professor. In our evidence class, he actually convinced the professor that an out-of-court statement fit into a hearsay exception that the professor had not previously considered. I liked his no-nonsense way of doing business.

Someone with thinner skin might have been offended by his comments. I was concerned that this incident could have forced a rift. But that afternoon he called back an apologized for being short and rude. I told him that there was no need to apologize and that much of what we do will be done without the benefit of precedent.

Due Date
Monday, May 31, 1999

Eight days after the excited students picked up their packets, the assignment was due. Each entrant had to turn in eight copies of the memos. They could be handed in in person or mailed in. Some were mailed, some were hand delivered. By the end of the week, we had 87. We waited until Monday before a final tally because of the mails. We got one more in the mail Monday with a valid post-mark. In all, only 88 essays were turned in.

As in past years, roughly half the people failed to follow through. Some people probably sat down and felt that the work would be too much. Others probably knew or thought they would grade on. Others probably just did not care. After a year of law school and a week of final exams, it was difficult to get motivated to spend another few days working on an essay, especially when the competition encroaches on a summer vacation.

Most summer jobs begin after Memorial Day. Thus, a week-long competition threatens to consume an already truncated summer vacation. Grading these essays would span the next two months. We set the middle of July as the deadline to have the grades. The graders were the six associate notes and comments editors, Nick, the notes and comments editor and me. We had eight separate people reading the essays. Because there were two hypothetical problems, which the entrants had 10 total pages to address, we decided to divide the grading. Four people read all of the essays for topic one; four read all the essays on topic two. The same people read each of the 88 essays. The only identification was the sign-up number. Nick held the number/id chart in a sealed envelope that would not be reviewed until after the scores were tallied and we had the names of the top 10 percent of the class.

Summer Reading
Saturday, July 10, 1999

Grading the essays was not too difficult. Connor's prophecy was not as ominous as he promised. Grading, however, was not that easy either. At least I had an idea for a good essay and I knew the material pretty well because I researched and wrote the problem that I graded. It was not difficult to differentiate the good from the bad from the ugly. Most of the essays were bland. A few were horrendous. There was one that was only two pages long. Entrants were allotted up to 10 pages for the entire assignment for both issues.

One essay stood out because it had a spelling, grammatical, typographical or citation error in every other sentence. Some people failed to use spell-check. Others used a spell checker but the essay had too many typos that would not have been caught: its, it's, their, there, they're, thee, four, for. Some just failed to state the law accurately while others had weak organization. Five pages are not too tight. There was enough space to be thorough. Logically, each essay should be five pages because each was worth the same amount of points.

Memorandum format also factored into the grading. This was an all-or-nothing section worth 40 points. Unless the format was completely ignored, practically every entrant got the full points on this category. Memo format, which was a staple in the first-year writing program, was basic formula structure: memorandum heading; questions presented; brief answers; statement of facts; discussion; point headings (indented paragraph blocks summarizing a section's arguments); and conclusion. This was the style and format taught in the first-year research and writing classes. This was also the format everyone would likely employ during summer clerkships at law firms or judges' chambers.

The format style was also relatively fair. Some law reviews allow students to turn in papers written for classes while some require essays in actual law review article form; that means Bluebook format for law review articles with Bluebook footnotes and rules. Citations for memos are considerably more manageable because they appear in the text and are not subject to the more complex Bluebook rules.

A detailed grading form governed the grading system with a top score of 500 points. Everything counted: point headings; topic sentences; grammar; spelling; legal citations; writing style; flow of the argument; use or misuse of materials. The highest score I gave was a 478. The lowest was a 28, but that was for the two-page entry.

After a while the essays blurred. But differentiating the good from the bad was not difficult. The good writing, clean essays, stood out like a sore thumb. The bad ones blended together. The horrendous ones blended in, too.

Cody, as an associate notes and comments editor, was one of the graders. He emailed me toward the end of his grading, saying that he was so appalled by the quality of the essays that he was afraid to have these people working on his soon-to-be-published note. "I read these essays, crumpled the paper and wiped my ass with them, they were that bad," he wrote. Cody's stellar use of hyperbole was not too far off.

All the graders turned in their scores on time. Although each grader applied his or her own criteria and graded through an individual lens, there was clear consensus for the best essays. The only slight differences came through on the two issues. Some entrants spent more time on one issue instead of the other. Overall, the graders were fairly consistent— some had consistently higher marks while others had consistently lower marks.

Nick ranked the top 30 scores. We would invite the top 14 write-ons.

The Collaborators: Scandal (#1)
Wednesday, August 4, 1999

The real fireworks with the competition exploded during the grading. Along with the eight essay graders, the Form and Accuracy Editor was responsible for grading the 10-question Bluebook editing exercise. George, the editor, with a meticulous eye and memory for detail, discovered that entries under numbers 100, 101 and 87 had made the same bizarre typographical and editing mistakes that no other entrants made. Plus, the Bluebook entries for two of the three were identical.

Two days later I got an email from Sofia, an associate notes and comments editor, who was grading the essays. She told me that she thought essays for 100 and 101 were similar.

When I initially read the essays, I noticed some textual similarities, but thought-proving collusion would be difficult, if not impossible. George mailed me the Bluebook entries, and I was convinced that these two had cheated and there was a possibility that number 87 had cheated, too.

George, Nick and I decided that we would disqualify 100 and 101 from the competition. Number 87's essay was so bad that this person would not write-on. We agreed that we would let the matter rest unless any of the three happened to grade on. "Best case scenario, these idiots do not grade on and we bury the matter here. Worst case scenario, they grade on and we have to make an evidentiary inquiry," I said.

In mid July, Nick received a list of the top 10 percent from the registrar. When he compared the grade-on names to the identities of the competition numbers, our fears came true. Number 101 graded on to law review. I drove to Syracuse that weekend to handle several administrative issues because we needed to send out the invitations to the new law review members. We wanted to get the letters out early so they could plan to get back early for the intensive orientation program.

A law review member who had recently graduated and was studying for the bar exam came into the office. She was a teaching assistant for 1Ls and wanted to see how many of her students made law review. Teaching assistants, many who are on law review, run the research and writing classes and take pride in having their students make law review. It is like an unofficial competition among teaching assistants. A couple of her students made it. One was Stacy. I mentioned that she was involved in "a slight situation." When I recited the nature of the situation, she, honed in on Keith, the other student involved. She said that Keith had sought help from Stacy all year and that they were friends. This unsolicited information corroborated what I had suspected.

I sent out letters to the top 28 students—the top 10 percent of the first year class. All the letters were standard congratulatory stuff and a schedule of orientation events and a biographical questionnaire that needed to be mailed back to me. Nick sent the letters out for the top 14 write-ons.

But my letter to Stacy was not quite as congratulatory. Basically, my letter said, "Congratulations, you graded on to law review but upon your return to Syracuse you will be brought up before the law review's sanctions committee for violating the rules of the writing competition, from which you were disqualified." I assured her that her case would be handled professionally with every effort to ensure her due process. I put my phone number on the letter and encouraged her to call me.

She received the letter on a Thursday. And she called me that night. I was not even out of my suit from work when the phone rang. She sounded slightly rehearsed and remarkably unfazed by the accusations. And, she immediately offered up Keith as a likely suspect.

"I never colluded with anyone. I did not show my paper to anyone," she said. After a few minutes of back-and-forth, she admitted that she worked in relatively close proximity with Keith and another student. She also admitted that they were in the same law firm class and that she printed out a copy of a class assignment to serve as a model for Keith. But she vehemently denied cheating during the competition and claimed to be an innocent victim of some sort of chicanery.

I told her that we would settle the matter with an investigation upon our return to school. I told her that if she was truly an unwitting victim, her close friend Keith "will stand up and assume responsibility for his actions if he has a modicum of integrity." I knew that I should not take her word for anything, but she sounded like she had been hoodwinked by her friend.

Keith called me that night at 11:30 p.m. He lived in the Mountain Time zone so it was not too late for him. He called to account for his actions and admit that he took a look at Stacy's Bluebook exercise when she was not in the room. He admitted that he cheated and that nobody else knew what he did.

"I assume full responsibility," he told me, then added that he was home in the west tending to his mother who was weeks away from surgery. He said that he might not even return to Syracuse in the fall. Keith added that he was prepared to accept whatever punishment came down.

"I just want to make sure this is correct, you are admitting to this and nobody else knew what you were up to?" I said, still incredulous.

I thanked him for coming forward and assuming responsibility. I told him my report would include a request for leniency but I could not promise that the administration would pay any heed to my request. He immediately asked whether he could serve a suspension during the semester that he planned to be away from school. The adjudication was completely out of my control, so there was nothing I could do about the punishment. I thanked him for standing up and taking the heat, but adding, "I wish you did not put me in this position because I have no other choice but to turn this over to the administration."

Before proceeding with the report, I asked him to put his confession in writing as soon as possible. His statement had to include a complete description of the events leading up to this and a detailed admission.

The confession arrived in overnight mail on Sunday morning. It was a three-page handwritten account in which Keith wrote that he cheated "in a moment of weakness."

By owning up to his actions, Keith made my investigation a little less complicated. But I still had an uneasy suspicion that the duo was not being entirely forthright. The guy openly admitted to cheating. Stacy did not seem too disturbed on the phone. In fact, she sounded a little too comfortable.

Both Keith and Stacy volunteered that a third person had nothing to do with the cheating even though she worked in close proximity and she had some of the same mistakes. But her essay was so bad that she would not have even had a prayer. I pretty much ignored her involvement.

In the following days, I had separate conversations with Professor Locknor, the law review's advisor, and the Dean. The report totaled eight pages complete with exhibits and copies of the documents. I even took a sheet of evidence exhibit stickers from the office supply closet at my law firm. It took me several hours late at night to complete the report. I mailed it overnight to the Dean and set the wheels in motion.

The case would later be presented to the law school's judicial board, which read the report and reviewed the evidence.

Keith opted not to return to testify before the panel of three professors, three students and two student prosecutors. One of the prosecutors later remarked to a friend that "law review takes things seriously" and that she could not believe the detail and length of my report. A month or two later, Cody read the report, calling it "overly officious."

Given the weight of the decision and the potential impact on the student's future, the report had to be well documented and professional. The implications that a guilty verdict could have on a law student's career are monumental. Expulsion from law school can alter a student's future career. A suspension or reprimand will appear on a student's transcript and could affect admission to the bar. The legal profession likes to deceive itself by instituting ethical guidelines.

[Another reason I wanted to document my report dated back to the beginning of my second year. I had been bumped out of a professional responsibility class and put into another when the administration overbooked a class. Then, the professor, a full-time tenured professor we were stuck with, abandoned the class after about a month. The professor just dropped the class about four weeks into the semester, that was after canceling about half the other classes. The classes we did have were utterly useless because she mostly rambled about alcoholism in the legal profession as though this class was one of the Twelve Steps. Then, suddenly, she left, allegedly to tend to the needs of an ill relative out of state. Throughout the semester, a classmate reported that he frequently saw her at a local fitness center.

The result of that was the administration throwing the rest of the class into another professor's class more than a month into the school year. The net effect of that would have been putting the moved students at a major disadvantage. The administration abandoned the class too. I wrote one of the most vitriolic letters I ever wrote and hand delivered it to the Dean and an associate dean.

My letter alleged that the professors and administration had abject disrespect for the students and nobody gave a damn about the students. I made the letter widely available to friends, too. One friend requested his own signed copy and made repeated references to the letter for the subsequent months. The letter prompted a meeting with an associate dean who took great offense and demanded specific evidence and examples of my allegations. "I read this like I would a memo to a judge and you cannot just make allegations without evidence," she lectured to me.

"I do not need to cite to evidence to express an opinion," I told her, adding that I was not the only bitter student around. That was true, I was just the only one crazy enough to put it in writing and sign his name to it.

Because I knew the associate dean would read my report, I made sure everything was documented. I would not give her another opportunity to take a shot at me.]

The eight-page investigative report laid out the case in a preliminary statement and discussed the mechanics of law review and the procedure for the write-on competition. The section headed "Facts of the Case," presented the findings, including excerpts from Keith's letter. Everything was formal, with titles, Ms. and Mr. The conclusion referred to Keith's letter saying that the case against Stacy would be dropped without prejudice. Because of Keith's cooperation, I requested that the judicial board apply a degree of leniency:

> His confession, which was sent in overnight mail, certainly facilitated resolution of this matter. There is no question that Mr. Keith could have easily been uncooperative and unavailable. His honesty and cooperation not only eased the investigation but his willingness to stand up and assume responsibility also saved his friend and classmate from further troubles. Without cooperation, the Law Review would have embarked on a difficult, bitter and time-consuming journey that may or may not have been resolved.

Keith wanted any suspension to be served during his planned absence from Syracuse. The board refused that. One professor scoffed at my report's request for leniency, I later learned. It was easy for the board to adopt a tough stance when I pitched a home-run softball.

I had my doubts about Keith's eagerness and willingness to take the heat and fall on the sword for his friend. Even under direct questioning, he denied it. At this point, I could only accept him at his word. At any rate, at least we got one fall guy.

[Months later I learned through another source that Keith took the fall for Stacy and he was bitter about it. This sounded like a soap opera, and according to a friend of Keith's who hated Stacy, they cheated together. Apparently after talking with me, Stacy threatened Keith, saying: "I spoke with the editor who said that he knows my class rank and that you are at the bottom of the class and nobody will believe you anyway." She encouraged him to take the heat for her while she walked away without even the implication of cheating. Meanwhile, she went on to land a job at a prestigious national law firm.

The thought that I was hoodwinked by a couple of cheaters makes my stomach turn. Not only did Stacy cheat and get away with it, but she sold out her friend, lied about our conversation and still got the kind of prized job many outside the Ivy League could only dream about.

The board suspended Keith for the spring semester and sentenced him to several hours of community service. This process, of course took months to complete.]

Summer: The Tale of Two Jobs
Saturday, August 7, 1999

It was the worst of summers; it was the worst of summers. I was the first and only summer associate in the New Jersey branch office of Dickman & Cherubb, a large New England-based law firm. I had my own office and a whole lot of assignments. I was in the office by 8:30 every morning and left anywhere between 6 and 9 at night. Lunch usually consisted of a buttered roll, a Coke and 30 minutes of checking my AOL email and responding to law review issues.

The firm-wide Intranet included profiles of the 20 summer associates throughout the half-dozen offices. Most of the others were on their school's specialized or secondary journals. I was the only one with a senior editing role on a law review. My title provided a tremendous amount of conversation fodder when they sent me to the New England office for the summer associates retreat. It was a nice event complete with a cocktail hour and a visit to a minor league baseball game. I thought I performed well enough.

A number of the firm's the senior partners approached me for some perfunctory conversations. The cachet of my title, compounded with my work in the exotic New Jersey location gave me quasi celebrity status. "I was just down in New Jersey office last month, the new building is great and they seem to be doing some good work there. It's about time we had a summer associate down there," a senior partner said. "Are you having fun there? Do they have enough work.?"

"It is great. I've been able to work for several different lawyers. I have a lot of responsibility. I even have my own office," I said.

One of the other summer associates, who spent the summer in the firm's Boston office, where she attended law school, held an editorial position on a specialized journal.

"Have you had to do a lot of work for law review over the summer," she asked.

"I spend at least one to three hours every night on things like grading the write-on competition, articles and staffing issues. Plus, some time on the weekend," I said, as I stuffed popcorn in my mouth at the baseball game.

"Wow, I cannot even imagine how much work and responsibility that is," she said.

Things were now winding down at the firm. Throughout the summer I kept in constant contact with the other law review members. Before leaving school for the summer, we compiled a list of summer phone numbers, workplaces and emails. In July, I wrote letters to the eight executive editors. In early August, I sent letters and emails to all the other staff members. By the end of August I had also spoken with almost every third-year staff member. I wanted a healthy turnout for orientation as well as the orientation barbecue. It was important to make sure the poor morale problems we encountered last year would be a thing of the past. Contact with the staff would be vital to that cause. Furthermore, I wanted to engage the unelected 3Ls in our plans for the 50th Anniversary project.

I also had at least two conversations with Chris, the head of the law school's community liaison office, an administrator I always liked, but could never get to do anything for me. Chris needed the list of who made law review so she could get the ball rolling for on-campus interviews with law firms. She had already heard about the write-on competition scandal.

The acceptance letters flowed into my hands in the following weeks. They were accompanied by the four-question questionnaire that included information on the students' undergraduate school, hometown, summer workplace and work prior to law school. A couple new members sent their resumes along. These were later typed up and included in the law review handbook. It would be a nice touch and a good way to get to know the staff. One of the problems during our second year was the lack of camaraderie. By the end of our second year of law school, there were law review members who did not know other law review members. I needed to not only know everybody but to know a little about everybody. Luckily, a graduating teaching assistant gave me his picture book, so I knew what everybody looked like, too.

With a couple weeks to go I still had not heard from four people. One guy from upstate New York was just in his own world. I located his telephone number through the registrar and spoke with him. One girl went home to South Korea and overnighted her acceptance the day before I left for school. Two students transferred, which required some dealing with the registrar. That meant that two students would move into the top 10 percent, and thus make it onto law review.

I exchanged an email with the registrar who promptly provided me with the names and telephone numbers for the next two students in line—one had already called me in Syracuse to see if she made it. I called her back at her workplace, and made her day.

The second new member was Hank. First, I spoke with his mother, who gave me the number to the family beach house in North Carolina, where Hank was recuperating from a summer of legal work. When I delivered the good news, he let out a big cheer. He was ecstatic. "That's really awesome. I was wondering whether I'd make it. That's awesome, yes!" he said. I could almost hear waves lapping up on the sand in the background. It was almost heartwarming calling someone with good news. I was still accustomed to the response I frequently got when I called people as a reporter, usually for bad news: curses and a click.

Last Rites or Wrongs
Thursday, August 12 , 1999

It was like a wrecking ball destroying a building. This was my last day as a summer associate for at Dickman & Cherubb. The partner-in-charge of the New Jersey branch office took me to lunch. This was it. This was the lunch, I hoped, would generate "the offer" for permanent employment.

Then Pat opened the conversation with, "Have you ever thought about clerking?" It was clear where it would go from there. She then asked, "I know you did good work for me, and the others you worked for raved about the work you did for them, but did Evans give you any feedback on your work?" She referred to partners and associate I did the bulk of my work for over the summer.

"No, Evans just gave me two assignments and that was it," I answered. "Ed told me that the work I did for him was as good as that he'd seen from any second or third-year associate that he'd seen in his 20 years in practice—lawyers who had worked for two or three years."

"I know that the others liked your work. But Evans, well, you have to take this criticism with a grain of salt because this is the same thing he has said about every new lawyer we've had here, but he said your work was not sophisticated enough," Pat said. "He said that this was not what he expected from the editor of a law review."

"Sophisticated? I don't even know what that means. If he had a problem, why didn't he just tell me, I would have stayed later and come in more on the weekends. I would have done whatever it took," I said.

"He is difficult to please. He never likes anyone, really," Pat said. "That's how he deals with things. He's not always right but he carries a lot of weight around here. Even though everyone else liked you and your work, we cannot bring in a new lawyer that we're going to have to train."

"Just for the record, I don't think he has good judgment with his cases," I said. "He's not going to win that malpractice case, it's very weak." A week earlier, he lost another malpractice case in federal court that he had me perform some clerical work on.

"He brings in a lot of business," Pat said.

The rest of the lunch was pleasant, but I had lost my appetite. For circumstances seemingly out of my control, I was the one summer associate at a big firm who did not get the offer. Even worse, I did not go down in a ball of flames like others that attained legendary status in the summer associate community. Usually, the only summer associates at big firms who fail to get offers at the end of the summer do crazy things like proposition a partner's wife, get sloppy drunk at a law firm event and piss in a punch bowl.

Then, again branch offices for law firms are a different animal. As the first summer associate in the New Jersey office of Dickman & Cherubb, the firm was not prepared for how to deal with me at the conclusion of the summer. There was never any representation that the firm could not absorb me at the end of the summer. Then again, the New Jersey office had just fired two lawyers for unspecified reasons, and Pat said nobody was eager to bring in a recent graduate who not only needed training, but brought in no new clients.

"We liked having you around. If you need a reference for a clerkship, please use my name," Pat said. "But whatever you do, don't say anything to Evans. You don't want to piss him off."

The old me probably would have marched right into Evans's office and let him have it. But after lunch, as I packed up my boxes of books and other stuff, I made the rounds, saying goodbye to the other lawyers and support staff.

When I went into Evans's office, he was leaning back in his chair cradling the phone between his shoulder and ear. Extending from the side of the desk were the hind quarters of a man, clearly on his hands and knees behind the desk. At first glance, the scene appeared extremely inappropriate. I thought it might have been a junior partner who followed Evans around like a puppy. Then, I realized that guy on his hands and knees was the shoe shine boy working on Evans's black loafers. I do not know what was more disturbing, the sight of a man on his hands and knees in front of a partner or the fact that the partner had a guy on his hands an knees in front of him shining his shoes while he talked on the phone.

The shoeshine boy came around the office twice a week. I never used his services.

Evans put the phone down and looked at me.

"Today's my last day, I just wanted to thank you for giving me all the work all summer," I said, attempting to be diplomatic.

"Good, goodbye and good luck," he said. "Have fun with that law review thing."

Office Time
Thursday, August 19, 1999

Upon my return to Syracuse, I headed straight to the office. It was finally mine. I sat down at my desk in the corner office and looked out the expansive vista of the Onondaga hills, the Brewster Boland freshman dorms and I-81. The other view consisted of Lawrinson dorm, the tallest building on campus, the walkway into the law school, the parking deck, the patio deck and the western end of the Carrier Dome.

The windows were tall and high, more than six feet from the sill to the ceiling. The corner office had the nicest view of any offices in the law school. The view was as nice as that from the Dean's office.

Four shelves lined the wall with the bound volumes of all 49 years of the Syracuse Law Review. I set up my polished wood desk set. I hung a frame with two early 1900s postcards of the university: one an aerial view of the university and the other a picture of the Carrier

Dome's predecessor, Archbold stadium. I pined my favorite Far Side card to the bulletin board: "Damned if you do, Damned if you don't"— my personal mantra.

For the next few hours, I reviewed the files and cleaned the office— scrubbed the tables, computers and cabinets with Windex and vacuumed the floors. I am fairly certain the editors of the Harvard Law Review probably do not clean their offices that thoroughly.

I hung some wonderful old black-and-white photos that were posted on foam core. Connor had obtained these great old law school pictures from the Law School's Centennial Anniversary from 1995. The administration was going to throw them out and he salvaged them, only to collect dust in a pile under his desk for a year.

The office's wide, unadorned walls left plenty of room for the pictures. They were: a photo of a stern-looking editorial board from 1964 with a stoic woman seated in the middle of a bunch of goofy-looking white guys; the first law school class from 1895 in their black suits and slicked hair; a collection of early university buildings; and a College of Law parade from the 1920s.

With four poster-size pictures hung in front of the computers, it would hardly be confused with an art gallery. Nevertheless, it made the office a more inviting place. Several senior members commented on them. The photos also generated plenty of conversations.

Operation Orientation
Friday, August 27, 1999

Orientation was no minor feat. Planning, organizing and rallying everyone to attend the three-day program a week before classes started was a monumental task. Surprisingly, everything proceeded relatively smoothly and effectively. One guy even showed up in a full, three-piece suit, which was a far departure from his usual dirty t-shirt and jeans.

The three-day program was intended to initiate people to law review, get them acquainted with each other as well as the work they would be performing. The program began with an hour-long informal presentation and ended three days later with an evening barbecue at my house. It was important to meet and greet as well as inform. I secured a pizza lunch from Lexis, a coldcuts platter from Westlaw and a bunch of Lexis T-shirts and mugs. We even began work on three Survey articles.

Day 1 was Wednesday, Aug. 25. I welcomed the more than 30 students to law review and introduced them to our system. "Membership is an honor and privilege and the work will be hard but quite worthwhile," I said. Several editors on hand also made similar introductions. We distributed the handbooks and complimentary Syracuse Law Review glass beer mugs—people love free stuff.

Training took place in three smaller groups in two classrooms and a computer cluster. One group met with Nick and heard about the note-writing process. One group went with George and learned about form and accuracy editing—indoctrination of the *Bluebook*, also known as subciting or cite-checking. The third group went with me and had Lexis training.

The format for Thursday would be similar, except with Westlaw instead of Lexis. While one group went to computer training the others stayed in a classroom and began editing two articles. I convinced the Westlaw representative to spring for lunch. He paid for a caterer to come in with a coldcut platter, chips and potato salad for more than 40 people.

Friday was more low-key with an afternoon session with the law school librarian. That night we had a barbecue at my house. I bought $120 worth of soda, chips, hotdogs, hamburgers and veggie-burgers. The funds would later be debited from my $500 editor's discretionary account. I also bought a couple bottles of wine with my own money. I lived in a converted ground-level basement in split-level house in a nice neighborhood five minutes from campus. It was fully-furnished with a three rooms, a kitchen, a bathroom and screened-in porch. My landlady, Mrs. C., got her daughter's old gas grill and then bought $10 worth of propane.

Light gray clouds hovered low all day. A slight drizzle, almost a mist, fell, deterring some 3Ls from stopping by the party. But overall, there was great turn out. Almost every 2L attended, some brought spouses or significant others. Most of the senior editors showed up.

I was pleased with how smoothly everything went. From booking the rooms to ensuring attendance to updating and printing out the handbook, everything worked. I shelled out $375 at the Campus Copy Center to get the handbook copied. I was reimbursed later from our printing budget. The Lexis and Westlaw sessions went well. People who showed up for the programs seemed enthusiastic.

The goal was to get people involved and interested early on. The bonuses came with the work on the articles. Our demands were quite tame compared to some law reviews that assign article editing to senior editors before they leave for the summer and require new members to do work immediately upon their invitation in the middle of the summer. If we had articles to assign then, I would have been more than happy to assign work in July.

Orientation took months to organize, but it was definitely worth it. If people felt like this was a worthwhile, professional and classy organization, their work and attitude would reflect that. At one point in my introduction, I said, "This is a prestigious organization, we will be publishing a book. We are putting out a product. If there are mistakes, all of our names are on that masthead. The school's reputation is on the line. So, remember that when the work seems boring or unimportant. There are no small mistakes."

Everyone wants to be on law review, but nobody knows what it really is. Then, once they find out the amount of work it requires, they get bent out of shape. The obligations of law review membership had to be articulated early on. They needed to know the policies, procedures and bylaws.

I wrote a brief note to the staff, intended to be an inspirational note, that appeared on the third page of the handbook. The letter welcomed the staff to the law review and remarked on the good fortune we encounter for the 50th Anniversary:

This is a special year for the Syracuse Law Review as we inherit the publication on its 50th Anniversary. This golden anniversary is a tribute to the Syracuse law students before us and a legacy for those who follow.

In his foreword to the Law Review's inaugural issue, Dean Andrews set forth the Law Review's purpose: "It hopes and expects to be a creditable addition to the field and to contribute something to legal scholarship; something by way of practical aid and interest to the practicing lawyer; something to the prestige of the Law college and the University."

Dean Andrews's proclamation is equally relevant 50 years later. Today's complex legal community demands accurate, timely and original legal scholarship.

It is our task and duty to continue the tradition of publishing a respectable, independent, interesting and scholarly Law Review. This is no easy task. But I am confident that this staff, comprised of the best students and writers in the College of Law will stand strong and deliver a quality product. The work will be hard and sometimes painstaking. But the rewards will be grand, for each staff member, the Law Review, the College of Law and the legal community.

It is also important to recognize that the Law Review is more than just a publication with a tradition. The Law Review is also a social organization. We work with a common goal of publishing the best product we can. Additionally, we hope to incorporate a number of social events throughout the year.

There will be many opportunities for fun, as well as, pride for alumni, the College of Law and most importantly, for us the members of the Syracuse Law Review.

I look forward to an enjoyable and productive year with each of you on the Syracuse Law Review.

I posted a similar version of this letter on the website. I had to craft the letter with a delicate balance of authority, gravity and pep. Much of my dealings with the general staff had to maintain a positive edge, kind of like a go-out-there-and-bring-home-the-gold speech. This was certainly a different tact for me. But this was also the first time in a long time -- or ever-- that I held a position of authority with figurehead ramifications.

Unlike my old college days as *Daily Orange* news editor, I had to be more diplomatic and more encouraging. At the DO, my student-writers needed me as much as I needed them. They needed the experience and the clips. I needed the news articles to fill the newspaper. The work was different, too. If bad copy came in, I had to make it better to put it in the newspaper and the writer got a better clip. If needed, I could easily re-write the lead or sections of a news article. That job was on the edge because of the daily deadlines. Plus, I had a lot of newspaper experience. I could be cantankerous and business-like. Newspaper editors are supposed to be like that anyway. But now, I not only had to be business-like, but I had to be diplomatic.

The top students at the law school did not need me, they had what they needed, good grades and law review membership. I needed them. With law review, the students get academic credit and valuable experience checking footnotes, editing articles and researching and writing. But they would be able to achieve professional success without law review. Once it was on their resumes, it was there. Thus, because of the size of the staff, the slow pace of work and the layers of editors, there was ample opportunity for a 2L to hide on law review or do poor work and escape any long-term repercussions. There would always be someone checking their work.

One of my biggest roles would have to be that of cheerleader. I had to reinforce that membership and the honor of performing this work really mattered.

As a 2L working on articles last year, I enjoyed finding mistakes in the articles I worked on. I enjoy editing. It was like an academic hunt. Also, this was the only venue in law school where a student can criticize a professor with impunity. When you are in a classroom with 80 other students, challenging a professor can end up being an exercise in futility. The Socratic method and repetition of the same material year after year ensures that law professors are *never* wrong, especially in classrooms. It is a different story in a law review office, though.

During the cite-checking and editing process, the students check every citation for Bluebook form, the accuracy of statements, quotes and parentheticals and the spelling and grammar of the text. Finding mistakes is the job. Not many students shared my zeal for doing this. Still, many others just are not that skilled at it.

Weighted Authority
Monday, August 30, 1999

When I was a reporter, I always cherished my outsider status. I was not from Ohio but moved there for the job. I did not live in parochial Lake County, 20 miles outside Cleveland, but was stationed there to work. I frequently disagreed with the policies and mandates sent down by the demi-powers at the paper, and was often at loggerheads with my boss, a suburban bureau chief whose skewed news judgment ranked multiple homicides with the same high-priority news value as a 20-foot snow dinosaur an unemployed man built on his front lawn after a winter storm. Sometimes I would adopt a contrarian stance just to buck the system and to irritate my boss.

During one of our many closed-door attitude discussions, my old boss, said, "You know, Roy, you could be one of the great reporters at this paper if you do not let your attitude problem get in the way." I told him that the paper has a built-in disincentive to do anything more than the bare minimum.

I preferred doing things my own way. I still do. I have often wondered whether I am suited to work for anybody but myself. But the second I was elected Editor-in-Chief of the law review, I instantly shed my outsider status. As editor, I was not only part of the system, but in many ways I controlled it.   This was an unusual position for me, especially after my disastrous first semester grades, which not only alienated me from the law school, but nearly made me reassess my decision to attend law school, in particular Syracuse, in the first place. Like the mythological phoenix, I not only rose from my own ashes, but I wrote onto the law review and navigated through the system to rise to the highest position on law review, arguably the highest profile leadership position in a law school.

Reflecting on his election as Editor-in-Chief of the Yale Law Journal, Alan Dershowitz, wrote: "That made me something of a celebrity in the small world in which we lived.   Professors called me Chief, directed the hardest questions at me in class and asked me to work as their research assistant."[8]   An author of a law review article about law reviews described law review members as an elite who are carry the school and its traditions forward.[9]   "Within the law schools, most students may feel their experience is mediocre, but law review members—particularly editors-in-chief—carry an aura of excellence.   Rightly or wrongly ..."[10]   Another author wrote: "Journal editors are viewed as the elites of the law student world."[11]

In the old days, the student chosen to lead the law review was also the valedictorian.   Some law reviews maintain this tradition, or a least require senior editors to maintain a certain class standing.   That was part of the prestige of the title.   Even though the majority of law reviews, Syracuse included, have long since dropped the grade requirement for senior editors, senior editor positions still possess the luster.

With a staff of 80 students, I had more people under me than any other organization in the law school and as many people as a small business.   I actually had a bigger staff than my old boss had, even in his hey-day at a small local newspaper before he made it to the Plain Dealer.

There were early indications, like the applause at the election or the big laughs and congratulations I received at the banquet.   Then, there were the little things like all the classmates who suddenly would greet me in the hallways or professors who looked at me differently in class.

---

[8] ALAN M. DERSHOWITZ, CHUTZPAH 50 (Touchstone Books 1991).
[9] Harper, 82 MINN. L. REV. at 1272-77.
[10] *Id.*
[11] Russell Korobkin, *Symposium: Ranking Journals: Some Thoughts on Theory and Methodology,* 26 FLA. ST. U. L.REV. 851, 854 (1999).

One professor even wrote a brief congratulatory note on a paper she graded and returned.

All this was somewhat daunting for me. Although I had always enjoyed the confidence for leadership, I preferred to just get things done. I have never been particularly adept at self-promotion or politics.

On the first day of class, the authority worked for me. I enrolled in copyright law, a subject that I always wanted to learn. Professor Sault, however, required intellectual property as a prerequisite, which could be taken concurrently with copyright. Although I was interested in IP, there was no room in my schedule for another class. Furthermore, I did not want to have the same professor for two classes in the same semester.

I approached Professor Sault after class. She was one of the toughest professors in the school. Her Socratic questioning could sometimes be cruel. A classmate who had Professor Sault the year before, and quipped that after she completed her questioning he realized he had been "As-Saulted." Her students learned the subject matter well but she was not too much fun.

"I am really interested in taking copyright. This was one of the reasons why I decided to go to law school," I told her in the hallway.

"Then you have to enroll in intellectual property, it's as easy as that. Why don't you want to take IP?" she said. "I've never had a student want to take copyright but not IP."

"I just cannot fit anything else into my schedule. It is too tight and it's balanced," I said.

Then, she asked, "How have you done in law school?" I almost felt odd using my position for a personal issue, but I had to. I looked her in the eye and said, "Well, I am the Editor-in-Chief of the law review." In a typical, succinct Sault answer, she responded, "Enough said. You're in."

The Prince
Monday, August 30, 1999

As the first day of class, today was also the first day of law review office hours. I opened the office up at 8 a.m., had my typical breakfast of Coke and cookies, and got ready for class and set up the computers. The computers were integrated into the law school's computer network but were password protected in our office, which gave us access to our own drive on the network. Things went smoothly: all the 2Ls on staff did their work, senior editors supervised and a number of returning 3Ls who held no official position streamed into the office to see how things were running. The thorough orientation regimen helped prepare everyone for the office hours work.

Everything ran smoothly until this afternoon. I knew we would be desperate for work because we only had two articles for the 2Ls to work on during office hours. Ideally, each of the six teams would have its own article to work on. Each team had an executive editor and between six to eight 2L members. But as of now, everyone was working on the same three articles.

There were things to be done, and if there was no work, there were discreet ways to kill time. Constructing a ball out of all the rubber bands in the supply closet certainly was not a discreet way to kill time.

Thus, my first encounter with Adam, who would become the Prince, at least privately. Every now and then in life you encounter a person who you just know is trouble. Sometimes you meet a person and you can just tell that there are troubles or scars behind the façade presented to the public. Others times, you can tell that a person is just a nudge away from shooting up an office. I honed this skill to a fine art as a reporter where I had to size up people in a matter of minutes or seconds.

From the moment I met him, it was abundantly clear that the Prince simply enjoyed being a pain in the ass. With an editorial staff of 42 second-year law students, it was reasonable to anticipate a mixed bag of personalities.

If I want to assign blame for the Prince, I can blame myself. We made the decision over the summer to accept 14 people from the write-on competition. We could have accepted any number we wanted. We chose 14 so our total staff of 2Ls would be 42. I wanted a large staff so we could process the articles faster. I also anticipated losing a couple of staff members over the course of the year. We lost two members from my class: one did not want to write the note so she could maintain her GPA and the other was kicked off because he failed to attend any office hours or submit any of the required note drafts. I expected the same nonfeasance from this batch of students.

After the write-on scores were ranked and we received the grade-on list from the registrar, we had to knock off four students from the top write-on scores because they had graded on. As much fun as law review membership was, nobody could make it onto law review twice.

The Prince, by virtue of excluding the highest ranking grade-ons from the competition, made it onto law review. He was the last person on. And, he was lucky. He learned that he was the last one on because a close friend, who was a senior editor, knew, and told him. Information about the write-on scores should have been kept confidential. We had inadvertently left the write-on rankings in a non-private file on one of the office computers. I was not sorry that he knew his standing.

If I learned that I was the last one on, I know I would have been grateful and obedient. But then again, I am not the Prince.

When I walked into the office, he was sitting at a computer terminal sucking on a Blow Pop. The wrapper of an already-eaten Blow Pop lay beside the computer mouse with the stick jutting out. He was liberally enjoying the candy supply from the bowl in the middle of the office table.

I ran a couple of errands around the building. I was in the process of obtaining office keys for all the senior editors and dealing with the locker situation. Several senior editors who had private offices would not get lockers this year because the administration admitted more first year students than they had lockers to accommodate. Because I was a student group leader with a private office and a desk, I would not get a locker. The building operations manager, Jackie, needed me to find a handful of other editors in the same boat. Five senior editors who had access to the private offices would not get lockers. Besides me, the others were the managing editor, the articles editors and business editor. This was fine with me because I was not planning on using my locker anyway. My private, corner office and a desk that could lock, would be fine. Running down to the first or second floor locker rooms two or three times a day would have wasted too much time, anyway.

But I was reluctant to accede without some kind of concession for the law review—*quid pro quo Dr. Lecter*. The office needed coat hooks—my office, the business/articles editors office and the main office. If people were not going to have lockers, they still needed to hang their coats someplace. I also wanted an additional file cabinet for the office. The desks in the private offices locked, so private items could be securely stored.

I spent about 20 minutes chatting with Jackie. We flipped through an office supply catalogue and settled on a series of wall-mounted coat hooks. She was eager to accommodate me and was pleased that I was not making an issue of the locker situation. Of course, I did not reveal that I was not even planning on using mine. I walked out of Jackie's office with an agreement and a wooden coat tree that would serve as a substitute until the permanent coat hooks were purchased and affixed. She said that would take several weeks.

When I returned to the office, I carried the coat tree and saw the Prince leaning back with a bag of rubber bands on his lap and a fist-size ball made from the rubber bands in his hand. He had raided the supply cabinet to find something to occupy his time. His industriousness was quite impressive. I asked whether there was any work for him to do and he said no. The team he was on was not yet assigned an article to edit and the other two articles were occupied by other teams. He attempted to justify his rubber band project. I told him to help whoever was working on an article and be more productive next time. He laughed at me.

Only a few minutes remained in his two-hour block. I told him to just put the rubber bands back when he left the office. "Those rubber bands belong to the law review." I added. He just smirked at me.

At exactly 5 p.m., when his office hours expired, he walked out with his new rubber band ball. Now, the supply closet had no rubber bands. I did not appreciate this; he was rude and defiant. I knew then and there that the Prince would be trouble.

The Prince was the youngest of a family of three children from Miami Beach. His father was an executive for a major multi-media company. Without meeting his parents, it was abundantly clear that he was the baby of the family, the focus of his parents' attention and obviously felt that the world owed him everything. A position on law review was an entitlement that he deserved. Rules or authority did not apply to the Prince. Office hours interfered with his smoking breaks. It was clear that what the Prince wanted, the Prince got. If the Beastie Boys bred with the British Royal Family, the Prince would have been the offspring. He was not sophisticated enough to be described as irreverent, and too crude and shallow to be aloof. He was just a pain in the ass, and he liked it that way. Nobody and no one would tell the Prince what to do, certainly not a fellow law student.

Chicanery, Shenanigans and Monkey Business
Wednesday, September 1, 1999

Sofia came into the office after hours while Sara and I were having a snack of pretzels, chocolate and Coca Cola. Sofia was a rare commodity in a law school: a perfectionist with almost straight As and a self-effacing and warm personality. Hailing from Eastern Europe, she was fluent in several languages, but sometimes mistook English colloquialisms. Once when I attempted to explain how Southern racists once condemned interracial dating, she thought I was propagating racist policies. American multiculturalism was like an all-you-can eat buffet for her, but she did not know the ingredients.

"Roy, I wanted to tell you that I heard a 2L in the hallway saying that he saw the write-on competition scores and he just missed making it onto law review," she said in a serious tone.

"That's impossible, nobody saw the write-on scores. That guy is full of baloney," I said.

"How do you know what he ate for lunch?" she said innocently.

"I'm sorry?" I said.

"You said he ate baloney and he's full," she said.

"No. That's an expression," Sara interjected.

" It means he's not telling the truth," I said.

"Oh, I see," she said.

Sofia was a dear friend to both Sara and me. With her future slated at a major Washington, D.C., law firm, I occasionally took it upon myself to brief Sofia on the nuances of American culture and the English language, which admittedly is difficult enough for native speakers to grasp. She also welcomed the informal lessons.

"There's some sort of chicanery here, and we'll have to get to the bottom of it," I said.

"Chicanery, what is that?"

"Chicanery is shenanigans."

"What are shenanigans?"

"That's monkey business," I said. I knew that I could play these word games with her in a way that was not condescending or mocking. "Sofia, chicanery means foul play or cheating. Shenanigans and monkey business are slang for playing around, foul play, trickery or cheating."

Ever since then, whenever it fit, Sofia interjected these words in conversations. One day she will be in a meeting with a partner at a law firm who will drop one of those words, and she will not miss a beat.

Race War
Friday, September 3, 1999

In an era of political correctness and affirmative action, the fact that the law review had no minority members was a source of criticism. Every year, whispers circulated that law review was racist and that the leadership deliberately excluded blacks, Hispanics and any other minorities we could think up. In the three years that I spent at the law school, there were only a handful of Asian students on staff. There were no blacks and I am not sure that there were any Hispanics. I read a study that found 76 percent of the law reviews in the United States had no black members while 69 percent had no Hispanic members and 85 percent had no Asian members.[12]

This was a sore spot for the law school administration. It was a sore spot at law schools across the country. I had heard rumors that the law school administration had expressed interest in establishing an affirmative action plan for law review. Some top-tier and state law schools set aside a handful of affirmative action positions on staff.[13] New York University ran a separate write-on competition for minorities.[14] Rutgers, in New Jersey, kept one slot available as a special affirmative action position.

According to information on its website, the Harvard Law Review reserves spots on staff for "discretionary" selection to fulfill its affirmative action policy. Other law reviews with affirmative action policies include Columbia, Cornell, Michigan, Penn and Virginia.[15]

Like many law reviews, however, the Syracuse Law Review had no such policy. The students who grade on make law review based on their grades and class performance. The write-on competition was completely anonymous and unbiased.

Despite the fairness of our competition and adherence to the grading system, we were under criticism. I was bracing for the allegations ever since I was elected. They certainly came, in the form of Wilfred.

A few days earlier, I received a note from an editor, Sofia, regarding a conversation she overheard in the student lounge. She overheard Wilfred discussing the write-on competition with friends of his. She heard him say that he had seen the list of the write-on scores and that he was only two points away from making it onto Law Review. Sofia approached him and asked him how he heard about this because she was interested in learning more about how she did in the write on competition. He told her that he saw the list from a friend he has on law review.

---

[12] Mark A. Godsey, *Educational Inequalities, the Myth of Meritocracy, and the Silencing of Minority Voices: the Need for Diversity on America's Law Reviews,* 12 HARV. BLACKLETTER J. 59, 61-62 (1995).

[13] *Id.; See also,* LAZARUS, at 237.

[14] According to the Law Review's website in 1999.

[15] Godsey, 12 HARV. BLACKLETTER J. at 90.

A day later, Annie, another associate editor who was a senior board member of another law school organization, came to my office to inform me about a conversation she had with Wilfred. She told me that he had questions about the write-on competition and was convinced that the editors miscalculated his score because his essay was superior. She added that he thought that he deserved reconsideration, and pointed out that law review lacked minority staff members.

"The law review will not reconsider Wilfred's or anybody's write-on essays," I told Annie. "If he has any questions about that or our policies, he can come talk with me. I'll talk to anybody."

A day later Wilfred came to my office. I shook his hand and offered him a seat. He wanted the door closed. Wilfred expressed his concern that he received no feedback on his essay. "As a lawyer, writing is very important and I believe it is very important to get feedback on writing," he said. "There was no feedback with the write on essay."

"The law review has a policy of not disclosing the details or grading of the write-on competition," I said. "We cannot provide people with feedback, it's not feasible."

With 80-plus entrants in the competition, it would be impractical to provide critiques of the essays, I added.

Then, I explained the competition grading procedures and assured him that it was completely anonymous and that each essay was read by eight separate readers. Each paper had an accompanying detailed score sheet. These scores were then transferred to a chart with the corresponding number. These charts were then faxed to the Notes and Comment editor on July 12.

"I assure you, the information was accurate and the scores were not erroneous or mixed up or otherwise compromised," I said.

He then asked whether the Law Review would publish a note that he wrote last year. "The only student notes we publish are the top notes from our spring competition and the law review does not ordinarily publish student work," I said, adding, "Feel free to send in your work for consideration. We receive about 20 or so submissions every week. But I'll be honest with you, the likelihood that it would be published is quite slim."

The Law Review stood by its judgment and would not reconsider Wilfred's, or anybody else's, entry. Even though there would be no reconsideration, Nick, the Notes and Comments editor, reviewed his accounting figures which were accurate. I wanted to ensure that we were on solid footing. I reviewed the calculations and spreadsheet data, too.

The night before I retrieved Wilfred's essay from the box of entries I stored in a crawlspace in my apartment. I was swamped enough, but I reviewed his essay anyway. I stood by my personal score. First, his essay contained several sections that were grossly overwritten. His use of transitional adverbs and conjunctions was excessive. Second, his misuse of commas was disturbing and grammatically incorrect.

Third, none of his citations conformed to proper *Bluebook* form (the courts and dates were omitted). Proper *Bluebook* citation form reads like a coded sentence: party v. party, reporter book volume; reporter book, page, court, jurisdiction and year. For example, *Smith v. Jones*, 1 Fed. 2d 100 (S.D.N.Y. 1999), stands for Smith versus Jones, reported in volume 1 of the federal reporter, second series at page 100 from the Southern District of New York in 1999. It is standard, logical and taught to all first year law students. Furthermore, it is all in the *Bluebook* or any legal writing manual. Fourth, his short citations were lacking. Short citations are subsequent citations after the case was initially cited.

Overall, his argument was not well-crafted either. His essay garnered average scores among the graders as well.

I withheld my detailed assessment of his essay. If he pressed me, I would have gleefully pointed out his essay's deficiencies. He obviously thought he was a writer's writer. Someone probably once told him that transition was good for arguments. But every other sentence, and this is not an exaggeration, began with a transition word. He was particularly fond of "on the other hand." The transition words were excessive and clumsy. In a memo designed to be persuasive, not every sentence needed to begin with *but, however, accordingly, moreover, furthermore, nevertheless, and, in so far as, because, since, neither, nor,* or *on the other hand.* Apparently, his did.

If pressed, I would have shredded his essay to his face, the way I inadvertently did with reporters at the *Daily Orange* as news editor or the way I sometimes did to the *News-Herald*, my newspaper competition in Cleveland. But Wilfred did not push me and there was no reason to be mean-spirited.

"We're not running a legal writing clinic here. If you want feedback, take your paper to a professor," I told him.

Based on the scoring, Wilfred was 56 points off the last score of the last write-on candidate invited on to law review. He was not even in the top 30 essays. Nick had ranked 1 through 30, and he was far below that.

As we sat there in my office, I was waiting for him to say it. After I completed my presentation on the grading system, we sat there looking each other in the eye. He looked like he wanted to say something but did not quite know how to broach the topic. To him, I was probably sitting there smugly.

"Anything else?" I said.

"No ..." he said. We shook hands and I opened the door for him. "Well, there is one last thing ... how many people of color do you have on your staff?"

"Oh, is that what this is about? I thought you wanted feedback on your essay," I said.

"It's a legitimate question. I'm just curious," he said.

"You already know the answer to that question, otherwise you wouldn't have asked it. If you are implying something about our selection process, you're off-base. Everybody has a shot through the write-on competition. If you have a problem with the way professors grade, I'm sure you could bring it up with the dean."

As he was leaving the office, I said, "Wait, I have a question ... I heard that you've been saying that you saw the write-on competition scores."

He just kind of looked at me blankly and said, "I never saw the scores."

"I know," I said.

The Law Review was an easy target for criticism on race-relations. If people were dissatisfied, they should have complained about the grading system to the administration. Plus, having a special slot solely for a person of color, to me, seemed unnecessary. Every law student had a shot at making law review, regardless of skin color or background. The writing competition alone was color blind.

Grading on and writing on were based on personal merit. One scholar critical of the lack of minority representation on law reviews denounced the lack of affirmative action policies at most law reviews as well as the notion of the law review as a meritorious honor society, writing that "'honor society' mentality makes two erroneous assumptions: (1) that 'grade-on' and 'write-on' selection methods identify the students who are able to do the best job as law review members, and (2) that anonymous 'merit'-based selection policies are inherently fair and impartial simply because they are blindly graded."[16]

---

[16] *Id.* at 62.

The article went on to discuss the implications of all-white law reviews which put minorities at competitive disadvantages in the job market while stifling the marketplace of ideas.[17]

Grades, I agree, may not always be the best indicator for whether a law student will be a good editor, proofreader or cite checker. I cannot speak for professors' grading systems, but I can say with complete certainty that the law review's writing competition was color blind. If a student was competent enough to be admitted into law school, and then survive the first year, there was no reason why any student was incapable of writing-on to the law review, regardless of race.

Writer's Market
Tuesday, September 7, 1999

It was a writer's market this year. We were systematically unable to secure articles for our first book. Every author we made an offer to came back with a negative response. The articles editors were reading the submissions, sending them to me for approval and then sending offer letters to the authors. By the time the letters got to the authors, the articles had already been snatched up by other journals. This happened with the first five articles we chose. Now, we were agreeing on the articles and negotiating over the telephone.

One scholar, Professor Lawrence Friedman, writing about legal scholarship pointed out the unique—"completely loco"—characteristics of the law review community; unparalleled in other areas of academia.[18] Law reviews present legal scholars with a potentially bottomless ocean of opportunities to get published: the country's law reviews combine to publish more than 150,000 pages every year.[19] Calling the law review industry a voracious behemoth, he pointed out that they are run by law students who choose articles based on their own judgment without the scholars subjecting their articles to peer review.[20]

The articles editors chose articles from a huge pile based on the topic addressed in the article, its overall quality, which also took into account how much editing work it would require and the author's

---

[17] *Id.* at 68.
[18] Lawrence M. Friedman, *Law Reviews and Legal Scholarship: Some Comments*, 75 DENV. U. L. REV. 661 (1998).
[19] *Id.* at 662.
[20] *Id.*

background and prior publications. Law reviews are judged by the quality of their articles and the quality of the authors. Good articles from prominent or up-and-coming authors would be cited in other articles, books and judicial opinions.

Despite the bottomless pit of law reviews, the competition was stiff. Professor Friedman described the massive volume of submissions law reviews receive: top journals receive as many as 1,200 submissions.[21] Authors, intent on getting their articles in the best journals, send out multiple submissions, which is anathema in other areas of academia.[22] The author illustrated the mentality of legal scholars, mostly law professors:

> Our author will print out fifty copies of her masterpiece, and send it off to fifty law reviews. If they all reject (or, more likely, ignore) her, she will crank up the Xerox machine and send it out to fifty more. You can't do that in journals that operate on the peer review system. But on law reviews, manuscripts are read not by faculty but by students, and nobody cares about wasting their time.[23]

Somebody had to care. After all, we usually received one to five unsolicited articles every day.

Without articles to edit, the 2L staff would be idle during office hours and our supply closet would be picked clean for such projects as paper clip necklaces. As it stood now, we had no rubber bands.

I set today for the deadline for revised student notes. This had given all the student authors, myself included, the Labor Day weekend to make some finishing touches on the notes. Sara and I spent the weekend revising our notes. We did take Sunday afternoon off to drive to Oswego, a city about 30 miles north of Syracuse on Lake Ontario. We toured the Revolutionary War era Fort Ontario and ate dinner at a riverfront restaurant.

The notes were due today, on disk and with any obscure materials needed for reference. I carted in four boxes full of cases and documents as well as a half-dozen books. Most of the other authors did likewise,

---

[21] *Id.* at 663-64.
[22] *Id.* at 664.
[23] *Id.*

except for Tom, a senior editor who went to Florida for the first 10 days of classes. He had missed orientation as well as his office hours. We needed his note, too.

Now, at least, each of the six teams had work to do. There would be no more rubber band ball incidents.

Buck-A-Roo
Monday, September 13, 1999

When I expressed displeasure with the Prince's rubber band project to Merry, an editor and the Prince's sometimes close friend, she passed the message on to him. I told her to convey to him that office hours were for law review work and that he owed the law review a bag of rubber bands.

The Prince was at a computer terminal working when I strolled into the office. I looked at him. As I stood in the middle of the office talking to another editor, the Prince approached. "Where are all those rubber bands?" I asked.

"I don't know," he said with a smirk.

"As far as the law review is concerned, you owe us a bag of rubber bands. As it is you wasted two hours last time and deliberately walked out with the rubber bands," I said.

Then, he reached into his wallet, pulling out a dollar bill and threw it at me. "Here, go buy some new rubber bands," he said.

I picked up the bill, attempted to hand it back to him and said, I did not appreciate this, "I am not joking with you."

He refused to take the dollar back. I simply placed it in the office candy bowl.

Throw the Book at Me
Monday, September 13, 1999

All the planning and meetings with the librarians paid off. A major plank in my campaign involved establishing an equitable policy with the library. The law library had an average-size collection. Thus, students could only check out books for about two weeks. This was hardly enough time for editing purposes. Furthermore, the law review team members needed books for months. In the past, individual team members or executive editors signed out books on their private accounts.

They became responsible and would incur late charges if books were not returned on time. At one point during my second year I had more than 80 books charged out on my account; at least two dozen were for books my team needed for editing articles.

Library fines could sometimes be whittled down, depending on the politeness of the student and the mood of the librarian. While students were required to keep a vigilant eye on the due dates and sat in fear of excessive library fines, faculty members enjoyed semester-long privileges.

In May, I submitted a report to Maggie, the head librarian, and arranged a meeting, to discuss establishing a policy for extended privileges. During a transition meeting, Connor, my predecessor, commented, "Dude, you'll never get that done. We've tried in the past and got nowhere."

After finals, I met with Maggie and the head circulation librarian, Becky, a pleasant, soft-spoken librarian. I proposed semester-long privileges for books used specifically for form and accuracy editing. The nature of the fact and citation checking required unfettered access to books and materials. They agreed.

"What law review editors do is important," Maggie said. "We want to help you. The library's concern is accountability. What are we going to do if books are stolen, lost or damaged?"

They wanted security. First, they wanted a $100 deposit. Edna, in the budget office, shrieked at the mention of a deposit system, and squelched the idea on the spot—"Unless, you want to take $100 out of the budget or your discretionary account," she said. I had neither the intention nor the authority to alter the budget that way, and was not going to waste 20 percent of my discretionary account on this.

We settled on an agreement of limited access. The library established a special account with a library card for the law review. This card was only accessible to the senior editors and executive editors. Only about 10 editors had privileges. Executive editors would be responsible for checking out the books their teams needed for editing. The library would have automatic recall priority. If someone needed the book, the librarians could automatically recall it. The library staff held a key to the office, accessible only to library staff and designated law review members. This gave staff members without keys access to the office on those rare occasions when it was locked.

The law review assumed responsibility for lost, stolen or damaged books, and we would deal with that on an ad hoc basis. Then, the law review could check out law library books for the entire semester. Maggie and Becky drew up a contract. I signed it.

Circulatory System
Tuesday, September 14, 1999

Despite being a law student, I was thinking like a publisher even though I had no pecuniary interest if we gained or lost subscribers. No one would send me a bonus for getting new subscribers and no one would fire me if we lost them. Increasing our circulation was something I wanted to work on; this was pure ego. The bigger our subscription list was, the more we could charge for advertising and the more recognition the law review and law school would receive.

This plan was entwined with a sense of bravado. Even though law reviews continue to publish traditional books, more and more legal content was appearing on the Internet.

Most lawyers researching issues run general searches on Lexis or Westlaw and use the materials that they retrieve. If a Lexis or Westlaw user accesses, downloads or prints an article from the Syracuse Law Review, they pay for it through the service and the law review gets a residual. Therefore, they will use our products when and if they need it. Most would not pay $27 for a subscription for books that they may or may not need, or have time or desire to read.

The Survey had close to 1,200 subscribers while our regular subscription base had about 800. Law review circulation cannot be compared to newspaper or general publication circulation. These are not mass-circulation, general interest publications.[24] The Harvard Law Review, with the highest circulation of any law review in the country, has a circulation of only 8,000. Interestingly, the Harvard Law Review proclaims that it is the only independent student-run law review in the country, even though it has a professional business staff to carry out day-to-day operations, according to material on the Harvard Law Review's website.

Shooting for 8,000 subscribers was not realistic, but we could at least market the Survey to more law firms throughout New York as well as larger firms in New Jersey and Connecticut with business in New York.

---

[24] *See generally* SELIGMAN, at 182; MAYER, at 110.

Throughout the course of the year, I anticipated losing a handful of subscribers. Like any publication, our subscription list would ebb and flow. Every law school library in the country subscribed. Many New York law libraries and judges' chambers subscribed. Even a few correctional facilities subscribed. Alumni comprised a substantial portion of our subscribers. The alumni office sent out subscription forms once a year.

Once someone subscribed, the subscription automatically renewed and invoices were automatically sent by the business editor. To be removed from the list, the subscriber must affirmatively cancel the subscription. This prompted a series of cancellation letters after last year's books were mailed out. It also meant that a fair number of people received Volume 49 without paying for it or sending it back. The widow of an alumnus subscriber who had recently died wrote to cancel her husband's subscription. I suppose the subscription was not something she wanted to inherit or pass on.

The business editor, Ally, maintained an up-to-date mailing list on a computerized database. She was also keeping track of who paid and who cancelled and who failed to get the books that they paid for. She agreed that in order to counter-balance lost subscribers we needed to do something to attract new subscribers.

Unless there was a specific problem with a subscriber or a faulty address, Ally and the law review, did not have to mail the books. The printer, Joe Christensen, Inc., in Lincoln, Nebraska, handled all the mailings. Christensen, a family-owned printer was founded in 1932 and prints more than 330 law reviews, journals and titles. Law reviews were their business, they knew it and they were professional, patient and accommodating to new staffs.

Paneling
Thursday, September 16, 1999

A 3L on law review who held no editorial position asked me to sit on a panel for a discussion undergraduates thinking about attending law school. Sandy, the undergraduate pre-law advisor, wanted a diverse cross-section for the panel, including students who had worked before going to law school. She also thought having the law review editor would give her panel some additional credibility. There were four other panelists, a couple who had gone right to law school from undergrad, me and Cole, another senior editor and good friend who worked before going to law school.

Each panelist spoke for about two or three minutes, then it went to question and answers. The only wisdom I could impart was telling the students that they had to do everything they could to prepare for the competition of getting into law school, which mostly meant preparing for the LSAT exam.

"You will be competing against people with better grades from better schools with better connections than you. You have to be prepared for this and do everything you can to distinguish your application from the others. Doing well on the LSATs is probably the best thing you can do," I said.

My parting wisdom was a word of caution. "Before you go into this, you really have to assess whether going to law school is the right thing for you to do. I know everybody thinks being a lawyer is a great thing. But unless you are really certain that this is what you want to do, don't do it. Don't do it because you don't know what else to do. Law school is an investment of three years of your life, lots of money and energy. You do not need to invest all the time and money and energy into something you are not completely sure of. It is not worth it," I said.

Diplomatic Immunity
Monday, September 20, 1999

In some countries, the only way to get things done is to grease the system: outright bribery. In many countries it is impossible to get simple things done without paying off someone. Here, bribery, kickbacks and influence peddling are technically illegal. That is not to say that it is not widespread, because in many circles it is.

Wrapped up in the illicit underworld of bribes, is the perplexing practice of tipping. If you do not tip your waiter, waitress (or gender-neutral server) at a restaurant, there is a good possibility that the next time you eat there someone will sneeze on your meal, drop it on the floor or serve you leftovers, or worse.

It is enigmatic that society dictates paying extra money, in the form of a tip, to someone for doing his or her job. As editor in chief, I could not distribute gratuitous payments to school administrators who did their jobs on law review matters. The best I could do was write a letter. That was why I wrote a gushing letter to the law school's Records Administration Manager.

To understand the import of this particular letter, it is important to understand the cantankerous personality of the Records Administration Manager, Bella. Talking to Bella, if she talked to a student instead of snapping, left the impression that life at Syracuse would cease if she failed to show up for work one day. She was always overworked and never had time for students. When she did have time for students she was rude, curt and mean. She embodied the worst elements of a civil servant with the attitude of a victim-turned-vigilante.

Students had to deal with her for a variety of reasons ranging from adding and dropping classes, to pass/fail forms, scheduling issues, credit issues, reviewing exams and a host of bar admission forms. In my years at the law school, she yelled at me once for asking to review an exam. I watched her berate students individually and in groups. At the end of my first year, she held a meeting in the auditorium to explain course selection procedures. She spent the first five minutes simply yelling at an auditorium full of law students.

In short, there was only one student known to have a positive experience with Bella. But this student, who graduated a year earlier, claimed to have a good relationship with Bella because she lavished her with chocolate. This student's success with Bella probably rested more with the student's father, a prominent alumnus, fundraiser and donor.

Over the summer, the law review needed Bella to provide us with the list of the top 10 percent. Nick and I had each written her and personally introduced ourselves to her in May. Nick stayed in touch with her over the summer. We needed the list, plus summer addresses as early as possible, and we made sure Bella realized that a lot hinged on this, including fall interviews for those students. We would also need to know whether students in the top 10 percent would transfer out of Syracuse and then we would need the next in line. Then, once the fall semester began, we needed to contact the new transfer students to Syracuse.

Connor complained about her foot-dragging and the near ensuing chaos. He reported that she delayed the release of the list and even excluded a name. Any delays in this process would have a domino effect that would set things back for the rest of the year. We were bracing for Bella to drag her feet with us, too.

But Bella came through. She had the list in Nick's hands a few days early and even gave me phone numbers for three hard-to-reach law review invitees. I was so appreciative of her promptness that I put it in writing. This two-paragraph letter was brief:

> On behalf of the Syracuse Law Review I would like to thank you for your invaluable assistance in identifying and locating the second year students who now comprise the law review's editorial staff.
>
> Your prompt notification of the students as well as the notification of those who transferred to and from the College of Law enabled the law review to convene early. Our early orientation program allowed the law review to begin our work before classes began. Again, thank you for your assistance.

I sent a copy of the letter to the Dean and included a cc mark on the bottom of the page. I hand delivered the note to Bella's secretary and returned to my office.

Within a minute of my return, Bella called to thank me for thanking her. "This is one of the nicest letters I've ever gotten. Thank you so much, Roy," she said. It was not chocolate, but was just as sweet.

The President of the College of Law's Associates Council, the junior board of visitors for the law school, called me to find out whether we had any plans for the law review that he might be able to include in a council mailing. I sent a brief letter announcing the notes chosen for publication while outlining the law review's plans for the year. This was one of my first opportunities to begin soliciting support for the 50th anniversary book. The information was included in the fall mailing of the Associates Council's newsletter. The law review would be available to assist in any associates council or homecoming events, I added.

At the very least, I offered to make sure the office would be open during homecoming if any alumni wanted to stop by and see the nice new office. The new office was about two-and-a-half years old, and a far cry from the tight, cinderblock, windowless dungeon of a room that the law review formerly inhabited in the old building.

The People's Editor
Wednesday, September 29, 1999

My friend, Cody, frequently criticized me for being "too accessible" and otherwise nice to the 2L editorial staff. Cody told me that I should not even talk to the 2Ls on staff. "You are the *fucking* Editor-in-Chief, you are so much above them. You bring down your office by even talking to them," he said. "You should march into the room, not even look at them and go into your office."

"I have to at least be nice to people, otherwise how can we expect them to do the work? I have to encourage them to do the work, otherwise, they'll just go through the motions," I answered, adding that part of my job entailed cheerleading. I reminded him that part of the problem with the staff malaise during our second year emanated from the attitude that the senior staff had toward the lower staff.

A cabal of senior editors the year before was largely credited with making the office inhospitable. There were other staff morale issues ranging from the condescending manner with which the sanctions committee meetings took place to the general intimidation factors. The year before, one editor rudely barked at everyone while another editor scared people because he knew the Bluebook so well that he could recite rules, complete with the section numbers right off the top of his head.

Many of my classmates simply felt that law review was not a place for them. Some classmates used these isolated incidents as excuses for not getting involved. Some were just plain old lazy. Part of it was general apathy and part of it was the arrogance of the senior staff before us. Regardless of the source, a number classmates did not want to have anything to do with law review during their third year. That, certainly, contributed to my successful election. But it also deterred some pretty good people from running for senior staff positions.

So, part of my job included motivating people any way I could. If being professional and nice to people helped motivate, so be it. After all, if people were excited and proud to be part of the organization, they would do better work. They would enjoy their work and feel a sense of camaraderie. If they felt that they had a vested interest in the articles, they would be better editors. Perhaps I was being naïve and optimistic (a first for me).

A seemingly endless supply of candy in the office should have been a substantial step toward this goal. I must have spent at least half of my discretionary funds on Blow Pops, Tootsie Pops and other assorted sweets that I kept in a bowl in the middle of the table in the middle of the office.

When Cody criticized me for being too involved with the staff, I bristled. As editor, I had to know everyone and welcome everyone to the staff and the office. I knew everyone by face even before they came back because I studied the face book. I remembered trivial facts about many people because I collected and typed up the questionnaires. I knew their hometowns, their summer workplaces and where they went to college. I had to know everyone and I was always pretty good at memorizing trivial facts about people.

This knowledge also helped when I divided everyone into the teams. I tried to match people with the right editors, and even bolster one team with stronger members to compensate for a flighty editor. This later helped when we assigned articles. For instance, we assigned an article with health care issues to the team with a 2L who was also a physician— this helped when the term myocardial infarction came up in the text of an article.

If the weight of my office was what it appeared to be, any contact I had with the junior staff would serve as additional motivation. Anyway, I liked being able to talk with the 42 editorial staff members. One 2L, Geneva, was even from Ashtabula, Ohio's largest but least populous county where I once covered a suspicious fire at landmark winery/restaurant and once got my car stuck in a muddy swamp after police found the body of a missing Cleveland girl. Geneva and her husband even grew up with a guy I knew from the News-Herald, the suburban paper my paper competed against.

It was this sort of familiarity and rapport that made the office, and my daily job, more pleasant. Nevertheless, Cody scoffed.

Reflecting on our second year, our junior year on law review, I remembered how cool it thought it was when Connor initiated a conversation with me in the parking lot during the fall semester and the time Connor approached me in the halls in February when I was contemplating running for editor. "It's really good that someone with leadership was stepping up," Connor told me.

As Cody, Sara and I sat around a table in the cafeteria, chewing Juicy Fruit gum, exchanging observations and sharing Seinfeld trivia questions—Cody and I spent the better part of a year-and-a-half testing our respective Seinfeld knowledge—he finally acquiesced, "You know what you are? You are the People's Editor."

Net-work
Monday, October 4, 1999

After weeks of waiting for the computer tech director to handle the updates for our website, I went directly to the webmaster, who fixed and updated everything practically as I waited. I learned that if I wanted anything done for the website to go directly to the webmaster.

Just about every law review has a presence on the web. Law review websites have everything from abstracts or synopses of articles to full text of articles and archives. Some law reviews list their upcoming articles and symposia and even post their bylaws or constitutions. Commonly posted information also includes mastheads or lists of the staff with email links, subscription information . Our site did not have a lot of usable content: mailing and subscription information, a list of the Survey authors, topics and affiliations, the masthead with email links, the student notes selected for publication and an editor's message. We could not give the articles away for free.

After updating the masthead, a 2L member emailed me to ask whether it would be possible to include her middle initial in her name. She apologized for making such a "stupid and trivial request." If the technical editor was available and attentive, he would have taken care of all of these little things. I jumped on it immediately because I certainly appreciated the necessity of using a middle initial. At the paper, I stewed whenever a copy editor or other reporter omitted my middle initial in a byline or tag line. My byline included the S. and I took it seriously— perhaps because my first name is so short.

Where There's Smoke ...
Wednesday, October 6, 1999

At this point, each of the six editing teams had been working on student notes, Survey articles and book 1 articles. In late August, the six student-authors turned in their notes, along with the piles of obscure materials such as cases, books and photo copies of excerpts. The team led by Deb, an executive editor, was working on Tom's note, which she reported was "not in good shape." Tom, who was also a senior editor, had the third-ranking note.

Tom had missed many of his office hours and did not even show up for the first 10 days of school. He was a nice guy, friendly and gregarious but not the most diligent person on staff. Deb approached him on several occasions for help in locating a book and that was not available in the law library or any of the other libraries on campus. There was a piece of legislation from California that was also unavailable in our libraries or online in Lexis or Westlaw.

"My people are stuck on a couple of footnotes and Tom hasn't been able to give me the information we need. He keeps on putting it off and this one book is not available," Deb told me late one afternoon. Deb was a serious editor with an eye for detail that was surely honed in by her years as an electrical engineer. She was business-like and always on top of her team's work. Her work was solid and beyond reproach, and she had a couple of people on her team who were among the best researches on staff.

The book in question was a well-known text on journalism ethics. I had read excerpts of the book for journalism classes at the S.I. Newhouse School of Public Communication. The book's author, a journalism professor at a southern university, once bought me dinner at a Society of Professional Journalists convention I attended as an undergrad. I considered obtaining a copy of his book for my own research for my note, but opted against it. I knew at least three professors at Newhouse who had the book on their office bookshelves. That book could have been in my hands in five minutes. But for some reason Tom was singularly unable to retrieve a copy of the book.

My editing philosophy was to assume that a footnote was wrong or inaccurate until I found the proper source to confirm the information. Because of my inherent suspicion, I asked Deb to personally check the footnotes in question by running searches in Lexis or Westlaw to see that the materials existed. "Try calling up a couple of the articles he cited and check them for citations to the book, or excerpts or the legislation. I bet it turns up there," I said.

There was no reason to suspect anything was afoul. I just wanted to help Deb and her team corroborate the information until Tom turned over the book.

Bill of Writes
Friday, October 8, 1999

Even though enthusiasm among the junior staff of 2Ls had not yet subsided, the panic was about to set in for the student note. For many who had never written anything resembling a heavily-footnoted scholarly piece like a law review article, it was easy to feel lost. Few had any specific interests, much less expertise in an area of law. Every year at about this time, the law review ran a note-writing workshop. About half the 2L staff showed up. It was a Friday afternoon, the other half of the staff was at outside jobs, externships and out of town interviewing.

Professor Fairmont, a popular professor around the school with a number of writing credits, gave such tips as choosing a narrow topic, having a thesis or an argument, writing about something interesting and creating a title that included at least one colon—nearly every law review title includes one in the title: it is practically pro-forma.

Before getting to useful advice, he liked to begin with a sobering message: "The law review editor can cover his ears for this, but I have to tell you, nobody is going to read your note. These are papers written for the sake of being written." Professor Fairmont was repeating the same arguments and criticisms that scholars have articulated for decades, mostly in the pages of law reviews.[25] The Dean of Northwestern Law School, as far back as 1956, wrote: "Whereas most periodicals are published primarily in order that they may be read, the law reviews are published primarily in order that they may be written."[26]

An introduction like Professor Fairmont's was about as inspiring as a standup comedian opening with Hitler jokes. Both professors were entirely correct. But there was a purpose to law review. Writing a law review article while in law school hones research and writing skills and builds an expertise in a topic. Getting published is as good as listing any other accolade on a resume.

And, despite the cynical analysis of the purpose of writing a law review article, it still has not stopped Professor Fairmont or thousands like him from continuing to write and publish such articles.

Author, Author
Monday, October 11, 1999

The law review could not sustain itself without articles. Between the four books, we publish about 35 articles, essays and student notes

---

[25] *See* Dean Havighurst, *Law Reviews and Legal Education*, 51 N.W. U. L. REV. 24 (1956); Reinhard Zimmermann, *Law Reviews: A Foray Through A Strange World*, 47 EMORY L.J. 659, 694-95 (1998).
[26] *Id.*

each year. Books 1, 3 and 4 each had two articles, one essay and two student notes. This was the system. The Survey had about 20 articles every year on recent developments in New York state and federal courts. Our 50th Anniversary book would have anywhere from 5 to 10 articles. This year's haul would be more than the usual hefty publication schedule.

Dealing with the authors had been more of a headache than was predicted or anticipated. It was more like a full body ache.

The aches started when we had to fill four spots in the Survey: administrative, employment, state tax and conflicts of law. The lead articles editors and I spent the first month of the year combing the Martindale Hubbell law directory and Lexis looking for potential authors. I spoke to some alumni editors who put the word out through their networks.

I landed a Harvard grad from a major New York law firm for administrative law and a local lawyer at a fancy Syracuse law firm for employment. It was odd making the sales pitch to lawyers and professors, especially when we were running up against a tight deadline. Our initial deadline for the Survey was early August. By the end of September, it was increasingly difficult to entice potential authors. We were additionally hampered by the fact that last year's Survey came out several months late—a feat I wanted to work hard not to repeat.

A nationally-known employment law lawyer from New York City expressed interest but declined because he was unable to undertake another writing project on such short notice. Then, I was able to sign a well-known employment litigator from Albany. But a month later she returned the contract and said that her court schedule was too clogged to actually fulfill her obligations. "Sorry," she wrote.

An alumnus, an editor the year before, at a prominent Syracuse law firm, helped secure a commitment from a partner who had written for the law review in the past. We set a January 17 deadline.

Three of our Survey authors actually met the initial August deadline. Others promised their articles would be forthcoming. Black's Law Dictionary should have an entry for the terms "forthcoming," "next week" and "soon." A clear definition of deadline might also be useful.

Still, other authors completely ignored the deadlines. Roughly half the Survey authors were law professors. There was absolutely no excuse for a professor to miss a deadline; especially when most were repeat authors who had written their respective articles for years. Law professors have nothing else to do but research and write. Our practitioner authors were often over-extended and viewed their article as the absolute last thing on their crowded agendas. A law review article could not be billed to a client, so it was expected that their writing would not be a priority in their lives.

One of the most outrageous complaints a handful of authors lodged was the timeliness of our publication. "You get the Survey out late every year anyway," one author complained to me during one of our deadline debates.

"The books come out late because authors submit their articles late," I replied.

Law review editors everywhere face the almost impossible challenge of publishing on time.

The difficulties we encountered securing articles for our first book began during the summer. In hindsight, our troubles began the day the staff was elected in late March because that was when we should have started nailing down authors.

Over the summer Walt and Vince, the articles editors, read through piles of potential articles. Then they sent me the ones they liked and once I read them and approved, we would write an offer letter to the author.

This is how their predecessors did it. This is how we would do it. It seemed like a good system. Only by the time everything got to me, not to mention by the time we had letters mailed to the prospective authors, the articles were already committed to other law journals. One author was being published by the Columbia Business Law Review. Others went elsewhere.

By the time we returned to school at the end of August, we had no articles for our first book. To expedite the process, they began calling authors of articles they liked. Then, it was the authors' turn to jerk us around. In the first month-and-a-half, we must have made offers to about 15 to 20 different authors. Most were clearly not interested in publishing with us. They would lead us along, ask for a week or two to consider the offer and weigh it against other offers. Some wanted a commitment for extra reprints. A reprint is a single, fully-paginated copy of the article in the law review's bound cover. They look fancy and authors give them out to their friends and colleagues. It is more cost-efficient to order the reprints when the book is printed, otherwise the printer has to make a separate, and costly print run.

Authors love their reprints. Reprints are like currency, the way cigarettes are in jail. The law review provided 50 free to the authors and allowed them to buy extras. For negotiation purposes, we were ready to throw in extra free reprints to sweeten the deal.

Dealing with authors intent on getting published at the best possible journals was frustrating. Many authors I dealt with were clearly more interested in using our offer to strong-arm some other journal, and had no intention of running with us.

One author, Professor Boscow, from Seton Hall University Law School in New Jersey, vacillated for almost two weeks before deciding to run his article in a Midwestern law review. We negotiated back and forth and had a contract drawn up and faxed to him. The article was interesting, too. Then, he called to tell me that he was accepting an offer from the other law review.

There was no convincing him, either. "That is not a better law school or law review. Our reach in this area of the country, where you live and work, is better than some Midwestern law school. We have better name recognition," I told him on the phone.

Unfazed, the next day Professor Boscow faxed me a letter explaining his decision; shifting the blame to the law school's tenure committee: "I wanted you to know, though, that it was a very tough decision to make, and that we have a great deal of fondness for your journal here at Seton Hall because of some work you did a few years back on housing issues ... I have a completed article on bankruptcy (which has some math and economics in it) and I'm working on a piece about the game theory behind presidential succession. If you're interested in either of those subjects please give me a call."

The decision, I am sure, was not too "tough." He probably faxed that same letter to a half-dozen other law reviews that he had jerked around. I did not call him for his bankruptcy or game theory articles.

Another author who evaded us and avoided us after we made him an offer seemed disappointed that we would want to run his article. He ended up putting us off until we had to force his hand. The frustrations were piling up, so I decided to be blunt: "Why would you send something to us if you really did not want to publish with us?" He was unable to give me an answer. "It's just unprofessional, and it's a waste of time and money," I added.

For many law professors, it was a game. Most of them left the legal profession after a couple years at prestigious law firms to teach law.

Most of them have research assistants to find the cases, brief or summarize cases and check the footnotes. Then, they posture and negotiate with law reviews to run their pieces. They call and ask for expedited review, pit law reviews against each other by dangling offers, whether genuine or fictitious. Some of the tricks they use would be grounds for disciplinary action if they pulled them on another lawyer or a court.

Academia pressures professors to publish or perish. Publishing articles eases the path to tenure. Some law schools even give their professors cash bonuses for published articles. Articles get the professor, and the law school's names into the world. Citations could influence the outcome of a judicial opinion. And, it all leads to more space on the professors' curricula vita.

With more than 400 law journals competing for articles, few professors find themselves totally excluded from publication. The only problem is that many of these professors only want their articles published in the top law schools' law reviews. All other takers are second-rate, so they look down their noses at the less prestigious law schools. Beggars cannot be choosers. Most of these articles are not even well-written and are pretty boring, anyway.

Maybe I should have solicited Seton Hall Professor Boscow's game-theory article, just to read and learn about game theory. Learning to play a game might have helped me deal with authors.

Spreading the Wealth

As if attracting authors was not a big enough hassle, Freddy, a 3L member who was an editor of one of the school's other journals, the Syracuse Law & Technology Journal, asked me for help with articles.

"Hey, if you have any extra articles on technology or intellectual property, could you send them over to us, we're having trouble getting articles," he asked me.

His journal was a new entity at Syracuse, begun the year before to replace a journal on legislation and public policy. The tech journal's niche was declared in its name, but its novelty was the fact that it was totally online. There was no hard copy book printed. Between the online nature and its new, unproven standing, it was not surprising why he was having trouble getting articles.

Politely, I told him that we were having our own troubles and had no extra articles to spare. "If we do, I will certainly send them over," I reassured, "but I can't promise you anything."

A day or two later, I remembered a conversation I had with Edith, my old friend from the *Daily Orange* who graduated a year earlier. She showed me a paper she had written for an independent study project on the copyrights associated with type fonts. This would certainly fit with the tech journal's focus and I knew that Edith would have great difficulty getting the article published elsewhere as a first-year lawyer coming out of Syracuse without other journal articles under her belt. She worked at a Syracuse law firm and was eager and appreciative that I remembered her article and volunteered to forward it to the tech journal.

I brokered the deal.

... There's Fire
Wednesday, October 13, 1999

Deb came into my office with a look of utter nausea. She told me that she followed my advice on checking the outstanding footnotes in Tom's note.

"I checked out his footnotes and they are similar to footnotes in another law review article from the Tulane Law Review," Deb said before handing me a copy of his note and a similar looking footnote from the Tulane Law Review.

The Tulane article was quite familiar because it was an expansive and comprehensive accounting of the same newsgathering and First Amendment issues I covered in my note. I had cited this article prominently in my own note. I mentioned the author by name before she even handed me the copy. Deb was surprised by my immediate recognition of the article but more disgusted by what she saw in her hands. The article had extensive footnotes that covered practically half of each page. They were lengthy string cites with parenthetical analysis and plenty of the author's own analysis.

I quickly scanned the footnote she marked on Tom's note and the one she marked on the Tulane article. They were verbatim copies without attribution to the Tulane article. This one footnote looked as if Tom had cut and copied the footnote from the Tulane article and pasted it into his note.

My stomach sank. "Deb, I think we might have a problem," I said.

"I think it is worse. I looked at a couple other footnotes and they looked the same too," she said.

I asked Deb to go through the note and make a list of the footnotes that were similar or identical to the Tulane article. If this was what I feared, we would have to proceed with caution and precision. I consulted with Mike, managing editor, and George, the form and accuracy editor. They agreed, this looked like plagiarism.

Conflagration
Thursday, October 14, 1999

Deb returned, armed with a list that she compiled after carefully comparing the footnotes in Tom's article to the footnotes in the Tulane article. The list revealed that at least 12 footnotes in Tom's note appeared practically identical to footnotes in the Tulane article. One footnote bore a distinct similarity to a footnote in a prominent public figure privacy opinion by the Second Circuit Court of Appeals.

Beyond the identical footnotes, Deb found several sentences in the text that bore a distinct similarity to statements contained in the Tulane article, without proper footnotes.

There would be a problem, a big problem. This note was clearly not his original research. Of the roughly 60 footnotes in Tom's note, 13 were apparently copied from another source, and most were copied verbatim. They were not just copies of a list of cases or string cites, a list of cases standing for a proposition. The copied material included the Tulane author's parenthetical summaries of the cases as well as extensive discussions within the footnotes themselves.

A typical law review article footnote would resemble this: Jones v. Smith, 1 State Rep. 100 (App. Ct. 1999) (holding that it is illegal to steal). Most parentheticals include lengthy quotes or an author's particular take on a case or article. This type of documentation shows that the writer performed extensive and thorough research and that the material cited adequately supports the statement or conclusion.

Obviously, part of the reason why Tom's note was chosen for publication by last year's editors was the impressive appearance of his long textual footnotes. The panel of judges, like critics of legal writing, gave points and credence to lengthy footnotes. That is why it is not uncommon to see some law review articles with as few as two or three words on a page and footnotes consuming the rest of the page. This zeal for documentation is sometimes pedantic and frequently criticized, but it is also a reflection on the amount of research performed.[27] If a footnote cites several cases, it stands for the proposition that the author read those cases and spent time digesting and understanding them. Those cited sources support the assertion in the text.

Even a cursory comparison of his footnotes to the Tulane footnotes revealed that the work was not his. *Black's Law Dictionary* defines plagiarism as: the act of appropriating the literary composition of another or parts or passages of writings or ideas or language of the same and passing them off as the product of one's own mind ... to be liable for plagiarism, it is not necessary to exactly duplicate another's literary work.[28]   A leading legal writing book provides a more laconic and conversational definition of plagiarism in its glossary:

> Plagiarism is copying someone else's ideas or words and claiming them as your own. In legal writing, this is as unacceptable as it is in any other kind of writing. But do not confuse plagiarism with paraphrasing; it is perfectly permissible to paraphrase someone else's words, that is, to put their ideas into your own words and then to acknowledge the source of that idea. Thus you may paraphrase and then cite to the authority for any holding, proposition, rule, quotation, or point of law.[29]

Unfortunately, the legal research and writing books used in our first year law school research and writing classes did not address plagiarism in their pages. But this was law school, I thought, that any person who had gotten this far in academia would not need a special lesson on the subject of plagiarism.

This was a serious matter because of the drastic implications a plagiarism charge could have on a burgeoning legal career. Much like the write-on scandal, this was not a charge I wanted to level. The implications could devastate Tom's career before it even started. Furthermore, the charge could embroil the law review, and me, in

---

[27] Abner J. Mikva, *Law Reviews, Judicial Opinions, and Their Relationship to Writing*, 30 STETSON L. REV. 521, 525 (2000).

[28] BLACK'S LAW DICTIONARY 1150 (6th Ed. 1990).

[29] MARY BARNARD RAY & JILL J. RAMSFIELD, LEGAL WRITING: GETTING IT RIGHT AND GETTING IT WRITTEN 223 (2d ed. 1993).

litigation. It was not uncommon for a person charged with academic fraud to hire counsel and sue everyone in sight.

I would have preferred not to have to be the executioner for a senior editor, a person I considered more than simply an acquaintance. I would have preferred to handle the matter internally but realized there were too many reasons why I could not simply ask him to withdraw his note from publication.

Anything short of a prosecution would be viewed as sweeping it under the rug. I was compelled to turn the case over to the Judicial Board for several reasons. First, because of the academic credit implication, law review members receive two academic credits: one credit is attributed to the law review note. Furthermore, writing a student note satisfies the law school writing requirement. This pushed it outside the scope of my authority.

Second, the Law Review's internal bylaws did not allow the Law Review to bring charges for removal against a Senior Board member without a finding of an appropriate adjudicative body except for gross dereliction of duties. Plagiarism for a senior editor fell outside the ambit of gross dereliction of duties. In order to remove Tom from his senior board position, we needed an adjudication by the Judicial Board.

Third, the members of the Law Review were bound by the New York Code of Professional Responsibility, which applied to law students and was expressly incorporated by the Law School's academic rules and code of student conduct. Specifically, the New York Code of Professional Responsibility DR 1—103 (a) and (b) attaches a duty to report to the appropriate authority wrongdoing or ethical violations by another lawyer. This provision required disclosure of evidence or knowledge of behavior that raises questions about another lawyer's honesty, trustworthiness or fitness in other respects.

I could have buried this matter. I took no glee in prosecuting another student for academic fraud. But I could not compromise my own integrity or the integrity of the law review by ignoring this matter. I would not implicate myself or the law review by turning a blind eye. If I did not prosecute, I would be guilty of abrogating the Code of Professional Responsibility. I had no choice, professionally or ethically.

The Good, The Bad and the Ugly
Tuesday, October 19, 1999

This morning, I scheduled a meeting with the Dean to address a number of issues including a presentation of the preliminary evidence in the our plagiarism case as well as the purchase of several off-budget items. His secretary booked me for the late afternoon.

Walking into the Dean's private office, we shook his hand, as we always did during such meetings. A year earlier, I noticed that the Dean and I both had the same shoes, a pair of black leather bucks made by the H.S. Trask company of Bozeman, Montana. I had seen them only once in a store in New Jersey. He was the only other person I ever saw wearing a pair of these shoes, made from buffalo leather. I always wore them when I met with him, but I do not think he ever noticed.

Regardless of whether he noticed my footwear, we exchanged brief pleasantries, very brief pleasantries. There was no polite chit-chat. Neither one of us seemed well-suited for small talk. Neither of us seemed to have time to engage in small talk either. Maybe he just did not like me. It did not matter since we both had plenty of business to attend to.

As I sank into his deep leather couch, which always made an awkward squeaking noise, I said, "What do you want first: the good, the bad or the ugly?"

With a pitch like that, he grimaced slightly as he said, "Let's start with the ugly."

At this point I had the two articles, with the footnotes highlighted for comparison, as well as the list prepared by Deb. I laid the three documents out on the table in front of him with the list in the middle.

"This is a student note slated for publication and this is a law review article published last year," I said, pointing to the documents like a waiter at a restaurant. "And, this is a list of footnotes that bear a distinct, if not identical, resemblance to the note and the article."

I paused to allow him a moment to absorb the materials before him. "Holy moly!" he said.

"We will not publish this note but I believe we have a plagiarism case and I wanted you to have a heads up before word gets out," I said.

He said he would inform the Associate Dean and told me that I had to prepare a report and turn it in to the Associate Dean so the Judicial Board could try the case.

My next order of business, the Bad, would be like a walk in the park on a sunny day. The Bad was a request for several off-budget book purchases: *Bluebooks*, a *Black's Law Dictionary*; a grammar manual and a modern dictionary to supplement our unabridged 1950 *Webster's Dictionary*.

After presenting a case of plagiarism to the Dean, I probably could have gotten approval to buy a car for the law review. By comparison, purchasing a car for the law review was much more appealing than charging a student with plagiarism. But then again, the law review had no need for a car. Nearly $200 in books, vital to editing legal articles, was nothing compared to a serious scandal.

The Dean also did not flinch at my memo informing him that I unilaterally ordered two hardcover *Bieber's Dictionary of Legal Citations* without pre-approval.

The Good news was glossed over: plans for our 50th Anniversary book. By the time I mentioned that we were contacting alumni to write articles for our 50th Anniversary book, I was practically out the door.

When I returned to the office, Tom was sitting at my desk talking on the telephone. I was surprised to see him because he was not frequently in the office for his office hours much less in the office after office hours were done for the day.

As he heard me approach, he quickly ended his phone conversation. I was dreading this moment. I did not feel comfortable confronting him but I had to do this eventually. I owed him the courtesy of keeping him informed. It was only fair. It was uncomfortable for me and it would be a shock to him. But it had to happen sooner rather than later.

I braced myself the same way I used to when I interviewed the family of a victim of a crime or a car accident. As a reporter, I was frequently at the scene of an accident or a crime or at the survivor's house seeking an interview for biographical information or gory details of the tragedy at hand. It was not the most appealing aspect of journalism, but a necessary part of the job. Sometimes people welcomed me into their homes, offered me coffee and permitted me to observe their grieving first-hand. Sometimes people slammed the door in my face, cursed at me or attempted to forcibly remove me from their front steps. Some were too distraught to talk and others designated family members. I never knew what kind of reaction awaited when I approached with my press pass dangling around my neck and a reporter's notebook in my hand.

Similarly, I had no idea how Tom would react or what he would say. So, I braced myself.

"I wanted to talk with you, Tom, because we have a serious problem," I said, closing the door to my office.

"Oh, I know I owe some office hours. I talked to Mike this week about coming in on Friday," he said.

"It's about your note, we have a problem."

"Yeah, I talked with Deb, I told her I'd get that stuff to her and forgot," he said.

I laid out the three documents as I did earlier with the Dean, pointing to the first footnote in question and asked him to read it. He read them both and said, "Yeah, so?"

I was taken aback and said, "Well, these footnotes are identical."

"So? I agree with that statement."

"I don't know a delicate way to say this, Tom, but this looks like plagiarism."

"What?"

"This is not your work," I said.

He attempted to explain the evidence by saying that he did not understand what I was saying. "Yes, I agree with these cases."

"But this is the same language. These are the same cases and the same words in the Tulane article and your article. It's verbatim."

"Yeah, so? I agree with the statements."

"But this is not your work, is it? Did you read this case?" I asked pointing to the first case in a footnote.

"No. But I agree with it."

"How about this article," I asked pointing to the next item in the lengthy citation.

"No, but I agree with it."

We went through a couple of the lengthy footnotes like that. I suppose I was somewhat pedantic at this point. But it had to be clear and straight with Tom.

"You cannot simply list this stuff without reading it. A footnote stands for the proposition that you read this case or that article and that this is what you gleaned from it. That is what a footnote means, that you read it and this is your interpretation. You cannot simply take someone else's interpretations. That is not your work. That is plagiarism.

"Well, this is news to me. I mean, you have a background in publishing. I didn't know any of this," he innocently said. "I'll do whatever it takes to fix this up."

"I am afraid it is a little too late for that," I said. "You had all summer and the first couple weeks in August to fix this up. I have to turn this over to the Judicial Board."

"Wait, can't we just fix it here? I'll do whatever I have to," he said, with a hint of desperation.

I felt the worst at this point. Here I was in my closed office with a classmate, a friend, whose career I was dangling in front of him, unable to yield an inch. At this point it was also too late. As much as I liked Tom and as much as I wanted to believe that he made an honest mistake, I had no other choice.

"I'm sorry, but this is out of my hands at this point," I said.

Given the extent of his plagiarism, I had difficulty believing his innocence or his explanation. Perhaps he really did not think that he did anything wrong. Even if he was being honest, I found it incomprehensible how someone could have lifted the wealth of material that he took without realizing what he had done. The extent of the similarities looked as if he downloaded the article from Lexis or Westlaw and cut and pasted the footnotes in their entirety. In a few cases, one or two words in a lengthy footnote were changed, as if he had looked up an applicable synonym. In another instance, one of the Tulane author's internal citations made an internal short citation to another law review article that was frequently cited in the article. So, Tom's article included a sentence referring to another article not cited in his article: "hereinafter ..."

The evidence was glaring and disturbing. I suspect that Tom cut corners but did not want to admit guilt. He was eager to have his article published. The five other law review members whose notes were chosen for publication, including Sara and me, spent a lot of time over the past six months revising, updating and double checking our notes. He, surely, could have done the same. At the very least Tom had more than six months to cover his tracks.

Tom probably did not have any willful intent. He was probably just caught up in the deadlines and cut corners. But plagiarism, like copyright infringement, does not have an intent or *mens rea* (guilty mind) requirement.[30] The mere act, even if inadvertent or accidental,[31] is enough to warrant infringement.

Shortly after this evidence surfaced, I supplemented my heavy reading load with some research into law student plagiarism and academic dishonesty.[32] As if I did not already have enough material to read, I had to become more than just familiar with the topic of plagiarism.

Thanks, but No Thanks (By the way, Screw You)
Tuesday, October 19, 1999

The epitome of unprofessional conduct was delivered by a character named Mr. Jeremy, a lawyer in the legal department of a famous Wall Street brokerage house. He submitted an article on management trends the year before, got an offer and signed a contract with our predecessors only to withdraw the article. He had a potential dispute with his superiors about publishing so he withdrew, Connor had told me.

---

[30] Terri LeClercq, *Failure to Teach: Due Process and Law School Plagiarism*, 49 J.LEGAL EDUC. 236, 244-46 (1999) (in a survey of 152 law schools, 91 law schools, the majority, reported that intent is not required to establish guilt for plagiarism under their academic rules or codes of student conduct. However, 42 schools required intent to be proven. The researchers sent the survey to 177 law schools, some failed to respond.) The Syracuse Code of Student Conduct had a knowing requirement that requires a slightly lower burden of proof.

[31] Robert D. Bills, *Plagiarism in Law School: Close Resemblance of the Worst Kind?*, 31 SANTA CLARA L. REV. 103, 114-15 (1990) ("Strict accountability regardless of intent gives a clear warning: 'Accidental plagiarism is plagiary nevertheless, but may not warrant an academic execution. Other sanctions will still be imposed.'").

[32] *See* LeClercq, 49 J. LEGAL EDUC. at 236, 244-46; Marilyn V. Yarbrough, *A Nation Under Lost Lawyers: The Legal Profession at the Close of the Twentieth Century: Do As I Say, Not As I Do: Mixed Messages for Law Students*, 100 DICK. L. REV. 677 (1996); Donald H. Stone, *The Bar Admission Process, Gatekeeper or Big Brother: An Empirical Study*, 15 N. ILL. U. L. REV. 331 (1995); Jan M. Levine, *Symposium on Legal Education: Response: "You Can't Please Everyone, So You'd Better Please Yourself: Directing (or Teaching In) A First-Year Legal Writing Program*, 29 VAL. U. L. REV. 611 (1995); Monroe H. Freedman, *The Professional Responsibility of the Law Professor: Three Neglected Questions*, 39 VAND. L. REV. 275 (1986).

He sent it back to us and called us to see if we were interested. We were. We read the article and decided to go for it. He orally agreed to run with us. Walt, the articles editors faxed him a contract to him on a Friday. We assigned it to Cole's F&A team and work began on it.

On Tuesday, Mr. Jeremy called back to withdraw. He said that he got an offer from the Stanford Business Law Review and was going to publish it there.

"We have a contract," I told him. "We have an agreement."

"No we don't," he said. "I never signed the contract."

"We had an oral contract. You agreed that we were publishing your article. That's a contract," I said.

"No, we don't have a contract," he said.

I told him that based on his conversation and agreement we assigned the article to a team that began working on it. "That's just too bad because we don't have a contract," he answered.

He basically said "too bad." That's when I unloaded. I told him that he was one of the most unethical people I ever dealt with in my professional life.

"You are so completely devoid of ethics and morality that you appall me," I calmly said. There was silence, so I continued. "You have no right to do this. This is an egregious breach and an unprofessional act." He disputed that and said, "I am sorry you feel like that."

"No. No, you are not sorry. You are not contrite. You are unprofessional and ethically-challenged. You do not care about anything but yourself. Do me a favor, don't ever send anything to the Syracuse Law Review again, never. Because I do not want to do business with someone as depraved as you," I said, never raising my voice.

I was going to put a similar letter in writing and cc to his superiors as well as contact the Stanford Business Law Review, but I had more pressing concerns. It was obvious that there was nothing I could do or say that would bother this guy or change his mind. What could I as a law review editor really do to an Ivy League snob at a giant investment brokerage house?

Despite his denial, the law review had a legitimate breach of contract claim. As much as I would have enjoyed raising hell with his superiors and even the Stanford journal, allocating my time and energy to an exercise in futility seemed wasteful. The more pressing task would be to find authors who *would* publish with us.

The Ringer (I)
Wednesday, October 20, 1999

One of the worst authors I had the pleasure of dealing with was, Mr. Ringer, our construction law author for our Survey. Ringer was a lawyer at a prestigious international law firm in New York City. Ringer's secretary called the office several times in the past week demanding that we make extra reprints for his article from volume 49. He had not even completed this year's article but wanted more reprints from last year's article.

When I spoke with her, the secretary was rude. She wanted the reprints printed and sent immediately and expected that I could quote her a price off the top of my head. "You are the editor, you should be able to tell me right now how much it will cost," she said. I explained to her that I might be the editor but I was not the printer and I could not give her a price because the price was contingent on the number of pages in the article. Furthermore, the printing also had to be done when the book is initially printed, otherwise it would cost more. I gave her a contact person at the printer in Nebraska and hoped she would be out of my hair.

The secretary also requested permission to post the article on the firm's website. I faxed back permission and added that we looked forward to receiving his article for this year's Survey.

The Report
Thursday, October 21, 1999

In the days before submitting my formal report on the plagiarism case, I individually briefed the senior board editors privately in my office. They needed to know about the matter because it involved an article slated for publication in our first book. They also needed to know about this because as long as this matter was pending, Tom, a senior editor, would not be performing his office hours, which meant we needed coverage. Additionally, enough people already knew and would know about the controversy because of Tom's friendships with editors and others on staff. I also welcomed the insight of the senior editors.

After each editor had a chance to review the material, each expressed a similar range of disgust and dismay. They were editors with a vested interest in the integrity of the law review. They were also law review members who wrote notes last year that were not chosen for publication. Essentially, their notes were runners up to someone who had cheated. These were editors who believed in their responsibilities and could sense that the law review was thrust into a precarious position.

One editor who was moderately friendly with Tom looked at the evidence and said, "I always thought he would do something like this. Fuck him." Another editor said, "This is a tough thing to do, I'm glad I'm not in your position. You have to do what's right." And another editor said, "I cannot believe that my note did not make it and his did, but I see why his was chosen, look at these footnotes, they look good. I'm shocked."

The Dean's office was quickly becoming acquainted with my investigative reports. I submitted my report to the Associate Dean today. This report was a tight three pages, single space, with three accompanying exhibits: the note; the article; and the chart. Cody did not read this one, but I suspect he would find it only slightly less "officious" than my previous report.

Nevertheless, I approached this report as I would have a regular legal brief: a preliminary statement; background; facts of the case; analysis; and conclusion. We were all law students and dealing with legal matters, the report needed to be comprehensive, objective, professional and properly supported. Too many reputations hung in the balance here, including mine.

In the preliminary statement, I leveled the charge of academic dishonesty, fraud and misrepresentation under the Code of Student Conduct § F 2(b) against Tom as a member of the law review. The Law Review, bound by the Syracuse University College of Law Academic Rules and Code of Student Conduct and the tenets of professional responsibility, presented this matter to the College of Law Judicial Board for adjudication, I wrote.

Because law review matters are often shrouded in mystery, I included a background section on law review policies, obligations and the note-writing process. The judicial board hearing the case would include law students who were not on law review and law professors who may or may not know how a law review operates. Here, I described the note-writing process and the requirements of law review members:

> Writing a student note comprises roughly half of the second-year editorial responsibilities for Law Review members.

As specified in the Syracuse Law Review bylaws, the student note must be an original scholarly paper of publishable quality.

The student works independently throughout the second year under the supervision of an Associate Notes and Comments editor, an elected third-year staff member. There are six AN&C editors who work with teams of eight second-year editorial staff members. The AN&C editor oversees the note-writing process and enforces deadlines to ensure that the editorial staff members meet deadlines and adequately progress with the project throughout the year.

Many Law Review members also enlist the supervision of a College of Law faculty member who helps direct, prod and otherwise mentor the student during the process. Additionally, the faculty supervisor certifies the student's work to satisfy the College of Law's writing requirement.

The note-writing project is essentially an independent study project. Writing a note of publishable quality requires intensive research and writing. Submissions are typically in the range of between 25 to 60 pages with complete footnotes and citations. Like all work in the Syracuse Law Review the student note must conform to *The Bluebook: A Uniform System of Citations.*

Because of the independent nature of the note-writing process, the student writer has flexibility with the subject matter, research materials and writing format. Students are encouraged to check for preemption by other law reviews or journals, changes in the law or changes in facts surrounding the note topic throughout the note-writing process. Fluidity with subject matter and the length of the publication schedule demands authors update and change their note well beyond the deadline for publication.

Second-year Law Review members earn two academic credits for satisfactorily completing the membership requirements.

The deadline for the 1998-99 Syracuse Law Review note writing competition was Friday, March 12, 1999. In the month following this deadline, a selection committee evaluated and ranked the notes. The Notes and Comments editor announced the top six chosen for publication on April 16, 1999 at the Law Review's annual banquet. Two alternates were also chosen.

Student notes were graded anonymously by the panel. The Editor-in-Chief is in possession of the scores and rankings for all the notes submitted.

The student notes selected for publication are subjected to rigorous editing for form and accuracy, colloquially referred to in-house as F&A. Student notes are subjected to the same editing processes and standards as the other articles selected for publication.

The F&A process ensures the accuracy of every author's propositions, quotes, spelling and grammar and Bluebook form. This editing work is performed during the editorial staff members' regularly-scheduled office hours. This work constitutes the other half of the editorial staff's duties and responsibilities during weekly office hours.

The facts of the case section objectively presented the matter. Probably the most strongly-worded portions of this section detailed Tom's inability to turn over documents:

> Deb attempted to solicit more information from Tom on several occasions. Tom was either unable or unwilling to provide materials. Acting on advice from the Editor-in-Chief, Deb searched online legal research databases for the information cited in the note. The Editor-in-Chief also recommended that Deb run specific searches for the unavailable books and resources through materials prominently cited in Tom's note.

> The Law Review does not take pleasure in presenting this case to the Judicial Board. Tom earned his way on to Law Review on his merits and to the best of the current administration's knowledge satisfactorily contributed to the publication throughout his second year. Additionally, Tom serves as a Senior Board Editor to which he was elected in March.

> The Law Review harbors no animosity or hostility toward Tom. The Law Review has not yet determined how it will deal with Tom upon adjudication by the Judicial Board. Nor has the Law Review adopted any recommendation to present to the Board regarding possible punishment should the Board find Tom guilty of a violation. The note will not be published in the Syracuse Law Review.

As regretful as this entire incident was, I could reflect upon this as an example of the safeguards of the editing process. Had this note been published, the reflection this would have cast on the Syracuse Law Review and the College of Law, and me personally, would have been one of complete embarrassment. With a scandal like that, word spreads fast. There might have even been publicity in the legal newspapers and magazines. People still talk about a law review editor at a well-regarded southern law school who was expelled during his third year for plagiarizing a portion of his note in the early 1980s.[33]

In many ways, we were lucky to catch this. Despite the seriousness of the copied material, this could have easily slipped through the gaps. His citations were good, except for the fact that they were identical to those of another author. Second-year staff members checked the form and accuracy of the citations for the first month of school and were unable to know that the footnotes were the same as footnotes in another article. Unless they were specifically looking, nobody would think that this event occurred.

In journalism circles, a phrase bandied about in the 1980s was "Afghanistan Journalism," a reference to the Soviet invasion of neighboring Afghanistan, which the western press largely ignored because nobody knew it was happening. Thus, if you are not looking for certain things, there is no way you would know it was there. Sort of like hearing a tree fall in the forest if nobody is there.

The thought of the chaos and embarrassment that could have ensued from publishing this piece frightened me. Once each single issue book was printed, the printer sent the entire book on computer disk to Lexis and Westlaw. The articles are immediately loaded into the immense database and incorporated into the vast body of legal scholarship. I know for a fact that almost every author who writes a law review article closely follows subsequent citations. The frequency of citation often appears on law professors' resumes or CVs. Frequent citation is a sign of respect and credibility. Some scholars even write law review articles analyzing the most-frequently cited law review articles.[34]

---

[33] David Berreby, *Student Withdraws in Plagiarism Uproar,* THE NATIONAL LAW JOURNAL, May 9, 1983, at 4.

[34] See e.g. William M. Landes & Richard A. Posner, *Citations, Age, Fame and the Web,* 29 J. LEGAL STUD. 319 (2000); Fred. R. Shapiro, *The Most-Cited Law Reviews,* 29 J. LEGAL STUD. 389 (2000); Fred R. Shapiro, *The Most-Cited Legal Scholars,* 29 J. LEGAL STUD. 409 (2000); Tracey E. George & Chris Guthrie, *An*

L.Rev.   87

Then there is the ego massage associated with other scholars referring or citing your work. I got a kick when I learned that news articles I wrote appeared in footnotes of five law review articles. I also hoped that my own law review note would be cited one day.

Electronic database services provide a mechanism akin to a clipping service. With Lexis, it is called Eclipse, a trademarked, automatic search engine of the service's expansive resources. This allows a person to insert search commands that automatically search databases. Then, Lexis either sends an email, electronically sends a copy of the article or source including the search commands or automatically prints the cited source on a designated printer.

This was an excellent tool. It was a way to stay on top of cases and subjects without logging onto Lexis every day. I had several Eclipse searches running to keep me up to date on issues covered in my note. Every news article mentioning the parties in the Chiquita Banana-Cincinnati Enquirer case was sent to me. Another search command involved several key cases I was following for my note, too.

The professor who wrote the Tulane article surely had her name, article title and citation locked into a Lexis Eclipse. I can only imagine the conversation I would have had with her after she read substantial portions of her work in Tom's article. The Tulane article was cited two or three times in the piece, but her footnotes appeared throughout Tom's note without citations. She would have easily recognized her work. Imitation may be the sincerest form of flattery, but in academia and publishing it is plagiarism, infringement and theft.

Empirical Evaluation of Specialized Law Reviews, 26 FLA. ST. U. L. REV. 813 (1999); Gregory Scott Crespi, *Ranking Specialized Law Reviews: A Methodological Critique*, 26 FLA. ST. U. L. REV. 836 (1999); Russell Korobkin, *Ranking Journals: Some Thoughts on Theory and Methodology*, 26 FLA. ST. U. L. REV. 851 (1999); Tracey E. George & Chris Guthrie, *In Defense of Author Prominence: A Reply to Crespi and Korobkin*, 26 FLA. ST. U. L. REV. 877 (1999); Bart Sloan, *What Are We Writing For? Student Works As Authority and Their Citation by the Federal Bench, 1986-1990*, 61 GEO. WASH. L. REV. 221 (1992); James Lindgren & Daniel Seltzer, *The Most Prolific Law Professors and Faculty*, 71 CHI-KENT L. REV. 781 (1996); J.M. Balkin & Sanford Levinson, *How to Win Cites and Influence People*, 71 CHI-KENT L. REV. 843 (1996); Fred R. Shapiro, *The Most-Cited Articles from the Yale Law Journal*, 100 YALE L. J. 1449 (1991).

Stupor Bowl
Sunday, October 24, 1999

One of the major complaints my classmates lodged at last year's election was the lack of social events. As the so-called "People's Editor," I made an effort to encourage social interaction among the staff. On the first day of orientation I tried to create an atmosphere of sociability: "Law review is more than just editing articles and writing your note."

The law review's bylaws mandated the formation of a social committee. Both second and third year staff members had to sign up for one of three standing committees. The social committee for the past two years had the largest roster, but had never done anything.

Unfortunately, I was one of the only people intent on socializing outside of the office. The law school held many social events. There were speakers, panel discussions, and a myriad of clubs and associations. Most of the socializing in the law school occurred at "bar nights," parties organized by the student government association, practically every Thursday at local bars. The goal was fundraising for student groups through a cover charge and heavy drinking, not necessarily in that order. I never attended a bar night. Unless I was out of town for a job interview, I tried to make it to my classes on Fridays.

A co-ed athletic event—flag football—against the Syracuse Journal of International Law and Commerce, our alleged rival with an office next to ours, gained support among the staff. The inter-journal trophies were at home in our office. When this was first discussed, there was widespread interest. At least 30 people signed up to play. Mike reserved an athletic field, borrowed flags and belts and traffic cones to mark the field from the school's intramural league.

By this afternoon, in the cold, gray drizzle of a late October afternoon in Syracuse, interest had waned. Only about a dozen people showed up. The turnout from the international journal was even thinner. The law review ended up loaning half our players to them so we could have a game. The people who played seemed to have fun. But it was certainly not the huge social event I envisioned.

The only real highlight, besides three days of charley horses, was the game summary I sent out over the listserv: a parody newspaper report of the game, complete with a Syracuse dateline and football nicknames for everyone that referenced their names and key plays. The style of the game report was straight sports news reporting of a recreational game, complete with sports-like nicknames: "Crazy Legs," for a guy who ran all over the place; "Red Lightening," for a red-haired guy who ran fast; "Hunchback," for an editor who graduated from Notre Dame; "It's Too Cold for Pom Poms," for a woman who came to watch and cheer but shivered instead.

The phony news report ended: "As the law review semi-stars doused each other with flat champagne, one unidentified voice said, 'You gotta believe ... we are going to be sore tomorrow.'"

That soreness would likely last more than just a couple of days.

Round 2
Monday, October 25, 1999

The key to running a smooth student organization should be professionalism. The law review, while essentially a student group, was also a business. Every student had responsibilities and we always tried to keep it business-like. This was something we tried to instill during orientation. Managing a staff of 80 personalities required delicate balancing.

Every 2L had the 100-page manual detailing the rights and responsibilities of law review membership. There was an irony that the reward for academic achievement that law review membership bestows is more work. The honor of being on law review overwhelmingly exceeded the duties and time commitment required. Two hours of office time each week and writing a heavily-footnoted 20 to 30 page article over the course of eight months is not too demanding. Some law reviews demand more than six hours a week of editing time, plus writing a note. Regardless of the time commitment fulfilling law review responsibilities was worth two academic credits. Senior board editors received an additional one credit.

For the majority of the membership, these requirements were not too demanding, either. Some students, like myself, actually enjoyed the work. Most did not enjoy the work, and law review became just another resume line while the work was relegated low priority status on the heap law school responsibilities.

Office hours were business hours, 9 to 5, even though I almost always opened it at 8 a.m.. Staff members signed up for two-hour blocks during orientation. There was plenty of flexibility, too, for people who had job interviews, sickness or sudden other pressing issues. We were not running a Soviet gulag, and recognized that law review was not always going to be a top priority. Any reasonable notice or legitimate emergency was enough to excuse office hours without penalties. Makeup hours were held on Fridays. Despite our flexibility, the hours had to be made up.

Accounting for office hour time was largely by the honor system. Members signed in at the beginning of their block, marked the time and signed out at the end, marking the time.

The Prince did not sign out properly and according to his own signature signed out at 4 p.m. rather than 5 one recent Monday. As such, he owed the law review an hour. This was a straight deal. We were not even making an issue of the two hours he wasted a month ago when he spent his hours building his rubber band ball. We were not making an issue of his liberal 15-minute smoking breaks either. We were cutting him a break, I thought.

As managing editor, Mike, maintained the records and accounting of everyone's office hours. Mike had the perfect personality for a managing editor. With All-American Golden Boy looks and a thoughtful, reliable outlook, he juggled the scheduling and monitored staff compliance. He had an affable disposition and was patient, easy going and fair, regularly giving people breaks when they did not give him adequate notice before skipping hours. He was realistic about where law review ranked with people's priorities. He made sure everyone on staff was up-to-date with their hours, and kept the staff members individually informed about what they were doing and what they were supposed to do.

And nobody complained. Until today.

Mike sent the Prince a note informing him of the hour he owed. This was the type of note that Mike sent to a handful of staff members who owed time. It was a brief, business-like note informing the Prince that he owed one hour of time. The Prince was not the only person who owed office hours. Fall interviews with law firms frequently encroached on office hours. Students travelling to New York City or Washington to interview at the big firms frequently missed their hours. This was expected and accommodated.

This afternoon during his office hours, the Prince, in front of a room full of other staff members, began loudly protesting about his lost hour.

"I don't owe you anything," he protested. "You fucked up with your counting. You made a mistake and you are wrong with your counting. I'm not making up anything," the Prince yelled.

"On this day you signed out an hour early," Mike said, calmly pointing to the sign-up sheet that he saved in his files. "It's pretty clear. This is your signature."

At this point, Mike asked the Prince to come into our office. This was when I entered the main office, and heard yelling through the closed door of the inner office Mike and I shared. I knew what was going on but did not enter the inner office because I not want to walk into the storm. Dealing with the 2L members' office hours was one task I avoided, leaving it totally in Mike's competent hands.

Then the door creaked opened and instantly slammed. There was more yelling, audible by all in the office. A minute later a red-faced, yet smirking, Prince emerged.

The Prince had accused Mike of erroneous accounting and refused to accept that he owed an hour. "You fucked this up and I'm not going to do any more time because you fucked up," the Prince added.

Mike was calm and said that the Prince's own handwriting marked the time. "This meeting is over," the Prince told Mike as he opened the door to the office to leave.

That was when Mike slammed the door and said the meeting was not over.

The Prince then asked Mike if he wanted to fight him. He extended his neck and stuck out his chin to challenge Mike, pointing to his face and said, "You wanna fight? Go ahead. Take the first shot."

It was clear that the Prince had no intention of listening. But challenging the managing editor to a fist fight seemed outright ludicrous. So much for professionalism. Mike chuckled, asking the Prince, "Are you serious?" The Prince was. He was seriously challenging Mike to a fist fight. As much as we both would have loved to take a shot at the Prince, Mike just let him go.

The Prince's behavior dumbfounded us. It is one thing to have a disagreement. But to escalate a minor thing like owing an office hour to a closed-door yelling match seemed a tad irrational. The Prince perceived everything we did as a personal affront to him. The law review bylaws were not written make his life more difficult. The bylaws did not address fisticuffs either. To push Mike to the point of yelling meant that the Prince really pushed him to his limit. Despite all the yelling, nothing was resolved, another frustration, for us, not the Prince.

Later that night I spoke with Merry, a senior editor and friend of the Prince who witnessed the incident. She also got the Prince's side of the issue. I told her that there was not a mistake and that the Prince really worked hard to infuriate Mike because he is such a calm and professional person.

"I don't' care what he thinks about Mike, me or law review, but he owes the law review an hour and he has to make it up," I told her. "We are not here to make his life difficult, but if he wants it that way we can. Tell him to just be a *mensch*."

"A what?" she asked.

"A *mensch*, he'll know what I mean. Use that word, please. Otherwise, it will be a long year," I told her.

Merry unwittingly became an intermediary between us and the Prince. It gave her something to talk about, which she must have appreciated.

Truth in Advertising
Wednesday, October 27, 1999

The quest for articles extended beyond the two articles editors. A handful of senior editors who held research assistantships or were close with professors were dispatched to see what they might turn up. Cole, an executive editor jointly enrolled in a graduate program, was a research assistant for a business and public policy professor outside the law school. The professor was actually an alumnus of the law school and had an article that she was ready to pitch to law reviews around the country.

Cole, who had instinctively promoted the Syracuse Law Review, wanted to show me an abstract of the article on product liability. Cole was one of the first students I became friendly with during first year, we were in an informal study group together. He, too, had worked prior to law school, mostly for law firms, and was mature, thorough, responsible and precise. Shortly before elections last year, he told me that he was not interested in holding a senior board position until I was nominated for editor in chief. He later confided that had I lost, he would have withdrawn his name, perhaps the greatest compliment anyone had paid me at the law school, and it meant a lot.

Cole had emailed himself the abstract. One computer was free in the main office. Three 2Ls worked at the others and two other senior editors worked at the table in the middle of the room. Cole called up the web-browser program and typed the address for his email service's website address. Only, in his haste, he transposed a few letters, quickly hit enter and waited for his email provider website to appear. The only problem was, the mistyped address was also an automatic default or secret link to a hard-core porn site, aptly titled "Massivecocks.com." There was no mistaking the service provided by the site, either.

"What the hell?" he exclaimed. A few heads turned, eyes focusing right on the computer screen. Recognizing the typo immediately, Cole stopped the download and retyped his intended address. Luckily nobody was offended by the material. At least the article looked interesting. The authors would be finished with it in a couple months, just in time for our third book.

Preparing the Prosecution
Thursday, October 28, 1999

The case against Tom proceeded. Ensuring procedural due process was crucial to the judicial process. [35] Due process meant that the defendant received proper notice, clear charges, the opportunity to respond, opportunity to review and challenge the evidence, motives and an opportunity to confront witnesses.[36]

---

[35] A recent case of academic fraud in New York, *Ma v. Columbia University*, NYLJ October 29, 1999, at 25 (New York County Supreme Court, October 29, 1999), reiterated the United States Supreme Court's pronouncement on academic fraud matters discussed in *University of Michigan v. Ewing*, 474 U.S. 214 (1985). For a charge of academic fraud to survive judicial review, the court must review whether "the challenged determination was arbitrary and capricious, irrational, made in bad faith or contrary to Constitution or statute." (citing *James v. Board of Education*, 42 NY2d 357, 365 (N.Y. 1977)); *see also* Scott R. Sinson, Note, *Judicial Intervention of Private University Expulsions: Traditional Remedies and a Solution Sounding in Tort*, 46 DRAKE L. REV. 195 (1997).

[36] I wanted to ensure fairness of the process. The last thing I wanted was to start a firestorm of litigation like the case I read about at Seton Hall University Law School where a student who was charged with plagiarism. After appealing his case to through the school's judicial process, the board voted not to enforce the student's suspension. Later, the school administration refused to send the New York Bar Examiners a "Certificate of Attendance." The student sued the school, the justices of New Jersey Supreme Court and the judges of the New York Court of Appeals. Defamation was part of the student's case. The appeals court

Enforcing the Code of Student Conduct and adhering to the rules of procedure, combined with the presentation of evidence would likely indemnify the school, prosecutor and myself from outside litigation. Courts are loath to overturn academic disciplinary actions as long as they were conducted fairly.

Academic discipline is often conducted under a cloak of mystery. Students' names are not publicly revealed. The identities of the three professors empanelled with three law students were not revealed. The members of the judicial board were drawn from the pool, much like the way cases are assigned to judges in real court. Faculty and the first, second and third year students each had their own small pool of potential panelists.

The cases were prosecuted by two student prosecutors, both third year law students. Andie, a cheerful, outgoing 3L with experience on another journal, and Greg, a dry, humorless guy, would team up for another law review prosecution. They were like a mismatched comedy duo: the comic and the straightman. They both read the report and the charges. Andie grasped the case upon her first reading. She understood the charge and the evidence. "This is as clear as sunlight. I can't believe someone was so stupid," she said.

Greg had concerns and questions. At Andie's request, I met with Greg in my office before classes one morning to discuss the case and further explain what actually happened.

"I read your report but I do not see the issue here," Greg said in his monotone voice.

As I had done before, I laid out the three damning documents on the desk in front of us.

"I don't see what is wrong," Greg said.

"First, these footnotes are identical to each other. Second, this clearly is not Tom's research but he is passing it off as his own," I said, allowing him more time to grasp the matter.

"But he cited the article up here," he said, pointing to one of the two citations of the Tulane article.

"Yes, but he copied the footnotes. Ordinarily, he could have listed a string of cases one after the other, just like the other author. He even could have put it this way: Smith, at 15 (citing White v. Black, Red v.

---

affirmed the district court's dismissal, after about three years of litigation. *In re Anonymous*, 1996 U.S. App. Lexis No. 33498 (2d Cir. 1996).

White, White v. Blue). He could have done that; it would have been a short cut and lazy and even questionable, but as you can see these footnotes are the same. He told me that he did not even read these cases."

Greg furrowed his brow in confusion as if I was speaking Chinese. I was not sure whether the art of footnoting ever really reached him. He squinted at the documents and said, "I never wrote a law review article."

"We covered stuff like this in first year research and writing classes," I reminded him. "A footnote documents and supports a proposition. When you put a case or article down in a footnote, that is a statement that you read the case and it supports your quote or proposition."

"I think I understand now," he said.

Greg's need for explanations caused concern. The evidence was strong, but I was afraid that the case would disintegrate, teetering due to prosecutorial mishaps, the same way the O.J. Simpson case crumbled. Nobody, here, to my knowledge wore any ugly-ass Bruno Magli shoes and nobody uttered "if the footnote doesn't fit you have to acquit." I was confident that Andie had a firm grasp and figured that she would be able to carry the case, if necessary.

Catch 44
Friday, November 5, 1999

My head ached and my nose would not stop running; a continuous stream of clear mucus. I could not stop sneezing. I sweated profusely even though I was shivering. I could barely keep my eyes open, but I had no choice. The flu hit me early this year, the first time I had such a debilitating sickness in nearly three years. There is never really a good time to get sick, much less sick with a 102.5 fever, but this was worse than others. My timing, as usual, was impeccable.

The day before, I had an interview with a federal judge in Utica. Spending a morning in Utica was a punishment that made Syracuse look like paradise. Even though the judge was a Syracuse alumnus, he had never hired a Syracuse law graduate as his law clerk. He never even interviewed a Syracuse law student before me, I was told.

Federal judges have budgets that allow them to employ a secretary and clerks. Some judges hire a term clerk for one- or two-year terms and a permanent clerk. Some judges hire two term clerks on overlapping terms. Here, the judge employed a term clerk and a permanent clerk.

And, it was clear that the permanent clerk was calling the shots. The clerk, a middle-aged woman who had gone to college and law school after she married and had a family, could barely muster a smile. She had a huge chip on her shoulder about something and regularly disregarded Syracuse, which was odd for someone without Ivy League credentials. A friend familiar with the chambers told me that she perceived the term clerks as a threat to her domain.

She interviewed me for about 25 minutes and was ready to pass me off to the judge, who was handling a case management conference that was running over. So, I had another half-hour of awkward small talk and odd glares to deal with.

The judge was pleasant enough. We spoke about Syracuse, the law review and writing. "Looks like your reporting background would be good for a clerk. I really want to work on my writing and that might really help," he said, while sitting on wingback chair across from me. His legs were crossed and his socks were short, resting down around his ankles, exposing his naked shins.

The sock problem aside, I thought my talk with the judge went well.

But I was really looking forward to my afternoon interview at Granmont, Boardman & Lipshitz. This was my dream law firm in New York City—a sizeable firm with one of the top First Amendment and media law practices in the country. This firm was the firm to work for if you wanted to get into media law. A personal letter declaring my interest in media law to the firm's top lawyer, a nationally-known expert on First Amendment law, got me in the door. There was no way my resume would get past the human resources screeners who disregard resumes by the hundreds based on where the student goes to law school and GPA.

I took the train down from Syracuse because I was too exhausted to make the four-hour drive. I spent the nearly six hours on the train sneezing and popping aspirin like Pez. The woman in the seat ahead of me winced and sneered at me with every sneeze. I arrived at Penn Station with more than two hours to kill before my 2 p.m. interview. I bought a hotdog at the Nathan's in the train station and tried to eat it.

As I sat there, staring at the meal, hoping not to throw up, an overweight gray-haired man wearing a bright yellow jacket and a black beret juggled his tray in one hand and a violin case in the other. He passed by my table, and stumbled. His tray went flying, landing about a foot away from me. His soda splashed my shoes, pants and trench coat while green-snot relish landed on my sleeve. I had never seen so much relish on a hotdog before in my life; the hotdog was barely visible under the heap of green slime. Rather than clean up the puddle of soda, fries and relish, the man threw the tray on top of the trash can and left. Being hit by a blob of relish seemed better than the entire load hitting me.

By the time I made it to the firm, I had completely sweated through my light blue shirt and dark suit. The receptionist asked whether I was feeling well. My aspirin had just worn off. The receptionist brought me a cup of water. I went to the men's room to try to compose myself. *"Just pull it together for the next two hours,"* I told myself. I thought I would be able to make it through and perform well in the interviews. I thought my experience and credentials would be able to speak for themselves. I thought the people at this prestigious law firm would recognize that my background at a major newspaper, coupled with my current position on law review, would compensate for other chinks in my armor, like my GPA or Syracuse law degree.

The interviewing process at Granmont, Boardman & Lipshitz was like most firms': the circuit. I started with a partner who opened the interview asking me why I went to law school instead of medical school. His second question was why I went to Syracuse. Then there was a young associate who was editor of her law review and empathized with the hours I kept. She chain-smoked about three cigarettes during the interview, flicking her ashes into an overfilled ashtray on her desk. I could barely breathe, and here was an associate blowing smoke right in my face and up my ass.

Then there was Jim, a sixth-year associate who took one look at my transcript and honed in on my Scarlet Letter. When Jim saw my contracts grade he started laughing. "What makes you think that you could work here with something like that on your transcript?" he asked, barely containing his smirk.

"Look, if you want to judge me based on one grade, there is nothing I can do about that," I said. "What I can tell you is that I have a professional background as a writer and I can find anything and write it up better than any of the lawyers you have here."

"Everyone here was on their law review. I mean, you don't have an offer from your summer firm, you have lousy grades and don't go to a top law school, I'm not sure why we would even take a chance on you," he said.

"Is there a question there?" I asked.

"Why should we take a chance on you?" he said, still barely containing his smirk.

"Because I am a hard-worker and a professional writer. I am the editor in chief of the law review. I earned my way onto law review because of my writing. I was sought out to be the editor. I didn't just win a popularity contest," I said. At this point, I was clearly agitated, whatever patience I had when I arrived at Granmont, Boardman & Lipshitz had by now worn off, along with my aspirin. "I'll put my writing up against anyone you have around here."

I could sense the futility. He had a decent circumstantial case: no offer from the big firm and a disastrous first semester transcript. Things did not look good and nobody was looking at the total package. My newspaper experience and awards seemed inconsequential in the face of one bad grade. Hawthorne himself could not have penned a more accurate tale.

The way Jim, and a handful of other lawyers, judges and law firms regarded me, it was as if I had pulled my pants down and took a dump right on someone's desk. It was one grade, based mostly on bad handwriting and exam essays that zeroed in on answer rather than vacillating back and forth.

Of all the lawyers who interviewed me at any law firm, Jim was the most gleeful. He seemed to enjoy tearing apart my resume. He was not the only one, however. And without family or alumni connections, or even legitimate support from the law school's placement office, I was alone when it came to getting a job.

My standing as editor of the law review helped me get in the door at a couple of firms, but it did not impress people from Harvard, Yale or Penn. Then, lawyers who held positions on their law school law reviews were unimpressed because I wrote-on, not graded-on. So, my grades killed me with those people. To further complicate the mess, there were those who interviewed me who did not even write-on to their law school's law reviews. Thus, those people resented me because I wrote on and then navigated the system to rise to the top of the staff.

It seemed like no matter what I did or said, there would be a barrier. It was complicated and not fully articulated by any of the culprits. Nobody had to verbalize it the way Jim did because the articulation came a week or two later in the form of a rejection letter. It was a Catch-44.

An Ounce of Prevention
Wednesday, November 10, 1999

Prompted by plagiarism controversy, the Associate Dean sent the editors of all the journals a brief primer on avoiding plagiarism. Her terse note implored distributing the material to the entire staff.[37] I put together a small packet for the entire staff including the primer and an article on confronting plagiarism from a legal writing newsletter that another professor gave me.[38]

The Associate Dean's four-page *Avoiding Plagiarism* primer was printed from the website of the Writing Place, Northwestern University.[39] The primer was clear and direct with tightly-written sections defining plagiarism, noting that there are two common types of plagiarism: paraphrasing with no citation and misplaced citations.[40] It also included tips for avoiding plagiarism and examples.[41]

It included a strong warning: "Whether you copy from a published essay, an encyclopedia article, or a paper from a fraternity's files, you are plagiarizing. If you do so, you run a terrible risk. You could be punished, suspended, or even expelled. Otherwise mild-mannered professors tend to turn into vigilantes when confronted with plagiarism. Why borrow trouble?"[42]

The article, *Confronting Inadvertent Plagiarism*, was more focused to law students and addressed the rigorous requirements for footnotes and documentation in legal writing.[43] A section on the time pressures that may propel a law student to plagiarize was particularly accurate: "Plagiarism, as a timesaving mechanism in legal writing, becomes an easy temptation. A student might ask why he or she should research, read, outline, draft and redraft, proofread, print and reprint when the

---

[37] The Writing Place, Northwestern University, published a four-page primer titled Avoiding Plagiarism on its website. (last updated 9/18/1996) ("Avoiding Plagiarism").
[38] M.C. Mirow, *Confronting Inadvertent Plagiarism*, PERSPECTIVES: TEACHING LEGAL RESEARCH AND WRITING (Winter 1998).
[39] Avoiding Plagiarism.
[40] *Id.*
[41] *Id.*
[42] *Id.*
[43] Mirow.

words of one court from one opinion seem to have already done all of this."[44]

Along with those two articles, I printed a New York Court of Appeals case that I stumbled upon in which an author sued a law journal after editors inserted errors into his article.[45] This was hardly a landmark opinion. And, the message may have been a little too subtle.

Whether anybody besides me read any of these materials remained a mystery. The 2L staff members received the copies in their office mailboxes. Some dutifully scanned it during office hours. Some stuffed it in their notebooks or folders and a few just threw it out. At least they could not say they were not given information. By now, the law school rumor-mill was rampant. It was difficult to keep secrets in the law school. Enough people on law review knew something was going on. The eight people on Deb's editing team knew something was up when they no longer had to work on the article they were editing for the past month. And Tom's friends knew what was going on. Nobody asked me anything, though, which was fine with me.

Emergency Beer
Tuesday, November 16, 1999

I am not a heavy drinker. In fact, I frequently go months without drinking alcohol. Nevertheless, I was not above using the occasional beer as a tool or an outright bribe. For one of the 50th anniversary meetings, I lured an apathetic 3L classmate to the meeting by promising him beer. I bought a six pack of Corona for the meeting and then had two extra, which I stashed in the office fridge, behind my supply of Coke cans.

They became the "Emergency Beers," kind of like a fire extinguisher or one of those oxygen masks that drops down in airplane disasters—"use in case of emergency."

About two weeks after stashing the Emergency Beers, an exasperated and frustrated 2L staff member, Erica, returned to the office after spending two-and-a-half hours working on some difficult footnotes in the library. She could not find the proper materials and looked like

---

[44] *Id.*

[45] Clevenger v. Baker Voorhis & Co., 197 N.E.2d 783 (N.Y. 1964).

she had just run the New York Marathon. It was after hours, about 5:30, and the only people in the office were Sara, Cody and me.

"You look beat," I said to Erica.

"I am lost on this. This is *so* frustrating," she said, looking as though she was on the verge of tears and a panic attack.

"Would you like one of the emergency beers?"

Deploying the Emergency Beer outraged Cody, not because he wanted the beer himself or held himself out as a temperance advocate, but because he thought it was beneath me.

"You are the editor, it's bad enough that you talk with all the 2Ls but now this girl will go around saying that the *Editor* gave her a beer," Cody said. "That is so beneath you. But you are the People's Editor, I almost forgot."

"It looked like she needed it," Sara added.

Inhuman Resources
Friday, November 19, 1999

A partner in the home office at Dickman & Cherubb emailed me to come to Providence for an interview. I was not too eager to relocate to Providence, but I liked the city. My brother went to the Rhode Island School of Design in Providence and it was closer to home than Cleveland. I briefly considered relocating there, but was not too eager.

The firm paid for my flight. I went through the usual battery of interviews but was unimpressed. I spent about 30 minutes with the firm's human resources director, Patrick, a middle-aged life-long New Englander who had been with the firm for a year or two. He was a nice enough guy to spend about five minutes with, but I got stuck with him for 30. Human resources people never ceased to amaze me.

Patrick and I talked about the dynamics of the firm's New Jersey office and various law school issues.

"What classes are you taking this semester?" he asked.

"I'm taking corporations, real estate transactions, copyright, trial practice and law review. I open the law review office every day at 8 in the morning and I'm there until seven, eight or nine each night," I said.

"You know Roy, I am not a lawyer, and we like interview and hire people who are on law review, but I really don't know what you do on law review," Patrick said.

His question shocked me. It sounded like a partial confession. At least he was not asking me whether the Plain Dealer was an aviation newsletter, as a human resources director at a major New Jersey firm once asked.

"The thumbnail sketch is: law review is an honor society, student group and legal publishing house all in one," I said. I described the publication and editing process and the nature of the articles.

"Wow, that sounds like a lot of work," he said.

"It is," I answered.

Going Medieval
Tuesday, November 30, 1999

By the time we landed authors, we were pretty desperate. We managed to land a few interesting articles: one on the Americans with Disabilities Act; one on the legal ramifications of kicking pregnant mothers off the national honor society; the development of the jury trial system.

The first two articles were interesting and presented no serious obstacles for the editing teams. The third article by Professor Martin, a professor at a southern law school, traced the origins of jury trials to religious ordeals in the Middle Ages. In the famous pawn shop dungeon scene in the movie, Pulp Fiction, the violent gangster, Marcellus, described his own brand of vengeance as "going medieval on his ass." Little did we know that Professor Martin's article would be "going medieval" on us.

First, the author cited a multitude of obscure texts ranging from a treatise on Hungarian law in Magyar, to the French civil code, in French, to a book on Roman law, in Latin to something in German. There were a series of obscure religious and religious history journals that were not available at the main campus library. The executive editor assigned to the article signed out about 50 books from the main library and about two dozen on inter-library loan from other colleges. Plus, he took out about another 50 books from our law library, of course, on the law review account.

Then, the real fun began. There were days when I emerged from my office to find exasperated 2L staff members struggling to find a source to cite or struggling to find the appropriate page number in an obscure text. Or simply struggling to comprehend the dense text. It was a trying article.

Many of the citations were long textual footnotes with general propositions and unspecific documentation. Many were inaccurate, too. A typical citation in the unedited version generally cited to a book or article without a specific page number. Thus, it needed to be more precise. This meant that students editing the article had to sift through arcane texts to find the precise page documenting the assertion. We were lucky to have one staff member who spoke French and German and two who spoke Italian. We were even luckier to have a senior board editor who knew Latin well enough to translate and confirm the translation of a 70-word blocked quote from a text in Latin.

Computer problems hastened by defective and virus-laden computer disks the author sent only exacerbated the situation. She seemed to be in her own world. Whenever we spoke, it sounded as if she just woke up. It was as if she had never worked with a law review before. The gaping holes in her article made it seem as though she had no prior writing experience. She had written articles before and had top clerking and law school credentials. But she had to know that there would be problems with her article. She had to know about her citations and the difficulty any editor would have checking them.

When we sent back the edited copy for her revisions and comments, she called back to tell me that the editors "made mistakes." I was shocked and asked for specific examples. "The editors had a lot of work to do on your article. The sources you used were not the easiest in the world to deal with. But I am concerned that you found mistakes, though," I said.

Then, she revealed the mistakes: the internal citations, the supra numbers, references in the footnotes to other footnotes, did not all correspond. "That's what you're calling mistakes? Those are the last things that get checked. The editors had to add a whole bunch of footnotes anyway, that's why they're not all right," I answered. I pressed her for other mistakes and she said that there were none and that she liked the changes.

I was relieved and agitated at the same time. I was confident that the editors did not make too many mistakes. However, I was disturbed that she would impute mistakes when the piece was such a mess anyway. Furthermore, the editor handling the article reported that the initial draft did not even have any supras or internal citations in her original draft.

The Hearing
Monday, December 6, 1999

The Judicial Board procedures were based on fairness. The Board must proceed with deliberate caution. There were built-in deadlines for the defendant's answers to the charges and inspection of evidence. Then there were the scheduling problems. The Board must accommodate the schedules of its six members, the student prosecutors, witnesses and the defendant.

Like any civil litigation, Tom's lawyer attempted to delay the hearing. As the semester waned, nobody wanted the matter to drift into finals. Nobody needed that headache at that time.

Today was the hearing, like it or not. I was not too nervous. Then, again, I did not know what to expect. There would be two witnesses: first Deb, then me. I wore my expensive suit. I might as well try to look good. I was eager for closure on this matter so I could find a replacement for Tom. As it stood, I was covering for Tom during his four office hours a week and also handling his duties as senior editor. I was also curious to see how I would fare against a real live lawyer in court. This was not a mock trial or Moot Court tryouts. This was for real. Someone's career and reputation could be affected here.

Tom hired Mr. Lerner, a local attorney and Syracuse law alumnus who was once counsel to a controversial, high-profile client who was recently involved in some shady business practices that spurred criminal charges. Tom also worked part-time for Mr. Lerner. I anticipated a shark who would attack me with impertinent and hostile questions. Maybe I watched too much *Law and Order* or OJ coverage on Court TV.

The Judicial Board was comprised of three law students and three law professors. I knew the identities of students on the board but did not know the professors until they marched past me in the hallway to the fourth-floor meeting room. One professor, the author of a casebook and numerous articles, held the editorship of a faculty-edited law journal. Another professor was a well-published author of several articles and eager to receive her tenure. The third professor was Professor Sault, who was currently teaching my copyright class.

The professors were drawn randomly from a pool of volunteers. Some professors at the law school were so indifferent and held the student body in such contempt that they actively avoided any service that would bring them in contact with students. A handful actually cared about the students and would do whatever they could to ensure the school's integrity.

A professor had the right to decline serving on the panel. A draw could empanel rigid professors who strictly interpreted ethics rules or empathetic professors with a predilection for mercy. There was an element of luck involved in who sat on the panel. It was abundantly clear that this was not a panel that would look sympathetically on a plagiarist.

Tom and his lawyer, Mr. Lerner, emerged from a nearby administrative office armed with folders and grim looks. Tom and I shook hands and he introduced me to Mr. Lerner, who quickly whisked Tom away.

The prosecutors, Andie and Greg, walked by and told me that Deb would testify first. The hearing was scheduled for 3 p.m. but did not get underway until about 3:30. I sat on a leather sofa in the hallway near the administrative offices. Deb was questioned for more than an hour and emerged from the room pale. She was smart and resilient, so I was concerned that she looked shaken. I told her I that I would call her later.

The room was stark, white painted cinderblock walls and a window overlooking the library's atrium. Along with the tables and chairs there was a blackboard and an easel. The Board members sat on my left facing Tom and Mr. Lerner across the room on my right. The two student prosecutors sat beside me. A large tape recorder operated in the middle. This was not like a formal trial with procedural and evidentiary rules.

The questions were not too grueling. Mr. Lerner was not the vicious shark I fretted about. He was actually mild-mannered and polite. I had definitely watched too much of the OJ trial.

The questions mostly related to my report, my thoughts and reactions. One professor sought a clarification about why I cited to the rules of professional responsibility. One student asked me to describe the note-writing process and the editing and fact checking process.

Lerner's best avenue of attack was to paint a picture of personal bias and failure of process. He insinuated that the case was mishandled.

"You went around the school, showing this to everyone before you even showed it to Tom, didn't you?" he said.

"Could you please define everyone, counselor?" I asked.

"You showed these documents to people before you confronted Tom, correct?"

"Yes. I showed the documents to the Dean, our adviser and my managing editor. I wanted their feedback to make sure I was not off base. I confronted Tom the first time I saw him in the office. Then, I submitted the report. I had to brief several senior board members because this involved an article that was being edited. Senior editors would also have to cover for Tom's office hours."

"You determined his guilt before you even confronted Tom, didn't you?" he said.

"I investigated the matter and submitted a report and evidence. This board will determine guilt or innocence," I answered.

"No, by showing this to your editors you determined by yourself that Tom was guilty?"

"No. This board is a fact finder. This board will determine guilt. I simply presented facts and evidence. I needed to keep my senior board apprised of important staff issues," I said.

"Before this event, how would you classify Tom's attendance and performance on law review?"

"Sparse. He frequently missed his office hours, he holds an outside job and took a trip. But that has no bearing on this matter. It is completely irrelevant," I answered. "As far as I am concerned, he is still a member of the law review, but I advised him to suspend his hours until this matter is completed because I thought it might be awkward for him. I actually considered Tom a friend. This is not a matter I took lightly, I gave this a lot of consideration and lost a lot of sleep about it."

"You are not the only one," he said.

I thought that I sufficiently disposed line of bias questions.

A student member asked, "I would like you to explain why you recommended Deb to investigate the matter the way you did?"

"I had editing and publishing experience before law school. When I edit, I work under the belief that something is incorrect unless proven otherwise. I just wanted to make sure that the materials that Tom failed to turn in actually existed. I had no suspicion other than that."

"Were you worried that his article was in jeopardy of preemption?" another student asked. Before I could even answer Prof. Sault cut off the student, berating him for asking a preemption question that she thought was impertinent. The Board chair directed me to answer the question anyway.

Then, Prof. Sault questioned me about how I confronted Tom. Her tone was accusatory, bordering on hostile, just like her class. She was cross examining me with the vigor of a district attorney in front of tv cameras. Her questions were not leading or traps. They were clear, just not asked too nicely.

"How did Tom react when you showed him the evidence?" she asked.

"He said that he did not see anything wrong. He said that he agreed with the propositions and that he did not see a problem."

"What did you say?"

"I explained what a footnote stands for and that it looks like he just cut and pasted the footnotes from Lexis or Westlaw. Then, I went through one footnote and asked him whether he read the cases. I went case by case and he said that he did not read them but that he agreed with the statement."

"Was he ingenuous?" she asked.

"I don't understand your question, professor."

"Did you believe him, that he did not know that he didn't do anything wrong?"

I paused and recounted his plea of ignorance to me that night in my office, "Yes, but ..."

She cut me off. "Thank you. That is enough."

I continued, "I believed that he was genuine but could not understand how someone had gotten to this level in academia and not have any understanding of footnotes and plagiarism. I wanted to believe him but could not fathom how a third year law student could not recognize what I was showing him."

The questioning lasted about 40 minutes. I thanked the Board and they thanked me. I told Andie and Greg that I would be available if the Board had any further questions. I had to stay in the office until about 9 p.m. anyway because Sara had a night class. Her night classes were a good reason to stay late and catch up on work.

Deliberations began the moment I left. By now it was about 5 p.m. Andie called my office at 9 p.m. to tell me that the Board was unable to render a verdict and would reconvene tomorrow.

More Deliberations
Tuesday, December 7, 1999

My appearance before Professor Sault and the Judicial Board earned me a Socratic barrage in copyright class. She was too predictable. I had a feeling that after my testimony, particularly my exchange with her, Professor Sault would come at me the next day.

In anticipation of the impending "As-Sault," I had prepared detailed briefs of the cases scheduled for today's class. At the end of yesterday's class she left us with three or four issues to "think about." That meant that she would grill us on the issues.

Class started at 9 a.m. She walked into class at 9:02 wearing her winter coat and carrying a canvas tote bag with her books. Before the bag was on the table and before her second arm was out of her coat, even before she turned around to face the class, the her first question was out: "Mr. Gutterman, if you were advising the client in the *Carter* case, what would you advise them about the moral rights of artists?"

"I would tell the client that in this country there are no moral rights."

"That is not enough. And, then what would you advise the client to do?"

"I would advise the client to avoid work made for hire status, avoid paying benefits, social security ..."

After about 10 minutes of questioning, I was off the hot seat. It was difficult to get a correct answer in her class. Nothing a student ever said was correct. In fact, it seemed as if the closer someone got to a correct answer the angrier she got. One morning she asked me a question about a particular rule hidden in the case. "Oh no Mr. Gutterman. That is not correct." Her reaction was loud and disapproving, as if she had just witnessed me stealing money from a crippled orphan. Then, five minutes later, as she lectured she made the exact same point, practically using the same words I had used. But I was the one who was wrong. The Socratic method will forever baffle me.

Professor Sault returned to me a couple more times in the class today, which was not uncommon. She frequently returned to her victims in class, like a serial killer returning to the scene of the crime.

At about 6:30 that night, I was flipping through a partially-edited article in my office when the phone rang. It was Andie. The Judicial Board had reached a verdict after about four more hours of deliberation. Andie was bound by confidentiality of the proceedings and could not reveal the verdict. The Board had to write its opinion, which would also render its punishment, if there would be any. The cloak of confidentiality and Tom's academic privacy could not be compromised. Technically, I could not learn about the outcome before the accused.

I did not want to put Andie in an awkward position. But I asked whether I would be surprised by the outcome.

"Probably not," she said. "The Board is pretty consistent."

"When will I be able to know for sure? I mean, there are staff implications here. I do not have a senior editor and I need to find a replacement or deal with it internally."

"The Board has to write the opinion. Plus, there is an appeals process," she said.

Without abrogating her duties, she told me what I needed to know. This was like "deep background," I could know it but not act on my knowledge. I could not begin looking for a new editor. I could not even mention what I knew to anyone.

The Board's verdict was a relief from a personal standpoint. Had the Board acquitted Tom, it would have made the charges appear bogus, trumped up or personal. There was no personal gratification for me on this. To a certain extent, I was relieved. But there was nothing to relish.

Into the Lion's Den: Roar
Wednesday, December 8, 1999

I was unwinding in my office with my afternoon Coke when Cody strolled in. Because he was an associate notes and comments editor, he occasionally stopped by the office, but it was mostly to hang out. I was particularly frazzled by this point in the afternoon. The usual hassles of the day had caught up with me along with a minor argument with Sara about "relationship things."

Sara, as quiet and shy as she was downright sweet, was stressing out about her trial practice class tonight. After class, she decided to barricade herself in her downstairs research assistantship office to avoid her trial practice teammates. Her trial practice final was tonight. She was confident but nervous and agitated by her teammates who demanded that they screen her questions and watch her rehearse in front of them. She would have a direct examination and cross examination in a mock trial of a rape case.

Although each person in the class was graded on his or her own performance and merits, it was also a team project. Her team's leaders were all over her because they were concerned that because of her demure personality, delicate appearance and quiet demeanor she would not perform well. Also, they simply thought they could run roughshod over her because of her appearance and demeanor. What her teammates overlooked in their zeal to boss someone around was that she had high honors at the law school that put her close to the top of the class.

I had to deal with Sara's fraying nerves along with all the other stresses in my life.

Then, as I sat in my office with Cody, Yoka, a friend of Sara's who was on her trial practice team, came into my office. Yoka often had difficulty understanding my bluntness and sarcasm, and thus did not really like me. I am not sure whether sarcasm translated well into Malaysian. But a month earlier, she liked me plenty when she asked me to proofread and critique her cover letter and resume.

"Where's Sara? We need her," Yoka said in a near panic, as if the world would collapse around us if Sara did not materialize within seconds. "We're meeting and Ed wants to go over her questions with her."

"I don't know where Sara is, but I'll tell you what, you and Ed should worry about your own questions rather than worrying Sara."

"We need to hear her questions," Yoka continued.

"She knows what she is doing better than any of you. She does not need you and Ed or anyone else to validate her performance or tell her what to do," I was practically yelling at her.

"But he wants to hear her questions before the trial. He is a team leader," she said.

"Which part of this don't you understand? You do not need to worry about Sara. She is more than competent and knows exactly what she is doing. Nobody has a damn right to question her ability or her skills. I saw her perform a cross examination a couple weeks ago in class and she was perfect. You worry about your own grade and leave Sara alone. You think that you guys have a right to impose yourselves on her for no apparent reasons, why don't you just worry about yourselves. Who do you think you are to question her ability? You have no right," I yelled.

"If you see her tell her we're in room 100," she said as she left.

"She knows where you are. And if any of you have any other questions or concerns about Sara and her ability to perform tonight, feel free to come back and talk with me," I said.

Cody looked at me and said, "That girl did not know what she was walking in to."

"I am tired of these assholes thinking they could push her around for no reason. I mean these people are idiots. Not one of them is on law review or moot court, yet they think they have a right to boss my girlfriend around. Then, she gets all pissed at me," I said. "Somebody has to pay for it all."

I nearly dropped the law review line on Yoka. That would have been the kind of condescending attitude that these people deserved. That would have ruffled them the same way they were ruffling Sara. However, as much as I wanted to really rub their faces in something like law school status, it was not my style. Instead, I simply unloaded the best I could. I knew the people in her class and wanted so much to tell her that nobody in her class has a right to question someone with Sara's standing in the class.

It was important to defend Sara against these people who obviously thought they could boss her around. However, I think it was equally important for me to yell at someone with impunity. I could not and would not yell at anybody on my staff the way that I just yelled at Yoka. And I really needed to unload on someone. It felt good, too.

A passage from John Grisham's *The Rainmaker*, characterizes the resentment and elitism that law review membership sometimes generates outside the confines of the law review office. Here, the working-class hero, Rudy Baylor, described a cabal of malicious snobs "all prickish sorts who write for the Law Review and frown upon those of us who don't."[46]

Later that night, at my own trial practice class, a woman in my class, Marie, who I did not know well but became conversationally-friendly with in class (we talked in class and in the hallways on occasion), approached me in the hall.

"Roy, I did not know you were the editor of the law review," she said, touching me on the shoulder. "That's great. I am so happy to know that a nice, regular guy is the editor, not some arrogant guy who refuses to talk with the regular people."

"Thanks, I only wear my law review jacket at home," I said.

There was a fine line between associating with elite people and being an elitist. Most of the people I was surrounded by on law review were at the top of the class and going to fancy law firms. These were the people who frequently had all the right answers in class. Even though I

---

[46] JOHN GRISHAM, THE RAINMAKER 27 (Double Day, New York, 1995).

frequently had the right answers, too, I was different because of the grades. In the old days, and at some today, the person selected to be editor in chief of the law review was also number one in the class. Things were different now, but the position maintains some of that old-time luster and prestige.

As a write-on, I recognized that even though I deserved to be up there on the law review based on my writing, there was plenty keeping me from getting too full of myself, mainly that one grade.

Outside the confines of the law review office, law review membership frequently met with resentment and jealousy. I was always cognizant of how people outside the office perceived and received the law review, and me. Most people in the law school knew who I was, so there was no reason to go around flaunting anything.

Live From Syracuse ...
Friday, December 10, 1999

The bylaws required monthly meetings for the entire staff. The entire staff was supposed to attend. We usually held them at about 5 p.m., after classes were done for the day or on Friday afternoons, when no classes were scheduled. Turnout was surprisingly good for most of the meetings thus far. Almost every 2L showed up, and we were doing a decent job of attracting 3Ls.

This was the fourth one and the last general meeting before the finals and the winter break. To reward the staff for the work thus far, Ally, the business editor, took care of the pizza and soda order.

I took to wearing ties and decent slacks for the meetings as a sign of professionalism and courtesy to the staff. Mike and I often walked into the room together. It was weird because once we entered the room and descended the stairs into the pit, most of the 50 to 70 staff members on hand hushed. I always brought my binder with bylaws and usually prepared a brief agenda of subjects to address.

"Thank you for coming. I know everybody has lots of other things to do and places to be, so we appreciate your attendance," I said. This was how I usually started the meetings, sort of like Jay Leno or David Letterman. These were my monthly monologues, and I appreciated the turnout. Law review competed with so many other things that it was important to be cordial and even gracious to the staff.

"This is where we stand ... " I reported that book 1 was late due our difficulties securing authors and problems with the articles we had. "We're behind schedule, which means when we get back, things will have to go faster."

Nick, the notes and comments editor, spoke briefly about the last note deadline and the next note deadline in January. He also distributed a list of everyone's note topics. "This is so everyone knows what everyone else is working on. Someone here or there might come across something that might help someone else," he said.

After Nick's speech, I added my own pitch for taking the note-writing process seriously. "Getting your note published will look as good on your resume as any other accolade," I said.

A significant portion of the staff was content with doing the bare minimum on the note because the odds for publication were not too favorable. Only six of the 42 entries would be chosen.

"There is a secondary market for your notes if you're not chosen for publication," I said, describing how one senior editor recently won $1,000 for his note in a legal writing contest.

Dozens of organizations, bar associations, journals, agencies and law schools offer cash, certificates and even trips to conventions for unpublished research papers. The career services office kept a binder of such contests and every time the law review received a mailing on one, I put it up on the bulletin board.

"Take this seriously, don't be discouraged," I said. "Do a good job, because there are opportunities out there."

Mike maintained the sign-in sheet and handled the excused absences. The unexcused absences were not really monitored. But if we needed, we could always refer to the sign-up sheets at a later time. He also talked about office hours, make-up office hours and signing up for next semester's office hours. "Some of you owe a lot of hours, just email me or drop a note in my mailbox and we'll work something out," he said.

As I prepared to close the meeting and get the pizza party started, I pitched the "perfect holiday gift idea." The law review ordered about 20 extra glass beer mugs, the same ones the 2Ls got on the first day of orientation. They were available for $5 in the office because, "Nothing says happy holidays like a Syracuse Law Review beer mug. It's better than a the Clapper and more useful than a Chia Pet," I said. For the half of the staff that did not think I was totally crazy, there were laughs. The other half was probably salivating for the pizza.

Once the pizzas arrived, I worked the room. One 2L wanted to buy two mugs. Another mocked, "Yeah, I want to buy a mug for everyone in my family."

As I reached for another piece of pizza, Lulu, an energetic 2L, tapped me on the shoulder. She had just pulled all the cheese off her slice of pizza. "You know, everyone really likes the way you run these meetings," she said.

"No, I didn't know that. Thanks. I'm just glad people come," I said.

"You're funny and it's so nice how you always thank people for coming," she said. "People like that. We appreciate it."

What Comes Around, Goes Around
Monday, December 13, 1999

The agreement with the library books was perfect. Library books collected on the shelf all semester to the point where two entire rows were full. The Martin article alone required more than 100 books from the law library, the main campus library, and inter-library loan, a reciprocal program between college libraries. The books for this article filled two, 10-foot-long books shelves in our office.

Accounting and otherwise keeping track of when these books had to be taken back to the library and renewed would have been an oppressive hassle. As the fall semester wound down, and the books became due on the last day of the semester, some of the executive editors collected and returned the books. But as finals approached and law review office hours ceased prior to the reading period, office appearances by other staff and editors also ceased. I brought several piles over to the library.

The librarians printed out a weekly list of the outstanding books on the account. I checked off the books I brought over. One book, however, failed to turn up on the shelf: Richard Epstein's *Takings: Private Property and the Power of Eminent Domain*. I feared it was lost, along with my pledge of responsibility. I scoured the shelves over and over. Perhaps it might have been returned but not properly checked in. I alerted the librarians who put a "check" on the book.

I went to the library shelves and found it. I brimmed with pride and relief when I presented it to the librarian. She scanned it and said, "Nice try, but this is a second copy of the book. We have two copies of it."

"Oh man," I said.

"Don't worry, I doubt anybody stole that book. It will turn up," she said.

Back in the office, I rearranged some loose papers on the shelves. Then, the green-covered book poked up through a pile of papers. My credibility was saved and the law review was spared the cost of replacing a book.

I strutted across the patio yard to the library and confidently handed the book over to the librarians, saying, "The book was buried under a pile of papers. It was not lost after all." I was happier than they were.

The Day Before the Night Before Christmas
Thursday, December 23, 1999

A fresh blanket of snow, only an inch or two, fell overnight. The campus was silent. The undergraduate exodus began close to 10 days earlier. The last of the law school finals was yesterday.

At 8:30 in the morning, I was the only person in the law school until one of my classmates, who happened to live in Syracuse arrived at 10 a.m. to work in the nearby computer cluster.

There was plenty of work for me—updating and fixing my note, reading and printing out several articles and handling some law review correspondence.

The souvenir order debacle was finally over. Every year the law review ordered shirts, sweatshirts, mugs and plaques. This year the university finally figured out that we were ordering things in Syracuse's orange and blue from a vendor that did not pay the university a license fee. The vendor was owned by a relative of a law review editor from the early 1990s. Only the plaques bore the university's logo. In the past, it was not a big deal, but this year the student handling the order decided to change the process.

This time, instead of each person writing a check directly to the vendor, we each wrote checks to the law review, which then sent one big check. Ordinarily, this should not have been a big deal. But when the university's budget office learned that we were buying stuff from a non-licensed vendor, the university refused to cut a check. This prompted protracted negotiations. Unfortunately, the student handling this project was not too efficient, either. This meant that the business editor and I had to deal with the problem. This also meant that souvenirs that should have been delivered in May arrived in December.

Now, I had to track down three alumni editors who paid for their stuff before graduation: one was in Syracuse; one Buffalo and the other New York City. I boxed and wrapped two law review mugs and sweatshirts.

After that, I surveyed our progress with the articles. Our production schedule was far behind. I wanted to take several home with me for the winter break and wanted to fill in a chart I made to help me gauge our status with the articles. I printed copies of the business associations, local government and environmental law survey articles, which had been through the system. I skimmed through two new articles that came in during finals, New York state tax and penal law.

Other miscellaneous paperwork included completing the form for my entry to the Scribes writing competition run by the University of Arkansas School of Law. The competition seeks entries from every law review in the country. My note was submitted because it received the highest ranking in last year's anonymous note writing competition. I briefly explained our selection procedures and note-writing process.

Then there were a handful of memos to write: one to Mike, the managing editor, who would be travelling to Washington D.C. for a two-week intensive study program; the other to Cole, an executive editor, who lived in Syracuse and was planning on working in the office during the break.

To prepare for the impending doom that the Y2K bug threatened, the law school's tech staff directed journal editors to clear off the all the computers' hard drives. The tech staff planned to back up the entire network before the millenium changed. All non-essential documents stored on the hard drives had to be saved to the network or floppy disk. All law review documents and articles were stored in the law school network. But I also saved all essential documents on floppy disks, just in case.

The last tasks I completed included a reimbursement report for $48 worth of soda, candy and office supplies I purchased since October. Finally, I sent about 10 holiday cards to several law school administrators and staff people who frequently made my life slightly easier, including the librarians, staff in the budget office, support services and the Dean's office. I also sent cards to our Lexis and Westlaw representatives and our point person at the printer in Nebraska. Why not? Professionals send out holiday cards, why not the law review? A little good will could not hurt.

Secretary of Administration
Tuesday, January 11, 2000

Winter vacation was short. I returned well before classes resumed to take care of a host of administrative tasks. There was never a lack of minor administrative tasks to coordinate events and copy flow of the articles. It required a constant stream of memoranda, notes and messages to the law review's listserve, an automatic e-mail list that sent the same message to the entire law review membership.

Because I practically lived in the office during the day and I had to be on top of just about everything, micro-managing without looking like a micro-manager. Someone had to respond to the inevitable questions about the 2Ls' notes or the articles they were editing or the time of the next meeting. Then, there were the external developments; whether it was an outside author or a subscriber calling with a question. Sometimes, it was just easier for me to deal with a matter right after fielding the phone call, than to write a message or memo to the editor who would handle the matter.

The little things piled up, such as requests to reprint or use past articles. As the Editor-in-Chief, I had the authority to grant or deny use of our articles. A handful of our past authors sought permission to reprint their articles, mostly on their law firm's websites, to show off to clients. Three publishers of specialty digests and books wanted to reprint student notes and articles from past volumes. The Copyright Clearance Office for the University of Pittsburgh wanted permission to copy a 1981 article for use in a law class.

The law review received requests like these about every week or two. The policy was to grant all reprint requests as long as proper credit was given to the Syracuse Law Review. Because law review was an academic endeavor and scholarly publication—and we were pleased that anybody wanted to read our articles—we declined to request royalties or remuneration.

My personal policy was to deal with these requests immediately or at least as quickly as possible—sign off and get it out of my hair and off my desk. When the requests involved student-written work, I forwarded the request and my response to the alumni-author. This was a simple courtesy. An editor who graduated the year before called me the minute he received my letter: "This is awesome!" he said. "I can't wait to show the partners [at his law firm], they will love it. Thanks for sending this to me."

Another burgeoning headache involved the back issue sales for volume 49. The law review always printed a fair number of extra books with every print run. Over the years, the law review acceded back issue responsibilities to the William S. Hein Company of Buffalo. The Hein company is one of the biggest publishers of law books in the country and also maintains back issues and single issues for practically every law review in the country. As part of our contract with the company, we designated back inside cover of our book as an advertisement: "Where can you get back volumes and issues? Order through Hein! We have obtained the entire back stock, reprint and microform rights to the Syracuse Law Review." Advertisements like this appear on the back inside cover of practically every law review published.

The company subscribed for an order of 50 books for its operation. Ally, the business editor, responded to a call from someone at Hein notifying her that the company never received its order of 50 books for 49:1 (the first book in volume 49). Thus, Hein needed 50 copies of that book. We were confused because the subscription mailing list showed the 50-book order. But that list was about 10 months old. The chaos of the past 10 months could not be explained. Our responsibilities often required us to solve problems we inherited from previous years. That is expected, given the fluid nature of the staff that sits for only a year. There is little continuity from staff-to-staff. By the time I really got a grasp of the issues and running the operation and business, my term as editor would be over.

Ally and I decided that we had no other choice but to refill the order for 50 books by pulling them off our shelves. We kept a sizeable chunk of the extra books. The only problem was that at this point, we did not have 50 to give. Over the course of the year, the extras that we had seemed to have disappeared from our office. Plenty of staff members helped themselves to what seemed like a never-ending supply of law reviews. We had a huge shelf full of them, it seemed obvious. It was nice for your family to see your name on the masthead. We scrounged around for them. I returned one I had at home and we sent what we had.

[Months later Ally learned that Hein actually had the complete order for 49:1 but had misplaced the box. And, we decided to add a liberal buffer of extra books for the single issues of volume 50. I did not want to run out of single issues again.]

Some of Our Most Devoted Readers are in Jail
Thursday, January 13, 2000

As I sorted through the pile of mail we received today, I came across a handwritten white envelope postmarked Amarillo, Texas. Most of our mail was institutional, meaning it usually came in stationery envelopes with business addresses.

This had a handwritten name and number and it was addressed to the Syracuse Law Review.

Inside was a terse handwritten letter on yellow notebook paper from a man named John, with a seven digit number next to his name, from Amarillo, Texas:

> Greetings. I am seeking a copy of "Mesmerizing Justice: The Use of Hypnotically Induced Testimony in Criminal Trials," 34 Syracuse L. Rev. 927-75 (1983).
>
> In my trial the state of Texas was allowed to hypnotize a person who suffers from depression. The subject prior to hypnosis claimed to see other people. Further there is no evidence to corroborate this testimony.
>
> Any other information on hypnosis—mainly dealing with criminal proceedings and on hypnosis of persons suffering from depression and new or current beliefs. Thank you for your help in this important matter. Respectfully, John.

There was not a lot of punctuation. I pulled volume 34 from my shelf to make sure the article really existed. It did. Then, I went to Lexis to see if I could learn anything about John. Nothing came up in the news data bases or court files for Texas. I wanted to know a little about this guy before I started sending anything to him.

I found the Amarillo Globe, the local newspaper on the web. Nothing came up in the online archives. I called to speak with the police reporter, who confirmed that the address was the local prison. But he never heard of this John. He said he would check out the paper's archives for me and get back to me.

That night my Uncle Irwin in El Paso called me. He needed legal information about New Jersey for my other uncle in New Jersey (who I rarely talk to). I asked him whether he had any contacts in Amarillo, where he worked as an assistant prosecutor in after he graduated from law school. He decided to fulfill his lifelong dream and attended law school after retiring from his career. As the inherently inquisitive individual he is, he called a friend who worked in the prosecutor's office and found out that John was convicted of murder and burglary and will be spending some time in the William Clements Unit of the local prison. That was enough information for me, although I was interested in learning some more specifics of the case as well as more detailed information about John. But the information satisfied my curiosity.

I sent him a copy of the article. My letter was brief:

> Dear Mr. John.,
> Please find a photo copy of the article you requested: Mickenberg, "Mesmerizing Justice: The Use of Hypnotically Induced Testimony in Criminal Trials," 34 Syracuse L. Rev. 927 (1983). Best of luck with your endeavors. The Editorial Board.

I opted to share the honor with the Editorial Board for a couple reasons. First, I did not want this guy attaching a name, particularly mine, to this organization in his attempts to enlist my individual services for his appeals. Second, I did not want to have my name attached to this just in case he got bent out of shape or somehow blamed the Syracuse Law Review for his failed appeal. One of the last things I want is some convict with a chip on his shoulder brooding over his failed appeal while thinking about me. I did not want some kind of Max Cady-Cape Fear vengeance attack later on.

Back in April, at the banquet, I hit some loud laughs when I cracked that our readers included lawyers, judges, professors and people in jail. If you are doing hard time and want to kill several hours, try reading a law review article. It might even constitute cruel and unusual punishment.

Credit Report
Friday, January 14, 2000

Because law review members receive two academic credits for their staff membership and requirements, the editor had to fill out a grade submission form from the registrar, then submit it to the law review's academic adviser. Professor Locknor, the adviser, signed off on the submission report.

Even an innocuous task like checking boxes on a form was not without hassles. All I had to do was check the "Pass" box for each member who successfully completed the law review requirements (satisfactory performance during office hours and writing the student note). Only 3Ls may apply their law review credit. So, you do the work during your second year but apply the credit during your third year.

It was all pretty simple. However, the Tom situation still lingered.

One senior board editor forgot to apply the credit during her fall semester (senior board editors received one extra credit for a grand total of three academic credits. But the registrar prohibited board members from applying all three credits in one semester).

Then, there were two 2L members enrolled in masters programs which technically gave them 3L standing because they had earned additional credits. Thus, their inadvertent registration for law review credit was not caught by the registrar. The registrar emailed me a nasty note earlier in the year after a couple 2Ls on staff improperly applied for law review credit.

I detailed these problems in a brief memo to Professor Locknor who would handle the matter with the registrar. Professor Locknor, our school's most distinguished professor, author of more than a dozen books, was our hands-off adviser. The role of adviser differs from law review to law review. Some advisers hold veto authority over what gets published. Some act as additional editors. Others are just on standby if problems arise.

For us, Professor Locknor was on standby. He never ventured upstairs to the law review office. I could never discern whether his laissez-faire attitude was based on indifference, contempt or an ideological belief that the law review should be run by the students without interference.

Professor Locknor was my favorite professor at the school. I went out of my way to take his classes and enjoyed his dry humor. But I never felt comfortable talking with him. He was very professorial, and spoke with intellectual authority. That was why he was the law review's adviser. That was why I enjoyed his classes.

His door was always open for me, and his advice always restrained, thoughtful and contemplative. I tried not to burden him with trivial issues, but the law review kept running into major problems, such as the cheating and plagiarism cases. He also helped land a 50th anniversary author and allowed the law review to publish a version of the opening chapter of his latest book in our 50th anniversary book.

Law Review: *the redux*
Tuesday, January 18, 2000

It all started again today, the first day of classes for the Spring Semester—my final semester as a law student. Crunch time for the law review. Even though I had been back for a week, office hours resumed today in earnest for the full staff.

A number of people also owed office hours. My welcome back message to the staff, via the email listserve, reiterated, "There is no millenial amnesty plan." I also detailed all the new office amenities, including the new dictionaries, Bluebooks and coat hooks. "We hope you take advantage of all the wonderful changes and additions to the law review office. We finally received our wall-mounted coat hooks. Feel free to hang your coats, hats or other winter regalia on the hooks behind the door." These acquisitions were minor victories, and I had to ensure that the staff was aware of everything. As with most of my staff-wide emails, I laced the message with a slight degree of sarcasm.

People would use the coat hooks, but rarely picked up the latest edition of *Black's Law Dictionary*.

Glorified Secretary
Wednesday, January 19, 2000

We always joked that we needed a secretary. We would get a secretary when I got my law review car.

A 1966 alumnus called the office because he wanted copies of the articles he wrote while on law review. His abruptness caught me by surprise. He was the one who called. He was the one asking for a favor, yet he had no interest in small talk. He gave me his name and address, which was in New Jersey. I told him I was from New Jersey, which normally would at least prompt a polite, "Oh yes."

I was slightly offended. The administrators at the law school boast about the loyal alumni. But all I encountered was rudeness. During my first year I even had two alumni refuse to talk with me after I sent them letters. It was not that they were busy. I told this one attorney's secretary that I would call back at a more convenient time. She said, "Don't!."

Here I was almost two years later, in a position that demanded politeness and a degree of diplomacy to our alumni. Mr. Flemington wanted no part of it. All he wanted was copies of his 24-year-old articles. Even more troubling, he offered not citation and was vague about what he actually wrote, describing an article on tribal lands zoning and international law.

I took down his address and told him I would get copies made. It took about an-hour-and-a-half of almost page-by-page leafing through Syracuse Law Review volumes 15, 16, 17, 18 and the 20 year index in volume 21. I found two Recent Decisions and a copy of an article on international law that he worked on. I found his name in a footnote. I also copied the masthead and sent it to him.

It was difficult to find the articles because student-written work in the older volumes spanned several years. Work prepared during a student's second or third year on staff might appear in a volume after the student graduated. Also, there were student notes, comments and recent decisions. In the old days, students wrote more. But the articles were shorter.

I sent Mr. Flemington his copies and dashed off a letter pitching the 50th anniversary book and banquet. I never heard from him again. Not even a thank you. I should have sent him a bill.

The day before performing Mr. Flemington's search and recovery mission, I delivered two boxes of documents to a lawyer downtown, Mr. DeVine, a local attorney and alumnus who was considering writing an article for our 50th book. A team of 2Ls prepared this research during office hours. At least DeVine thanked me. But I never received an article from him.

Days of Chaos
Thursday, January 20, 2000

This was not an extraordinary day in my life. But chaos that followed me from 8 a.m. to the time I went to sleep.

Like most days, I opened the office up at 8. This semester, I had about 2 1/2 hours to read for class and set up the computers and other stuff.

I wrote a memo for a research assignment for a potential 50th anniversary book author who needed to know whether there were any law review articles on the topic of the contingent workforce. An editing team without an article did the work during office hours.

A few days earlier, the librarians printed out a list of who signed out the law review office key on reserve in the library. The key could be checked out by staff members like a book. Thus, there was a record of who checked out the key. I wanted a listing of who had checked out the key for general accounting purposes and found someone who is not on law review had checked it out on Nov. 18. I was perturbed and sent the librarian an email to see if this person was a library employee or a Lexis representative. This mystery student was on one of the other journals, so the librarian said it was just a mistake.

The next two hours were a mix of reading for my securities class and answering various questions from staff members.

I fielded a phone call from one of our Survey authors who was past his deadline by about five months.

"I recently had eye surgery and had other work and that the deadlines," he whined in the best Woody Allen impression I ever heard. "Anyway, your deadlines don't mean anything. I mean, the Survey comes out late every year anyway."

"The reason it comes out late every year is because authors ignore deadlines," I said. He wanted a few weeks to finish it, and finally agreed to deliver the article in two. I said it was important to get his article and thanked him.

I checked the mail and then went to class.

Liz, an associate notes and comments editor who had been an absentee staff member since her election, was in the class. It was time to deal with her for the last time. She had systematically ignored her 2L students assigned to her for note-writing mentoring and failed to perform her duties. She even blew off the writing competition scoring which sent us into a tailspin early on. Both Mike and Nick had talked to her about her responsibilities, but got nowhere with her.

The question prevailed: how could we expect 2Ls to meet all of their note-writing requirements and deadlines, if their editor failed to contact them or otherwise perform her responsibilities?

After class, I approached her and asked her if she had a few minutes to talk. She said no. "Fine I will walk with you," I offered. In the crowded hallway, I took a deep breath and said, "I think we have to reassess your commitment to law review."

"What are you talking about?" she said.

"We have heard from the 2Ls on your team that you had not contacted them and that some had been seeking help," I said.

She looked at me with a vacant glare, "I have contacted them and sent them emails. They have my email address and telephone number, they can contact me if they want."

"You know, we have been over this repeatedly with you before," I said. "Enough is enough."

"If you guys want me to quit, I will. I have better things to do with my time," she said, verbalizing what I wanted to hear.

"Fine. That's fine," I said. By now, her eyes were starting to well up. I was not quite sure why she started to cry. She never lifted a finger in her editorial capacity.

She ran for several senior board positions, but failed to present one cogent reason why she wanted to hold any position. She had several outside commitments including a couple of part-time jobs. Law review clearly was not a priority. But there were several editors with outside jobs, internships, research assistantships, families and other commitments. One senior editor had a one-hour commute, a part-time job and a wife and kids at home, but it never once encroached on his law review duties.

Later that afternoon, we had several people in the office but no 3L senior board member scheduled. I talked Merry, an executive editor, into hanging around until about 4 p.m. because I had class from 2:30 to 3:45. There were plenty of the usual crazy things going on. One 2L was having trouble with her Westlaw printing which sent documents to the law review's office printer instead of the designated Westlaw printer. Whenever Westlaw or Lexis printouts went to the office printer instead of the designated Lexis or Westlaw printers, it would jam up the printer, drain the toner and consume massive amounts of the paper that the law review had to pay for out of our budget. The Lexis and Westlaw printers were housed in our office but maintained by the two companies and consumed their own paper, an endless supply of free paper. This was a problem that I thought we had fixed. Several memos and emails to the staff detailing the printer routing should have resolved this.

Then an editor checked a direct quote on Westlaw and found a typo. I told her to go to the library and check the reporter volume to see if it was in the official copy as well. It was not. I told her to call Westlaw and point out the error. "Westlaw offers rewards for such error-spotting," I joked. After making the call the editor said the Westlaw representative she spoke with said there were no rewards but that she made her day.

"Well, there should be," I told her.

I visited the school's computer tech guy who installed three new (refurbished) computers in our office before the break. The computers were new to our office and better than the ones we had but they were still at least five years old. They were computers used in the former library computer lab that had not been thrown out. The computers were not configured to accept the law review logons or passwords and were of no use for certain tasks which required access to the law review's network. I sent him an email more than 10 days ago; got no response. So I went to his office. He said he would jump on it Friday morning. This was frustrating because people needed to use the computers, otherwise they could not work during their office hours. Then, they would complain that the computers were no good.

Then I met with Caitlin, Tom's girlfriend in my office. Since the plagiarism incident, she had been icy. There had been concerns because she was on the editing team that uncovered the evidence. I was ready to switch teams and place her on another team because she was friends with another editor.

"If you would be more comfortable on a different team, we're more willing to accommodate you. It would not be a problem," I told her.

"No," she said, walking out of the office. That was the extent of the conversation. It would likely be the only conversation I ever had with her because Tom's expulsion appeal was temporarily scheduled for next week.

When I went to inquire about Tom's appeal, I first went to the Associate Dean, who had told me that the appeal would be this week. She was not available so her secretary sent me to Beth-Ellen, a school administrator involved in student disciplinary and enrollment matters. She was one of those administrators with a nebulous job that nobody could specifically identify but was always in the midst of things.

Knocking on her open door, I asked her about the status of Tom's appeal. "I was told the appeal was supposed to be completed this week," I said.

She immediately got defensive and started yelling at me. "You have no right to come in here and demand information about this." I was shocked that she instantly became so hostile. She said I was accusatory and had no right to any information. "That is confidential student information and you have no right to march in here and demand that I tell you this information," she yelled at me.

Perhaps she did not recognize me or she forgot who I was. "Do you know who I am?" I asked.

"Yes I do," she said.

"Wait a second here. Maybe we are not on the same page here." I could not believe she was so hostile. On the few occasions I had spoken with her this year, she had been polite and pleasant, almost nice. "First of all, I am the one who brought the charges. I have staff concerns here because this is a position that has responsibilities. I need to know what's going on because I am the one who has to deal with all of this and I am the one who will be up in my office in August, after I graduate and after I take the bar exam doing this work because I could not get someone to do this work now. And, I am the last person to find anything out."

She demanded to know who told me the faculty appeal would be this week. "The Associate Dean," I said.

"You have no right to any information or criticism about this process," she yelled at me, again.

"I'm not criticizing anybody. I just want to know what the process is," I said, adding that I did not even know what the process was.

Then, she backtracked and apologized for yelling at me. At this point, I was so angry that I shrugged my shoulders and said I did not care about her apology. She proceeded to tell me where things stood and that I had to understand that the faculty and administrators have personal lives. I wanted to explain to her that she should address students, particularly me as the editor of the law review, with a modicum of respect. I did not tell her that, though.

She attempted to explain that the Associate Dean was in the process of moving. It seemed like the Associate Dean was always in the middle of something that demanded more attention than student issues: an article, a move, a symposium, a hangnail. That did not explain Beth-Ellen's verbal explosion toward me.

Then, she said that the administration could not even get the appeal underway until they notified and convened the faculty and allowed the student prosecutor time to prepare for the appeal.

The appeal would take place before the entire faculty at a meeting (or at least whichever faculty members decide to show up). Each member would get a copy of the complete packet of evidence, including my report and Tom's appeals papers and other evidence. They would read the materials, probably at least two days before the meeting and then hear oral arguments. There would be no further evidence or testimony. The faculty would only consider the merits of the punishment, which in this case was the suspension of a third-year student for his last semester and a sizeable chunk of community service.

For all the administration's concerns about confidentiality, the appeal would expose the case to between 30 to 50 faculty members. This meant a substantial portion of the faculty would now read my report and review the evidence. I never anticipated so many people getting involved in this.

I had lost enough sleep over this matter and was frustrated with the pace and dissemination of information. I resented that law school administrators kept me in the dark about this, and then had the audacity to verbally assault me. I had valid staffing concerns because once we got ready to get out book to the printer, we would need the senior editor to assist with several intensive aspects of production. As it stood, I had to shoulder an excessive amount of additional work because of Tom's absence.

Hare-raising Midnight Encounter
Friday, January 21, 2000

The reverberations from the chaotic day jostled me awake at 3:20 a.m. This was not the first time I had trouble sleeping because of law review problems bouncing around in my head or my law review nightmares.

My room was hot because I had kept my little space heater on at high overnight and I was thirsty. I had not been sleeping well since coming back to Syracuse from the winter break. It had been really cold—wind chills 20 degrees below zero some nights and plenty of snow.

It was cold and it had snowed all day and night. I got a glass of water and went to my large picture window which rested at ground level. As I drew back the curtain with one hand I startled a little bunny rabbit foraging for spilled birdseed from the bird feeder above. It stood less than a foot away from me but was separated by the glass. It stood still and looked at me. Its ears twitched. I let the curtain go, leaving a sliver of space between each side.

The snow flurries and inches of snow covering the ground brightened the midnight darkness. It was the kind of darkness that made everything visible, including the bunny. I looked at the rabbit and it looked back at me. The bunny hopped around and I crawled back into bed.

Pile-on
Wednesday, January 26, 2000

Walt, one of the two articles editors, was flipping through piles of submissions on his desk. The articles editors and business editor shared an office on the other side of the wall from mine, just off the main law review room. Even though the law review had two elected articles editors, Walt had been pretty much running the show with article selection and author-relations since last year's elections. His counterpart, Vince, rarely showed up for office hours, despite the four-hour required office hours and my constant urgings. Walt was displeased with his counterpart's absenteeism, but seemed content sharing the workload with me.

"Anything good in the pile?" I asked, hoping that there were at least a couple worthy submissions among the hundred or so there before him.

"A couple, we got this one on the Uniform Commercial Code," he said, lifting up an 80-page manuscript. "I spoke to the author this afternoon. He's interested, but this is only the first part and it's not done. He has a second 80-page manuscript and he said it needs a lot of work. I looked through it and the footnotes need a lot of work."

"Would he want to publish with us?"

"Yes, but it needs work. I'm talking to him tomorrow, what do you think we should do?"

The article was interesting and from a young professor at a respectable Midwestern law school. But after a quick glance, it was clear that the article was not in good shape. There were gaping holes where footnotes were needed. Dozens of footnotes were half-completed and needed substantial editing. Plus, the article was huge. A quick cost-benefit analysis, a favorite way to analyze a torts case, determined that it would just be too much of a headache to publish. Several staff members were still smarting from the medieval article. We needed articles for our third book, but that one would take too much work for little return.

"It's a good topic but this article is not nearly ready and we cannot re-write this guy's article," I said. "Let's make our life easier and take a pass on this one. Tell him to get a research assistant, too."

"Yeah, that's what I was thinking. The professor told me he did not think it was ready," Walt said.

"What else do we have there?"

He flipped through the piles. He arranged the submissions in three piles: the day's new submissions;   articles written by potentially reputable authors with interesting topics; and borderline articles, written by authors, mostly professors at second, third and fourth-tier law schools, young associates at major national law firms and law clerks to federal circuit court judges.

The latter submissions from young associates and law clerks usually ended up in the recycling basket beside the trash. We received several submissions weekly from this population of budding scholars, usually their unpublished law review articles, law school independent study projects or extensions of research memos written for their bosses. Some of the names in that pile would undoubtedly one day become names in legal scholarship, but I was not sure the Syracuse Law Review would be the starting point for them.

Because law reviews are partly judged by the quality of their authors, for better or for worse, we usually avoided these types of submissions until we were desperate. Instead, we were hoping to attract authors with a couple of other articles on their resumes or at least professors from other second tier or even lower-first tier law schools. The Syracuse Law Review was not receiving submissions from faculty at Harvard or Yale.

Walt was in negotiations with a young associate from a major New York law firm for an article on substantive due process. The author had a couple other articles under his belt along with two judicial clerkships, including one with a well-known circuit court judge. He wanted to be a law professor and, more important, he jumped at the opportunity to publish with us.

"We did get one interesting one here, it looks like it's from a guy in jail," Walt said, handing me a 35-page hand-typed article on the Eighth Amendment and cruel and unusual punishment. The author was doing time in a state prison in Florida.

The footnotes were not long and expansive but the form was proper. The article looked interesting and was written by someone with first-hand experience in the penal system. There was an unmistakable air of expertise behind the article. Few law professors spend much time in jail, even if some should be locked up. This author knew what he was writing about.

The novelty of publishing an article written about the prison system by someone inside the system was quite appealing. But the article was not available on computer disk and would have had to be typed into our computers. Communicating with the author also seemed to be a problem. Even though many of our authors ignored our telephone calls or made themselves unavailable, we could eventually get them on the phone. An author behind bars who is allocated an equal number of telephone calls as showers per week, seemed like a lot to deal with.

"What do you think about it," I asked.

"Too much of a headache," he said.

Telephone Roulette
Saturday, January 29, 2000

Answering the telephone in the office was like playing Russian Roulette, anybody could be at the other end. At least once every two weeks we got some kind of strange caller looking for free legal advice. One morning, a woman with a heavy foreign accent called because she wanted to "buy our books for her bar review preparation." She said that somebody told her to buy our "review" books, obviously mistaking the law review for bar review. I explained that she had the wrong idea about the law review and I told her that Bar Bri would be better. I gave her the 1-800 telephone number for her. I should have sold her a subscription, too. BarBri should have given me a commission.

On another occasion, I found a voicemail message from a guy looking for free divorce information. I called the number back, as a courtesy to give him the clinic's number. A kid answered so I hung up.

Whenever anybody called with a legal question, I directed them to law school's free legal clinic, an office in which students, supervised by full-time faculty lawyers, provided free legal services on a variety of subjects. That was about as much information as I or anyone else on law review would provide. I regularly reminded the staff of this. Nobody on law review needed to be accused of unauthorized practice of law.

A few days ago, I fielded an odd call from a local man named Frank who had a question about whether a defendant in a capital murder case in

New York could represent himself in court. Frank said that he needed the information to make his screenplay authentic.

A screenplay loosely based on a 40-year-old film and murder trial sounded intriguing. Frank, a recently-retired law enforcement official, had an agent and studio in Hollywood was working with him. The story had lengthy courtroom scenes set in New York courts, and he needed some accurate information on the topic to make the dialogue and descriptions authentic.

I offered to research the topic for him, in exchange for something akin to a movie credit as "Legal Consultant." I stressed that nothing I would provide could be construed as legal advice. It was still early in the semester, so I had a little flexibility with my personal schedule. It was a lot more interesting reading about the Sixth Amendment and capital murder trials than the assigned reading for tax or decedents.

My 8-page report titled, "The Defendant as His Own Lawyer in New York," really hammered it up:

> The American courtroom has been the backdrop for many classic tales in literature and screen. Many courtroom trials contain raw drama and gripping emotions touching on every aspect of life. Litigants engage in spirited intellectual inquiry into public policy and the human condition. The most basic principles facing humanity rest at the core of this inquiry: right vs. wrong; morality vs. depravity and good vs. evil.
>
> These are the basic tenets of any judicial proceeding. A capital murder trial magnifies these most basic human elements.

For the lay audience, I defined pro se representation and briefed a handful of leading cases on the topic of pro se defendants in murder cases. I included several blocked quotes of material that could easily be incorporated into his movie dialogue. I also added a brief synopsis of the Colin Ferguson case, the lunatic who killed six when he shot up a Long Island Railroad car in 1995 and acted as his own counsel.

This was probably the sort of research that the writers of *Law & Order* do. I had no idea whether Frank was legitimate or whether his movie would ever get done. If it did, great, if it did not get made, then I spent a couple hours researching topics that I may never need to know, certainly not the first or last time I did that.

[Frank called me the day he received the report and thanked me profusely for "writing such a professional report." He promised to keep me apprised of his project's progress.]

Nice Guys Finish Last
Monday, January 31, 2000

In an attempt to be a nice guy, I gave the Prince an assignment that would allow him to leave the office for a portion of his office hours. His team had about 50 books charged out of the main library. The books were kept on the shelf in the office and referred to during the fact-checking and editing process. The article had already been edited and sent to the author for revisions. Thus, the books were no longer needed in the office. They were due in a couple of days anyway.

The bulk of the books were charged from the main campus library, Bird Library. Retrieving or returning books from or to the main library was a plum assignment. It meant a 10 minute walk through campus. It meant that the lucky staff member got out of the office for a while and did not have to spend time working on detail-oriented fact-checking and editing. There were several occasions during my second year when I had the opportunity to go to the library and retrieve books.

One of those times I also spent an extra hour sifting through microfiche cards to find an incomprehensible 18th-century religion-philosophy book. I found the citation and read the text on the page of Jonathan Edwards' 1758 work, *The Great Christian Doctrine of Original Sin Defended.* I read it, checked it to make sure the text in the article and the proposition stated in the article matched, but made little sense.

Going to the library was not always a blow-off assignment. This time, however, it was a blow-off assignment. All he had to do was take back a pile of books. Things with the Prince had settled down after his challenge to fisticuffs and my "Just be a *mensch*" message. He even reluctantly made up the hour he owed. He was still on thin ice and knew it, but obviously did not care.

Returning books to the campus library consumed a half-hour, at the most, and that was walking really slow. I even gave him my backpack and Plain Dealer duffel bag to carry the books.

The Prince and another student, Scott, departed on the hour, 3 p.m. Scott returned about 40 minutes later and went to work cite-checking. The Prince did not return. The Prince vaporized.

I was had, again.

Not Quite Human
Tuesday, February 1, 2000

As I stood in the Dean's office antechamber waiting for his frazzled secretary to schedule me for a meeting, Elaine, another secretary, offered me a piece of chocolate. I cradled the Ferrerro Rocher chocolate-covered nut in my hand along with a folder and my little blue memo pad.

Jackie, the law school's building manager, came in and inquired about the chocolate, saying that it seemed completely out of character for me to be holding a gold foil-covered candy. I said that I eat a lot of candy: "I live on candy, and have Coke for breakfast."

"That is the most human thing I've heard from you yet," she said.

"What do you mean by that?" I asked.

"You are always so serious and business-like. You are always so busy and never look happy. I always see you walking and looking determined," she said motioned with her head-down with her arms straight like a robot. "You are always here, too. I see your office light on in the morning and at night."

She was correct about the hours I was keeping. It seemed like I was always there, even on the weekends. I reassured her that was human and serious by nature: "I like candy, soda and puppies. Really, I am a person. I just usually have a lot on my mind."

"I always thought you were human," Elaine said. Elaine was always eager to give me candy or cookies or whatever was stocked in the office's kitchenette every time I visited the Dean's office. It was her maternal instinct to feed. Elaine was easily the friendliest person in the building. She was fun and interesting to talk with. She knew about the law and lawyers and frequently took interesting graduate classes at the university. I would always make a point to poke my head in the office to say hello whenever I happened to be on that side of the building.

She was also new to the school, which explained why she was nice. She wore a pleasant smile, which few of the administrators or support staff rarely had for students. The first time I encountered Elaine I was turning in my report and documents regarding the plagiarism case. I needed to hand it directly to the Associate Dean, who was in a meeting. I was reluctant to hand it over to a new secretary.

"This is important and private material," I said.

"Don't worry, you can trust me. I used to work for lawyers. I know all about confidential and privileged documents," she said. "I'll even lock it up for you until the Associate Dean is available." I watched her lock it in her desk. I had a feeling I could trust her.

Later that night, over dinner at one of our usual dining spots, Cosmo's, a campus greasy spoon-pizza place, I relayed Jackie's comments to Sara. She then repeated a conversation she had the day before with Art, a friendly and skilled second year law review member, who did some of the best editing on staff but never took himself too seriously. Art engaged Sara in a conversation and repeatedly asked her fairly personal questions about me and us. "What is it like going out with him? Is he always like *that*?" he asked her.

I am not sure what "that" meant, but I have a pretty good idea. His questioning made it sound like spending time with me was tantamount to hard time in prison—like I was some kind of miserable tyrant.

"Art and a couple of others are concerned and scared by some of the things you said at one of the last staff meetings," she said.

Apparently, my recent speeches at staff meetings imploring careful scrutiny of work had sunk in. In recent weeks, I reviewed several articles that the 2Ls had already worked on and found numerous mistakes: errant citations, wrong page numbers, misspellings, misquotes and more.

These mistakes and lack of precision irked me. The law review staff was comprised of the best students in the law school. These were people who should not have been making mistakes. If there were mistakes, everyone's name would be on the masthead in the front of the book along with the university's, along with mine. Mistakes would be a poor reflection on everyone. And these top students destined for top law firms were making basic mistakes that a fifth-grader would be equally equipped to recognize. These were the top students the placement office raved about and promoted to the big firms, yet they could not properly Bluebook an article.

Even more troubling was the fact that most of the editing was technical, with little substantive critiquing of the articles' text or theses. The law review had a policy to try to preserve the author's voice and intent, which meant little substantive editing and minimal rewriting of the text. Substantive editing was more complex and strenuous.

Mistakes happen. I certainly was not infallible. But the law review's demands on staff members were not too rigorous. Two office hours a week in return for a golden resume line is still a great deal. Expecting a degree of perfection, or even professional pride, among these top students was not asking for too much.

So 2L staff members like Art wondered why I was wound so tightly or why I was so serious about accuracy or the lack of accuracy. There was no reason for the 2Ls on staff to have any comprehension of my job.

Law review editors absorb a tremendous amount of pressure simply publishing a journal under normal law school conditions. But the responsibility of publishing the annual 20-article *Survey of New York Law* along with the 50th anniversary book intensified the pressures. The collateral pressures of the cheating and plagiarism cases added immeasurable worries.

To add insult to injury, I had the additional burden of worrying about landing a job.

Today was also the day after Tom's final appeal before the entire faculty. His conviction was upheld, which meant he would be suspended. An Associate Dean finally revealed the disposition to me when I went to her office. She was unaware that the law review might have to handle his suspension with internal administrative procedures formally removing him from the staff. But she finally said I could let the cat out of the bag. The senior board already knew and the law school rumor mill disseminated the information to many more.

I am not sure how much of the faculty turned out to hear the case. Mike told me that his dad, who taught courses on federal law, recused himself. The professor that Mike served as a research assistant informed him of the outcome.

The faculty read the report and reviewed the evidence. I was certain they would not overturn the judicial board's guilty verdict. That would be tantamount to overruling their own faculty brothers and sisters, which is practically anathema in the colluded world of academia. If law professors do one thing well, it is circle the wagons for self-preservation. It happens with academic standards decisions, sexual harassment or discrimination cases. They watch their backs. This time, they were also watching mine.

I am fairly certain my tax professor, who was a visiting for the year, sat in on the decision because he had called on me twice already. We had only had two classes with discussions and he was one of those professors who taught Socratically. He seemed pretty even-handed with his questions and I was prepared. But still, I did not enjoy being called on two days in a row in a class of 80 students. So far, I was the only student he had come back to for a second round of questions.

This was, of course, no surprise. If I was a law professor with the editor-in-chief of the law review in my class, I would probably go after him, too. I probably would not be as kind as he had been thus far. At least he was not "As-Saulting" the class Socratically.

Taxing Duties
Wednesday, February 2, 2000

Art just finished his two-hour block of office hours and kicked back to talk. I sat on the big table in the main office while he sat at a computer terminal. Another 2L, a quiet, almost silent guy, sat beside him. Nick, the Notes and Comments editor, sat at the table.

Art's team had the New York State Tax article for the Survey. The author was new to us and the citation form was extremely troubling. Every year, the tax article cited to a loose-leaf reporter of tax cases from state tax courts, tax appeals tribunals, administrative hearings and regular courts. Some of these cases never make it into traditional court reporters. Some are on Lexis and Westlaw, but are not very accessible and are difficult to find.

These difficulties were extremely frustrating to Art. He pointed out how some of the citations within the article were inconsistent. One person went through and started to put in Westlaw citations. Another person marked on the cover sheet that he did 50 citations during his office hours. But few were marked. The articles editors, who pick the articles and deal with the authors, had faxed a list of cases to the author that we needed to review because we were systematically unable to find them and the law library did not subscribe to the specialized loose-leaf service.

Then, Art said that he was surprised that there were so many mistakes in the article, especially after "your make-sure-everything-is-correct riot act speech." He added hand quotation marks and a Richard Nixon impression to his description.

"Don't dance around it, what are you really trying to say," I asked, adding that I did not appreciate the Nixon analogy.

"The staff is scared of you," he said, laughing.

"You're kidding. I find it really hard to believe that the people who are at the top of the class and the best writers in the school, are scared of me," I said. "Anyway, the work product thus far had been somewhat disappointing."

I reiterated that I did not appreciate the Nixon comparison. I really did not appreciate the Nixon comparison. I mean, I am not a Red baiting, anti-Communist. I do not believe that communism worked and may be a tad paranoid, but I was not the complete power monger lunatic that Nixon was.

Art's Nixon analogy jostled my memory. I remembered reading a biography of Nixon for an undergrad political science class that described the president as never being satisfied, dissatisfied when his plans failed to proceed as he envisioned while he was constantly concerned about what people thought of him.[47] I guess I could relate to that. The comparison should end there.

Later, after office hours ended for the day and I had time to kill before my 6 p.m. New York Civil Practice class, Nick lingered around to talk. Nick spent a couple hours in the office working and answering 2L questions. "Spending time in here must be like some of the pressures you get in a small private practice with people always asking you questions and taking your attention away every minute and expecting expert answers."

---

[47] RICHARD E. NEUSTADT, PRESIDENTIAL POWER AND THE MODERN PRESIDENTS 203-24 (1990). In a lengthy analysis comparing Presidents Johnson and Nixon, Neustadt wrote:

> Back of their bad grace when things went wrong lay insecurity, or so it seems, a stressful inner turmoil that would go away only when things went right. Apparently both men were in the grip of human hungers they endeavored to appease by being President: Johnson always seeking to assure himself that he had performed wonders and won love, Nixon always demonstrating to himself that he had retained mastery and kept cool. Nothing in the Presidency guaranteed them constant satisfaction, rather the reverse. Yet they were constantly in need.

Id. at 206.

Neustadt also wrote, in a discussion about Presidents Harding, Johnson and Nixon:

> [P]residents were men who victimized themselves, men of intelligence and acuity, determinedly pursuing a great cause which they themselves endangered by their moves in its defense, moves prompted by their insecurities.

Id. at 208.

He seemed surprised by the constant minute-by-minute demand for answers or questions or telephone calls or emails or problems. "This must be crazy for you every day," he said. "It is," I responded. "It is."

Leadership is alluring. But my law review experience elucidated one understated element about leadership: disappointment. Because my job was somewhat political—I was elected and I had to deal with a wide array of people on a daily basis—I reflected on the lives of politicians. When I was a reporter I covered a presidential primary and aspects of a United States senate campaign and a multitude of state, city and municipal politics. For many politicians, politics is a job that brings great public exposure and massages for massive egos.

But there are really politicians who believe in leadership and campaign for office and enter office with ambitious plans to change a system, implement plans, influence policy and generally help people and serve the country. In 1992, when Bill Clinton campaigned for president, he promised that he would fix the economy, fix taxes, provide universal health care, and save the world. Ambitious plans that mesmerized the nation, some which he actually believed in.

For the most part, all he really did was survive impeachment, "smoke a cigar" and prove that Gap dresses are not stain-resistant. Politics fouled his glorious plans, which, I believe, perhaps naively, must lead to personal disappointment. This sort of disappointment rests deep inside the hearts of these leaders. They rarely articulate this disappointment but keep on going, or else they will lose their job.

Surely, it is a stretch to equate a law review editorship with the Presidency of the United States. But there are parallels involving leadership and authority. Power is power and disappointment is disappointment. The roadblocks that lead to disappointment transcend levels of leadership.

With all the daily frustrations and minor setbacks, I could sense I was losing my focus. I held a purportedly prestigious title, and all I could do was see staff members missing bad citations, ignoring typos and authors blowing off deadlines.

The senior staff made a concerted effort to make the office hospitable. The staff had all the resources necessary, including lots of candy. Memos, meetings and the handbook provided everyone with all the information they needed.

Then there were my speeches and pep talks at the staff meetings, in which I attempted to convey serious information laced with occasional humor. I had an open-door policy and practically lived in the office. But, for months, I could see that I was one of the few people who took things seriously. I could see now that leadership can only lead to disappointment.

I could talk until I expired. I could talk about the gravity of the mistakes I found. I could even scare the staff. I was beginning to realize that I could not make people more competent editors. But even worse, I could not make people care about the jobs they did.

Book'em
Friday, February 4, 2000

The law library was searching for a new director. In an effort to generate student input, or at least throw a bone to the students, the administration scheduled informal question and answer breakfast meetings for students and candidates. They were Friday mornings at 9. Student attendance on Fridays is meager enough. Expecting students to attend anything that did not have the prefix "Mandatory" was overly optimistic, if not unrealistic.

I felt partially obligated to represent the students and the school. My official capacity would lend a moderate degree of credibility to an interview. The image that an empty room conveyed was enough to get me there. I was usually in the office by 8 a.m., even on Fridays when I did not have classes. Plus, I could get a doughnut and juice from the Dean's office. What a deal.

There were four candidates who met with whatever students showed up or could be scrounged up for informal discussions and questions and answers. I knew the library well. So I participated and asked the first candidate several questions, over breakfast, about increasing the size of the collection; balancing technology growth with traditional books and dealing with the massive tensions of a large university.

I did not mention law review. But I was quite pleased to see the books I delivered to the Dean's office a month earlier resting comfortably on a coffee table in the richly paneled Dean's conference room. They sat between the *National Law Journal* and the *Chronicle of Higher Education*. The Survey was on top of a slimmer book, at a slight angle, as if Martha Stewart herself had placed them there for both a utilitarian and ornamental appearance.

It was nice to see our books there, especially because a magazine rack near the door had two volumes of law reviews from Harvard, Yale, Columbia, Michigan and Stanford.

About a month ago, I was surprised to learn that the Dean's office did not have copies of our books. A 2L on staff who attended a meeting in the conference room observed the absence of our books, saying "Why aren't our books in there, too. If they have all those other law reviews in the conference room, they should have the Syracuse Law Review. That does not seem right."

He was correct. When I checked our subscription list with the business editor, we realized the Dean did not subscribe. I immediately brought a handful of copies over in January. We added the Dean's office to the subscription listing for two complimentary copies. The school pays for much of this stuff anyway.

Some law school deans and faculty members eagerly read and follow their law reviews. Lucas A. Powe, Jr. illustrated this point in his recent book about the Warren Court.[48] In a discussion about the noted reproductive rights case, *Griswold v. Connecticut*, Powe described the relationship between the *Harvard Law Review* and its dean in the 1960s:

> At the time when virtually no law review was published on time, Harvard's legendary dean, Erwin Griswold, was best known for demanding that his copy of the *Harvard Law Review* arrive on his desk during the month listed on its cover. He was also known for reading every word in every issue immediately and conveying his opinions to the editors.[49]

I am not sure whether the absence of our books in the Dean's office was an oversight, or whether he read them online or in the library, or whether this was simply another example of the administration's abject disrespect for the student body. Several faculty members at this

---

[48] LUCAS A. POWE, JR., THE WARREN COURT AND AMERICAN POLITICS 376-77 (2000). This anecdote was part of an extended discussion of reproductive rights involving the case *Griswold v. Connecticut* and the controversy that followed a humorous footnote included in the Harvard Law Review's casenote on the case. *Griswold v. Connecticut: The Supreme Court, 1964 Term*, 79 HARV. L. REV. 56, 165, n. 22 (1965)).
[49] *Id.*

law school had difficulty masking their distaste for the student body. It was part of the problem when people with credentials from Ivy League law schools and top law firms settle in a depressing city in Central New York that receives snow from Halloween to May Day.

Let's not mince words: Syracuse was not Yale. But it is a solid place to learn the law and a nice private university. We learned the same cases and rules that they teach everywhere else, from the same books. There were students who could easily fit in comfortably at the top tier schools. In fact, there were certain areas which I believe SU taught better than the Ivy League schools, mainly legal research and writing. Every year students returned from their summer associate jobs at top firms in New York City or Washington with stories about how some hot-shot from an Ivy did not know how to log on to Lexis, Shepardize a case or perform a mundane legal research task.

My theory was difficult to prove, and when articulated, sounded almost paranoid. And, an Associate Dean once lambasted me for a letter I wrote alleging this disrespect. The disrespect was subtle. It took the form of unprepared professors, unfocused classes, limited office hours. It took the form of a professor telling a first year student, in front of the whole class, that he should have gone to art school instead of law school.

This was a system that permitted a professor to waste a portion of nearly every lecture by first showing up late, and then debating the attributes of soft drinks, in between rants about the coolness of baseball. I had a tenured professor who literally debated the qualities of Diet Pepsi vs. Lipton Iced Tea, "both good drinks," he concluded. Surprisingly, the merits of soft drinks never showed up on the final exam. But neither did his other hobbies: flirting and looking down young women's blouses. I had several professors who had not even published an article in more than 10 years.

This was also the same system that permitted professors to use their grade books to right the past wrongs of racial and gender discrimination or spend more than a week of a first-year criminal law class discussing the ruling in *Bowers v. Hardwick*, which is barely a criminal law case. The controversial holding in *Bowers* was that there is no constitutional right to homosexual sodomy; an interesting case, but not worthy of that much discussion in a criminal law class.[50]

---

[50] 478 U.S. 186 (1986).

The disrespect also came in the form of a C curve for first year classes while a school like Harvard graduates 76 percent of its law school classes with honors.[51] Then, our professors complained about grade inflation.

In the grand scheme of our law school, it should not have been a surprise that our books were not up there on the shelf, right next to the Harvard, Yale, Penn and Stanford journals. Nevertheless, it was disheartening.

Final Verdict
Monday, February 7, 2000

The Judicial Board's opinion was posted in the glass cabinet in the main hallway, across from the lounge, and published in The Docket, the law school newsletter. The opinion posted in the locked cabinet had the names of the parties and other confidential information blacked out, like those FBI documents shown on *60 Minutes.* The names of the prosecutors and the law review were the only identifiable proper nouns on the paper.

The Board handed down a one-semester suspension, loss of credit for law review work, removal from law review and 50 hours of community service. The finding and penalty had been affirmed by the entire faculty in January. The punishment and the subsequent affirmation were not surprising.

The opinion laid out the charges and the sections of the Code of Student Conduct that were in play. One particularly harsh paragraph lambasted the student and even described his conduct as "intolerable to the legal profession."

The Board found that "the evidence showed beyond a reasonable doubt that the student willingly and knowingly inserted material portions of another published law review article in both the text and footnotes of the note submitted for publication in the Syracuse Law Review."

The Board reviewed the evidence so closely that members found several examples of similarities that I had overlooked. The Board deliberated on the knowing requirement: whether Tom knowingly and intentionally plagiarized. Despite his statements and pleas, the Board determined that he exhibited sufficient *mens rea* (guilty mind). Intent is

---

[51] Ethan Bronner, *A Limit on Honors,* THE NEW YORK TIMES, June 9, 1999, at B11.

required for conviction of most crimes. There are, however, strict liability crimes, which do not require intent, for example speeding. Even for some intentional crimes, proving intent does not have to be black and white. For example, pointing a gun at someone and having the gun shoot a bullet that kills the victim. There might not have been intent to kill the person but there was enough knowledge and intent to constitute murder, or at least manslaughter.

Plagiarism is not as serious as murder, except for law professors, and possibly law review editors. In the grand scheme of things, it really was not that important. The only bullets that flew were the ones Tom shot into his own foot.

Only time will determine the impact this sad event will have on Tom's career. He certainly was not the first person to get caught plagiarizing, and likely will not be the last. In fact, one of Syracuse College of Law's most distinguished alums was embroiled in a highly-publicized plagiarism scandal decades after he graduated.

In 1987, Senator Joseph Biden's presidential aspirations were snuffed out after word leaked that he failed a class, and was forced to repeat it for lifting five pages of text from a published law review article and submitting it under his own name.[52] This was one of those embarrassing anecdotes haunting the university. I was aware of this scandal when I was an undergraduate at Syracuse.

---

[52] Paul Taylor, *Biden: A "Regular Guy" With Regular-Guy Flaws; Judgments Diverge on Democrat's Conduct*, THE WASHINGTON POST, Sept. 20, 1987, at A16;   James R. Dickenson, *Biden: Academic Claims "Inaccurate:" Misrepresentations at Videotaped Political Gathering Are Admitted*, THE WASHINGTON POST, Sept. 22, 1987, at A1; Paul Taylor, *Biden Admits Plagiarizing in Law School*, THE WASHINGTON POST, Sept. 18, 1987, at A1;David S. Broder & Eleanor Randolph, *Biden Calls News Conference to Answer Plagiarism Charges*, THE WASHINGTON POST, Sept. 17, 1987, at A1; Robin Toner, *Biden Assails New Report of Dishonesty*, THE NEW YORK TIMES, Sept. 21, 1987, at A16, E.J. Dionne, Jr., *Biden Admits Plagiarism in School But Says It Was not "Malevolent,"* THE NEW YORK TIMES, Sept. 18, 1987, at A1; Richard J. Meislin, *In Hindsight, Biden's Law Teacher Sees Offense as Minor*, THE NEW YORK TIMES, Sept. 18, 1987, at A23; E.J. Dionne, Jr., *Biden Was Accused of Plagiarism in Law School*, THE NEW YORK TIMES, Sept. 17, 1987, at A1; Mickey Kaus, *Biden's Belly Flop*, NEWSWEEK, Sept. 28, 1987, at 23.

It was an ugly affair. The way the information was leaked, allegedly accidentally by a former dean,[53] certainly influenced the way that the law school now approached disciplinary matters with confidentiality and secrecy. Academic institutions, especially law schools, take academic privacy seriously, sometimes to extreme and dangerous proportions.

The same administrators who yelled at me because they thought I was talking about confidential matters of student conduct, charges that I filed on behalf of the law review, were also the same people who dragged their feet during my first and second year when a classmate frequently spazzed in class at professors, threatened to kill a professor and physically attacked and threatened to kill, hit and rape several female classmates. The law school finally reacted, after months of complaints, when police got involved. Police were called after the student stood on a girl's car, threatened her in a parking lot and chased her in his car, ramming his car into hers. The law school confronted the student. The administration wanted to be fair to the student while a dozen female students were living in fear.

A federal law, known as the Buckley Amendment, protects students' privacy and ensures that academic records remain confidential.[54] The law school certainly would not want to inadvertently allow an internal matter to explode into a federal case.

The competitive rigors of law school and the life-altering impact of grades and academic honors make people do weird things, desperate things. It was inevitable that people would not follow the rules; some cheat, others plagiarize. In a field that was totally based on interpretation of words, facts, rules and situations, people inherently push the envelope to see how much they can get away with. Then, if they get caught, they argue about it.

Rather than push the envelope, others simply ignored the rules and cheated. I witnessed students exit closed-book exams several times during the exam and return. How many times does someone have to relieve him or herself in three or four hours? Law school caused me

---

[53] Jill Abramson & James Lyons, *Former Law Dean's Indiscretion? Behind the Biden Plagiarism Flap*, LEGAL TIMES, Sept. 21, 1987, at 1; David A. Kaplan, Biden Brouhaha, THE NATIONAL LAW JOURNAL, Oct. 12, 1987, at 4; Edward A. Adams, *Biden Could Face Bar Disciplinary Action*, THE NATIONAL LAW JOURNAL, Nov. 9, 1987, at 4.
[54] Family Educational Rights and Privacy Act of 1974 (Buckley Amendment), 20 U.S.C. 1232g (2000).

serious stomach problems but I never left an exam to go to the bathroom, I simply did not eat before an exam. I heard of students talking about exams during 24-hour take-home periods. I knew students were known to collaborate on papers and extra credit papers. I heard of people referring to cheat sheets during closed-book exams. There was even an incident in which a few students left exams to cajole information from the professors during the exam. A huge controversy broke out during my first year when students in another Constitutional Law class altered the font-size and margins to squeeze more into the page count. The professor "pooh-poohed" the complaints by students who followed the rules and the students who manipulated the rules got As on the exam.

A study by a Rutgers University provost found that 70 percent of the 1,800 students he surveyed at nine campuses in 1993 cheated at least once in college.[55] A study of plagiarism in the nation's law schools reported that one "Eastern law school" had 14 plagiarism cases pending in the spring of 1996.[56] It happens at bottom-tier and elite law schools.[57] I know it happens. A lot of things happen.

I made it through law school without cheating. I certainly could have used a helping hand during a couple of first-year exams, or at least someone to translate my handwriting. I could have exited the room, gone to the men's room and refreshed my failing memory on some forgotten rule. I certainly could have boosted a few grades here and there. Perhaps, crossing the line then, would have opened the doors to the "right" job later.

These are just the facts. I am not trying to boast about any self-righteous morality. It disturbed me knowing that students cheated and got away with it. I was intent on not permitting it to happen on the law review, however. There was too much to protect. If the students who were supposed to be the best students in the school failed to uphold the tenets of professional responsibility and academic honesty, how could anybody else be expected to? If the people in charge of the law review, did not uphold the rules, how could the administration and other professors respect anybody at the school? As it stood, they barely respected the students anyway.

---

[55] Alison Schneider, *Why Professors Don't Do More to Stop Students Who Cheat*, THE CHRONICLE OF HIGHER EDUCATION, January 22, 1999 at A8.
[56] *See* LeClercq, at 236.
[57] *Id.* at 239.

I was not a vigilante. Other students at the school, even on my own staff, may regard me as arrogant and officious with a stick up his butt for the rules. Some may even perceive my actions as a grand exercise in self-promotion. One professor approached me in the hallway this morning and said, "That was a very difficult thing you had to do, but you did the right thing."

I hope that I did not ruin Tom's future. Tom will probably rise to some high level of professional achievement, perhaps riches and fame, and for the rest of my life, I will be the arrogant, officious guy with a stick up his butt for the rules who got Tom kicked out of school for a semester.

Meeting
Monday, February 7, 2000

The executive board met to discuss various staff and production issues. At the request of one of editor I ordered two pizzas (one plain the other half pepperoni, half vegetable). We used the requisition form provided by the budget office. This process relieved me from paying cash and getting reimbursed. But it also required the approval of the Dean, who had the last word over dispersal of the editor's discretionary fund. I spent portions of my $500 discretionary fund on the barbecue, pizza for a staff meeting and the all the Blow Pops, Tootsie Pops and individually wrapped LifeSavers.

"It's nice to know the dean isn't micromanaging this institution," Cole said when I mentioned that the Dean had to approve all the requisition slips.

The law review's bylaws required the executive board to meet weekly. We did it as needed, close to every three weeks. We discussed the status of articles and exchanged thoughts on staff issues. The executive editors joked about trading certain team members. Actually, it was more like unloading team members.

Most everyone took their jobs very seriously, which was reassuring. The executive editors were the real workhorses of the staff and ensured the quality of the articles. Merry liked to discuss minutiae such as policy implications of italicizing the period after an *id* in footnotes. Matt liked to make jokes about everything and proposed an incentive plan for staff members based solely on providing free pornography as a reward for good editing. Most of the other editors were very serious.

Before the break, Marcia assigned the commercial law Survey article as a take home and was pleased to report that everyone on her team turned it in on time, except one guy. "He emailed me the day before it was due and said he needed the weekend. I thought he had blown it off and was going to turn in garbage. But his editing was almost perfect. I am very pleased."

We spoke about other staff issues, including the disposition of Tom's case. "The judicial opinion was posted late on Friday. The administration took out the trash. If you haven't read it yet, you should," I said. Questions from staff members would surely follow, I warned. "Just be discreet," I said.

Somebody asked whether the law review's sanctions committee, comprised of the executive board and three other members, would have to act on Tom's case. They were relieved to learn that part of his punishment included removal from law review. At this point, the case was closed.

I also informed the editors that Liz stepped down from her position of Associate Notes and Comments editor. My use of the term "stepped down" prompted a few snickers because everyone knew that she never fulfilled any of her obligations.

The banquet plans and upcoming staff election piqued interest. Everyone seemed interested in making sure we enticed good people to run and got them excited about it early. Cole said he was going to start talking to individuals on his team. Marcia said the same.

It was important to capitalize on the eagerness and excitement and competition. Hopefully, this would spur people to better performance. Self-interest, I hoped, would motivate people to do a better job.

Pre-Game Analysis

The SU basketball team took its 19-0 record to the Carrier Dome this evening to play Seton Hall. It was another Big Monday game. This was the third Monday in a row that I attended a game. In one month, I attended more basketball games than I did my entire four years as an undergrad here and two years of law school. In retrospect, I felt as though I missed out on some fun as an undergraduate at a Big East basketball powerhouse.

Mike and I took the short walk over to the Dome, talking about ethics in the legal profession and how we had been personally pushed to the brink by the unusual circumstances we encountered with our two scandals.

"This is crazy stuff. But I think it will prepare us for what we'll see in the profession," he said.

I agreed. "People push the boundaries of right and wrong and never think they are going to get caught. Stuff worse than plagiarism takes place every day."

"It will be interesting to deal with stuff like this as lawyers," he said.

"It has been stressful and traumatic dealing with this as law students. It consumes so much time, time that we could spend editing or doing other work," I said.

"And, all the other work is still there," he added.

We split up. He went into the Dome and I went to the box office to buy my ticket. The game was a heart-stopper. We were behind for most of the game, despite our number 4 standing in the national rankings and our home-court advantage. I sat in the upper deck and then moved down closer to the floor after half-time with some classmates.

The game came down to one play with 16 seconds left and the ball bounced off the rim. We lost our first game of the year by two points. I could certainly empathize with coming close but coming up short.

A Beautiful Day in the Rage Cage
Tuesday, February 8, 2000

It was a beautiful day in the neighborhood. Like a typical Syracuse winter, several inches of slush covered everything. Syracuse weather required boots. But because I spent more than 12 hours a day in the law school, I kept a pair of shoes in my office, and changed into them every morning, just like Mr. Rogers—no zipper cardigan, though.

I was switching footwear when Marcia came into the my office. A down-to-earth and subdued executive editor, Marcia, frequently came into my office to chat during office hours. She was one of the senior editors I did not know until we began working together on law review. It was quite nice to get to know her. Last semester, we were in the same real estate class, and would often talk about the mind-numbing reading assignments before class. She knew her real estate law quite well and she was serious about the law review work.

Midway through unlacing one boot, a Survey author called, expecting to leave a voicemail message. Instead, he got me on the phone, only to tell me that his article would be coming in late, several months overdue. I expressed my displeasure to him. After the conversation ended, I slammed down the phone muttered some curses to myself and watched Marcia, easing herself into the spare chair in my office.

"You have a lot of rage, Roy, don't you?" she said with a slight chuckle.

"I wouldn't call it rage, how about heightened frustration?"

"No, I see how you sometimes stew in here over how things are going," she said. "You shouldn't' let it get to you."

"I can't help it, it drives me nuts when people don't do what is expected or required or treat me like I'm some sort of idiot."

"Why?"

"I just want things to work out and go smoothly. I get bent out of shape when things don't go smoothly," I said.

"You can't expect everything to go smoothly."

"It just bothers me that some people shirk their responsibilities and I'm going to end up cleaning up the whole mess later on," I said.

"Not everybody cares about all the editing and note writing and stuff, but don't worry about it," she said. "We're here for you, and when it's all done, it will be done, we all know it. Don't rage."

Marcia then turned our conversation into a confession.

"I did something very evil," she said. Her confession: she sent her team members individual notes about getting ready for elections, which still would not take place until April. "Basically, I sent the same note to everyone but sent it individually," she added.

"There's nothing evil about telling people you think they're doing a good job and should think about staying involved in law review," I answered.

Awkward Moments
Wednesday, February 9, 2000

In our quest to make the law review office a warmer, gentler place where people felt welcome, we encouraged friendly conversations. When I was a 2L, office hours were often quiet, bordering on nerve-wracking. Many of my classmates complained that they were afraid to even get up and go to the bathroom during office hours for fear of rebuke by the senior editor on duty. Some of my classmates were intimidated by our senior board predecessors. And, some feared being insulted by some of the ruder senior members.

There were a couple of senior editors who would shoot a glare at you just for walking in the door. One editor was so cold and abrasive that the utterance of her name sent shivers down people's spines. People complained that she would snap at them when they asked a question or that she was simply mean, and said things like, "Go look it up in the Bluebook yourself."

One of these editors oversaw the hours I worked as a 2L. I worked diligently and avoided asking her questions unless I was at a complete loss. I never liked interrupting her as she checked her email or surfed the web for low air fares or shoes. One time I asked the her a question and she told me to look in the Bluebook. I had already scanned several sections of the Bluebook and showed her the page that was giving me a problem. She simply told me to follow my own interpretation.

This year, the office hours were different. For one thing, many of the senior editors, while intensely diligent, were also quite approachable. Merry, an executive, was more than just approachable, she was an open book. She was garrulous and was known to ramble and ramble and ramble. The first time I met her during the law review orientation barbecue on the first day the year before, she just started talking to me and kept talking to me. I thought she might have been flirting with me and unaware that I was attached. She just talked a lot.

Talking with her took on almost a free-association approach. She would start with a question about a citation and end up telling you how some guy she knew in college swallowed live goldfish at a sorority party. She would tell you that she gained weight over the holidays or that she clogged up her toilet and had to borrow a plunger from her insomniac neighbor.

At times, she was loud and distracting. But I was convinced that she did not have an ounce of maliciousness in her body. She added a lot to the office environment and made it a warmer place. However, there were times when her James Joyceian ramblings derailed my train of thought in my secluded office.

On several occasions, I subtly encouraged her to tone it down and keep it professional in the office after witnessing childish arguments between her and her sometimes ex-boyfriend, an unproductive, 2L on staff. At one point I emerged from my office and said, "You two are like little children. Knock it off."

One day in early February, it just reached the point of no return. One afternoon she was just talking and talking and talking about everything but law review work. She talked about fighting with her ex-boyfriend. She talked about prom dresses for the upcoming Barrister's Ball. It became so distracting that nobody could get any work done. Even I had trouble concentrating, and I used to conduct interviews and write news articles with the cacophony of a newsroom behind me.

Two other editors approached me to ask me to talk to her. Then, a 2L who at this point had missed enough office hours last semester that he owed the law review about 16 hours of work, approached me to lodge his own complaint. "She was so fucking loud that it took me 10 minutes to read one sentence," he said. This is the same guy who smoked so much that his clothes stunk up the entire office during his hours. He also took liberal cigarette breaks. I assured him that I would talk with her.

The next day at about 5 p.m. as Merry was leaving I asked her whether we could talk during her next office hours. I sounded ominous, she said. So, she called me at home that night at 9:30, just as *Sports Night* was about to start.

"I was afraid that I made a big mistake or got in trouble," she prefaced.

I took a deep breath and began my pitch. "I am not quite sure how to say this, but I know you like to talk a lot in the office and you are so friendly that it really makes the office a hospitable place, but I think some of your conversations about non-law review issues are distracting people. Please do not take this the wrong way because I really like the way you lighten up the office. But we really need to tone it down a little because people are having trouble concentrating."

To my surprise and delight, she did not take offense and apologized. She said that she did not realize that she was distracting people. "This makes me feel somewhat awkward," I said. But I was less concerned with hurting her feelings than I was about irritating her and damaging her morale.

After that was out of the way, she talked for the next 29 minutes, until *Sports Night's* credits started rolling. As a precaution, I taped the show anyway.

This situation reminded me of the difficult predicament my old boss at The Plain Dealer's Lake County Bureau occasionally confronted.

With a small office of 15 reporters in close quarters, my old boss, along with his editorial responsibilities, had to deal with such staff issues as a reporter with an unhealthy, rancid body odor problem and another who frequently clogged the office's toilet.

Sometimes there is no comfortable way to deal with certain staff issues. Asking someone to be less sociable was a lot easier than some of the other staff issues we had. We had a guy who smelled, but I was relieved that the law review office did not have toilets.

Expunging Fines
Thursday, February 10, 2000

A 2L incurred a $5 fine for a book she had taken out in October for work on an article. The book was *Of Civil Government*, a two treatise set by John Locke. The law review's semester-long privileges did not extend to Bird Library, the main campus library. I promised to get this fixed. I felt uncomfortable having a staff member incur a fine for an overdue book that sat on the shelf of the office.

The law school librarian, Maggie, gave me the name of a librarian at Bird, and assured me to drop her name if problems arose. I called Lenore, the Bird Library contact, three times before getting her on the phone. I explained the situation, and with remarkable ease, she erased the fine on the 2L's account.

Lenore asked whether there were any other fines I needed fixed. I thanked her and said that we did a pretty good job of keeping track of our books from the library.

I was very pleased I could deliver such results without a headache. But the very next day, Marcus, an executive editor, presented an overdue notice for a book that was supposed to have been taken back to the library.

I called Lenore again and conveyed the information. She said she would get to the bottom of the missing book and call me back.

About 10 minutes later, she called me back to tell me that the book had been checked in and placed on the shelf but not recorded in the computer system. When she called me back, she asked for "Professor Gutterman." I laughed and told her that I was only a student, not a professor. Thanking her profusely for solving a second problem, I joked that I knew the minute I got off the phone with her last time that we would have another problem.

"Problem solved," she said.

Hard Questions
Friday, February 11, 2000

Attendance was thin for another library candidate this morning. Actually, only three students counting myself, showed up. This candidate, an assistant library director at a top-tier southern law school, seemed somewhat aloof and detached, if not downright creepy. He barely contained his arrogance during the hour-long discussion.

He really touched a nerve with me, so I laid the cards right on the table with a zinger question: "I would like to hear your thoughts and perceptions on leaving your top tier law school, and coming here to Syracuse, a, let's be frank, second tier law school."

This unexpected and direct question caught him off-guard. One of the other students, a 2L gasped and said "great question." The candidate paused for about 20 seconds, smirked and said, "I see Syracuse as a stepping stone to a library directorship at a top tier law school."

A blunt answer for a blunt question. My report following the interview questioned whether it would be wise to hire someone who would leave as soon as a more attractive job elsewhere opened up.

As I left the conference room in the Dean's office, Elaine loaded me up with two extra doughnuts.

Equipment Violation
Friday, February, 11, 2000

The budget office called as the staff there engaged in an accounting of office equipment. The only law review equipment that qualified was an old electric typewriter and an old fax machine.

Joan, a part-time secretary, came over to check the serial numbers with the school's budget records. The typewriter was ok. The business editor used the typewriter for business forms, particularly the official Statement of Ownership, Management and Circulation form on file with the U.S. Postal Service. The law review also had to publish this as the last page in the first book listing all sorts of relevant information: the editor-in-chief; managing editor; business manager; the printer; the publication schedule; domestic and international circulation. This was required under postal rules. It looked more professional to type it.

Joan also wanted to check the fax machine, which I kept in a file cabinet with a pile of other junk. When she asked to see the fax, I opened up the cabinet. It was an old fax machine, at least 15 years old—the kind that used the rolls of shiny paper. "It is really useless," I told her. "Anyway, the office does not have an available telephone jack to hook it up to."

The next day, Edna, budget director, called to repossess the old machine.

While I stood in the budget office, returning the machine and handling an overnight UPS mailing, Edna yelled out from her office, "Roy, why am I the last one around here to hear the dirt."

"Which dirt are you talking about?" I asked. She lifted up the green Docket, the in-school newsletter, with the suspension announcement.

"No wonder you look so sad all the time. What a crazy year it has been for you. That is so awful," she said.

I asked her whether she heard who the student was and then promptly informed her that she knew the student. She had been around the block a couple times with Tom over his complicated management of our souvenir orders over the summer. She said that she first heard about the case when the Dean and an Associate Dean edited down the original judicial board opinion to fit into the Docket. They edited out the strongly-worded paragraphs which called the actions "intolerable to the profession" and offensive to the ethics.

"This sure isn't the first time something like this happened around here," Edna said, recounting the case from the 1980s of alumnus who accepted an $80,000 a year job at one of the fancy law firms in Syracuse before he got caught cheating on the bar exam.

Edna said that cheating goes on all the time. And, I responded, "You don't know the beginning of it."

The Photo Shoot
Wednesday, February 16, 2000

The Advance Sheet was a colorful brochure mailed to the law school alumni highlighting student programs and events at the school. After months of discussions with one of the associate deans, the administration took up the cause of the Law Review's 50th Anniversary. The administration was ready to promote 50th Anniversary Committee's slate of alumni authors for the book and the plans for the banquet.

An associate dean wrote a piece based on some information I provided. He emailed a draft for my review. It looked fine, including my less-than-dramatic quote: "We want to commemorate this milestone the best we can."

The law school's development director also wanted to photograph law review members in action. Law review was not necessarily synonymous with action. Mike and I coordinated a time when we would both be in the office. He also tried to stack the office with senior editors. Only a couple were there. Nick had an exam to study for and was spending his afternoon in the office. Others had class. Others did not care. The official university photographer came to the office and had us pose in artificial settings: sitting at a table reading an article; sitting at a computer; reaching for a book on a shelf. It felt extremely silly. I was not accustomed to posing for photos.

With four men in the office, we obviously needed women. Sara was working in the lounge outside the office on the fourth floor but expressed moderate disinterest in participating in the photo shoot. I made an off-handed crack to Mike about drafting her for the photo shoot. Then, instantly, the development director went out in the hallway called for her and dragged her by the arm into the room. Sara and I posed at a computer screen, pretending to edit an article. The previous edition of the Advance Sheet featured two prominent photos of Sara in an article-photo spread on an international law program for which she was a research assistant. She was on her way, albeit reluctantly, to becoming the Advance Sheet's covergirl.

Voice of Reason
Thursday, February 17, 2000

On the way out of the building this evening, Sara and I stopped by the second floor lounge. We saw the opening scene of *Friends* on the lounge tv. A first year student, an older woman, was starting her dinner and said, "You are the editor of the law review, right? I wanted to thank you for your speech and advice at the exam workshop. It helped a lot of people, especially me. I liked what you said at the end."

Every December, a week or two before first year students took their final exams, the law review held an exam writing workshop. Students with the best grades, presumably, had the best advice about taking an exam.

A handful of law review members gave exam writing and preparation tips to eager, nervous 1Ls—the nuances professors demand for exams but never articulate. A handful of panelists described the traditional exam answer formula: I.R.A.C. whereby the student identifies every Issue, states the Rule, Analyzes the issue back and forth, then Concludes. One student talked about outline preparation, another recommended putting tabs in the casebook for the open book exams and another recommended bringing a snack into the four-hour exam.

Students also asked questions about specific professors. It was a helpful service at a desperate moment for 1Ls. For weeks, at staff meetings, office hours and through emails, I sought volunteers. About 15 staff members turned out for a group of about 40 or 50 1Ls.

As the event's moderator, I had the last word. The best advice I could offer was an ounce of common sense: "Get a good night's sleep, don't stay up all night cramming because if you don't know it by then, you won't get it. You're better off being fresh so your mind operates faster. And, concentrate on your handwriting because these professors have 80 exams to read and you don't want to give them any excuses."

As the event was about to close, I added a note to assuage these nervous souls, "Just stay calm. A lot rides on these exams, but remember, no matter what you do or what you get, you are still the same person that you were before your exams."

Entire legal careers are made or lost based on that first set of exams. Someone had to lend a little perspective amid the chaos.

I was pleased that at least one person appreciated the discussion. I thanked her and said, "I just hope it helped. People get all stressed out at exam time, so it's a service the law review does every year."

Ambassadorship
Friday, February 18, 2000

Nobody else showed up to interview the third library candidate. The Dean's secretary scrambled to get students to meet with the candidates. She asked me to find some more students. I obliged, and dragged over a 2L from the law review and another from another journal. Sometimes even free doughnuts and juice was not enough to entice students.

The Dean's office openly informed the candidates, almost boastfully, that the editor-in-chief of the law review would be interviewing them. As I walked into the Dean's conference room, an associate dean finished up his meeting with the candidate and said, in my presence, "There is nobody better to meet with than the editor-in-chief of our law review."

Casting aside the figurehead elements of my position, even before I made law review I spent a lot of time in the library. I frequently just walked through the shelves looking at the collection. I knew what we had or did not have in the library and where to find it.

The Nutcracker
Friday, February 18, 2000

The telephone lottery continued on this quiet Friday afternoon when a confused-sounding woman named Judith called. She read part of an article in the 1989 law review about an article 78 proceeding. She wanted to talk to the author to get help during her legal fight.

I told her that the author of the article was a student who graduated in 1989. She was surprised that it was written by a student, but still wanted to talk to him.

She sounded like a nut. An article 78 proceeding is a special action against a municipality in New York state under the New York Civil Practice Laws and Rules. Most people suing the government seem to be a little nuts. I remember all the nuts I covered at the newspaper who sued the government: a self-declared Freeman who refused to acknowledge the judicial system, except to sue the government; a band of local militia men fighting the government and a bike repairman who dressed up like Santa Claus to attend a city council meetings to protest a road-widening project. Absolute nuts. Judith sounded no different. But I did not want to have anything to do with her or her legal action. Despite my curiosity, I resisted asking her any questions about her dispute.

The author now worked for the Justice Department in Washington, DC. I did not tell her that, but said that I would contact him and then see if he felt comfortable talking to her. I needed until Monday, I told her. She seemed put off.

The author did not call me back by the end of the day on Monday, so I called Judith back. I told her that the author did not return my call and doubted that he would be able to help her anyway. I told her that he worked for the government and probably would not be able to talk to her. She seemed angrier now. "I don't see why he can't talk with me and help me," she said.

"Maybe you should engage a lawyer," I told her.

"I was married once, I'm not getting engaged to a lawyer," she said.

"No. I mean, maybe you should hire a lawyer. I think you would be better served by hiring a lawyer," I clarified.

Then, she hung up the phone. Not even a goodbye.

Later in the afternoon, Professor Saccomano called inquiring about the status of his latest submissions. At the beginning of the year, Professor Saccomano held the distinct honor of being the sole standout on the Syracuse Law Review's Blacklist. The list seemed to be growing, however. During transition, I posed the question about a Blacklist to Connor, who warned: never accept an article from Professor Saccomano. A professor at a non-accredited western law school, Professor Saccomano was a prolific writer, submitting two articles every semester, then following up with a half-dozen calls on each one. According to Connor, his articles were weak and years earlier he screwed over the law review after the editors accepted an article for publication. "Plus, he's just a pain in the ass," Connor said.

Walt and Vince, the articles editors, usually handled his calls. I spoke to him a couple times, too.

"This is Professor Saccomano, I submitted two articles and would like expedited review on them. I have an offer from another journal on one of them," he said. "Can I speak with Walt or Vince about expedited review?"

"The articles editors are not in the office this afternoon. But if you have an offer, I would suggest you accept it," I said. "I'll give the articles editors your message."

Professor Saccomano was persistent and at least deserved credit for remembering the names of the articles editors. I neglected telling him that his articles had already tossed in the recycling bin. He would probably call back in a week or two.

Subscription Drive
Monday, February 21, 2000

One of my side projects this year was to increase our subscription base. We had a 2L on staff, Trent, who was fluent with database and mail merge programs. Furthermore, Trent was a co-owner of a business that marketed lists of law firms to students looking for jobs. He had access to a database listing practically every law firm in the country and he was more than eager to negotiate for this work. Trent had missed numerous office hours and owed the law review about 10 hours, without any penalties.

"I'll do it, but I want to get out of the rest of my hours for the year," he said.

"That's not going to happen," I said.

"Ok, this is going to be like $1,000 worth of work," he said.

"Then, we can apply the work you perform to the 10 office hours that you owe. You own the database, you're not going to lose any money by doing this," I said.

"That's fair," he said.

Trent created a mailing list of nearly 500 New York City law firms that we would send a subscription letter. I made a similar list of about 40 law firms in northern New Jersey. We compared the list with our current subscription list and ran a mail merge.

Trent performed a search and mail merge for the Syracuse Law Review, in exchange for wiping out the hours he owed. By the time we were done with the mail merge and the envelope stuffing, Trent worked off all his hours and then some.

My letter addressed to "Legal Community Member" was a clear business pitch. I laid out the types of articles we publish and the value of our 20-article annual Survey of New York law. Our price was only $27 for all four books or $15 for only the Survey: "The Survey graces the shelves of judges' chambers and law libraries in the public and private sectors. It should be on your shelves too ... This is a small investment to stay on top of the law in New York and to serve our clients with an appropriate level of knowledge."

I anticipated that we might generate about 30 or 40 new subscribers. In the end, I think we only got about 12 new subscribers. The envelopes were addressed to the librarian at the law firm. Part of the problem was that the letters probably never made it into the hands of the people making the library purchasing decisions. I will never know.

Deadline? What's a Deadline
Monday, February 21, 2000

Survey articles, according to the contracts the authors signed, were due in late-August. Here we were at the end of February, about a week before the date initially envisioned for the Survey's publication. According to our statement of ownership form, our second book should be published in March. This was definitely an unattainable goal. At this point, we were shooting for getting the book out before graduation. Book 1 still had not even been sent the to the printer.

The two most egregious deadline deadbeats were our legal ethics author, an attorney at a big Syracuse firm and our evidence author, a professor, who wrote from his ivy-covered office at one of New York's more prestigious law schools.

The legal ethics author, Clay, derided the initial August deadline from the outset. He made snide comments to the articles editors as well as another editor clerking at his firm. Then, he continually postponed the deadline. We gave him a deadline later than most of the other authors. He systematically abused the December deadline. He called the office one Saturday in December, not expecting to reach anyone. I spoke with him. When he told me that he would not meet the deadline, I kind of grunted and he seemed offended. "It becomes impossible for us to get the books out on time if authors ignore the deadlines," I said.

I reminded him that he was critical of the fact that last year's book came out late. "The only reason these books come out late is because our authors fail to adhere to the deadlines," I said, just as I told another delinquent author. "So, don't complain when the book comes out late." He was unsympathetic. I had a similar conversation with him in late January when he called to ask for another extension. He told me that he was undergoing some major personal "change in my life" that would become apparent in the near future. "You can go find another author if you want," he told me, with full knowledge that the law review would be unable find someone to write an article in a week.

What lay ahead in Clay's life? Divorce? He had just gotten married. Terminal cancer? He was too glib to be seriously ill. Two weeks later he announced that he was quitting his job at the Syracuse law firm to teach law.

Walt and Vince, the articles editors, and I discussed firing him after we got his article. As a new member of academia where publishing counted and professional pressures were relaxed, if not removed, we could get rid of him and it would sting. I salivated at the opportunity. But since it was the end of February I was not sure whether we would cut him. Right now, we needed his article.

Our evidence author was also a friendly chap to Walt and Vince on the phone as he systematically pushed his deadline. He said that he would not be able to write his article until he read our criminal procedure article to make sure he did not cover anything that the criminal procedure author covered. We got the crim pro in early February and overnighted a copy to him. That was one more excuse eliminated.

Last month, the real estate author blamed his delay on eye surgery. But a few days ago reported that he was almost done. The civil practice author said that he was really busy but was nearly done and would have his associate check the citations. When that article came in, the first person who worked on it found a dozen mistakes on the first two pages. He remarked, "This is exciting. I prefer an article that I can find things in."

I spoke with the employment author, who said that he knew he owed us the article and that he would have it to us on Presidents' Day, via messenger. It never arrived.

Half our job entailed countering the excuses. I was expecting at least one author to say "My dog ate my article."

Prince and the Devolution
Wednesday, February 23, 2000

I went around the block with the Prince for weeks about the new hour he owed the law review for his library frolic and diversion. I also spent considerable time retrieving my backpack and bag. Both were my personal property. The backpack, which I was not actively using now because I rarely brought books home at night, usually rested comfortably on the floor in my office. Whatever work I did for class, I did in my office. By the time I got home at 9 or 10 at night, I was not hitting the books. I usually hit the sofa and fell asleep by 11.

My Plain Dealer bag was one of the few PD items I owned. This cheap, blue nylon bag was a trophy from a year of perfect attendance. In fact, I had perfect attendance for three full years and three-quarters of my first year (from June to December). As a result, I own three Cross pens bearing the PD logo and my initials and a couple nylon bags that I occasionally used. I was not eager to part with either my bag or my backpack, especially to the Prince.

The Prince willfully held on to my bags for a couple of weeks. Every time I asked him about it, he played dumb. He knew he was irritating me by not returning them. They were probably in the back seat of his sport utility vehicle.

The conversation was the same every time: "I would appreciate you returning my bag."

"Yeah, I have it," he said.

"Well, please return it to me. I gave you the bag to make your trip to the library easier," I said.

"Yeah. I'll try to remember."

"I am not joking. Try to remember, okay. I need them and one of them has sentimental value."

"Yeah, right."

Finally, after going around the block with him on my bag, I enlisted Merry, his friend, who I told that I would file sanctions charges against him if I did not get my property back.

The next day, the Prince came into the office and threw my empty bags at me. "Here are your damn bags," he said. I thanked him and he walked out. The bags smelled like smoke. The smaller blue nylon bag had the acrid smell of stale marijuana. He probably used it as a bong filter. A couple of other people, at my request, smelled the bag and agreed that it smelled peculiar. I was happy he gave me back my bags. I just better not walk past any drug-sniffing dogs for a while.

Despite my success in retrieving my personal property, we were unsuccessful in getting him to make up his hour. Exasperated, Mike and I decided to charge him with sanctions. The law review was charging four 2L staff members for failing to turn in drafts of their notes. The sanctions committee had been convened for an imminent meeting anyway. The goal was not to cause a ruckus but to send the Prince a message and have him complete what he owed, like everyone else.

The charge itself was not lengthy, most of the language was boilerplate. It cited the bylaws and the charge: failure to complete office hours to the satisfaction of the managing editor. It recounted the facts and stated:

This complaint arises out of your unsatisfactory performance of your office hours for Monday, January 31, 2000. On that day, Roy Gutterman instructed you and another member of the law review to return a number of books to Bird Library during your two office hours. The other member returned from this trip within one hour. You, however, did not return to the office after returning the books to the library. The excessive amount of time you spent performing this task was an unsatisfactory performance of your office hours for that day.

An objective analysis of the Prince's actions that day supported the charge. I knew that he knew he was up to no good. I was stunned when he barged into the our office to dispute the charge. It was about 3:50, Mike and I were at our desks working when the Prince entered, guns-drawn, clutching a partially-crumbled paper, the actual letter charging him.

"What the fuck is this," he said, thrusting the paper toward Mike, but looking at me.

"It's a formal complaint," Mike said.

"You guys are dipshits. You sit up here all day and jerk each other off," the Prince he yelled at us.

I stood up and said, "What do you think the box of tissues is for?"

"This is bullshit, man. I don't owe you anything. I didn't think it was worth it coming back to the office for 20 minutes," he yelled.

"The guy who went with you returned to the office within an hour. You took advantage of the situation and you took advantage of me. I gave you something to do that would get you out of the office because I know you don't like being in the office. I tried to give you a break and you took advantage of me," I said calmly.

"Fuck you. I did not take advantage of you."

"Yes you did. You knew exactly what you were doing," I said.

At that point, Nick, who had watched the entire event transpire from the main office, came in, grabbed the Prince by the elbow and shoulder and escorted him out of the office, telling him: "This is not the time or the place for this. Come to the sanctions committee meeting and we will hear your side of it. But this is not the time or the place."

"Stay out of this. This does not concern you," the Prince said to Nick.

Mike told the Prince that it did concern Nick because he is on the Sanctions Committee.

As he was led out of the office, the Prince's parting words were, "You guys are tools."

Serenity Now, Insanity Later
Wednesday, February 23, 2000

Minutes after the Prince's outburst, Mike and I typed up a report documenting the incident in our office. Just as the report came out of the printer, my friend, Cody walked into the office to say hello. Because he had been a friend and a confidante, as well as a member of the sanctions committee, I showed him the report.

He immediately laughed and asked for a copy. I said that he did not need a copy. "Come on, I want to show Jen. She knows this guy," he said. With Mike standing beside me, trying to ignore the conversation, I said, no. Cody asked again and I said that it was not appropriate to show his girlfriend.

He stormed out of the office only to call back five minutes later to scream at me. "I am stepping down from the sanctions committee and as associate notes and comments editor," he said.

"I am so tired of your dramatics," I said.

"Hey man, if I'm not good enough to have a copy of a report then I don't want to be part of the committee," he said.

"This is a report for the law review, not for your girlfriend," I said.

Like any argument with Cody, he vehemently protested, claiming that he never said he wanted to show it to his girlfriend.

"That was the first thing you said to me."

"No way. Yo man, you are on a fucking kangaroo power trip," he spit into the phone. "You are on a major ego trip. You act like you have some kind of top secret CIA report."

"It is not top secret, but it is not anything your girlfriend needs to read," I responded.

"I don't see how it's any different from Sara reading it," he said.

First, I told him that Sara had not read it. Second, Sara was on law review as well as the sanctions committee.

He continued ranting about my ego-power trip.

"I know you might find this hard to believe, but, the sun and the world do not revolve around Cody," I said. By not giving Cody a copy of the internal report for his girlfriend, I had somehow personally attacked him.

I told him that I was tired of dealing with his egocentric lunacy, and ended the conversation by saying, "Go to hell." I hung up the phone.

This latest spat with my good friend followed one from the week before in which Cody took personal offense with the possible seating arrangement for the law review banquet in April, a good two months away. He told me that I snubbed him by not having him sit at the front table with me and whatever "VIPs" planned to attend. The banquet had not even been planned and he was already making waves. He told me that he was not going to attend, "on principle." Later, he confessed that he had to attend a big birthday party for his father.

"There have been no assignment of seats, yet. You're coming," I told him, adding that it was far too early to make an issue out of arrangements for a banquet that had not even been planned.

Cody was an expert debater, the kind of superstar devil's advocate that lay-people typically envision as lawyers. A conversation with Cody could turn into a Lincoln-Douglas debate in a matter of seconds. He could argue about sports, politics, the weather. He had a well-informed opinion on most topics and deftly manipulated facts of every situation to suit the needs of any particular argument. In class, he was not one of those students who spoke to hear his own voice. He did not participate in class discussions unless called upon, and it was a pleasure to hear him. He had soundly won the law school's appellate advocacy competition and came within a point of winning the school's trial practice competition.

Sometimes the debating wore me out.

Cody had branded me "The People's Editor" but then derided me for adhering to the procedures of the bylaws. Another journal was embroiled in a staff dispute that threatened to end up in court because an editor was removed without due process. The Moot Court rarely followed procedure, which Cody, repeatedly scoffed.

Despite his rage and attempted insults, he was still my good friend and I valued his opinions. There is nobody else I would rather have on my side in litigation or a street fight. If I was on death row, Cody is the guy I would want defending my case.

Cody was the only person I ever met who defended bestiality as a natural property right. This defense came after I reviewed a submission from a property professor who wrote an article condemning same-sex marriages. The article had a lengthy section on property rights and the taboo of bestiality. Cody found a property right in the act and refused to hear any other arguments.

"If you own a dog, it's your property, and can do whatever you want with it," he said.

"I think it's abusive toward the animal," I said.

"How? I don't think that's abuse. It's property. You can do anything you want to things you own," he said, adding, with a straight face, "It could also be a sign of affection."

There was no arguing with him, so I ended the conversation by saying, "It's got to violate some health code ... By the way, I will never let you within 10 feet of my dog."

By the time the commotion settled down in the office, it was time for the monthly general staff meeting. As we progressed with the publishing, my updates became more detailed: the book 1 articles had been sent back to the authors for their review; 12 of the 20 Survey articles were in and at various stages of editing; the articles editors signed one author for book 3 and had offers out on two others; book 4, the 50th Anniversary book had a March deadline.

I added my requisite "work fast but accurately" message before turning the floor over to Mike, who announced April 7 as the election day. Nick spoke about the next note deadline. The 20-page draft was coming up and would be the last deadline before final papers were due after Spring Break.

Other messages included talk about the banquet and law review souvenirs. My pep talk on notes was: "Try not to get discouraged or overwhelmed. Writing a note is an excellent opportunity, don't let it slip through your hands."

I concluded the meeting, with another oddball message, offering the staff some of the extra cardboard stationery boxes thanks to Westlaw. The free paper Westlaw supplied came in great little boxes that I began stockpiling. "We have a whole bunch in one of the cabinets in the office. They're great for storing papers. I have all sorts of documents for my note in some of these. Just holler if you want any," I said. Of course, I was only half-serious.

Dropping the Ball
Saturday, February 26, 2000

This evening, we attended the annual law school prom, a.k.a. the Barrister's Ball. The Multi-state Professional Responsibility and Ethics test review was this morning. Sara and I were resigned to the fact that we would not be sitting with our good friend Cody for this event as we previously planned. We sat with Cody and his girlfriend last year and had a great time. But last week's discord over the memo created a rift. Cody informed Sara that we no longer on speaking terms and no longer friends. Sara and I prepared to sit with other people.

After the review session, Cody followed me to the elevator. "Do you want my resignation from the sanctions committee in writing, fax or email?" he asked, barely containing his wide grin and laughter.

"How about smoke signals?" I answered. "You can tender it anyway you want, but I will not accept your resignation. You're too important to the law review."

He followed me into the elevator and up to the office, and expressed his dissatisfaction with the way I treated him.

"You have been privy to more information about law review than anybody else outside the senior staff," I said. "Asking for an internal document solely to show your girlfriend was inappropriate and you know it. You are always deriding other student organizations for airing their dirty laundry in public and not following procedure. I cannot allow our internal information to go out there like that."

He knew what I was talking about because he frequently criticized moot court for flouting procedure. I told him that law review took enough criticism from disgruntled students, "I am not about to add fuel to the fire."

Cody got prosecutorial on me: "First, if I wanted to take a copy of that document, would you or would you not give it to me? Second, if this was a confidential document, do you or do you not trust me to keep it confidential? You made a presumption that I would take this document and show it to other people."

"If this was a privileged document, something for a client and you were in practice, you would be in breach of your fiduciary duty if you showed it to anyone," I countered.

Again, he accused me of making a presumption and that he should have been entrusted with the document. "I did not make a presumption. You openly told me that you wanted a copy of the document so you could show Jen because she knows the guy," I said. "You told me that's why you wanted it and that is why I did not give you a copy. You read it and you digested the information. I knew you would tell her anyway, right?"

"Yes, but I wanted to show her the writing for comedic effect," he said.

"That is not appropriate and you know it. Anyway, wasn't it funny enough verbally?"

I finally had him on the ropes, and he knew it. My *coup de grace* followed: "For the past six months you have been telling me that I should not even talk to the 2L staff, that I am the editor and that I should not even associate with them because I have this higher authority. Then, you accuse me of being on a 'kangaroo power trip.' I'm damned if I do, damned if I don't. What do you want from me? By the way, you misused kangaroo. It is really a kangaroo court, which is a sham court absent rules or procedure. Here I am adhering to procedure. But I knew what you were getting at."

Cody immediately consulted the dictionary. I told him that kangaroo was right next to "ji" in the dictionary. [A month earlier Cody came over to my apartment to watch an SU basketball game with me and Sara. After the game, he noticed a my Scrabble game on my bookshelf and challenged me to a game. I did not want to play. But he persisted and persisted. He told me that nobody ever beats him. I resisted, telling him it would probably get competitive and possibly ugly.

Nevertheless, we played a marathon scrabble match that ended in controversy when he put the letters J and I together on a double word score, absolutely convinced that ji is a word, a type of plant, he said. We referred to two separate dictionaries, a modern Webster's and a classic Webster's from the 1950s. I let the ji slide because he argued so vehemently that I actually believed him, and did not want to risk losing a turn on a mistaken challenge. Cody earned another 18 points, which still was not enough to overcome my 60 point lead.]

After some more talk, he told me that he saved two seats for us at his table at the ball. I thanked him but told him that we had just made plans to sit with some other people.

He asked when I made those plans. "Yesterday," I told him.

"Damn, if I knew you were going to sit with other people, I would have kept the Cold War going a little longer."

The seating arrangements would come back to haunt us, I just had a feeling. When we got to the ball, the couple we arranged to sit with had already gotten a table. There were two other couples at the table who I really did not like and we opted to sit with a quasi friend of Sara's. We put our stuff down at the table and went to mingle. The bar was packed. The five-hour open bar attracted a thirsty crowd.

With law review elections around the corner, many of the 2L law review staff were pretty friendly. Lots of people stopped to shake hands and talk. It was weird how people you see every day in school suddenly start shaking hands because you put on a tuxedo.

I navigated through the bar crowd and got Sara a Cosmopolitan Martini and me a cranberry and vodka. We stood in the crowd and talked with people. Tom, currently out of school on his suspension, walked up to us with his girlfriend. We shook hands. I asked him how he was doing and holding up. He seemed as upbeat as usual. His girlfriend did not acknowledge me. Such a meeting was surely not surprising. It was nice that he was not harboring any outright hostility. But I certainly understood if he did.

By the time dinner was ready, we moved back to the table, which had filled up. Another couple, friendly with Tom, lured him and his girlfriend, to our table. There they were sitting right next to my seat. Both our mouths dropped. Luckily, there was one seat separating us.

As I went to sit down and said to Tom, "Look, I understand this will be awkward, so Sara and I can go someplace else if you want, no hard feelings."

He was amiable and said that it would be ok. As we sat there, struggling to eke out a polite conversation, he said, "What are the odds of this?"

Luckily, a 2L, Sandra, who I had never met before needed a place to sit and took the seat between us. Sandra was interesting because she was even older than me, probably in her mid 40s and was an antique dealer. We talked antiques.

Aside from the awkward seating arrangement, the night was pretty nice: decent food; a couple of drinks; and a crowded dance floor, even though the DJ refused my request for the theme from *Dirty Dancing*, a song that had become an inside joke between Sara and me.

It was comforting to learn that Cody's seating arrangement was as disturbing to him as mine was to me. The empty space at his table was filled by a classmate that could only be described as his nemesis. He spent the night seated next to a guy he hated, almost with a passion, and I sat next to a guy who most likely hated me. We both appreciated the irony.

What Goes Up, Must Come Down
Monday, February 28, 2000

The other chap that I got suspended from school this year reappeared in Syracuse at the beginning of the semester. Keith was suspended but seemed to be hanging around with his friends at the law school. I saw him at the ball. At least he did not sit at my table, too. I felt lucky that I had not run into him personally until this afternoon.

I had to take one of my many trips up to the alumni office on the fourth floor of the old building. Then, I had to take the elevator down to support services to pick up some more paper—our office was going through paper like it grew on trees.

As I turned the corner to the elevator, there he was standing there waiting. I nearly ran right into him. I gave him a polite hi, the kind that you give to someone you do not really know but feel compelled to because of the close quarters. He shot me a look of utter disgust. I could have easily turned around and walked, but I was not going to give an inch. I had no reason to feel intimidated, ashamed or uncomfortable.

We both stepped into the elevator. It was just the two of us looking at the numbers light up. Out of the corner of his eye, he looked over and grimaced. "You're Roy Gutterman aren't you?"

"Yes. You're Keith right?"

We shook hands. I asked him how things were going and how his mother was. He said things were fine and his mother was better. I said that was nice and then we got to the first floor. It was a long ride for the three floors. I was eager to get moving.

The Adam Bomb
Monday, February 28, 2000

It was not enough for the Prince to ignore his duties on law review, and verbally abuse Mike and me in our office in front of people. He spent part of his office hours drafting a vitriolic letter to the Sanctions Committee. He abstained from attending the meeting to defend himself in person, but asked that his page-long rant about me and Mike be read in his absence.

His letter denied any wrongdoing and disputed the accuracy of the charge. He even said that Scott, the guy who accompanied him to the library, did not return within the hour. Scott returned because I saw him walk in and then glanced at the clock. We also interviewed Scott about the incident. The bulk of the letter was a diatribe against me and Mike who "chose instead to bring charges—likely as a way to force their petty authority upon a hard-working and diligent member of law review." He further added that our charge was "a display lacking any sort of professionalism on the part of the editor and his staff ... the fact that my time as well as the time of the Sanctions Committee has been wasted and misused in such a flagrant manner speaks to the lack of professionalism exhibited by Roy Gutterman and Mike."

In his conclusion, he added that the attack on him was a result of "the petty insecurities of the current Editor in Chief and Managing Editor."

The Sanctions Committee is composed of all senior board members and three members of the overall law review staff: an associate editor, a third-year un-elected member and a second-year member. The Committee discussed the matter. Everyone on the committee was aware of the Prince's previous chicanery: the rubber band ball incident; his frequent and lengthy smoking breaks; his rudeness; lagging work ethic and his two outbursts.

"I do not like the way he is disrespecting the law review, the editors and his responsibilities. I don't think we should put up with it," one editor said. Another editor said, "He is really immature. We should just kick him off."

That was when Merry came to his defense to tell us that he thought we, meaning me and Mike, were picking on him and that we were out to get him. I responded, not even commenting on his letter or abusive outbursts, "Nobody's picking on him. I think that we've been quite accommodating. We had grounds to charge him months ago, you know it and he knows it."

I added, "We may or may not have grounds to kick him off today because of the nature of the charge. All I want to do is have the hour made up and the message sent. There will not be another incident with him."

This joker had already gotten kicked off moot court for nonfeasance and was close to getting booted off law review and all he could do is pick fights and verbally abuse us. Some of his overreactions and outbursts hinted at erratic behavior. I had heard some other stories about other bizarre behavior at bar nights and off-campus parties, but mostly ignored it.

The Prince was wearing out his welcome on law review and my patience were wearing thin. I repeated this to Merry privately, with the intent that she would forward the information to the Prince, adding, "If I were out to 'get' him, I would have brought the charges four months ago. He's pissing off a lot of people and we have the votes to kick him off. I don't care who his father is or what law firm he works for because if we kick him off, I will make sure that he cannot put membership on the

Syracuse Law Review on his resume. I will report him to bar examiners if I learn that he did. Then, he will never be certified. If he even looks at me cross-eyed, I will move to have him kicked off. I have the votes and the cause. I've been a nice guy up until now. So, has Mike. But there is an imbalance of power here and if he wants to test it, he's going to lose. I have had enough."

Other Sanctions
Monday, February 28, 2000

As a completely voluntary organization, the law review had very little authority over its members. It was implied that the honor of being a member should have been more than sufficient incentive to get people to perform. When I was a 2L, I was so happy to be on law review that in the first months, I came in on a weekend to do some work. The bulk of the 2L staff was not too eager to do the work. For most, law review was just a line on the resume and a lot of nit-picking, uninteresting, drudge work.

There was practically nothing I could do when a senior editor failed to perform his or her duties. Midway through last semester it became clear that there were two senior editors who would not complete their jobs. We could manage the load of one of the editors, charged with picking the articles. The other editor, who had proofreading responsibilities, would be sorely missed, and there was nothing I or anybody else could do about it.

The law review's arsenal was stocked with more weapons for dealing with the 2L staff. There were occasions when people willfully missed office hours or failed to adequately do the work during hours. The most common violation of law review rules and responsibilities came through missed deadlines for drafts of the notes.

The note was one of the biggest things 2Ls do for law review. The top six notes selected through the competition were published in the next year's volume. The note-writing process spanned the entire year with periodic deadlines for outlines and drafts. The drafts were turned in to the associate notes and comments editors. We were pretty lenient with the deadlines during the fall semester. To some degree, the 2Ls took advantage of the deadlines. Several just took offense, viewing the deadlines as superfluous and rigid. In separate discussions, two 2Ls informed the notes and comments editor that they regarded the draft deadlines as "unnecessary hand-holding."

The two most vocal deadline scofflaws were almost defiant in the way they ignored the deadlines and flaunted their intent to ignore the deadlines. When it came time for sanctions, they would become even more adversarial than they ordinarily would have or should have been.

When appealing to the students' consciences and professional pride failed, the only way to enforce the law review bylaws and policies was through the Sanctions Committee.

The charges, written by the Managing Editor, and delivered with sufficient notice, were straightforward. The procedures afforded the accused the opportunity to appear before the committee or to write a written response that was read to the committee. Two of the charged appeared, one responded in writing and two chose to ignore the body altogether.

First to appear was Martha, a stuck-up 2L who was unable to meet the earlier deadlines because of her obligations as a teaching assistant, class work and her grandmother's death several days before the end of the semester when the 10-page draft was due. She informed the committee of all these extenuating circumstances . She also informed us that she intended to mail a copy of her draft to her editor over the winter break, but forgot her editor's address. She was polite and convincing. I was a tad skeptical, but reserved judgment or comment. A couple of editors asked polite questions.

Then, came Celeste, who sat down and proceeded to tell the board that she was offended by the deadlines and the charges because she "was out in the real world before going to law school. I worked for a few years. And, when I came to law school I did *really* well my first year— *really* well!" She established a totally adversarial position from the beginning and made the mistake of shifting part of the blame to her associate notes and comments editor. Cody, her editor, was innately contentious with most issues anyway; the last thing she needed to do was publicly challenge him, especially when she was on shaky ground.

"I emailed Cody and he never responded. I never received any emails from him about deadlines or anything," Celeste said. The excuses poured on. In October, she began working on her note. In November, she learned that there were many articles written on the same subject and that she was preempted. Thus, she lost valuable time and had to start over again. She attacked the law review's deadlines and procedures.

"These deadlines are stupid. I was angry and crushed when I got this letter," she said. "I am angry that I came in here to do my office hours each week, and I did all of my requirements well, and nobody said anything to me about this. I have a real problem with the way this was handled."

Her excuses flowed further. The week before the 8-page deadline her brother-in-law was in a bad car accident. She had offered Cody a copy of the newspaper police blotter account. It seemed that every time there was a deadline she had an excuse. She proclaimed her offense and distaste for deadlines. "I will not submit substandard work for a draft. I mean, I have the freak'in eight pages, if that's what you want," she said pulling out a packet of papers from a folder on her lap.

Then, the questions began. Cody was the first and he was typically prosecutorial. "I sent individual emails about the deadlines and meetings several times. Did you not also get the staff-wide emails about the deadlines?" he asked.

"You did not send any to me," she said.

Ron, the only 2L on the committee, had specific questions about what she turned in and when she turned it in.

Cody dug in again. He logged onto one of the computers while someone else asked questions to see if and when she sent him an email and vice versa. He pointed out the specific dates that he had sent the messages. She had not sent him any seeking assistance or direction. Then, Cody asked, "Can I see your *freak'in* eight pages?"

My only contribution to the discussion involved detailing the organizational management so Celeste understood that an executive editor in the office during her office hours would not be in a position to know about her note status or whether she was facing impending sanctions.

After Celeste was finished, I read a letter written by Tina, seemingly the busiest and flirtiest 2L on staff. Law review competed with Tina's other activities ranging from research assistant to teaching assistant to student government association and more. A consummate joiner, with enthusiasm so gushing it had to be phony, it seemed fitting that she failed appear before the committee. Instead, she submitted a rambling page-long letter explaining why she was unable to turn in a draft on time. Her letter praised her international civil rights seminar professor as a wonderful influence on her note, her life and her future. But she had not met him until the Spring semester began and he was unavailable to help her in the crucial early stages of her note.

The bylaws required the committee elect a chair. The bylaws explicitly prohibited the editor-in-chief from chairing the committee, which was fine with me. Before we began the meeting, while everyone was still chomping on the cookies, pretzels and Tootsie Pops, we elected a chair. I asked for volunteers. Nobody stepped up. Then, I asked for nominations. Someone nominated Cody. But he declined. Somebody nominated George, he declined. I again requested volunteers and looked around the room. Finally, Cole, reluctantly, raised his hand, "If nobody else will do it, I will."

The chair was responsible for keeping minutes and writing whatever punishment the committee meted out.

Nobody on the committee enjoyed cutting time out of their schedule to deal with the minutiae of enforcing the law review's rules and deadlines. Each of us had better ways to kill two hours in the middle of the week.

The year before, the Sanctions Committee was more active. More people were brought before the committee. Some people sanctioned last year described procedures as abusive. One senior board editor ran the panel like the Nuremberg trials, vigorously interrogating the charged 2L. Another senior editor berated other students. We did not have time to berate people. We just needed to make sure people were on top of their responsibilities.

The Sanctions Committee could vote and mete out a host of punishments ranging from written reprimands to extra office hours to suspension and expulsion from law review. Last year, one person was sanctioned and kicked off the law review for not attending office hours or submitting drafts of notes. Several others racked up a bunch of extra office hours. Last year's committee sentenced a classmate to 10 extra hours, plus make up hours for missing office hours after his mother died. By the end of last year, he had not made up all his hours. Technically, he never completed his requirements and owed time. There was a brief note left in his office mailbox at the end of the year, which I found and destroyed.

Once we completed our interviews with the charged 2Ls, we discussed and deliberated the possible punishments for each case. I was less concerned about sentencing people to extra office hours than I was about sending a message to the entire staff.   With the last two note deadlines weeks away and the bulk of the editing work still ahead of us, I wanted the staff to be on notice: no more sliding by.

The Sanctions Committee voted unanimously not to sanction Martha and only to issue written reprimands to everyone charged, including the Prince. Our goal was not to be officious, but to make sure people knew that there would be no second chances.

The next day I made a point of approaching Celeste and another student who appeared before the committee to make sure they understood that we were not playing arbitrary power games and that they were treated with more respect than many of my classmates were treated by our predecessors. "Last year, people who missed deadlines in the fall were sanctioned with extra office hours and berated for it," I said. "This is the spring and you only got a written warning. We have these deadlines in place because if we didn't, people would wait until the end of February to begin their notes and then they would all realize that something was already written and they'd say they were preempted. Then, the quality of the notes would go down. Then where would they be?"

She was not the only staff member to cry preemption. Students who write law review notes frequently begin with a broad topic. Initial research on broad topics generally produced dozens, sometimes hundreds of articles, on the same topic. Thus, they panic and fear that this wonderful topic has been preempted. One way to avoid the preemption panic, aside from choosing a totally unique topic, is to have a well-crafted and unique thesis. A number of 2Ls who cried preemption later lost time changing topics. If they only thought about what they were really doing, they would have avoided such problems.

A few days later, I met with Chris in the liaison office, for some potential alumni contacts in New Jersey. Chris, a staunch supporter of the law review's grade-on contingent, criticized the law review, and me personally, for charging such good, responsible students, like Celeste. "How dare you sanction someone like Celesete. That was not right. She is one of the best students in the class," she said.

Chris frequently learned precious details of many confidential matters around the law school, most likely from an aggrieved source. "Just because someone has good grades, does that mean they should get a free pass with law review requirements?" I answered. There was no response.

Law Revue: The Musical
Wednesday, March 1, 2000

One of the more affable 2L staff members, Ernie, began humming, then singing this afternoon during his office hours. Ernie's enthusiasm made him a welcome addition to the office hours. As he hummed a whimsical tune, he asked whether he could be excused from his office hour editing duties to begin work on his new idea, writing: "Law Review: The Musical."

"Yeah, it's about an up-and-comer who makes through the cruel world onto law review," he said with a wide smile.

"As long as it's spelled Law R-e-v-u-e," I said.

The wheels immediately started turning inside my head. My superficial knowledge of musical theater, conjured up a production loosely resembling "42nd Street," a show I saw from the front row of a theater in Cleveland.

The Playbill could be in *Bluebook* form, complete with extensive footnotes and citations. All the editors could have roles: the Editor-in-Chief would be like the producer; the senior board one chorus line and the editorial staff another chorus line.

The story and protagonist: the small-town legal-et who comes all the way to the big law school and works her way on to law review, then gets her big break and makes it to the top. "Come on along and listen to the lullaby of law review." It lacks the ring of "Broadway," the meter may be awkward, but it almost rhymes.

Pledge of Allegiance
Friday, Marcy 3, 2000

The law review's advisor, Professor Locknor, emailed me announcing that Lexis wanted to donate a complete set of Moore's Federal Practice to the law review. The gift came out of the blue and there were no strings attached. I would never turn away a donation to the law review, even if a 30-book treatise on federal law might not be used by the staff.

The two main online legal database companies, Lexis and Westlaw, have been jostling for the loyalties of law students for decades. The indoctrination began midway through the first year for the research and writing classes. Once we learned how to research and Shepardize with books, they brought in Lexis and Westlaw.

I learned Lexis-Nexis about eight years earlier for some journalism classes at Syracuse's Newhouse school. I had frequently used it at newspapers, too.

The two services dispatched representatives to every law school in the country, carving up the law student population, much like the way the United States and the Soviet Union cut up Third World countries during the Cold War. By buying the allegiances of some two-bit dictator, the Super Powers bought the loyalty of the country.

As editor, I was the point-man for the staff with these legal research Super Powers. I was on great terms with representatives from Lexis and Westlaw who serviced the law schools and law firms in Central New York. Besides the free lunches for orientation, they were always throwing things our way: t-shirts, coffee mugs, pens, pads and other tchotkees. Westlaw had donated a printer for our office a couple years earlier, so my friendly Lexis rep wanted to bestow the same offer. The printers were only for downloading documents from the respective services, but it saved our office printer. Plus, there was the paper. Tons of paper with the distinctive logos.

All this was to make sure the law students who would be expected to do the most research used their service. They whet your appetite with the free access during law school, the way the neighborhood crack dealer gives away the first hit for free, so you keep coming back for more. So by the time law students graduate, they are addicted to the service and then rack up huge fees when their law firms assign them to research.

I spoke with the representatives every week or two. They frequently called to see how things were going and I called if I had a problem. They were quite helpful.

Promises, Promises
Tuesday, March 7, 2000

Five Survey articles were still outstanding—insurance, employment, evidence, torts and professional responsibility. I was hoping to have all the articles together before Spring Break. I really wanted to have book 1 to the printer before Spring Break, too. Those early delays, coupled with the bizarre difficulties of the Martin article and the absence of a technical editor, all stymied production.

Calls to the five authors prompted more frustration. I had another round with Clay, the legal ethics author. Clay had systematically ignored our deadlines for months. In October, he asked for an extension until November. In November, it was December. December it was January. He kept on procrastinating. He was callous and obstinate about the deadlines. He was even a tad belligerent on the telephone.

With Spring Break days away, I finally reached him at his office after several calls and messages with his secretary were not returned. He finally returned my calls. He said that when I called earlier that day, he was on the phone closing on a house and that he was hoping to get to his article in the next couple of days, possibly get it to us "shortly."

"Do you think you could give me a clearer definition of shortly," I asked.

Then, he tossed the deadline ball back to me: "When would you like the article?"

"How about September," I said.

"That's really funny. I will try to get it in next week. Maybe the middle of the week."

"Clay, at the risk of giving you yet another excuse ... I am only telling you this as a courtesy to a professional, but next week is our Spring Break. Can you get the article to us first thing Monday, March 20."

"I like the way you delivered that," he said. "I will get it to you on that Monday."

Then, I asked what the condition or quality of the piece would be because, "We've been getting a few articles in that are in pretty bad shape. One article in particular was awful. I do not know whether the author scoured a middle school or hired a room full of chimps to write it for him, but it was horrible and unprofessional. I mean, there was a mistake in every sentence. I hope your article will be in better shape."

He laughed and said that it will be in good shape.

D-Day
Monday, March 20, 2000

The student notes were due by the end of the day. The final deadline: no excuses. This was the moment toward which they had all worked. All those nights staring at the computer, surrounded by piles of books, papers and articles. This was the day.

The senior board, particularly Nick, the Notes and Comments Editor, decided to give the 2Ls the Spring Break to work on their notes. A year before, my class's notes were due the day before Spring Break. Some people expressed interest in having the vacation to finalize the notes. So, Nick set the due date on the day after spring break. The rationale was simple: those who wanted to work on their notes over spring break could and would; those who did not could turn it in before leaving town. Surprisingly, two students turned their notes in several days before the break and one came in over the break.

The others trickled in over the course of the day. A handful of 2Ls blew off their office hours. By the end of the day, 41 of 42 notes were turned in. All those cantankerous bodies who complained with each and every deadline and even the five who met with the sanctions committee turned their notes in.

Throughout the day, the atmosphere in the office hovered between jubilation and relief. Many grinned widely as they came in with their stacks of papers. Some were pale with exhaustion and a couple had that all-nighter look, bags under their eyes, unkempt greasy hair and sweatpants.

The students had to turn in six copies (one with their name, the other five anonymous). Along with the relief, there were many congratulations. The note-writing process was extremely valuable. There is immeasurable value to any exercise that demands a student be completely immersed in a topic that requires painstaking research and precise writing. For many 2Ls, the student note is a first opportunity to write a substantial paper and have it compete. It is the only opportunity to write something for publication and one of the only opportunities to do any substantive writing after the first-year research and writing class.

In the legal community and academia, being published is just as valuable as any award. Publication appears on the resume, along with the citation. It looks neat, law firms and law schools like it. The goal of scholarly writing in law reviews is to be cited or excerpted in other law reviews, books and occasionally a judicial opinion.

Being cited by a judge or a court is the ultimate coup. In one of my conversations with Mr. Bogin, one of the editors in chief for volume 1, he enthusiastically recounted the attention and praise he received when the United States Supreme Court cited his student note. Fifty years later, his excitement and pride still resonated. "I could not believe it when I found out," he told me, with a slight chuckle. "All these people came up to me and congratulated me. Everyone was very excited about that."

This was a tremendous honor, especially for a fledgling law review. The reality, however, is that most law review articles will never be read by anyone beyond the grading committee, the student, the student's adviser and, possibly family members.

To my disappointment, a handful of 2Ls had said that they hoped that their notes would not be chosen for publication because they feared that they would be expelled for plagiarism. Anyone who thought like that obviously did not have any confidence in his or her own work. When one editor recounted this to me, I said, "Wouldn't it just be easier to make sure that you do not plagiarize and double check everything?"

"They are scared because they do not know what plagiarism is," the editor, Merry, said.

"Every person on law review was given a four-page primer on plagiarism. I personally distributed it," I said.

"They are all worried because of the Tom thing," Merry said.

"Anyone who is that worried should double check everything before turning it in. Anyway, the evidence in Tom's case, as you know, was stark," I said.

Again, despite all the information we disseminated all year, these ingrates failed to take heed or even think rationally. These few staff members were publicly insulating themselves in the likely event that their notes did not get chosen. There were plenty of interesting topics. But too many people just did not put in the time or the effort to write a substantive piece. Most of the notes were less than 30 pages. The first two sections of my note were more than 30 pages. I flipped through the pile as they came in. It was disappointing to see that so many people did not really expend anything more than the bare minimum. I just hoped that we had at least six publishable notes.

As everyone flowed in and out of the office today, this was one of the few days that every 2L appeared in the office at one point or another. It was nice to see them enjoying themselves. I remember the relief I felt after completing my note in an exhausting all-night marathon session in which Sara and I spent 16 straight hours in the library. We stayed there working on our lap tops, hunkered down behind a bunker of books, until the library closed. Then, we took our materials to the 24-hour computer cluster.

From midnight until 8 a.m., it was only us and some creepy guy sitting in the back of the computer cluster sleeping with his eyes open.

There was a heavy snowfall that night. At about 3 a.m., we took a break to watch the snow falling on the parking lot. At one point, I was working on three computers simultaneously, having my note on one and Lexis and Westlaw on two others to assist with the final checking of quotes and footnotes.

By the time I was done, I had enough time to print off the seven copies and go to class. I stayed up all night and know that I looked like it. A friend of mine, Rory, who sat next to me in Labor Law, remarked on my noticeably disheveled appearance and saw the pile of copies I was carrying. He asked to read it and enjoyed the opening paragraphs. "That opening page is hilarious. That kicks ass," he said. Even a year later, he was talking about it.

Pep and Prep
Wednesday, March 22, 2000

Today was the first day of the Bar Exam Accelerated Training (BEAT) program offered by the law school. In order to attend the introductory class and still take care of several pending law review items, I skipped tax.

A BarBri representative ran the class, introducing the room full of third year law students to the bar exam. He sought to assuage some of our fears of this massive exam by saying that "everyone walks out thinking they failed." Then he proceeded to detail the three scenarios under which people fail: 1) people who do nothing; 2) people who have major tragedies or crises; 3) people who freak out. To illustrate his first point he said, "At a school that was not Syracuse, the editor-in-chief of the law review failed. Is the editor in chief here?"

At that moment all the eyes in the classroom, full with roughly 60 to 70 students, focused in on me. The rep looked around the room, and again said, "Is the editor here?"

I half raised my hand and said, "Yes, thanks." He proceeded, "Well, the editor of the law review at that school, which shall remain nameless, did not do anything. That summer he skipped the classes and went to the golf course and he failed. He took the exam again and studied and passed."

I really did not need that attention for this situation.

Minutes after returning to the office, the phone rang. It was Judge Frank, a judge who interviewed me for a clerkship over spring break.

The meeting seemed so positive that I thought I really had the job. He heaped lots of praise on me and lauded me for my professional background and position on law review. He heaped even more praise on me because in February, I had cancelled our initial meeting because we were facing a blizzard and snow storm for the entire weekend. "Your credibility and worth with me grew exponentially that day," he said. "At first I was a bit angry that someone would cancel an interview. But I thought about it and talked it over with my wife. I thought that anybody who shows that kind of sensibility and judgment is the kind of person I want working for me. I had to have you in after that because you made a difficult but smart decision."

After all that, I thought I had the clerkship in the bag. Reality returned with the phone call. "Roy, I am sorry but I do not have good news. I am going with someone else. You were a very, very close second. This was a really tough decision. But if I hear of anything I will pass your name along."

I thanked him and he seemed ready to hang up and I asked what kind of person he went with. He paused, almost surprised by my question, and proceeded to describe his choice as "someone with similar credentials as you." Except that he wrote for his college newspaper, attended law school in the Washington area, served on moot court and worked as a mentor with underprivileged inner city kids. Working with underprivileged inner city kids spelled it all out—what a farce.

This news came as a shock. I really thought I landed this job. And, even worse, I actually liked Judge Frank after meeting with him. Initially, I did not even want the job in a northern New Jersey state court, but then wanted it after I met the judge. Although I had become accustomed to rejection at this point I got nauseous.

I really wanted to just go home and leave. I was nauseous. But it was Wednesday, I had a night class in three hours and the monthly general staff meeting in about 20 minutes.

This was an important meeting because we were getting ready to send the first book to the printer. I was still finding numerous mistakes in the articles. Plus, the law review elections were in two weeks. I had to give another "accuracy is important" speech as well as a pre-election inspirational pep talk to entice quality 2Ls to run for office. Every year a number of good candidates balked at seeking positions because of the time commitment or general apathy.

The agenda covered several topics. I started with a brief discussion of the recently-completed note writing project: "I would like to start by offering the 2Ls congratulations on completing your notes. We received notes from everybody. You deserve congratulations and a pat on the back because writing a note is quite an accomplishment. Regardless of whether you are published here or elsewhere, your student note is an accolade you will have for the rest of your career. Congratulations."

I started applauding. Some sporadic applause followed. I think they thought I was idiotic. Then, I went through my general announcements with dates to remember like the upcoming volleyball game and the banquet. I provided a brief update regarding the status of books, articles and survey articles.

"Now that your notes are done, I would like to turn to the other half of your law review responsibilities, form and accuracy work during office hours," I said. Then, I went into the accuracy counts portion of my speech: "I cannot stress this enough. But everything counts. I know we have tried to keep the atmosphere loose in the office but please be careful when you are editing and checking. I should not have to find mistakes. By the time an article gets to me, I should not have to go on Lexis and find cases. I have found wrong citations, wrong page numbers, quotes. These are basic issues. When you are doing your office hours, please be aware of what you are doing and double check everything you do. Review what you type in because some people are good typists, some people are not. We are getting close to crunch time here and do not have time to make mistakes. This is not a race, but we have to work quickly. Accuracy counts and all of our names go on these books."

Mike, who organized the "Election 2000" bulletin board and procedures, wrote a memo outlining election procedures. There had been a buzz about elections. Mike described the election process and urged people not to be intimidated by the speeches and question-and-answer period. "I know that some of you are concerned about the speech," Mike said. "Let me tell you, public speaking is not favorite thing to do or something I like, so don't be concerned. You can go up there and read your personal statement. If you guys have any questions about the jobs or the time commitment, talk to me or any of the editors."

He handed the floor back to me. When I addressed the group I stood in the middle of the floor, close to the first row of seats. I looked around the room, sometimes making eye contact.

"Mike mentioned commitment. Each and every one of you made a commitment to this organization, to yourselves and to each other by joining law review. Each of you fulfilled a good portion of that commitment this week when you completed and handed in your notes. And, for the most part each of you has worked toward the other portion of that commitment each week during your office hours. But that commitment does not cease when your second year is complete.

"Being a member of law review will accompany you throughout your career. You have a vested interest in this publication. Each and every one of you should fulfill that commitment during your third year. You should seek a position and be involved even if you do not seek an elected position. You should want to ensure the quality of this publication.

"This year, we had unprecedented involvement from 3Ls who did not seek elected office. Most of that involvement was a function of the 50th anniversary. But in the past 3Ls have read the notes, staffed office hours and helped proofread. So, there is no reason why each of you is not involved with this publication next year.

"Yes, this is work, hard work. Most of you always see me up there in the office. But I will tell you that this is rewarding. I enjoy the work and I have enjoyed working with you. The editorial positions on law review are unique. I hope all of you will capitalize on this opportunity and continue with the law review. So, sign up or nominate yourself or your friends. I'll see you in the office"

There was a smattering of applause, probably in partial derision. I am not sure whether the 2Ls thought I was full of baloney or full of myself. But that was not my main concern. I was elected. I sought this position. If I did not take it seriously, and enthusiastically promote law review membership, why should anyone else?

After the meeting broke up. Sara and Sofia, who were seated in the upper right corner of the room, smiled at me. As I scaled the steps up to their perch, they quietly applauded. Sara gave me a high five and tugged on my tie, "Did you really believe all that stuff you said? We liked it."

Through the Ringer
Thursday, March 23, 2000

After weeks of voicemail messages and messages left with our construction author's secretary, I decided to enlist the support and assistance of an alumnus editor who also worked at the author's prestigious international law firm.

Benedict, who graduated last year, was the editor who made a giant point during the election, questioning whether I would be intimidated by authors. I called Benedict to see if he could help get in touch with Ringer. He told me that Ringer left the firm the week before to take a job with "a very important client." I told him that for the past three months, the author ignored us and refused to return calls.

Benedict was the editor who brought Ringer aboard to write the construction law article the year before. He said he would call him to find our where the article stood. He said that he was friends with Ringer. I thanked him.

Fifteen minutes later, Benedict called back to tell me that it was likely that the article would not be forthcoming. I expressed my disappointment and began to vent. "When exactly was he planning on informing us that he was not going to write the article?" I asked. "He signed a contract. As far as I am concerned he is in breach of contract."

Benedict took offense and urged me not to create trouble for him. "Don't call him. Be creative with how you contact him," he said. "I don't want any repercussions on me."

"What are you saying, that I cannot call him and ask where the article is that we were supposed to have in August?" I asked.

"Just do not get me stuck in the middle of this. I do not want this to reflect poorly on me. He is a powerful client who I respect now," Benedict said.

The conversation got progressively abrasive. I did not appreciate this arrogant former editor talking down to me about contacting an author who flouted professionalism and broke a contract. I did not like a former editor telling me not to call someone because it might impact on his career, which was a tenuous argument anyway. Benedict's pleading bordered on threatening, "Do not get me stuck in the middle of this, I'm warning you. You will regret it."

"Is that some sort of threat? Hey, he signed a contract. If he did not want to write the article, he should not have signed the contract," I said. "Either way you are stuck in the middle of it because he was your author. You brought him in."

"What are you going to say to him?" he asked.

"I am going to remind him that he had a contract and a responsibility and that this is unprofessional. What do you think I'm going to do, sue him? I don't have the time to sue him. It's an empty contract and I do not have the time, anyway?" I said.

"What are you going to do, sue for specific performance? He'll write 10 words," he said.

After five minutes with Benedict, I had had enough. Ringer was an author Benedict signed up, undoubtedly, as a way to ingratiate himself with the management at the prestigious international law firm during his summer there. Ringer was his author and I was going to let him have it.

"This is what happens with the Survey. That's why I don't like that we publish the Survey," Benedict said, as if his opinion mattered to me. He was always one to grace everyone in the room with his opinion.

The Survey was the best thing the Syracuse Law Review produced, I told him. The only problem with it was that half-dozen authors who did not have the decency to fulfill their obligations to meet the deadlines.

In a patronizing left-handed way, he said that being editor is a thankless job but he would tell the Dean that I was "doing a great job." He was either deluding himself or deriding me, not sure which.

"That's really great. I'm sure the Dean is waiting to hear from you,." I said. I thanked him for his kind remarks, but I doubt he recognized the sarcasm.

Then, he turned the conversation to gossip. He knew about Tom's plagiarism case, "I heard you had a problem with Tom."

"Yes, that's true," I said.

"What happened?" he asked.

"What did you hear?" I said.

"That he got kicked out for a semester."

"That's what happened," I said.

I was one sentence fragment away from telling him that it was a confidential law review matter that was none of his business and that I did not want him to get stuck in the middle of a law review matter. Instead, I simply ended the conversation.

At this point I was livid. The author completely ignored his obligation. I wanted to talk with him on the phone but never got around to it. Instead, I drafted a scathing letter. I was so furious that I wanted to send the letter to Ringer, the managing partners at the prestigious international law firm as well as his current bosses at the "very important client" of the prestigious international law firm.

Don't Piss in the Pool
Friday, March 24, 2000

The next day, I went to talk with Chris in the liaison office. I wanted to probe her on the power structure of a law firm like the prestigious international law firm where Ringer and Benedict worked. I explained the construction law article predicament, my anger and dissatisfaction. Chris became hostile when I mentioned my plan to write to the managing partners. She warned me not to write them a letter, presumably, because it might effect her relations with a law firm. Then, she told me that it would be acceptable to write to the author, but that she wanted to read the letter before I sent it. That was all I needed, prior restraint by a human resources expert.

She implied that a letter to the brass at the firm might have a deleterious effect on my career. "Why, that law firm will never hire me. Those pricks would not even have me in their lobby," I said.

"Just don't do it," she added.

The letter was a scathing rant, full of venomous and righteous indignation. The hole created by his missing article hurt our reputation because consistency is one of the hallmarks of our book. The editors before me made calculated effort to expand the Survey to include construction law.

Even the Editor's Note in Volume 49 made a grandiose pronouncement that the editorial board decided to add this topic "due to popular request." I liked the idea of expanding the Survey, especially with a topic that was widely litigated because it involves disputes between contractors, insurers and builders. However, one student editor's proclivity for self-promotion and sycophancy should not equal "popular request."

The letter to Ringer was so bitter that I held off on sending it. My letter was one of my finest pieces of indignation:

> It has become abundantly clear that you unilaterally decided to disregard your agreement with the Syracuse Law Review to write the Construction Law article for the Syracuse Law Review 1998-99 Survey of New York Law.
>
> This letter is an expression of our extreme displeasure with your unprofessional and irresponsible conduct. Your refusal to fulfill your obligations, to which you agreed, should be considered a breach of contract.

But your abject disregard for your commitment is more than simply a breach of contract. Your actions besmirch your professional reputation as well as the reputation of your prestigious law firm. Your callous disregard of our agreement, coupled with the way you repeatedly ignored telephone and voicemail messages left by our articles editors and myself, typifies your impropriety and lack of professional ethics.

Your calumny is not only directed to the editorial board of the Syracuse Law Review, but to each and every subscriber of the annual Survey of New York Law. Consistency is one of the Survey's hallmarks. The Survey has published certain survey topics for 50 years. Over that time, the Survey has expanded to meet the needs of the legal community. Last year's editorial board decided to include Construction Law as a new annual topic. The Editor's Note in the Survey attributed your addition to "popular request." I cannot investigate the verity of that statement.

However, because of your insolence and lack of professionalism, this year's Survey will not be able to include Construction Law. Your actions left us with no time to seek a substitute author.

I am curious to know when you intended to inform us that you decided to disregard our agreement. Is this also how you served your clients?

I certainly hope this letter reaches you at your new workplace. I would welcome the opportunity to discuss this with you. But, like the many previous attempts to reach you, I am fairly confident that this letter will be summarily disregarded as well.

I never showed it to Chris. But, I also never sent it. By the time I simmered down, other matters occupied my attention. No matter what I wrote to this self-centered ingrate, nothing would change. Like many of these authors, there was only one thing that mattered, and it was certainly not the predicament of the Syracuse Law Review.

Un-Civil Practice
Friday, March 24, 2000

The New York Civil Practice article had an August deadline. I spoke with the author in January and he said he would get it to us by early February. When February came and he did not send the article I called again.

He told me he was almost finished and just needed to have his clerk spell check and cite check the article. It came in and went to Cole's team. Cole assigned it to his team as a take home project. Each team member had a block of pages and a due date.

One 2L working on the piece showed me some of the corrections. Literally, every sentence had a spelling or grammatical mistake. It was in worse shape than the rough draft of a junior high school term paper. It was appalling.

By the time the first round of editing changes were made, the article was completely covered with editing marks, re-written sentences, added footnotes and arrows pointing in every direction.

Cole warned that this article needed substantial work. "My team is has a lot to fix on this. I cannot believe that a professional adult, who claims to take pride in his work, would send this out," he said. "This is a complete embarrassment."

The article was an abomination. Sentences just ended in the middle of a phrase without punctuation. There were misspelled words, misused words—their, there and they're were regularly interchanged. There were assertions without footnotes. There were footnotes not in proper Bluebook form and no parallel citations.

After flipping through the marked up copy, I added, "This looks like he gave typewriters to a room full of chimpanzees." It was obscene. I planned on calling the author and giving him a piece of my mind. But I needed to be on good terms with him because I would need his cooperation when we would send an edited draft for his review later on. I would need a quick turn-around on that.

Conversely, our new administrative law author delivered her article to the law review a full day before her deadline, along with copies of cases and materials. Her package included two disks, three copies of the piece and copies of all the cases she cited. She was a delight. But there were several minor problems. The biggest problem involved the discussion of a case that repeated details of another case. The second case, however, was not fully cited in the first case. The editor processing this article, brought it to my attention. I read the case and could not find two key details about the case that the author cited. The editor and a team member did a word search on Westlaw and failed to turn up the information.

I asked a student working on the article to search the text of the lower court opinion. That proved fruitless. I then directed the student to search through New York secondary sources including newspapers and the New York Law Journal to find the information and slap a *see also* cite on to the footnote. It worked.

Similarly, our commercial law author, Professor Nelson, a long-time Syracuse professor and his wife, presented a comprehensive accounting of developments in commercial law. I worked on this article during my second year and it was frustrating. I remembered tracking down a citation that my editor spent the previous two hours working on. The author had quoted from a state opinion of a remanded case but gave a citation to a federal case involving the same parties. The citation misstated the page numbers to the wrong volume of the reporter. It was a complete botch but I located the correct quote from the correct opinion. There were dozens of examples like that.

I dreaded the article we would receive this year. Luckily, many of last year's errors were attributed to his research assistant, a self-impressed blow-hard who did not know how to check citations or write a lucid sentence. His research assistant this year was a little more conscientious, at least I hoped so.

Professor Nelson's best attribute was his eagerness to continue writing the article. He was an expert in commercial law and had written this article for years, decades. It was refreshing to have someone interested in an authoritative piece year-after-year.

Dateline 2000
Saturday, March 25, 2000

As a quarterly publication, the law review should traditionally publish one or two books in the fall and one or two books in the spring. Book 1, we initially hoped would be published by the end of October. So much for ideals.

We were eager to have everything done the week we returned from Spring Break. Even though we would be sending the book to the publisher in the spring of 2000, we would still slap a 1999 date on the cover. That was until the Ninth Circuit Court of Appeals issued an opinion on the *Martin v. PGA Tour* case. Our lead article devoted about three pages of text and roughly 15 footnotes to discussing the district court opinion. Cole, the editor who processed the article by Professor Harrison, learned of the appeals court's decision, which was released within the past week.

There were two ways we could handle this now: we could ignore it or we could rewrite the section of the article. If we rewrote the section, it would effect our volume date. According to the Statement of Ownership, Management and Circulation, the postal system form in the back of the first book, the law review had to have a 1999 date on the first book.

If we included a citation with a 2000 date, it would look ridiculous, especially if a subsequent author or court cited the law review discussing this opinion. This is the kind of minutiae that only an editor could care about.

When I spoke with Professor Harrison I hinted that we could avoid rewriting the section if we ignored the opinion.

"I can't believe that that is an option," she said.

The other option, I told her, was that she could rewrite the entire section of the article, which at this point had already been formatted. The best remedy I recommended was to summarize the opinion in a long footnote and keep the text of the article as it stood.

Professor Harrison and Cole agreed with my recommendation. She told me she would get me her rewritten footnote within days.

Thus, Syracuse Law Review, Volume 50, book 1, would be dated 2000, not 1999 because of one footnote. I was the only person who worried about this.

Spike!
Monday, March 27, 2000

The law review experience abounded with irony. The paramount irony was that everybody wanted to be on law review but once they made it, a disturbing portion disregarded the responsibility. Others, often those who graded-on, regarded the work as trifling, boring, unimportant or otherwise beneath them. The bulk of the members who earned their way on via the write-on competition, seemed to approach the work with slightly more alacrity and interest. For a portion of both grade-ons and write-ons, the work was completely disregarded or they simply lacked the eye or desire to do detailed editing.

Office hours were not for socializing. But it seemed like this was when people were most inclined to socialize. After days of wiping mustard and mayonnaise off the computer keyboards and attempts to concentrate despite the office cacophony, it was no surprise mistakes popped up in articles. One of the honors of being editor meant that at the end of the day I had the privilege of disposing of an array of candy wrappers, food crumbs, coffee cups and various condiments left behind. It was bad enough my memos were disregarded, but so were the signs I printed and placed beside the computers. I borrowed from one of my favorite public service campaigns: "Put Trash in its Place." I also inserted clipart of a garbage can with odor lines emanating from the top.

When I was not serving as Custodian-in-Chief, on occasion, I evicted intruders at will. One recent afternoon, a 2L staff member had a visitor come into the office and stand in the middle of the room talking with her for about 10 minutes. The couple was flirting. The staff member, giggled and looked coquettishly at the guy, who wore shorts and a sweatshirt—he looked like he just returned from the gym.

My subtle glances in his direction failed to elicit an appropriate response, his exit. Subtlety rarely works with meatheads like this guy. They were just gabbing and gabbing, as if nobody else existed. Finally, I approached him and said, "I don't mean to be a dick about this, but people are here doing work. These are their office hours."

He quickly picked up his gym bag and weightlifter's belt, apologized and left. The girl looked at me and also apologized. I simply said, "Socialize on your own time." My patience at this point in the year was clearly wearing thin.

The truly ironic aspect of all this was that when social activities were organized, few people showed up. This was especially troubling because of the complaints levied the year before that there were no adequate social events. As the "People's Editor," the senior editors and I made the office a more hospitable place.

Our second foray into the social/athletic arena was a co-ed volleyball game against the other journals. Again, many law review members, as well as other journal members expressed interest. Celeste, the 2L who had her icy show-down with the Sanctions Committee, thawed and volunteered to make all the arrangements to reserve the volleyball court in a campus gymnasium. I made sure she knew that how much I appreciated her efforts and olive branch.

I sent out emails on the listserve and printed up posters, replete with clip art volleyball players. The sign-up sheet was on the bulletin board for weeks, right next to the office hours sign-in sheet and the law-related articles I clipped and posted from the Wall Street Journal.

The editors of the International Journal, the Tech Journal and the Digest, a student and faculty-edited journal of the Italian-American lawyer's association, expressed interest. They were all excited. We were excited. By the end of the week, I envisioned that we would have enough people to field several teams and have a round-robin tournament.

By game time, Sunday, 5 p.m., we only had a total of eight people, including me and Sara. Sara did not even want to play and ended up stewing about it for days. At about 5-feet-tall, she was not too eager to play volleyball. Nevertheless, she showed up because it was a law review event that I planned. What had been slated as the First Annual Inter-Journal Volleyball Extravaganza ended up a disappointing side out.

Expecting people to want to socialize with the same people they sit next to Monday through Friday in law school classes was unrealistic in many ways. I always cringed when I ran into law students, or worse, professors, off campus. Sara and I regularly encountered professors at dinner and movies, especially at the small independent artsy theater. Most of the time the encounters were ignored by the professors. One time a professor refused to even respond to a greeting after a movie. But another time, the movie *Primary Colors* spurred an interesting exchange of emails with my Constitutional Law professor assessing the movie.

The compulsory elements of law review membership competed with a host of other obligations. We were lucky that people fulfilled the obligations they were required to complete to earn the credit. Enticing law students to carve out a block of their weekend schedule for a recreational event was too ambitious. People went to bar nights, why not volleyball? Even the upcoming staff election was not enough to spark a healthy turnout. I am sure that if I bargained away office hours for volleyball participation, we would have had a full complement of teams.

Stretch Armstrong
Monday, March 27, 2000

A typical afternoon. I juggled about a half-dozen tasks simultaneously today in the span of about a half-hour: 1) I was going through the Martin article page-by-page with Marcus, the executive editor who handled the piece, because I needed to overnight the article to the author today; 2) Lulu, the new T-shirt and souvenir designee had questions about the color scheme for the shirts and the school-sanctioned purchasing rules; 3) the poster photo debacle; 4) the Lexis rep came in to help trouble-shoot the Cite-Check program; 5) a 3L who was judging the note competition came in to retrieve her copies; 6) a 2L had questions about citing to sections of the new revised Uniform Commercial Code; 7) the telephone rang with another author.

This was a typical sliver of a typical day in the three-ring circus of the law review.   I felt like a I was being pulled in about 20 different directions.   In the 1970s, Stretch Armstrong was a superhero with the power to stretch into extreme positions. The Stretch Armstrong toy was a slime-filled rubber doll that would could stretch to extremes, too. It was a couple of feet long and could stretch another foot or two. It was fun, but now I felt like one.

Election Connection—Secret Ballot
Monday, April 3, 2000

As the clock ticked down for the Election 2000 deadline, a handful of 2Ls appeared in the office to drop off their letters of intent and resumes, as well as to check out the other candidates.

The final deadline was 5 p.m., and this year's horserace was winding down.   There was speculation that one highly-respected 2L would run for my job, but he was keeping it to himself. He had been nominated and had plenty of support on staff, but privately admitted that he did not want all the additional pressures and headaches that came with the office.   Another potential candidate told me that she was not sure whether she wanted the additional responsibility, either, but was seriously considering her nomination. And one other 2L had his name in the ring for the job. The handful of people interested in my job were eminently qualified and were equipped to manage the Three Ring Circus if elected.

The quality of the people interested in the top staff positions was not keeping me up at night worrying. They were some of the best and most dedicated 2Ls on the staff, which was reassuring to me and my senior board.

Then, there was a knock on my door. Hoyt, a brash Texan who reportedly had a photographic memory, stood in the doorway holding a manila folder. "Got a minute?" he asked.

"Sure, what's up?"

He stepped in, closed the door and sat down in the extra chair. "I wanted to know your opinion on this. Today is the last day to sign up and I wanted to know what you thought about your position as editor-in-chief and whether you think I would be good for it."

"I can talk to you objectively about this job ... it is a lot of work. You know I am always here," I said.

"Yeah, but it is a hell of a feather to wear in your cap," he said.

"This is a serious job. It's not brain surgery, but I am here at 8 in the morning and leave anywhere from 8 to 10 at night, plus every weekend, Saturdays and Sundays. The editor wears a lot of hats. There is a lot of paperwork and management stuff. It's serious and if the editor does not take it all seriously, nobody else will."

"I know. What do you think about me for this job?" he asked.

"Hoyt, I cannot endorse anybody and will not tell you to run or not to run. I have to remain neutral. But what I will tell you is, you missed a lot of office hours, many of which you have made up, and you were the only person not to turn your note in on time. That sort of stuff will be addressed at the election."

"Yes, but I made up or will make up all the time and had computer problems that day, " he said.

"Again, I'm not going to tell you whether or not to run, but if you do you have to be 100 percent behind your decision because this is not a job that you can do half-ass. If the editor in chief is dropping the ball there's nobody else there to pick it up. Plus, the honor of being editor is paltry compared to all the work. But if you think you're the right person for the job, go for it," I said.

Hoyt was an intelligent and competitive guy who presented the aura of a student who did not work too hard, have to work too hard or care too much. He knew his law, perhaps too well, and was on his way to a top national law firm. His editing was pretty good. But he missed a whole bunch of hours and turned his note in a day late. His 11th-hour venture into the Election game seemed disingenuous. He probably would not have fared well with the rest of the staff, either. I was not sure he could carry the requisite personality points with the rest of the staff.

Plus, for weeks, months practically, the staff had been gearing up for the election, with candidate names being whispered and support being amassed. Then, Hoyt opportunistically tried to sneak in at the last minute. That's politics.

Wanted: Poster
Thursday, April 6, 2000

One of my *brilliant* ideas for the 50th anniversary celebration was a commemorative poster. I should have had my head examined for this crazy thought. The poster would feature the six previous law review covers along with photos of the new building and historic photos of old law review action photos. An action photo for law review was people sitting around a table.

The law school's development and alumni office had three photos in its file cabinet archives. There was a 1957 photo of the law review members sitting around with typewriters. The members were men in suits and thick horn-rim glasses. It was a great photo, but between last week and today someone there lost it. The other photos were similar.

A designer in the university publications office, Jane, quickly picked up on the idea and modified my rough sketch outlining the poster vision. We met on a Monday morning. I gave her all the materials, including slides of the new building, recent photos taken by a university photographer (with Mike, Sara, Nick and me) and the law review covers.

Jane called me this afternoon because the photos of the building showed construction workers and orange construction fencing. She had problems with the old black and white photos, too. Her complaint: "They are just a bunch of white guys, there is no diversity and since this is a university project, someone at the meeting this morning raised this as an issue. This is not going to be an inclusive poster."

"There is very little I can do about the racial and gender composition of the staff from 40 years ago," I said, adding that at least the photo from the early 1960s featured a woman who was the editor.

"Yes, I see that photo, but the concern is, is this the message and image that a Syracuse publication wants to send out?" she said.

I was annoyed at the thought of a bunch of designers wringing their hands because 40-year-old photographs were not "inclusive" enough. I was not surprised that she raised this issue, and admit that I anticipated the question. But I was agitated that I had to articulate a defense that made me sound insensitive. My only answer was direct: "There is very little I can do about the past. These are the only photos we have, these are the only photos we can use."

The great photo debacle was just that: a debacle. I wanted some photos of the new law school building that opened almost two years ago. I started with the dean's secretary who pushed me to an associate dean who directed me to the computer guy who was scanning building photos for the law school's website. He had photos, but the people in the printing office objected because construction worker and orange construction fencing were visible in the photos.

The poster designer sent me back to the law school to locate the good building photos which were used for official law school brochures. The same people, including the dean and development director in the alumni and development office could not locate anything. They sent me back to the secretary and associate dean, neither of whom could help.

The dean of alumni affairs hypothesized that the original photos or negatives or digital images were on file with the university printers. I went back to the poster designer the next day with copies of the university brochures. No luck. The designer dug out a copy of the law school's holiday card with a nice picture on it showing portions of the old building and the new building.

In the meantime, I ventured over to the university archives to see what they had on file there. The archives sit on top of the university on the sixth floor of Bird Library, the main campus library. An extremely helpful archival specialist, Maryanne, brought me the law school photo box and let me root through it. There, I found a fresh copy and negative to the 1957 photo that the law school development office recently lost. I was quite pleased.

Maryanne then brought me a complete photo archive listing. The listing consisted of about two-dozen yellow, or once-yellow-now-brown, legal pads with a chronological listing and brief one- to three-word descriptions of every photo in the university archives since 1950. Each photo had an identification number. "It would be kind of a daunting job, but you could do it if you want to," Maryanne told me.

The job of visually scanning page after page, pad after pad, was not daunting, but kind of like searching for a needle in a haystack. It reminded me of my reporter days when I would scour documents or reams of records, searching for a smoking gun or golden nugget of information. Occasionally, I would find something useful. But not this day. I found a 1962 photo of the law review, but it was only a "firing squad" photo—the staff lined up against the wall. I wanted action, or the illusion of action.

Going to the archives was actually fun. I skipped my securities regulation class. My adventure in the university history was more interesting than a lecture on prospectus disclosure. Archives procedure required registering with the office. The office banned all bags and coats anywhere near the large tables. I even flipped through the *Onondagan*, the university yearbook for the years my friends graduated.

The university had every yearbook since the university's founding in 1870, except one from the 1890s, when Stephen Crane attended the university. "Someone walked off with that one years ago because it had pictures of him, including pictures of him on the baseball team. We've been trying to get one for years," Maryanne said. I asked her whether she tried Ebay because there are usually several *Onondagans* for sale at any time. "If you see one, buy it and sell it to us," she said.

It was so refreshing to deal with someone who seemed so eager to help. I only wish that I had ventured into the archives when I was at the *Daily Orange* 10 years earlier. What a resource.

I signed out the photograph and headed back to the law school to find the photos of the building. I also wanted to show the development office personnel a copy of the photo I found (the same one they lost).

Back at the law school, I resumed my search with the usual suspects and sought their assistance. The dean's secretary again rooted through some files for the building photo, after again directing me to the associate dean, the computer guy and the alumni office. EUREKA! The building photo magically appeared.

The poster project would cost $1,016 for 500 or $1,025 for 1,000. There was no explanation why it only cost $9 more for an additional 500. The designer in the printing office said the disparity had something to do with the printer's scheduling and set-up costs for the full-color poster.

Because the poster project was not a budgeted expense, the Dean needed to approve. The money would have to be drawn from the law review's "Restricted Account." This account was a repository for funds donated to the law review itself or alumni donations specifically earmarked for the law review.

Only a handful of people even knew about this money. The law school's budget manager first informed me about the Restricted Account in August when we spoke about purchasing new computers. In the past, this was how the law review bought new computers. The account had about $18,000, not the wealth of an endowment, but enough that $1,000 for posters would not break it. I was personally reluctant to dig too deep into the account. I did not want to be the editor who drained the account. Only the Dean could authorize expenditures from the Restricted Account, anyway. I could not have drained it even if I intended to drain it.

Any concerns about dipping into the account for the 50th anniversary poster or celebration would be counter-balanced by the good will and alumni support we might generate from the event. At least I hoped. The law school administration already had an item for two alumni newsletters, one with full-color glossy photographs.

Election 2000
Friday, April 7, 2000

Today was the first step in passing the torch. The election proceeded pretty smoothly. The senior board met two days earlier to discuss possible contingencies, such as how to handle the executive and associate positions that might not have enough candidates. We agreed that if we did not have enough candidates, we would vote on the nominees and then open the floor to nominations and have a vote on the floor nominees. The bylaws required a supplemental election, which last year proved futile because it was just as difficult to lure people to run for the positions. We ended up voting in the only people who sought positions anyway. It was difficult enough to get enough people in one room for one election. It would be practically impossible to get everyone together for a second election for a few positions.

This was a one-day offer. Unlike those New York City stores that sell cheap tourist souvenirs and stuff like ceramic elephants under a perpetual red "Going Out of Business" banner, there would be no second-day sale.

The senior board also agreed that there would be no public discussion following the candidate speeches and the question-and-answer period. We instituted a "No Sandbag" policy because last year a candidate was subjected to some pretty frank discussions about her qualifications, commitment and performance on law review while the candidates waited outside the room for the vote.

Halie was elected to a position despite the apparent sandbag, but she was reduced to tears after she learned that an editor's boyfriend publicly questioned her commitment and qualifications. The boyfriend announced that Halie failed to turn in a draft of her note, missed deadlines and might not have the skills necessary to perform in a senior editor's capacity. As such, Halie never had the opportunity to answer the accusations. The accusations were truthful and the concerns were valid. But they should have been raised by the editor, not the editor's boyfriend, to Hallie's face

The executive board agreed that if anyone had a complaint, concern or accusation, it should be made publicly to the candidate's face. If it was good enough for a criminal defendant to face an accuser, it should have been good enough for a law review candidate. If anything, it was fair. As Justice Brandeis wrote, sunlight is the best disinfectant.[58]

The meeting was scheduled for 2 p.m. Annie, the editor organizing the banquet, recommended that before we began the election proceedings we have the staff collate, stuff and label the invitations for the banquet—all 1,500. As people filtered into the room, we began distributing the materials. Cole assumed the lead on this and directed the process while I ran around making final arrangements such as getting the $30 worth of soda and a 24-pack of beer out of my car. Ally, the business editor, coordinated the pizza order and delivery.

The scene took on a chaotic, yet festive atmosphere. It was reminiscent of the scene where Tom Sawyer convinced all the neighborhood kids to whitewash a fence. Few were pleased about the extra work, but nobody complained either. Sometimes some mind-numbing work was a welcome respite. A few people looked like they were actually enjoying it.

Cole patrolled the room, clutching handfuls of envelopes and invitations. Someone needed more return envelopes, Cole was there. Someone needed more invitations, but had too many outer envelopes, he was there. Then, he retrieved piles of sealed envelopes. Annie also collected the envelopes, and got them ready for mailing. The group completed the project in about 40 minutes, just in time for the 10 pizzas to arrive. As the envelopes were boxed and removed, the pizzas were opened and consumed.

Once the pizzas were gone, it was show time.

The elections went relatively smoothly, at least as smoothly as any four-hour event could go. Despite the serious business taking place and

---

[58] BRANDEIS, OTHER PEOPLE'S MONEY 62 (1933).

the personal questions, the entire event had a party-like air. Almost the entire staff attended the meeting, at least 75 people out of 79. There were a handful of people who had not been to one meeting all year, mostly third year students, who showed up for election day. I could count the truants on one hand. It warmed me to see so many people there, even staff members who showed little interest all year.

This successful attendance followed plenty of prepping, emails and telephone calls and outright begging to get some people there. I even had to call one editor who overslept that morning to get her to the meeting, which was ironic because she was most vocal about the No-Sandbag policy. A couple of others I enticed with the promise of beer.

The candidates wore business attire. I wore a tie and nice slacks, as I did for all meetings. I tried to dress professionally even as most law firms instituted casual dress policies.

There were plenty of sodas, ice and beer available for the first couple of hours. I borrowed a giant bowl from the cafeteria kitchen and filled it with ice, which prompted some wisecracks from the cafeteria manager. Like last year, a couple of guys had too much beer and got silly. There was plenty of laughter, too.

The candidates gave their speeches, some laden with the obvious criticism of my administration and all the problems we encountered: article selection, particularly the medieval article; the debilitated computers; the inefficient editing system. Overall, the questions were relatively benign.

One candidate complained that there was not enough information disseminated about the note-writing process and guidelines. Another candidate criticized our plagiarism policy and complained that there was not enough information presented about what constituted plagiarism. One candidate had the audacity to complain that the law review failed to have any social activities.

I tried not to take the criticism personally because every candidate needed a campaign platform. A year earlier, I leveled some mild criticism about our predecessors. This year's operation was so different from last year's that I was mildly peeved by the critique. It was always easy to shoot something down from the outside. Sure, everything could have run more efficiently, but too many extrinsic forces wreaked havoc this year, just like last year and just like next year.

The criticism was similar to watching Weather Channel video of extreme conditions—hurricanes, floods, heat or cold—which never looks quite as bad on television in your living room thousands of miles away. Set foot into 100-mile winds, three feet of rushing water in the middle of your street or temperature extremes, and it is a different story. There was no way the candidates could have enough insight into the pressures and tensions of the day-to-day operations of the law review.

There were a couple of candidates who failed to meet deadlines for notes but were not questioned publicly. One candidate who missed more than 12 office hours was questioned publicly about his attendance. The No-Sandbag policy which mandated leveling accusations to the person's face rather than during deliberations was more humane but may have enabled a couple of shady figures to slide by. Halie later complained to me about one candidate who missed a deadline for a draft of the note.

"Somebody should have said something," she told me.

"You could have," I responded.

"I was going to but I didn't want to do it in front of everyone," she said.

"I guess it would have been better to say it when she wasn't around, right?"

The irony failed to register with her.

Cody, the senior devil's advocate, also expressed concern that he wanted to challenge a candidate but balked at the prospect of appearing mean-spirited in front of the entire law review staff. This was the kinder, gentler law review, I reminded him. It must have rubbed off on him, too.

Most of the questions delved into the candidates' other commitments for the next year: moot court; classes and credits; externships; outside jobs; management philosophy. A hypothetical question I posed to managing editor candidates asking them how they would handle a staff member "who barges into your office, cursing at you and insulting you because there was a discrepancy between his accounting and your accounting of office hours." This drew laughter from many of the senior editors who understood my allusion.

"I will not be abused," said one candidate with certitude, which also drew laughs.

A 3L, half on his way after three beers, asked the perennial odd-ball question of the candidates for Form and Accuracy editor: which federal court had jurisdiction over the Panama Canal Zone. One candidate, without taking a second to digest the bizarre factoid, responded, "Before or after unification with Panama?" There was instant applause. The answer, which nobody ever knew until after such a quirky question was asked, is Louisiana. Over the years, asking this question became part of the election day tradition.

The senior editors took charge of the event, collecting and counting the ballots and assisting in ad hoc interpretations of the bylaws when minor controversies broke out.

The votes were tallied on scrap paper. Counting them got a bit tedious, especially when people started getting funny. For one position both candidates had the same first name, so someone voted for John—which one we will never know. I even got one vote for a senior board position. On another vote, one of the counters unfolded a ballot paper, revealing "I love Roy" in red pen. Sara denied responsibility, it was not her handwriting anyway. The perpetrator of this obvious joke never stepped forward.

One subtle act I encouraged, yet nobody recognized, was having the sitting editor from our staff go out to the hall to inform the candidates of the winner and bestow the first congratulatory handshake. Last year, the managing editor went out to the hallway for each position. This year, I went out to congratulate the editor in chief. Mike went out for the Managing Editor, Nick went out for the Notes and Comments editor, and so on and so on. It was a nice way to initiate the passing of the torch.

Each newly-elected editor returned to the room to be greeted by applause.

Several people remarked about how gently the event played out. We were relieved that we did not need to hold a supplemental election. Several staff members also stayed after to help clean up the mess and dispose of the numerous beer cans and an empty bottle of Captain Morgan Rum.

Nobody left the room crying this time. They might cry when they figured out what they had ahead of them on law review. A group of the new senior board editors invited Sara and me to join them at a nearby campus bar. We graciously declined the invitation. It was their celebration, not ours.

Sara and I got far away from campus for Chinese food at an authentic restaurant near the airport. A chef from New York City owns this restaurant where there is always a line out the door and a menu with exotic dishes like duck bill casserole.

Our first book was still on the table in the office, not yet sent to Nebraska. But my membership was about to expire and I could see the end was approaching. If all the work did not exist, I could have been a lame duck. Nevertheless, I began to sense how a lame duck president feels. I should have ordered lame duck casserole.

Letting Go
Monday, April 10, 2000

The first book was finally ready to go to the printer. After all the computer troubles, editing roadblocks and management headaches, 50:1 was going to Nebraska. Mike and I pulled a couple of late shifts reading the articles with a fine-tooth comb last week. We laid out the articles on the long office table and repeatedly read them.

I must have screened book 1 articles a dozen times. I read everything several times. The authors read their own edited work at least twice. Mike, as managing editor, George, the form and accuracy editor, and each executive editor read the final proofs. Yet, every time I picked up the 314-page book, I found something new—something wrong.

There was always something, whether it was a supra that did not correspond to a proper footnote number or a misspelled word or an errant citation. A few times I found footnote citations that needed a pin cite. In the medieval article, I was about to collate the pages and nearly dropped them. As my hands caught the falling pages, my eye caught a citation to a law review article that had the Cardozo Law Review spelled "Cardoza." Upon further investigation, I found that the Cardozo article's title was also wrong.

I also found little minor mistakes in my own note. Little things like an extra space, an unabbreviated name in a case name citation. Just little things. The little things make the difference between reliability and the Amateur Hour. I was elected because I presented a confident image that I would catch mistakes. I did catch mistakes, many of them. But I was scared, maybe paranoid, that no matter how many times I read the articles, no matter how many memos I wrote or speeches I gave, there would still be mistakes. Mistakes will happen. But if the law review published mistakes, it was an embarrassment to the law review, and personally myself. As editor in chief, I was the guarantor.

As the editor whose name appears at the top of the masthead and as one of the authors, I had a responsibility. My article was the lead note, chosen by last year's editorial board. My concerns were laced with self-interest and self-less interest. There could be no excuses and only blame. If there was blame to assign, it would come right to me. I could live with that. But I wanted to make sure that I would not have to.

Ted, an involved 2L who assumed some of the responsibilities in the technical editor vacancy, watched me laboring over the copy and said, "Look in last year's book and you will find mistakes. Eventually you have to let go." He was sincere but I would like to come back next year and see if he is as cavalier about mistakes he finds.

I have been known to make my fair share of mistakes. There were numerous occasions when the Plain Dealer's copy editors saved me from minor and major embarrassment. There were times when the Plain Dealer's copy editors were the cause of embarrassment. Errors in the newspaper business are embarrassing, but corrected in the next day's paper. A mistake in the law review will perpetuate for as long as these documents exist or until the article or the law discussed is supplanted by precedent. Or, until human history ceases.

The first book should have been printed in October or November. Here we were in April and it still had not been sent to Nebraska. There could be no more excuses. With a book this late, there could be no mistakes.

I finished up the accompanying paperwork, including the reprint order form, order of pages form and title page. I put the 314 pages into a stationery box, labeled it Syracuse Law Review, 50:1 and placed it into an overnight envelope. It was time to let go.

At the end of the day, I picked at the crunchy noodles when the waiter brought over the wanton soup. Sara sipped the warm tea.

Panda West, a classy Chinese restaurant on Marshall Street, just off the main campus, was one of our regular dining spots. Since we started dating more than two years ago, barely a week had gone by without a stop at the restaurant.

"I think we're going to put the camera-ready copy of the book in the mail tomorrow," I said.

"It's about time," she said.

"Yeah. I think it has to go now."

Our notes would appear as one and two in the notes section.

"If it's not ready by now, you can't worry about it. You're too much of a perfectionist," she said.

"If I was a perfectionist, my life would be significantly different. I just don't want to send the book with typos or mistakes."

"It will be fine. You worry too much."

"I keep catching little things here and there. I'm afraid there are things that I'm missing," I said. "Aren't you worried? I mean, your note is in there. I've read it at least two or three times in the last two weeks."

"I'm not worried. I know that you read it a few times."

"That's what I'm afraid of. I can't catch everything. I mean, when I was a goalie, I got scored on, even if I made a dozen saves in a game. I can't stop everything."

"Well, I'm not scared," she said as the waiter placed two bowls of steaming rice in front of us and our usual dishes of Mala Chicken, a delicious spicy garlic dish and her Chicken Amazing.

Alumni Achievement Award
Thursday, April 20, 2000

Every year, the law review recognized a past law review member with the Alumni Achievement Award. In the past a panel of law review members combed the alumni records and the old law review books to come up with a worthy recipient. This year it was as easy as walking down the hallway.

For months I knew who I wanted to nominate as the recipient, I only wanted the clearance from the one person who might not want the attention, my managing editor, Mike. I wanted to make sure Mike was comfortable with my plan because I wanted to make his dad the Alumni Achievement Award recipient. Mike's dad, now a full-time professor at the law school, recently stepped down from his position as United States Attorney for the Northern District of New York. He served as an editor on law review in the early 1960s and held occasional stints teaching law at our school over the years.

If Mike expressed discomfort with my decision because of the appearance, I would have found someone else. Luckily, he liked the idea.

I drafted a brief letter and brought it down to the mailroom. As I checked the law review mail, I ran into Mike's dad, Professor Maroney, as he checked his mail, too. I had already engaged him to write an article for our 50th anniversary book. I told him that I just put something in his mailbox. "I hope it's not bad news," he said. I assured him that it was not bad news.

I liked the idea of having Professor Maroney as our recipient. Aside from family-connection, which I thought would be a nice way for one of my most-valued law review staff members to honor his father, I liked the idea of honoring one of the few faculty members who was truly loyal to the law school. Professor Maroney was well-known in the region and was influential in attracting Attorney General Janet Reno to speak at commencement two years earlier. He also did not hesitate to volunteer his services to our 50th anniversary book. And on top of all that, he seemed like a really nice guy.

Mike later told me that his dad felt honored and excited about the award. I was touched, too, because this was a man with a public career who received numerous honors and awards.

Caught
Tuesday, April 25, 2000

Our contract with the printer in Nebraska did not include layout and copy editing services. We sent a camera-ready proof, our final version—edited and formatted. The staff at Joe Christensen Inc., the largest printer of legal and scholarly publications in the country, visually scanned what we sent. They went through the book page-by-page checking the folios, page numbers, headings and other layout items. But they did not read it. They made sure the pages lined up and that the page numbers were coordinated. Occasionally, they found little things that we missed. In the fall, I handled several little printing problems for Connor for books 2, 3, and 4 of volume 49.

Our point person in Nebraska, Kristi, called and later faxed me the problems they found, which included an extra space between the footnote number and the footnote text in the Martin article as well as two mistakes in the tables of contents of two articles. The extra space problem required manually deleting the extra spaces in the article and then printing out the fixed pages. There were also two page 192 because the printer ran out of paper and as such ended up reprinting the page when new paper was added.

When I sent back the revisions, I thanked Kristi for her "attentive eye." I frequently talked with Kristi and she always had the information I needed. I tacked a company promotional brochure with her photo to my bulletin board. I figured if I was going to talk with her several times a month, I should at least know what she looked like. I should have sent her my photo for her bulletin board.

The Banquet—50 Years and Beyond
Saturday, April 29, 2000

This was going to be the big 50th Anniversary Law Review banquet. The banquet was an annual event, but this year it was supposed to be a big deal. We printed fancy invitations through the university printing office and sent out more than 1,500 to all the law review alumni. The law review and the law school administration pitched the event as the big celebration. Over the course of the year, every time I interacted with a law review alumnus, I promoted the banquet. Information about the anniversary banquet was distributed to alumni as far back as September and the law review website had information about it. Every faculty member received a personal invitation, too.

The posters came in a couple days earlier. The event program, on fancy bond-paper, was printed up and ready. The banquet center, partially owned by the university, had handled everything quite well. The law review's budget had $2,500 earmarked specifically for the banquet, but the Dean's office frequently covered additional costs.

The two staff members who coordinated the menu planning with the banquet staff had done their jobs. There were three choices for the entry: London broil, chicken and vegetarian. I never figured out what the vegetarian meal was.

There was a lot of planning for this event. For the first time in a while, my nerves actually caught up with me. By today, we had about 130 people signed up and paid for, including law review staff, family, alumni and faculty. This was between 30 to 40 people more than the year before. Connor, my predecessor, drove up from Virginia. He brought another editor with him. Connor's predecessor, June, drove up from New York City. A couple of other alumni from New York made it as well as a handful of locals from the Syracuse region. I even talked Elaine, my favorite secretary in the Dean's office, into attending. This would be her first law school event, she told me.

Up until about two days ago, we even had an editor from Volume 1 committed to attend. When we spoke on the telephone, he said he was excited about driving up from New Jersey. He agreed to speak at the banquet about the founding. But two days ago, he called to say that he sick with shingles, and unable to attend.

When planning began, we envisioned an event with more than 200, possibly 300 guests. Unfortunately, we sent the invitations a little too late, giving people slightly more than three weeks official notice. Despite all the information disseminated all year, the invitations were the only things people considered.

I purchased six fancy pens at the university bookstore to present to several editors as a token of my appreciation. I had the gift for the Alumni Achievement Award recipient, a brass business card holder bearing university crest. I had to make a quick run this morning to a trophy store to have it engraved. The engraver decided to do it on a plate that would stick to the holder. The engraving was clear: "Syracuse Law Review, Alumni Achievement Award, 2000." It took about an hour and the engraver spelled it "Revue." I was relieved that he only did it on a plate. He would have ruined the entire thing if it was done to the holder itself. He redid it correctly.

The party began at 6 p.m. with an hour-long open bar. Sara and I arrived at about 5 p.m. to set up the greeting table, where we had the posters on display, the sign-in sheet and a handful of law review coffee and beer mugs available for purchase. I was anxious and wanted to make sure that the banquet center had everything properly set up. The banquet center coordinator, Adele, a nice elderly woman, grabbed me by the shoulder and said, "Don't worry, we have taken care of everything." She was right, they took care of everything, but she did not have to give two speeches.

I stood at the sign-in table greeting the guests and handed out the banquet programs titled "50 Years and Beyond." I was nervous. My parents came up for the event. I figured that they suffered through the last three years of the miseries of my law school experience, they might as well witness the only decent thing that I experienced. They chatted with Sara while I had to greet the guests.

As the emcee, I gave two speeches and introduced the other speakers. One speech, I titled "Introduction" and the other was my "Reflections" speech.

Once everyone took their seats, I began my introduction. I was nervous, but I was ready. I could perform. I stood at the lectern, gripping the side with my right hand and proceeded:

We are here tonight for two reasons, to celebrate the Law Review's 50th anniversary by looking back and to step forward to honor the new staff.

In 1949, a group of roughly 30 students executed plans that had been envisioned and discussed for years. It was part honor society, part student group, part scholarly journal. It was the Syracuse Law Review.

Those first editors published this book without the luxuries of computers, Lexis or Westlaw or even an office. Those first editors gathered wherever they could in that dank building at 400 Montgomery Street—across from the courthouse. They met, edited and published the first book from rickety tables in the· library and student lounge. Those first editors, with whom I have had the pleasure of speaking this year, downplay their roles in establishing a legacy.

Both Mr. Asher Bogin and Prof. Martin Fogelman, who were two of the first editors in 1949-50, told me that this publication was not born from a moment of clarity or divine inspiration—they claim, that they were just trying to keep up. A solid law school, they said, needed a visible law review.

They were right. And they took that bold step.

Publishing a law review, even with today's technological amenities is no easy task—imagine what it must have been like without an office from which to Sheparadize cases using books while writing and editing with typewriters. I shudder at the thought.

But over the past 50 years, the Law Review has changed, much like the legal landscape the we chronicle and question. In 1960, the Law Review became a quarterly publication. In 1984, the editors introduced computer technology to the publishing process. Anyone who has worked on the computers in the office this year might think that we are using the same computers. We're not. Several years ago, we established a presence on the Internet with our website.

Over the years, the articles, like the legal world itself have grown more and more complex. Our Survey of New York law has grown to 20 articles on everything from administrative to zoning law.

For this anniversary, we also reached out to the same group of people who faithfully published this review—our alumni. Some in this room wrote articles for our 50th anniversary book. Some lent their moral support and some joined us here tonight to look back over the past 50 years and beyond to the next. Thank you for coming

I introduced the Dean who gave a nice introduction about the importance of the law review to the law school. He recited a quote from the dean's foreword in the first volume and thanked everyone for coming. It was similar to his speech a year ago.

Then we had dinner. I was a little too nervous to eat my entire meal. I glanced at Mike who was taking a final look at his speech while his dad jotted a couple of last minute notes on his speech. As desert followed, I introduced Nick, the notes and comments editor, who announced the winning notes. Then, I introduced the Alumni Achievement Award, and Mike, who personally introduced his father. It was a touching moment, as Mike spoke about his dad's achievements and all the honors he accumulated over his very public career.

Professor Maroney delivered a hilarious speech touching on everything from his law review note on the death of a pet dog that was transported in an airplane, to his personal and familial devotion to Syracuse University. He estimated that between all the members of his family, they had accumulated more than two dozen degrees from Syracuse University.

"We may buy in bulk from Syracuse, but we are quite fond and proud of Syracuse," he said. He also commented on an anecdote I conveyed to him months earlier about a conversation I had with one of his classmates who made a derisive comment about the Syracuse Law Review. "This is the only law publication I've ever written for, and I am very proud of that," he said.

So was I.

It was no easy task following such an inspired and polished speech. After Professor Maroney returned to his seat at our table, I had to recall him to the lectern to collect our gift to him.

Then, I delivered my "Reflections" speech:

> Over the course of this year, we discussed some pretty weighty issues in the law review office: whether a period following an id is italicized, property rights associated with

certain types of animal abuse and the likelihood of getting Coca Cola to buy an ad in the back of the book.

Between all of the challenging legal debates, we met the daily challenge of balancing numerous tasks; sometimes the office felt like a three-ring circus. Nevertheless, we gathered the articles, edited them and sent them to Nebraska—to our publisher. At least we did that with book one. There were bumps, impediments and daily frustration. But the staff was dedicated. There was a lot of energy in the office this year. There was also a lot of energy expended on our behalf outside of room 414.

I specifically named and thanked close to a dozen law school staff and administrators who made our job of publishing a lot smoother. Then, I switched gears and thanked the dedicated staff, naming each senior editor by name and describing a little about what they did:

But, equally without the dedicated staff of second and third year law students, their efforts would be in vain. Law review is an honor, privilege and a burden. Our responsibilities encroach on many aspects of our lives and studies. Law Review is one of the few places where the reward for academic success is more work. And it is a lot of work. But it is visible, valuable and rewarding. We represent the school and serve the legal community—it is quite an honor.

For the senior board, the work spans more than a year. From spring through summer and fall and winter.

This year went very quickly. The work was difficult. But I would not trade the experience of working with all of you for anything. Believe it or not, I enjoy reading and editing these articles. It was an honor to work with you and represent the law review.

As we stand here tonight, looking backward to the past and the origins of this publication, we adopt a similar outlook of the law review and look forward. The first step in going forward is handing over the office. Our successors are worthy and competent. I am certain that we are handing the law review over to safe hands in Betty and her staff.

I knew Betty would be good for the job when her team was stuck in a footnote formatting problem for about two weeks.

Nobody could figure out how to fix it until she stepped up and fixed it. That was just the first problem you got to solve on Law Review, I promise there will be many opportunities to resolve problems in the coming year. But with this incoming staff, the problems, should be few and far between.

Blah, blah, blah. I was enjoying the public speaking. I could not believe that I really publicly said some of this stuff, and that a room full of people actually listened, occasionally laughed and applauded. Without Cody in the audience—he attended a family event out of town, and regretted missing the banquet—the laugh-track was subdued. A couple of people even took photographs while I stood at the lectern. It was nice.

After Betty gave her speech, I was all ready to wrap up the event. As I was about to stand and return to the dais, Mike motioned to me to wait. Unbeknownst to me, Mike had prepared a few words about me.

"A lot of people were recognized tonight. But there is one more person who needs to be recognized and thanked tonight ... before this year, I really did not know Roy at all. I have had the opportunity to work closely with Roy this year. A lot of people know he is always in the office but a lot of people do not know how much Roy does for the law review. There is nobody who works harder for the law review than Roy ...."

Mike's unexpected speech reduced my mom to tears and generated a nice round of applause. I stood half-way up and waved. Then, I returned to the lectern to thank Mike for the kind and unexpected words and thanked everyone for coming.

Afterward, I straightened out the bill with Adele. I found pearl necklace on the floor and searched the room for its owner. I had a hunch that it fell off one of our local attorney alumni guests, and was right.

As I gathered the extra posters and the mugs, I realized that someone had walked off with two of the glass beer mugs. Figures. But at least we had extra posters, probably more than 900. Enough for the next 50 years, and possibly beyond.

DEFCON 4
Tuesday, May 2, 2000

The plagiarism incident had most of the staff on high alert, if not on pins and needles. The team working on the insurance law article for the

Survey noticed that many passages in the text of the article resembled the actual verbiage of the headnotes found in Westlaw. Westlaw headnotes, summaries of the case and sections of the case, are copyrighted property of Westlaw. The headnotes are written by the editors employed by Westlaw. Headnotes offer no precedential value for citations, but help the reader get to the point of the case before wading through the entire judicial opinion. Often, the language in the headnotes can be found within the case. Sometimes the language in the headnotes is not taken verbatim from the case.

After spending several hours reviewing the allegations made by the editors working on the article, I was not comfortable with the draft the authors provided. There were numerous passages that were taken verbatim from the headnotes. The bulk of these examples were headnotes that had the same language as the case itself.

Additionally, the article lacked many pin cites and did not have parallel citations. The most troubling aspect of this article, however, was the liberal mimicry of the headnotes. This was so, even though the authors submitted the article about six months late. Maybe that was why, because it was late.

I called the authors, Carolyn and Ned, lawyers at a large New York City law firm. They were appalled and shocked when I leveled the allegation. They acted as if I had personally insulted them. They immediately took a defensive tone and the conversation got icier and icier as we progressed.

"I am flummoxed. I cannot believe this. I am totally shocked," Carolyn said.

"We have some editors who are a little sensitive about this sort of thing because we had an editor expelled for plagiarism," I said.

"We didn't plagiarize anything," she said.

"Yeah," said Ned.

"I did not accuse you of plagiarizing. I am just telling you that significant portions of your article are similar to headnotes. I think this is probably more of a case of cutting corners," I said. "Headnotes are not cases, they are copyrighted."

They promised to drop everything they were working on to review their article. They told me that they had a part-time lawyer working on the article. My suspicion was their part-timer cut the corners and they never double checked. In their defense, many of the judicial opinions they cited were only one or two pages long.

"When this is done, I want you to write a letter of apology," she said.

"What? All I want is the article fixed. I'm not reporting you to any ethics committee or anything if that's what you're worried about. I have nothing to apologize for," I said.

"I want it for my records," she said.

"Yeah," Ned said.

"I want a clean article as quickly as possible. This is what happens when deadlines are ignored," I responded.

Arrival
Wednesday, May 3, 2000

There was a small box, waiting for me today in the support services mailroom.

The box was about 11 inches by 8 inches by 12 inches deep. The light blue return address label was from Joe Christensen, Lincoln, Nebraska.

"Woah, this is small but heavy," said Robert, the director of support services, as he handed me the box with a smile.

"This is our first book," I said.

"Congratulations."

I thanked him, told him he can expect a couple of large boxes in the next couple days and returned to the office. I slit open the box with a small pocket knife I keep on my key chain and pulled out the book. The familiar navy blue cover and orange outline looked just like all the other books from the past four years, except this was volume 50. My name was right on the front with the lead note. The book arrived.

I placed one at Mike's desk and two in the business office/articles editors office. I placed one in the middle of the table on a typists easel. I quickly flipped through it. I had read it so many times before, I did not need to read it again. Back to work.

Everyone picked up the book and flipped through it.

Ted, a 2L recently elected to a senior position, picked it up, sat back in a chair and went through with boyish enthusiasm. With his military background, Ted was normally reserved. His reaction took me by surprise me because he rarely expressed excitement. But as he cradled the book in his hands, he said, "Are you psyched? This is awesome. This is your book. You did this."

"Yeah, it's my book and any mistakes anyone finds, they're all mine, too," I answered.

"Well, I think this is really cool," he said. "Take a break and enjoy it for a minute."

Another 2L who was elected to a senior position approached me after seeing the book and said, "How cool is it to see your name on that cover. You must really be excited."

"I have seen my name on the front page of newspapers. I can temper the excitement," I said.

In fact the arrival of this book, while exciting on its face, was difficult to enjoy. This was one of my chronic problems: an inability to fully appreciate a moment. I was either too preoccupied with the disappointing past or the uncertain future. Sara frequently reminded me of this character flaw.

The law review still had too much unfinished business with the Survey and the third and fourth books. It was difficult to sit back and relish the moment knowing the imminent headaches. Finals were barely a couple of weeks away and I had a lot of catching up to do. Those were just the short-term diversions.

As rewarding as it was to have the first book completed, published and in our hands, there were too many other distractions. I felt like the relish had to be on hold until after book 4 came back from Nebraska. That would be months away.

R. S.V. Peed off
Friday, May 19, 2000

Nearly 1,500 invitations went out for the banquet. Among the responses we received were a $75 donation, a $50 donation and about a dozen subscriptions. Along with the traditional information on the RSVP card such as choice of chicken, beef or vegetarian, I included two boxes for subscriptions: one for all four books and one for the Survey only.

A handful of alumni sent back the self-addressed RSVP envelope with a note of apology for not being able to attend. By the time we got to sending out the invitations in early April, I knew we might have been pushing it a little too close.

But Mr. Gold of Maryland, was another story. He actually took the time to scrawl a nasty note on the card accusing the law review of intentionally sending late invitations in "another typical scheme to raise funds." "You should be ashamed. This is yet another example of the disappointing way you treat alumni," he wrote.

There was obvious anger in his handwriting. The letters and words were scrawled and there were marks showing that he pressed hard when he wrote, as though he was in an all-out rage. I was offended. I felt bad enough that circumstances prevented us from mailing the invitations earlier. But one school administrator reassured me that if we sent the invitations out too early, people would have complained about that, too.

I drafted a brief letter to Mr. Gold and put it in an envelope with one of the hundreds of extra posters:

> Thank you for your note in response to our invitation to the Law Review's 50th anniversary banquet held last month. I, too, share your anxiety over receiving the invitation on short notice. I regret our inability to get the invitations in the mail earlier. However, notice of the banquet had been publicized in at least two prior law school mailings as well as on our website.
>
> Unfortunately, the Law Review editors are students. Aside from our normal responsibilities as students, some of us are charged with the sometimes insurmountable duties associated with publishing a book. Thus, full-time banquet planning was not really an option.
>
> Additionally, I would like to reiterate that the Law Review editors are students. I am offended by your implication that the Law Review editors are complicit in a university fundraising scheme. I attended Syracuse University as an undergraduate and returned for law school. I empathize with you over your concerns about fundraising. But I assure you that the motive for the invitation and the banquet was not a ruse but an attempt to commemorate a respectable milestone in the Syracuse Law Review's history.
>
> Enclosed is the commemorative poster that we designed and printed for the occasion. It is free.

DEFCON 1
Friday, May 19, 2000

Our insurance authors returned a revised copy of their heavily-scrutinized article. They gleefully called me a couple days earlier. "We went through our article footnote-by-footnote and are happy to report to you that we are confident that we did not plagiarize anything. You were wrong. You and your editors were over-sensitive about all that," Carolyn said. Ned, also on the phone via conference call, said, "Yes."

"I am glad that you are confident that your article is clean," I said. "This is what the editing process is all about."

"I want your letter apologizing to me immediately," she said.

Fine. I wrote a direct letter thanking them for their "prompt attention." I went on:

> I understand your concerns and appreciate all of your extra work. I agree that we may have been overly sensitive. But I would always prefer to exercise caution and employ additional scrutiny to ensure the integrity and accuracy of our articles. I am equally pleased that your additional review found no problems.

I was not convinced that they were genuine with their findings. They may have felt vindicated, which pleased me. But I did not appreciate their tone, especially because time was running short. It was obvious that they cut corners in their writing. Legal writers often paraphrase judicial opinions. Paraphrasing by using practically identical words and then dropping a footnote at the end of the sentence, almost exclusively throughout the piece, is not good writing. Many writers are often confounded because the original wording is frequently regarded as the best way to say something, rather than rewriting it. Nevertheless, there are ways to maintain the integrity of both a proposition and a piece of writing referring to it. Unfortunately, Carolyn and Ned were not aware of that.

I was pleased that we had a new team of authors ready to contract with for next year's Survey.

Honors Convocation
Saturday, May 20, 2000

The festivities for graduation weekend would begin this morning. The Honors Convocation was at 1 p.m. at Hendricks Chapel, the landmark in the center of the quad, an ivy-covered octagonal building with a silver dome.

The awards ceremony preceded graduation by a day and was followed by a cocktail and buffet on the patio at the law school. This was the ceremony where the milestones from the past three years were rewarded: high grades in classes; special scholarships; student club membership; moot court and law review membership.

Except for naming the valedictorian and salutatorian, the bulk of the honors bestowed today would be artificial feel-good awards. Certificates with a university seal to hang on the wall next to a diploma.

I spent the morning in the office formatting the Survey articles and checking footnotes. My parents met me at the office when they arrived, then we strolled over to Hendricks for the awards. I was so disgusted with the way my law school experience was winding down that I almost urged my folks not to attend graduation. I was one step away from boycotting the event.   My future employment situation, or lack of employment situation, was weighing heavily and there was no support from the institution.   It was impossible to get excited about a meaningless ceremony when the bar exam loomed. All this ceremony meant was that I, and the 200-plus other graduates, paid tuition for three years. The degree was virtually meaningless unless and until you pass the bar exam.

On top of all that, I could see what the summer portended: all the work that should have been done all year had to be done now. There was a lot of it, too.

It was like staring into a black hole and I had to put on a nice smile to attend an awards ceremony.

I knew ahead of time that I would receive two awards: one for holding the senior position on law review and the other for having my note published. I had to provide a list of recipients to the alumni and development office. I also named the recipients of the Law Review Editor's Award. In the past, that award was given to the associate notes and comments editors and anyone else the editor-in-chief designated. I chose to award a large group of 3L staff members who worked on the 50th Anniversary project. A few of the recipients were even appreciative. That could have also been the crowning moment on my authority as editor; to be able to tell the law school who to give certificates to. What power.

The administration worked hard to keep the ceremony to one hour. I was thankful for that. There were probably about 100 awards handed out. One law school office administrator who was partially responsible for the awards lamented to me a couple days earlier, "If you sneeze around here, they give you an award." There were even two people receiving awards who I never saw before that day, yet they were in my class.

I got to go on stage twice and shake hands with a couple of professors. Perhaps that would be my crowning moment in my legal career and I did not even know it. I just could not care less.

I wanted to return to the office to do some more work but joined my parents at their hotel and then took my folks with Sara's family to dinner in Skaneateles, a quaint town on a picturesque lake. As dejected as I felt, I guess I could not be rude to my family and hers.

Graduation Day
Sunday, May 21, 2000

I decided not to go to the office today. As the editor, I was invited to a brunch at the Hotel Syracuse with the law school faculty, the dean, the graduation speaker, other dignitaries and a handful of student leaders. I was allowed up to two guests and took Sara instead of my parents. It never occurred to me to take anyone other than Sara.

This event did not spark tremendous excitement either. But I would accept any opportunity to meet someone even moderately important like our commencement speaker, an alumnus who sits as a judge on the Third Circuit Court of Appeals.

There was nothing on the buffet menu that appealed to me, hashbrowns, cantaloupe, and some kind of melted-cheese bread. I could not even get a Coke. I picked at some grapes and strawberries. We sat with another law review editor and her mother, and were joined by a couple of professors. I was sandwiched between a professor and Sara. This professor sitting next to me spent about 15 minutes talking with Sara, right over me. He was one of a handful of lecherous professors who rarely engaged a male student in a conversation but would not shut up when he was in the presence of a cute young woman. I had nothing to say to this guy anyway.

By the time the brunch was completed, it was time to walk over to the downtown theater which served as the situs of the perfunctory ceremony. I waited for Sara to emerge from the ladies' room when the Dean and the judge walked past me. I greeted the Dean and hoped he would introduce me. They both walked right by me.

I never met the speaker. I had nothing to say to this guy either, I guess.

The graduation ceremony was nothing special. The speeches by the administrators and the student leaders were uninspired. The keynote speaker, the judge, admitted that nobody would likely remember his speech. Admitting defeat is hardly a way to grab attention. The substance of his speech focused on the extrinsic political forces facing federal judges. He credited a professor at another law school for scrounging up the examples. There was enough substance for me to agree to publish the speech in one of our books.

Graduation ceremonies always amused me because the people who get on stage and usually make the biggest spectacle of themselves are often the ones who accomplished the least in school. The people who get the biggest cheers, are also frequently not that special either. I was eager to graduate and get on with my life, and I did not necessarily need to wear a goofy robe to do that.

The Call
Wednesday, June 21, 2000

The bar exam was slightly more than a month away. Sara and I had a tight daily routine: mornings in the three-to-four hour BarBri lectures; lunch for about an hour-and –a-half, usually with Cody; four to six hours in the library; one hour for dinner and another hour or two back in the library.

During the roughly two months of bar preparation, my only time in the law review office was each morning from 8:20 to about 8:59 and about 10 to 15 minutes before lunch. I checked the mail, the voice mail and email. I made sure the small contingent of 2L volunteers had work and that everything would be on schedule so I could fast-track everything when the exam was done. The minor administrative tasks were just that, minor. I did not intend to sacrifice my bar exam for the good of the law review. As it was, the exam would be hard enough.

When I cleared off the office voicemail this morning, there was a mysterious call from the Dean's office. I waded through the usual batch of hang-ups and subscription problems and called back the Dean's office. One of the secretaries wanted to know my mailing address. I asked whether she meant my permanent mailing address, for such eagerly-anticipated (and inevitable) mailings as alumni fundraisers. She said the Dean's office wanted my local mailing address. I thought this was peculiar because it was in the law school's records, the campus directory and the local White Pages. I gave her my address and gave it no further consideration.

When I returned home that night at around 8:30, there was an equally cryptic message on my answering machine, a British-sounding gentleman calling from Long Island who identified himself as a volunteer from the William C. Burton Foundation, congratulating me for my winning entry in the competition. "It is urgent that you call me back as soon as you get this message," he said to my answering machine.

I was intrigued and immediately returned the phone call.

"Thank you for calling me back. You are a difficult person to reach. I have been trying to reach you for five days," Mr. Drukker said as classical music played in the background on his end.

"I've been in the library studying, I have a little exam to take next month," I said.

"Congratulations, you are a winner of the William C. Burton Award for Legal Achievement. We hope that you can attend the awards ceremony in Washington, D.C. on July 12," he said.

In the midst of studying for the bar exam, the last thing I expected at this point was to win an award. I knew that the Dean had submitted my law review article, as the lead note, but that was way back in January. I had completely forgotten about the competition.

Mr. Drukker told me that he had sent a letter to the Dean's office the week before informing the school of the award. He proceeded to give me all the relevant information including the overnight accommodations at the Hotel Washington, the $250 travel stipend and the time and location of the banquet dinner: cocktails at 6 p.m., dinner at 7 p.m. at the National Press Club. I could even bring a guest, he told me, but the guest would have to pay the $1,000 a plate fee. "That is a tax-deductible donation, of course," he reassured me.

I graciously thanked him and told him that I hoped I could make it even though I would be in the final stages of the bar preparation at that point. He said that he would mark me down, and if my plans changed, to call and cancel.

"There are 10 law school recipients, would you like to hear about the others?" he said.

"Sure."

He recited a list of law schools: Stanford, William & Mary, Duke, Emory, Vanderbilt, Fordham, Iowa, Valparaiso, University of Arkansas, and me, Syracuse.

Just out of curiosity, I inquired about the winner from Stanford because a week before my mom read me a wedding announcement for a girl who lived around the corner from me who went to Stanford. This girl's mother was a professional writer who taught an after-school creative writing class at my elementary school more than 20 years ago. I was in that class, which, upon reflection, was probably my first real writing experience. She won, too. Small world. Eventually, all roads lead to Scotch Plains, New Jersey.

Winning this award was an honor. Getting excited about it when the bar exam loomed was another story.

Official Notification
Thursday, June 22, 2000

A nice letter came from the Dean in the next day's mail: "Dear Roy, I learned recently that you were one of 10 law students in the country to be selected for the Burton Award for Legal Achievement. Congratulations and best wishes for future successes." Sincerely, the Dean." What a truly proud moment. Finally, the Dean's affirmation.

The Dean also enclosed a photocopy of the award, an impressive glass prism and a copy of the June 13 letter from William C. Burton informing the school of the award. Interestingly, the school knew about this for about five days, even before I learned about it.

The letter from Mr. Burton to the Dean explained that I was one of 10 students from entries from the 181 accredited law schools from across the country, "In the meantime, I wanted to convey the good news to you, and let you announce the decision."

Everything about this was gracious. I was the only person harboring any kind of circumspect curiosity, which I mostly reserved for myself and my parents. My folks were ecstatic, probably more excited about it than I was. When I relayed the news to them, I openly questioned the value of this honor, I mean, it would not help me pass the bar exam.

Then, they put the award into real perspective. They were both on the telephone and they were tag-teaming me with the information.

My mom: "Think about how many law review notes are written each year."

My dad: "With 181 law schools and everyone with a law review. How many notes are published by each law review four or five?"

Me: "Yeah, and that does not include the internal competitions to get the notes published."

My mom: "So, you're talking about more than 1,000 student notes."

Me: "Yeah, and every law school has more than one journal, so it's really like a few thousand. [veiled sarcasm].

My dad: "This is so great. I'm so proud of you."

Me: "Thanks, I am sure this will change my life. [blatant sarcasm].

In reality, yes, winning the Burton Award was a wonderful honor. If you actually play with the numbers there are anywhere from 800 to 2,500 student-written law review articles published each year. There are close to 500 law reviews and specialized law journals published across the country.[59] Many law reviews publish four to eight student articles each year, which are generally the result of an internal competition. Almost every student-run journal requires its members to write at least one article. Some journals require a writing assignment during the second-year of law school as well as the third year in order to maintain law review standing.

In the old days at Syracuse, second year staff members would write at least one "Recent Decision," a brief synopsis of a recent judicial opinion. During the third year, the staff members would write a Note, the student's analogue to a law review article. Some journals also require a Comment, which is more analytical than a note. Others publish essays and book reviews.

To be one of 10 out of all the thousands of student-written notes, comments and articles published sounds a hell of a lot more impressive than it may really be. At any rate, I was proud that my note was published as the lead note in the Syracuse Law Review, it really made that 24-hour all-nighter stretch at the end worth it.

Besides my folks, the only other person I told was Sara. I really wanted to stay focused on the bar exam.

---

[59] George & Guthrie, 26 Fla. St. U. L. Rev. at 821-22 (authors calculated that there are 330 specialized law journals annually published).

Word on the Street
Thursday, June 22, 2000

The Dean's office sent out a system-wide email to faculty, administrators and staff announcing the award. I got an email from a professor who I did not even think knew me, much less liked me, especially after a huge argument after class during my second year over an extra credit assignment. He offered congratulations, calling the award "a signal honor."

As I turned a corner in the hallway, I ran into Chris, from the law school's liaison office, who had seemingly ignored me for three years, except when I went into her office. "Congratulations, this is great, are you psyched?"

I shrugged my shoulders and grunted. "It won't help me pass the bar exam and I still don't have a job. This isn't the first award I've won," I said, trying to seem cool and nonchalant.

Whenever I interacted with Chris I tried to appear like nothing affected me—never let them see you sweat. She had written me off two-and-a-half years earlier after a disastrous first semester grades. Because I was not in the top 10 percent of the class there was either nothing she wanted to do, or could do for me. Writing onto the law review, doing good work and navigating the system to rise to the top really seemed of little value to her or anyone else in the legal community. My Scarlet Letter had made me *persona non grata* to her and anyone else who mattered.

The sad thing is, I liked Chris a whole lot. She told me she liked me, too. She frequently asked me to bring her short stories I had written years before. After she read my story about my grandmother which won a cash award a year earlier, she told me, "I was reading that on a plane and it made me cry. I couldn't believe it. I never read anything that jars me like that."

Despite her praises and honesty, I never quite received the same kind of service that others around the law school got from the administration. Besides those in the top 10 percent of the class, a handful of sycophants also received pretty good service from administrators like Chris. There were no calls on my behalf to well-established alumni, nobody aggressively pushing my resume to a law firm's hiring partner. The best I got was a call to that Utica judge's term clerk who hated Syracuse students.

1-800 High Airfare
Thursday, June 29, 2000

Syracuse's Hancock Airport does not experience the kind of high-volume air traffic that would allow airlines to keep fares affordable. In fact, airfare out of Syracuse is among the highest in the country. I spent about an hour on the phone inquiring about reasonable fares from Syracuse to D.C. The best I could get was $740. It was obvious that the lawyers in the Justice Department's antitrust division flew on government planes, or flew on government travel vouchers—maybe they just drove everywhere.

The Burton Foundation would defray $250. My folks told me that they would cover the costs if I needed them to. I figured I would see if the school would help me out as well. I wrote the Dean a brief memo outlining the finances, requesting assistance on this mission. I wrote that I was "eager to represent the College of Law at this prestigious event" and explained that I did not have the time to drive to Washington because of the bar exam.

The College of Law regularly paid for student trips to moot court competitions. In fact, every year, the school sent a team of about four or five students to Vienna, Austria, for an international moot court competition, which to the best of my knowledge they never won. Also, another team of up to 10 students traveled to Toronto for a similar competition every Spring. Then, there were the other moot court competitions all over the country in places like Florida in late November or Seattle. All I was asking for was enough to defray an airplane ticket and taxi service, at tops no more than $550. The Foundation covered hotel accommodations, dinner at the banquet and the continental breakfast the next morning at the hotel. Therefore, no meals would need to be expensed.

I never really knew what to expect from the administration at the law school, even though I got everything I needed for the law review. The law review needed a new *Black's Law Dictionary*, the seventh edition. I asked for them. We got them. New *Bluebooks*. I asked for them. We got them. New dictionaries. We got it. Expensive banquet invitations. We got them. Approval for special commemorative posters. We got them.

The law review got all the support that it needed all year from the administration. I must give credit where credit was due. But this request was not for the benefit of the law review as an organization, it was really just for me. I never really sought anything for myself. Not that there was really anything to get. I always tried to be cognizant of using my position for personal benefit. Really, the only thing that I wanted for personal benefit anyway, was a job. Likewise, I always tried to attend law school events. It looked good for the law school if the editor-in-chief of the law review attended an event like the first-year orientation barbecue or the library candidate selection meetings or the big speaker events. When the Chairman of the FCC came to the law school, I was invited to attend a luncheon with him. But that was cancelled because he had to meet with President Clinton.

With the airfare, I was bracing for fight that never came. The budget office called me this afternoon and left a message on the voicemail that the Dean approved my travel request. All I had to do was submit receipts after the trip. I was relieved that I did not have to argue with anyone over this.

Capital Gang
Wednesday, July 12, 2000

BarBri's lecture for the last day of the course was domestic relations. I never took a family law class in law school because I never planned on doing anything in the family law arena. Domestic Relations was one of the 17 topics that the bar examiners could test on, and I really did not know anything about it other than New York is not a community property state and any decision involving child custody must be made in the best interest of the child.

That was pretty much the gist of three hours of family law, minus the tangential rants of the lecturer who used an entire body of law as one big stand-up routine. There is not really too much you can lecture on jacktitation of marriage, other than it sounds like a funny word and it is no longer a legitimate cause of action.[60] I attended the first hour of the lecture and departed for the airport after the first break.

I engaged in a self-imposed embargo on disseminating information about the award. Sara had finally let the cat out of the bag to Cody one

---

[60] This antiquated cause of action means boasting of a false marriage. This tort was believed to damage or defame a reputation, and traces its roots to English ecclesiastical law. BLACK'S LAW DICTIONARY 834 (Sixth ed. 1991).

day at lunch while I bought ice cream pops for us. "That is awesome and great 'props' for the school," he said.

Enough passengers fluttered around the gate to make it nearly impossible for me to study my note cards and outlines at the airport. The flight was quick, no more than 90 minutes. Washington in July was hot. It waš a lot hotter and more humid than Syracuse. Check in at the Hotel Washington was not until 3 p.m.

I strolled around the White House where I saw a crazy lady being arrested after she refused to leave the fenced-in area around a sentry booth at one of the east gates. I watched, along with a group of bloated lady tourists, as police interrogated the crazy lady. I cracked them up when I said out-loud, "I am sure that on her planet she's acting rationally."

As I basked in the sun in Lafayette Park, sweating through my shirt, I downed a hot dog. At 2:50, I returned to the hotel to check in. Upon checking in, I was handed a shopping bag with Burton Awards programs, an envelope with the stipend and a canister of chocolate-covered pretzels. I went to my room and took a nap.

I had a 4 p.m. informal reunion with a former Plain Dealer Lake County Bureau colleague, Steve, who was now bureau chief of the PD's Washington operation. My interaction with the PD's Washington bureau was limited when I was a reporter. The only time I dealt with the big bureau was when some piece of legislation made it through from the local congressman or federal funds were awarded to county projects. There were years when I had more bylines than half the reporters in the Washington bureau. Things were different at the PD now—new management had an aggressive outlook. And, it was a different story with Steve; he was a real reporter and a genuine nice guy. I spoke with him a few days before to see if he would be free. We were going to have a drink, but some news broke. The managing editor had also been fired earlier in the afternoon. There was no time to socialize outside the office.

It was nice to talk about news and the PD. Steve was getting ready to go to Philadelphia for the Republican National Convention and then to LA for the Democratic National Convention—a long way from Painesville, Ohio, where he covered the county courts when I first moved to the bureau.

Steve was the first person I saw when I handed in my letter of resignation about three years and one month earlier. Only four of my closest friends at the PD had any knowledge of my law school plans (I did not want management, or my boss to find out too early and assign me to cover nighttime obituaries for my last months in Cleveland). Steve, whose wife was a non-practicing lawyer, had a cup of coffee with me in the cafeteria the day I turned in my letter of resignation. When I spilled the beans, he said, "That's great. You wouldn't be the first reporter to go to law school."

I found my way up to National Press Club for the cocktail hour, checked in and got my name tag. The woman checking off names asked my affiliation, "Are you with a law firm? Or are you an award recipient?" She gave me my name tag. As I struggled to clip my tag onto my lapel, a woman stopped me and greeted me. Her son was also a recipient and she recognized me from my picture in the awards program. She was very friendly, and as it turned out, also from New Jersey. Not from Scotch Plains, though. Later, her son was introduced to me during the cocktail hour. Nice guy, pretty confident sounding. He should be. He was the editor-in-chief of his law review, summer associate at one of the top law firms in the country and soon to be clerk for a federal judge.

All of the winners had impressive credentials and wonderful jobs ahead of them. One girl was clerking for the Court of Appeals for the Washington, D.C., circuit before taking her clerkship with Justice Sandra Day O'Connor. One guy was clerking for the 11th Circuit Court of Appeals. Another was clerking for another circuit court. One woman was even clerking for the federal judge who presided over all of the President Clinton/Paula Jones shenanigans in Arkansas.

Then, there was me. It was almost embarrassing and humorous at the same time. Here I was surrounded by all these impressive law students with great jobs from great schools with great futures ahead of them. And, I could not seem to get anywhere with any decent law firm, much less a federal judge. Unfortunately, I could not put "job interview with federal judges and New Jersey Supreme Court justice" on my resume. It was beginning to seem as though my job search had become somewhat of a personal joke on top of a tremendous disappointment.

I mingled with a few people and met William C. Burton, the founder of the foundation and namesake for the award. He was tremendously amiable, polite and classy. "I was so thrilled that someone from Syracuse won. I love Syracuse. I did not go there but I have relatives who did," he told me, adding that he had season's tickets to Syracuse football games. I thanked him and told him that I truly appreciated this honor.

Mr. Burton, a New York City lawyer with a firm that specializes in insurance matters, wrote *Burton's Legal Thesaurus*. He created his award in an effort to recognize and improve writing in the legal profession. He contacted the American Lawyer Top 100 law firms for support and article submissions, raised more than $75,000 and composed a panel of judges including a Harvard law professor, a judge and an expert on legal writing who is a descendant of Noah Webster.[61]

He and the foundation were featured in a front page article in the *National Law Journal*.[62]   The online version listed all the winning articles. The law journal article was objective and addressed the overall topic of legal writing including lawyers' desire, but inability, to adhere to plain language.[63]

Lawyers are notoriously awful writers.[64]   It is ironic that as professionals who use language, and twist and mold words to fit the facts of their case, most lawyers really are poor writers. No other profession would permit such deficiencies. The lawyer's tools are words. Court papers laden with poorly constructed sentences, typos, misused words, are commonplace.[65]   A legal ethics treatise stated that a lawyer must merely be competent—have knowledge, legal skills, capability, office management and good character.[66] Good writing may be entwined in the requisite minimum skills a lawyer needs, but it is not compulsory or prima facie cause for legal malpractice.

A friend who clerked for a federal judge confessed that every week he read a multitude of poorly-written briefs, motions and pleadings with typos, poor grammar and misstatements of law. Covering courts as a reporter, I read a lot of substandard legal briefs and documents for news articles or background research. At my summer clerkship for a county prosecutor, I read briefs prepared by lawyers, prosecutors and even pro se prisoner appellants. Sometimes the pro se briefs by the prisoners were no worse that those prepared by the lawyers.

---

[61] Matt Fleischer, *Herein the Said Answer*, THE NATIONAL LAW JOURNAL, July 17, 2000, at A1.

[62] *Id.*

[63] *Id.*

[64] *Id.*; *see also* TOM GOLDSTEIN & JETHRO K. LIEBERMAN, LAWYER'S GUIDE TO WRITING WELL 3 (1989).

[65] *See* GOLDSTEIN & LIEBERMAN, at 3.

[66] CHARLES W. WOLFRAM, MODERN LEGAL ETHICS 185-89 (1986).

Then, there was my experience in private practice at Dickman & Cherubb, which exposed me to not only horrendous writing but also snobbery. There may be nothing worse than a lawyer with a weak case, a massive ego and a run-on sentence. In court papers, even memos, it seemed as though deliberate obfuscation was just as much a lawyer's tool as clarity. The message, however, was clear: the work seemed so much more complicated and the case so much more important when the sentences were long and confusing. The billable hours were thus justified.

Sitting atop the law review topped off my exposure to the deficiencies of many legal writers. A submission was destined for the recycling pile when I could not even make sense of the piece from the cover letter. The fate was the same with typos in the cover letter. If the "roadmap" paragraph was not within the first few pages, it usually got tossed, too. In a law review article, the roadmap summarizes the sections of the article and the theory being argued. "Section one argues this ....; Section two argues that ....; Section three calls for ....." The roadmap tells the reader where the author is going. It should be the easiest part of the article to read and write.

Legal writing is different from other forms of writing. It is not like a newspaper article and it is certainly not poetry. Legal writing includes narrative style, persuasive writing and strong topic sentences. Active prose and active verbs are key. I always thought that a good writer was a good writer and could transcend boundaries and style. A good writer can communicate thoughts and convey a message in any format. But for a bad writer, it does not matter what format or style you use. Bad writing is bad writing. Many lawyers write in a style that is dense and confusing. Long, complex and drawn-out sentences will not help a client or the judge you are before. Clarity is more valuable than clutter. (Yes, a platitude and cliché).

A former Justice Department lawyer wrote of the conflicting messages he received at his law firm after partners regularly criticized his writing, in both polite and more direct terms, such as: his writing "stank."[67] After being dispatched to legal writing seminars, the attorney

---

[67] Ken Bresler, *Pursuant to Partners' Directive, I Learned to Obfuscate*, 7 SCRIBES J. OF LEGAL WRITING 29 (1998-2000). *See also* Richard Bingler, *Now Comes the Unbending Boss*, 7 SCRIBES J. OF LEGAL WRITING 37 (1998-2000);

sought to please his bosses by combining two sentences into one, "padded sentences with excess verbiage," "separated subjects and objects with conditional clauses and interjections" and threw in some passive voice and Latin expressions.[68]   This strategy garnered kudos from the partners.[69]

Nevertheless, any lawyer who has spent more than 10 minutes reading legal briefs, motions, contracts or law reviews knows how boring, dry and unclear most legal writing can be. And, if someone were to conduct a poll of lawyers or law students, asking them whether they thought they were good writers, I am certain that 99.9 percent would respond in the affirmative.

A legal writing consultant quoted in the *National Law Journal* article lamented that many lawyers are addicted to the 400-word sentence.[70] Joseph Kimble, a professor at Cooley Law School, quoted in the article, cited a poll of lawyers who were presented with two pieces of prose: one in plain language, the other laden with legalese.[71]   Of the 1,400 lawyers polled, 80 percent said they preferred the plain language. Professor Kimble added: "When they sit down to write, they forget that little lesson."[72]

Will William C. Burton save the world or the legal profession? Doubtful. One critic, Ross Davies, editor of an independent law journal, classified the Burton Foundation Award as "a terrible mistake," adding, "law reviews are far less important to law, to clients, to the pursuit of justice, to professionalism and so on than filings are. How many practitioners read law review articles anyway?"[73]   Mr. Davies's points are not too far off, but he downplays the role of law reviews in influencing the law and training of young lawyers. He also ignores the awards for court filings; it is called winning in court.

More problematic in the fight against bad writing is the fact that many of the worst writers do not even know they are poor writers. Most

---

Frederick Doherty, *The Headless Snake of Law-Firm Editing*, 7 SCRIBES J. OF LEGAL WRITING 43 (1998-2000).

[68] Bresler, at 30.

[69] *Id.*

[70] Fleischer, THE NATIONAL LAW JOURNAL, July 17, 2000, at A1.

[71] *Id.*

[72] *Id.*

[73] *Id.* (quoting Ross Davies, editor-in-chief of *The Green Bag*, an independent "entertaining journal of law."

of the others do not care anyway as long as they bill enough hours and get a year-end bonus. Law professors boast that good writing is important on exams. But good writing is less important than spitting back the professor's own words on an exam in a wishy-washy argument that points out what all the issues could be, rather than what the answers actually are. The accepted law school exam template vacillates from one hand to the other hand and back to the first hand is not an exercise in legal writing. That is supposed to teach legal analysis and lawyering skills?

Law firms boast that good writing is important, if not vital to the practice. But good writing for a law firm is subservient to who the candidate knows and where the candidate went.

Mr. Burton might be spinning his wheels. His intentions are idealistic. His results are yet to be seen, or read, but at least he is trying to improve an area of legal practice that needs help, and I am proud to be a winner.

The award's banquet dinner was wonderful. Filet mignon and some kind of crab cakes, green beans and a sea food ravioli appetizer.

I sat at table six with three other winners and their families. The conversation over dinner was nice. We shared law review stories, two of the others held the top position at their respective law reviews: author problems, recalcitrant staff members and hours upon hours in the office. Somehow my stories seemed the craziest.

After dinner wound down, it was awards time. The welcome bag included stage directions for the banquet: the recipient was to proceed across the room to receive the awards while the speaker read a brief bio. The student awards came first. Paul Duke, host of *Washington Week in Review*, was the moderator. As a journalist, both for the Associated Press and in television news, he spoke of the importance of clear, good writing. He made a few lawyer jokes, too.

Then, the awards were distributed. As my name was called I strolled straight across the room in front of the dais while the room of more than 150 guests watched. It was certainly an odd feeling walking across the room while Mr. Duke read my bio: "Roy recently graduated from Syracuse University College of Law where he was Editor in Chief of the law review ... Before law school, Roy was a newspaper reporter for the Cleveland Plain Dealer where he won many, many, many awards for his writing," he said, pausing long enough for the requisite applause. "Looks like journalism lost another good writer."

As Mr. Burton handed me my award, we shook hands and posed for a meet-and-greet photo. Mr. Duke finished his reading and the applause died down while I strolled back to my seat with the heavy prism award in my hands. Before I even returned to my seat, my greasy fingerprints already smudged the Plexiglas trophy.

The awards for the law firms followed. Each law firm winner also got a few minutes to present an acceptance speech. The law firm winners mostly represented large national, corporate law firms. I never heard of a lawyer who would not accept an award or a few minutes to speak. The acceptance speeches were like the Oscars, minus the tears and gratitude to their lord-savior. I do not know what I would have said if given the opportunity to make an acceptance speech. I probably would have kept it short and pithy, something like, "I never realized how close I got to breaking the law when I was a reporter ... ."

That night, at about 11 p.m., I called my answering machine to check my messages. I was awaiting word from my dry cleaner who lost my favorite Brooks Brothers shirt. This morning, I stopped by to inquire about the week-long search for my missing shirt and the woman said she would call me. I never had a dry cleaner lose a shirt before, but it had to happen eventually, and with one of my favorite shirts. The dry cleaner apparently switched my shirt with someone else's because I found a Lord & Taylor pink and white broadcloth, two sizes too big for me in the box. I returned the shirt, hoping that whoever had mine would do the same. The woman explained that the clothing is sent to a central dry cleaning facility.

"I'll put a search order in for it," she said. If the shirt did not turn up, the company's policy was to give a store credit or pro-rated value of the shirt.

"This is going to sound phony, but that shirt was one of my favorite shirts," I said.

"Yeah, and it was brand new," she smugly retorted.

"I did not say it was new, I said it was my favorite," I said, tempering my hostility because I just wanted my shirt back. She asked me how much it cost. I said it was a gift from my dad about four years ago and it was probably about $45.

"I don't believe that you paid that much for a shirt," she said.

"It was a nice shirt, just find it," I said, restraining myself letting the situation turn personal. I could not believe that they lost my shirt and now I was taking heat from the lady for the shirt's value.

Big surprise, there was no call from the dry cleaner but a call from Judge Borris, a newly-appointed federal judge. I had applied for a clerkship with Judge Borris a month ago. He would take the bench in the one of the New York federal court districts once he completed his duties for a federal agency for which he was counsel. He wanted to meet me and he was in his office in Washington.

I could not believe the timing. This was perfect.

Fortuitous Timing
Thursday, July 13, 2000

I spoke with Judge Borris first thing in the morning and we scheduled at 10:45 meeting. I could not believe the good timing. We had a great discussion about journalism and the law. He told me that he liked reporters even though he frequently argued with them over stories involving his agency. I was part of a team of reporters at the PD that broke a huge story involving his federal agency, and we just talked. He even told me he was friends with one of Syracuse's famous alums, former Senator Al D'amato.

We talked about grades, which he said were not important to be a good clerk, "Or," he added, "even a judge." He asked me what I thought a clerk would do, "I see the job of a clerk as doing whatever is necessary to make sure you get all the information you need to make your job easier." I thought that was a good answer. "I am a writer and can find anything you would need, and get it to you quickly and thoroughly."

He described that he did not yet have chambers and did not know what his chambers would look like. "I have a laptop; all I need is a chair," I said. "There were stories I had to dictate over a pay phone. I do not need too many accommodations." He said that he had no doubt that I could do that. He even praised me as a top candidate and said he was happy I applied and had not already accepted a job elsewhere.

The judge told me that he had not made a decision on his clerks despite two telephone calls from the dean of Columbia Law School. The dean had called him to pitch Columbia students to him. I am sure he also had some heavy political debts to pay back.

At the end of the meeting, we both said the same thing at the simultaneously, "This was fortuitous timing." Of all the interviews I had over the course of the past year, I thought this was the best.

Barbells
Thursday, July 27, 2000

After two days of the New York and multi-state sections of the bar exam, Sara and I ventured to New Jersey for the fun-filled day of the New Jersey bar exam. There were two other Syracuse students there as well as more than 2,000 others from various local law schools. We just wanted to get through it and move on. Law review was the last thing on my mind.

During the lunch break, we met up with the other two Syracuse students. When you are in a foreign land, you cozy up with anyone with whom you have anything in common. One classmate, Sara and I were friends with, Gretta. The other classmate was Glen, someone I knew by name and face only. I had never spoken a word with him over the course of three years. Glen was engaged to Liz, the associate editor whose absenteeism forced me to ask for her resignation. He actually seemed like a nice guy.

He and Liz were preparing to move to New Jersey so I gave him my phone number and told him he could call any time if he ran into problems or needed information about the area. He seemed surprised.

Liz came to visit during the lunch break. She was not taking this exam and was resting from the late-night drive from Buffalo to Somerset, New Jersey. The conversation turned to our respective plans for the next week. Gretta was going home to Maine for a week or two. Glen and Liz were looking for apartments in New Jersey. Sara was going home to Baltimore. I was going back to Syracuse to finish the law review.

"You still have work to do on all of that?" Glen asked.

"Yeah, there is a lot of work to do," I answered.

"Jeez, that's too bad. What, do you have to do all the work that nobody did all year? Did a lot of people not do their jobs?" he said.

Because I did not know Glen, I was not sure if he was making a sly crack about law review or whether he was simply being genuine. Liz, I knew, was not happy with how things went with her. I was not sure whether Glen even realized that his girlfriend did not do her job on law review and was asked to step down from her position.

Avoiding eye contact with Liz, I could sense her eyes drop toward the floor. I was kind of embarrassed that he would say something like that with his fiancée standing beside him.

"There is a lot of work to do," I answered.

Buy the Book
Wednesday, August 2, 2000

On a recent trip to the University Bookstore, formerly called the Syracuse University Bookstore (SUB), it dawned on me that the law review should be available there. I frequently browsed through the university publications section, which offers books published by the university press and faculty. I frequently looked at the five-volume history of Syracuse University, but never bought one. A footnote in the most recent volume disparaged the accuracy of the Daily Orange, irritating me so much that I refused to purchase the book. I was not too interested in shelling out more than $100 for the set.

But the law review should be available, after all it was a university product. And the bookstore sold several scholarly journals. Why not the law review?

Throughout the year, I had established a conversational friendship with the woman in charge of the bookstore's academic support section, Louisa. Last August, she set up the law school bookstore across the lobby from the law review office in the fourth floor lounge. Ever since I borrowed her vacuum to clean the office, I talked with her every time I stopped into the store.

Louisa agreed that my proposal was an interesting prospect. I drew up a one-page proposal, which included the details about our publication, tax information, the possible interest among the bookstore's shoppers and my successor's name. There was no money down, so there was nothing to lose. She accepted two copies of our first book, and we would see what would happen thereafter.

This was certainly not a circulation-builder, but the plan meshed with my goal for exposure. Who knew who might want a copy: maybe an alumnus at homecoming; maybe a parent dropping off a child for school; maybe a masochistic pseudo-intellectual. If the bookstore sold books by professors on arcane or obscure academic topics, well, the Syracuse Law Review should be right there, too.

Beyond Fifty Years
Tuesday, August 8, 2000

As the person who was making the biggest deal about the 50th Anniversary, a considerable portion of the burden fell on my shoulders. This anniversary allowed me to delve into the history of the law review, probably more than anybody else ever had. I began by researching how other law reviews commemorated their own milestones. Some did it with simple, modest introductions, others did it with brief histories of their journals and touching dedications by alumni who went on to hold jobs like Supreme Court Justice.[74] Some held symposia and some ignored it completely.

The 50th Anniversary plans took root pretty early in September and October. A panel of about 20 3L staff members who held no other elected positions worked on the project. Ordinarily, these staff members would have nothing to do with law review during their third year. I was

---

[74] Barbara Aronstein Black, *From The Archives (Such As They Are)*, 100 COLUM. L. REV. 1 (2000); The Editors, *Seventy-fifth Anniversary Retrospective: Most Influential Articles*, 75 N.Y.U. L. REV. 1517 (2000); Colleen Kristl Pauwels, *Hepburn's Dream: The History of the Indiana Law Journal*, 75 INDIANA L. J. i (2000); *Introduction, Hastings Law Journal 50th Anniversary Issue*, 50 HASTINGS L. J. (1999); Mary Kay Kane, *Introductory Remarks*, 50 HASTINGS L. J. (1999); Editor's Note, 75 DENVER L. REV. 305 (1998); Sandra Day O'Connor, *Fiftieth Anniversary Remarks*, 50 STAN.L. REV. 1 (1997); Charles H. Warfield, *Preface, Proofitatus Est Puddinatis*, 50 VAND. L. REV. x (1997); Thomas R. Phillips, *Foreword to Volume 75: A Law Review for Texas*, 75 TEX. L. REV. 1 (1996); Lewis F. Powell, Jr., *Congratulatory Note*, 50 WASH. & LEE. L. REV. 3 (1993); Fred R. Shapiro, *The Most Cited Articles from the Yale Law Journal*, 100 YALE L.J. 1449 (1991); N. William Hines, *The Iowa Law Review: A Tradition of Excellence*, 75 IOWA L. REV. 821 (1990); Randall P. Bezanson, *Reflections on the Iowa Law Review Past and Future*, 75 IOWA L. REV. 829 (1990); Erwin N. Griswold, *Essays Commemorating the One Hundredth Anniversary of the Harvard Law Review*, 100 HARV. L. REV. 728 (1987); Gerhard Casper, *Foreword*, 50 U. OF CHI. L. REV. 405 (1983); John Paul Stevens, *Introductory Comment*, 75 N.W. U. L. REV. 977 (1981); *Foreword*, 50 ST. JOHN'S L. REV. 431 (1976); The Editors, *Introductory Note*, 50 VIRGINIA L. REV. 1 (1964); Ray Forrester, *Introduction to Volume 50 Cornell Law Quarterly*, 50 CORNELL L. REV. 1 (1964); E. Blythe Stason, *The Law Review—Its First Fifty Years*, 50 MICH. L. REV. 1134 (1952); William O Douglas, *1901-1950*, 50 COLUM. L. REV. (No. 8, 1950).

lucky to enlist their support. Two committee chairs helped out, but as part-timers were unable to do too much work.

The plan was to attract a panel of law review alumni to write a variety of articles, essays and reflections on major developments in the law over the past 50 years.

The project was quite ambitious, especially on short notice. In reality, to do this properly, the mechanism should have begun one or two years earlier. Authors need more than a year to work on these types of articmles. I learned that in past years, there was at least one project that began with one staff and was handed off to another; that was computerization in 1984. According to an editor's note, the staff for volume 34 got the ball rolling on computerization and the staff for volume 35 was the first full volume to be published with the new technology.

There was no pre-planning for the 50th Anniversary. The panel was charged with compiling a list of possible authors. The alumni and development office searched the alumni database, printing out the names, addresses, telephone numbers and year of graduation for every alumnus who served on law review.

To find authors we used the list and cross-referenced it with the annual alumni director to find alumni who were now law professors. Some volunteers and 2Ls who needed work during office hours searched Lexis and Westlaw databases to locate alumni authors who frequently wrote articles. The volunteers delivered a list of about 20 or 30 potential authors. The Dean recommended a couple names as did our advisor, Professor Locknor. The two committee chairs and I began calling. I was working on my own list that I compiled through word-of-mouth, our alumni directory and the American Association of Law Schools directory.

I personally approached the three faculty members who were on law review. Mike's dad agreed immediately. Another, Professor Van Nostron, a renowned international law scholar who held emeritus status, was in Europe for the year. I contacted him via email and he agreed. The third professor, Professor Beyliss, was intrigued by my proposal and had a wonderful idea for an article about the anniversary of the *Gideon v. Wainwright* case. She thought it over for about a week and then politely declined.

But in January, Professor Beyliss approached me with a proposal to write an article about new technology in the legal profession. She was working on an article for an upcoming seminar, and this was perfect for the book. While most of the articles looked backward to developments and history of the law, this article would look forward. I nearly salivated at the prospect. It was exactly what the book needed. The only hitch was that her research assistant was already burdened by other projects and she needed additionally help with her citations. The text of the article was mostly completed. She needed to insert footnotes. She had a separate document, a roughly 50-page list of citations, documents and resources that she compiled.

Sara, the most-dedicated volunteer on the committee, also volunteered to do the work on this article. This was a lot of work, so I agreed to give Sara a hand and work closely with her on the article. I had taken a computer law class in my second year and was familiar with several cases and materials that I recommended Professor Beyliss include cite in footnotes. She actually appreciated my recommendations. After one meeting between Sara and Professor Beyliss, Sara relayed to me that I had convinced the professor to write for us because she "could not turn down my big weepy blue eyes."

Throughout the year, every time I spoke to a candidate-author, I asked whether they knew of anyone else who might be interested in writing for us. I spoke to about 30 possible authors. I kept a log in one of my law review notebooks. Two authors agreed immediately. A few vacillated. One prospect wanted a list of other authors and the alumni list because wanted to write a reflective piece on the history of the Syracuse Law Review. He planned on interviewing other alumni. He later declined.

One alumnus-candidate, was so annoying he was offensive. I spoke with Professor Stiner, a well-published professor at a California law school, one afternoon. I gave him my pitch, which was getting as polished as a used car salesman's. I was also getting good at determining the level of interest on the telephone. Professor Stiner said he was intrigued by the prospect and that he had a draft of an article that he was ready to send out to law reviews. His article involved developments in mental health and mental illness and the law.

"I will send this to you, but I do not think that I'm ready to commit yet" he said.

"This sounds like it would be good for our book. When can you commit?" I said.

"I haven't had a chance to send it out yet. I want to try to get it in a more prestigious law journal," he said.

"What, you don't think the Syracuse Law Review is a prestigious journal?" I said, coyly.

There was a long pause, followed by his raised voice, an indication of clear annoyance, "I am really surprised that you would say that. You are not being realistic then."

"Oh, I am being realistic, I just like to know how our alumni perceive their law review. We get this type of disrespect from everyone else, I don't expect it from our own alumni. But this is very telling," I said.

He stumbled around and told me that he would get back to me when he decided where his article would run. Professor Stiner called me in early March to see if the law review would be interested in running another article he had recently written.

"Sure, but only if you sent it to the more prestigious journals first," I said. I told him to mail it so the articles editors could review it. But it never came.

I relayed this conversation to a handful of people, all of whom were equally perplexed and disturbed by his comments and perceptions. I was deeply disturbed because this was the same disrespect I, and many Syracuse law students, received in the legal community. We did not need it from our alumni, too.

One of the other 50th anniversary authors replied to one of my emails, which relayed this story by saying, "Hmmm, I've never met a law and mental health person who wasn't crazy as a bedbug. I'm sure it's very satisfying to sneer at the place that gave him his start in the law, but it isn't very attractive."

Professor Maroney referenced my conversation with Professor Stiner during his speech at the banquet. He repeated Professor Stiner's comments verbatim, and answered by saying, "This is the only law review I have ever written for and I am proud of that."

By the time the book was set, we had six substantive law review articles on topics ranging from the state of the world in 1949 to the future with technological advances in the legal profession. The other articles included developments in conflict of laws, informed consent and health law. Mr. Bogin, one of the first editors-in-chief for Volume 1, wrote a reflective piece. In the early years a different staff of editors published each book, the hierarchy was chosen from the same pool of students, but the mastheads were different. Because there were three editors for

Volume 1, I was able to locate two of the first three: one was a retired tax lawyer; the other a professor at a New York City law school. The alumni office told me that the third editor had died.

By March, the deadline for the articles, only one of the first two editors came through, but it was a touching contribution detailing the inauspicious founding of the law review. In my conversations with Mr. Bogin over the course of the year, he was hard-pressed for stories about the founding. I wanted to hear about the struggle and hard-fought battles to start the law review—the moments of the epiphany, the grandiose pronouncements by students or that EUREKA moment that led to the founding.

Instead, Mr. Bogin described the founding as the realization that the law school needed it. "We were really just trying to keep up with the other law schools. Its time had come," he told me. By 1949, nearly every decent law school had a law review. If Syracuse wanted to compete, it needed a law review, too.

A note in the first edition, written by Mr. Bogin, caught the attention of the United States Supreme Court and was cited in the opinion to the case *Brooks v. United States.*[75] This was the first of 11 citations by the Court to date. Eleven citations is not bad, but it is not the volume of "the more prestigious journals" that Professor Stiner likes.

The final two pieces for the 50th anniversary book were written by the Dean and me. I was determined to write the authoritative history of the Syracuse Law Review at 50. Titled "Fifty Years and Beyond," the piece came to 11 pages, complete with footnotes. This was the same slogan we put on the posters.

Over the year, I had the opportunity to flip through almost every law review book. All 50 years of bound volumes rested in my office. The articles editors/business editor's office had almost every single issue of the law review. A handful of early editions were missing, but an alumnus donated his collection in April. The recent widow of a 1948 alumnus also contacted me last summer. Over the Fourth of July last summer, Sara and I drove to Bethesda, Maryland, to save the collection from the trash. Now, those books clutter a shelf in my home.

There were a few interesting items wrapped up in those 50 years of books. Many of the preliminary pages from the single issue books were removed for the binding. That meant the bound volumes, which adorn

---

[75] Brooks v. United States, 337 U.S. 49 (1949).

the shelves of practically every law school library, most likely did not include many mastheads, editor's notes and advertisements.

I discovered that the early mastheads were not in the front of the book, as they were today; but appeared on the first page before the student notes, somewhere in the middle. Plus, there were frequently different mastheads for each single issue. The same staff members comprised the staffs for the different editions in the volumes, but the hierarchy changed between the editions.

The most humorous items I found were the old advertisements. Today, most advertisements in law reviews are for the two legal database services, Lexis and Westlaw, as well as the printers. Some of the larger law schools at colleges with large university publishing houses also run ads for the year's new publications. Over the years, the Syracuse Law Review published the same types of advertisements that practically every other law review published: databases, printers, archive specialists, Shepard's citations and McKinney's.

But my favorite advertisement was from the 1960s for the Marine Midland Trust Company:

> Daddy ... what is a lawyer?
>
> A lawyer is many things, son. He's a man who spends many years of study to protect you and me.
>
> A lawyer writes the laws, protects the innocent, prosecutes the guilty.
>
> I refer my legal problems to him. He helps people with contracts, leases, agreements, wills, and advises me on my rights as a citizen.
>
> He's the man I turn to for advice and guidance in planning the future for you and Mommy. For example, son, our lawyer, together with my bank, have set up a trust fund for you. Among other things, this trust fund will make your college education possible.
>
> Preparing my Will, so you and Mommy are relieved of all problems, is a valuable service of our lawyer. In other words son, a lawyer makes our country, our state, our city and our neighborhood a better place to live.

The ad read as though a cardigan-wearing Ward Cleaver himself delivered the message of our most valued citizen. All it needed was "God Bless America" in the background. The only other people singing such magnanimous praises for lawyers are law school admissions officers.

Because the law review was a student publication, there were no special file cabinets with interesting odds and ends of the law review's history. Even the editors of the Columbia Law Review, which celebrated its 100th anniversary this year, lamented that as law students, they had difficulty maintaining its files for archival purposes.[76] Nevertheless, the Columbia Law Review still had better records and history than we did. We did not have letters from Supreme Court Justices on file in our file cabinets. There was barely anything from the editor before me, Connor.

In my search for interesting tidbits for the article, which I would publish unsigned on behalf of the staff, I learned that Syracuse began publishing the Survey in 1962 after the New York University Law Review became overburdened with its annual *Survey of American Law*. I scoured the books for editors' notes that would tell the story of the law review: in 1960 it switched to quarterly publication; in 1984 the editors first used computers to compose the books and in 1989 on the 40th anniversary the editors sent a message "to uphold and improve the high standards evident in past issues."

Throughout the year, as we were bombarded on a daily basis, it was often difficult to look at the big picture of what we were doing. Even as some of our authors openly ignored their responsibilities and disregarded our mission, the judges of the New York Court of Appeals, New York's highest court, lent perspective to our task.

Researching the development of the annual *Survey of New York Law*, I found forewords and introductions written by several judges, who respected and praised our publication. Judge Judith S. Kaye regarded the Survey as a reflection of the state high court's role in the democracy.[77] Judge Joseph W. Bellacosa described the Survey as a "fine way station in that journey towards the destination of better understanding and achievement of the ideal."[78] And, Judge Sol Wachtler called the Survey a yearly evaluation, "something like a report card" for the state's highest court.[79]

---

[76] See Aronstein Black, 100 COLUM. L. REV. at 1.

[77] Judith S. Kaye, *Foreword: State Courts in Our Federal System: The Contribution of the New York Court of Appeals, 1995 Survey of New York Law*, 46 SYRACUSE L. REV. 217, 217-18 (1995).

[78] Judge Joseph W. Bellacosa, *Foreword*, 44 SYRACUSE L. REV. 1, 2 (1993).

[79] Judge Sol Wachtler, *Foreword*, 43 SYRACUSE L. REV. 1 (1992).

The preliminary unnumbered pages for Volume 20 in 1969 reprinted two congratulatory letters by New York Governor Nelson Rockefeller and United States Attorney General John N. Mitchell. They were brief, but quite interesting. Mitchell's letter was also amusing:

> President Nixon and I would like to congratulate the Syracuse Law Review on its twentieth anniversary. During the past two decades, the Review has grown both in size and in excellence. The annual survey of New York law has been particularly helpful to practicing attorneys, judges and scholars who are interested in following the development of the law in our state. You may be proud of your contribution to legal literature.

Whether the President and Attorney General actually read the Syracuse Law Review will never be known. Perhaps, a discussion of our law review was on the missing 18 ½ minutes of tape.[80] It will be a mystery lost to history.

Framed
Tuesday, August 15, 2000

I unilaterally decided to purchase frames for the 50th Anniversary posters from the University Bookstore framers. The office needed at least two framed copies of the posters. I wanted one framed for myself.

I needed three, which included a custom-cut mat. I paid for mine as well as one of the two for the office. This would be my approximation of a lasting legacy for the law review office. The law review would pay for the third, but I was walking a precarious line without the Dean's pre-approval. Employing executive efficiency, I went to the bookstore, told the woman in the framing department that I was the editor of the law review at the law school, requested the 10 percent university employee discount and ordered the framing job.

A few days later, the framer cut the mat and framed the posters. I paid for two, which came to about $70, and had the bookstore send a bill for the third to the law review. In essence, I walked out of the bookstore with an item without paying for it.

---

[80] *See* CARL BERNSTEIN & BOB WOODWARD, ALL THE PRESIDENT'S MEN 334 (First Touchstone 1987).

When Edna, the law school's budget manager, received my memo on this unorthodox transaction, she told me that this was a first. "Nobody has ever gotten the bookstore to allow someone out without paying for something," she said. "How the hell did you do that?"

"I paid cash for mine and convinced them that I had the authority to have the law school pay for the third. I even got the 10 percent discount," I said.

"That was amazing," she said.

"If I get in trouble, guess what, they can fire me," I said. I was leaving town in a couple of days anyway.

How I Spent My Summer Vacation
Tuesday, August 15, 2000

In the weeks following the bar exam, many of my classmates took trips. One senior editor went to Europe. My good friend Cody spent several weeks at home, then went to California with his girlfriend. One friend started a job a few days after the exam, another moved to Washington. Sara went home to Baltimore. Most recent law school graduates enjoy a period of peace and relaxation following the bar exam.

Unfortunately, I was not one of them.

My three-day bar experience ended on July 27 in Somerset, New Jersey. I spent the next day at a job interview and the day after that accompanying Sara on her quest to find an apartment in New York City. Then, I returned to my office to finish the books.

On Monday, July 31, my first weekday back after the bar exam, I was in the office at 8 a.m., ready to put the finishing touches on books 2, 3 and 4. I was fortunate to have the assistance of a 2L, now a 3L, who worked every day over the summer on articles. I was fortunate, too, to have Mike right there beside me in the trenches following a couple of vacations.

There we were, confronted by the Survey with 18 articles in various stages of disrepair. I estimated there were about five to 10 days to finish it. The Survey had been our second book for years. According to the Statement of Ownership form, the second book should be published in December.

As a chronicle of developments in New York law for a period of July 1, 1998 to June 30, 1999, the Survey was a valuable resource, that should be in the hands of our 1,100 subscribers as quickly as possible. All this was in theory.

In reality, the bulk of the authors systematically ignored the deadlines. What many submitted would receive failing grades for grammar, style and Bluebook format if they were being graded. Some articles were more comprehensive than others.

Now, I had to go through 18 of the 20 articles. The law review never did receive the construction law article. And, I eagerly awaited the torts article. I nearly visited our torts author, Professor Woodson, during the lunch break on the second day of the bar exam at the University of Buffalo. She was not in her office.

Back in Syracuse, I had 18 articles at my disposal. Some had been completely edited and formatted for weeks. A couple had even been processed for months and just needed final formatting and pagination. At least that was what I thought. I kept a chart in a binder listing the status of every Survey article all year. Some were done. Before I began BarBri, that week between graduation and the review class, I sent drafts and letters to most of the authors. They faxed back or sent back corrections or amendments.

Now, I had to make sure everything was perfect. I did not think it would take a lot of time or effort.

I printed out copies of each article and laid them out on the long wide table in order as they would appear in the book. I left blank pages with Construction Law and Torts scrawled in green highlighter in the spaces where these articles would have been.

As I started reading and editing the articles my stomach sank. There were holes and little niggling problems. One article did not have pin cites, precise citations to specific pages, and in another article all of the journal citations were not in small capital letters. Some citations lacked parallel cites. For the Survey, every New York Court of Appeals case was also cited to the New York Reporter, the Northeast reporter and the New York State reporter. Every New York Appellate Division citation was also cited to the Appellate Division reporter and New York State reporter, along with a designation of which of the four New York appellate division departments the opinion emanated from.

Several articles lacked the parallel cites, which meant someone had to read each case and find the proper page to cite to. Some of the authors simply left blanks in front of and behind the latter two reporters, so the cite looked like: __ NE2d __ or __ NYS2d __. With those types of omissions, the author's intent was clear: "You look it up for me." Still other authors omitted the parallel citations altogether. Several authors dutifully supplied the parallel citations. These were rules only a law review editor could worry about. And none of this even concerned the substance of the articles, which seemed to hinge on each author's work ethic.

Two articles, administrative law and conflicts of law, were corrupted when they were converted from WordPerfect to MS Word and every typographical symbol (quotation marks, dashes, section symbols and dollar signs) was replaced by a weird hollow box. The editor in charge of these articles should have made these changes. Unfortunately, Merry, the editor in charge of these articles, was not around. Even during the school year, she really was not all there. Merry's team was responsible for four articles this year, but she failed to complete the editing on any of them. I finished them for her. So much for my dedicated staff.

Here I was supposedly performing the final editing read on these articles which had "been through the system." But it quickly became apparent that my "final read" would have to be more comprehensive. This made me nauseous, hostile and depressed all at once.

Out of shear carefulness and paranoia, I decided to plug a few citations into Lexis just to see if they were correct and that the names of the parties were correct. This form and accuracy or subciting was the same work the 2L staff performed all year during office hours. This was the same type of editing that I performed a year and a half earlier as a 2L on law review. It was not difficult work, especially with the modern conveniences of online databases like Lexis and Westlaw. In the old days, this work was done in the library, where the editor physically pulled the thick reporter volumes off the shelves in the library, leafed through to the specific page. Then, the editor or fact-checker laboriously paged through volumes of Shepard's citators to determine whether the case is still good law. This was painstaking work. Some law reviews still require their editors to cite check with books, the famous official reporters that line library and law firm bookshelves. Now, a couple of key strokes on a computer yields more information in about 5 seconds than 20 minutes of work in the library.[81]

---

[81] *See* PAUL HOFFMAN, LIONS OF THE EIGHTIES: THE INSIDE STORY OF THE POWERHOUSE LAW FIRMS 30 (Double Day & Co. 1982).

All the student editor had to do was read the case, check the facts, the names and the citations. It was not rocket science. Apparently it was too much to ask because what I started finding was appalling.

As I plugged a couple of citations into the Lexis document retriever, I noticed a couple of misspelled party names here and there and a couple of errant parallel citations here and there. Mistakes happen, I admit and accept that. A glance at page A-2 of any day's New York Times corroborates this. On any given day, "the newspaper of record" publishes a number of corrections, sometimes even an "Editor's Clarification," meant to clear up an issue or appease some hostile source. Even as I flipped through some of the old volumes of the law review, I stumbled across an Errata page, correcting a gaffe in the prior issue. But the volume of little mistakes at this point was outrageous.

These articles had been worked on for weeks and months by 2L law review members during office hours. Then, the executive editors read through and made changes or corrections. Then, the authors review their work. By this time, the articles should be as close to perfect as they would ever be. I, as the editor in chief, should not have to do the same kind of editing work that the 2Ls do.

But as the person at the top, I was the guarantor of the accuracy of our books. I could not let these articles go to press with the kinds of mistakes I was finding and the only way to find these mistakes was to check every citation the way it should have been done the first time around.

The government sets minimum standards for just about everything like the daily recommended allowance of riboflavin in your cereal (whatever riboflavin is or does) or how many parts per million of carbon monoxide your car can emit or the permissible amount of rat hair in your chocolate bar. But how many mistakes can a law review publish? It is difficult to quantify how many mistakes would be permissible without completely eroding credibility. A sizeable portion of the 2Ls on staff and a handful my classmates on staff, the law review's accuracy was not a major concern. Even Chris, in liaison office, told me that it did not matter how many mistakes got published. Her direct quote was, "Nobody gives a shit how many mistakes there are." But to me and a handful of editors it mattered.

It was difficult enough gaining respect in the legal community after coming out of a school like Syracuse. I did not want the Syracuse Law Review name tarnished by mistakes and errors in our books. Our subscribers paid $28 for a subscription. Other readers pay exorbitant fees to Lexis or Westlaw to access these articles. Members of the legal community rely on the accuracy of these books, if and when they actually read them. And, in some regards my personal credibility was on the line. My name was at the top of the masthead, just like my byline was when I was a reporter. If there was a mistake, I had to take the heat, no matter who made it—the privilege of leadership.

I remember the dreadful mistakes copy editors occasionally inserted into my news articles. One time, an overzealous assistant city editor changed the address of a 1 million-square-foot factory, which I originally located in the lead of my article. The lead originally read: "The 1 million square-foot Tyler Blvd. building ." The edited lead read: "The 1 million square-foot Tyler Blvd. building located on Heisley Blvd. ..." This was in the first paragraph of a news article, right under my byline. I looked like a moron and had to run a correction. Even worse, I then faced my sources that day and looked like an idiot for putting wrong information into my story, information that I knew by heart. The road the editor relocated the building to was on the opposite side of the city, it was not even close. There was no simple way to explain that to someone outside the newspaper, so you take a hit and brace for the criticism.

Likewise, I remember the times when a copy editor gleefully pointed out a typo or misspelling that I sent along in my copy. I remember how thankful and relieved I was when they found and corrected such mistakes. But that seemed like a long, long time ago because now there were no copy editors, there was nobody looking over my shoulder.

The more time I spent screening a year's worth of work from my law school's elite, the more and more bitter I became. These students were working at some of the best law firms in New York and Washington, one student was even going to work in the New England office for the law firm that screwed me the summer before. These were people who had the kinds of jobs that pay $2,400 a week for an experience tantamount to a summer internship. Yet, their law review editing was deficient if not outright negligent.

Academic performance in the artificial world of a law school exam obviously does not translate to editing, writing and cite-checking skill. Many in the vaunted top 10 percent, could not take care of basic tasks when it came to editing. The work is dull, and law review members everywhere lament the drudgery of the work. It seemed that the entitlement of being on law review was enough and they could skate by as long as they got to put it on their resume. I know exactly how they thought: *This is boring work. There will always be someone else there to catch any mistakes. Who cares, anyway, I already have my resume line. I already have my title for next year. I do not have to care if I don't do my job because I already have my job at the firm, my paycheck for two grand a week. Anyway, if I don't do my job, nobody will know, nobody will be able to do anything to me and someone else will catch the mistakes.*

There were a couple of senior board editors on my staff who clearly shared this view of the work: *if I don't check, I'm sure Roy will catch it.* Many of the mistakes I was finding were not things the executive editors would catch unless they specifically checked online. They, too, were duped by the students they oversaw. There were other mistakes that they could have found. But by now, four of my executive editors were gone, one was still in town but for all intents and purposes gone, and one was finishing up a summer job and was available, Cole. Cole, a pillar of reliability all year, was still around because he had a fourth year to complete because of a joint masters degree program. His articles were always clean, too.

None of this should have surprised me. The cutthroat environment of law school bred a competitiveness unparalleled in most other educational disciplines. The vast majority of law students care about one thing and one thing only: themselves. For many, being thrust into a team-like organization, where the competition should not really matter seemed like a foreign concept. When I was a 2L I was very competitive. I thought that the more mistakes I found in the articles, the better I would look to the senior staff. For me, that meant a couple of weekends in the law review office, it meant typing up a detailed memo to my executive editor when I found a sentence or citation that required editorial judgment. I had writing and editing experience, though. Not many other students in the law school, much less on the law review, had my kind of publishing experience.

Publishing experience aside, law review work is the same kind of work summer associates, law clerks and first year associates perform. Most legal work is research, writing, editing and fact-checking. Law firms say these are sought-after skills. The law review experience provides a venue to hone and develop these skills. As crucial as these skills are to professional success, after the first-year research class, there were few other opportunities to practice these skills.

With the exception of two weekend trips—one San Francisco to attend a wedding and see my old friend Ian and the other to Cleveland to see a bunch of my other friends—I spent the bulk of August in the office, side-by-side with Mike, editing the articles. There were many 12 hour days, a couple 15 hour days. Often there was no lunch. Just hour after hour reading the articles and checking the cites against whatever came up on Lexis. I would log on to Lexis first thing in the morning and log off when I left. If this was real research that was being billed to a law firm or client, each day would have cost someone $10,000, at least.

One article had 53 mistakes ranging from misspelled party names in cases to numbers transposed in the citations to page numbers missing in citations. The article was one of the longest, roughly 600 footnotes. I know the executive editor in charge of the article caught a lot of mistakes. However, 53 mistakes seemed inexcusable. I just hope I caught everything.

The insurance article, which was problematic earlier on, had 800 footnotes. The authors made such a stink on the phone with me about our concerns with their use of headnotes and stressed to me that they had gone through the article, footnote-by-footnote to ensure its accuracy. Yet, there were more than a couple dozen errors.

We were relieved to read a short article. We only had two: health law and penal, each about 12 pages. After Mike read the penal article, he said, "Wow, the penal article is short." I said, "You know, they say that it's not the size of the penal article that is important but what you do with the penal article that counts." He laughed so hard that he nearly spit on the computer.

Then, there was the legal ethics article. The rough draft did not come in until after Spring Break toward the end of March. The article was never assigned to a team and floated around during office hours. I do not know who worked on it or who did anything to it. All I know is that the author was less than pleased when I faxed him what I hoped would be the final draft.

Clay had been a persistent thorn in my side all year. The contract with the authors set late-August as the deadline. For months, Clay, kept putting off the deadline. Shortly after Clay announced that he was leaving his present law firm for the relaxing confines of academia, his excuses started flowing. That was, when I could even speak with him on the phone. I was quite familiar with his voicemail and his secretary.

One week it was, "I will get you the article next week." The next week it was "I will get you the article in two weeks." Another time his excuses ranged from problems with the real estate closing to a problem with the contractor to a problem with a client to other outside commitments.

He frequently apologized. "Roy, I am so sorry. This is embarrassing. I promise, you will have the article soon. I promise, this won't happen again." Talking with him started to sound like a transcript from "Cops," possibly Oprah: the remorseful alcoholic wife beater, breaks down on camera with a pathetic vow—"It won't happen again, I promise." Maybe I watched too much daytime television over the years, or talked to one too many alcoholics. I knew Clay would never change. What I did not expect, however, was how quickly he could turn from apologetic to belligerent.

He submitted his article in three drafts. Then, he submitted the article on disk but in WordPerfect, which meant that it had to be converted. Conversion, as we learned earlier, erased embedded codes and symbol and character signs while also removing footnote codes. It was a hassle. I had to send the article to our de facto technical editor, Ted, a summer associate at a big firm in Washington. As a volunteer, doing me and the law review a favor while working long hours at the firm, Ted, had to fit the special formatting project into his spare time.

I was behind schedule in getting the article back to Clay. In mid August, I faxed the draft to Clay for final review and told him that I needed corrections or amendments in 24 hours. He just about blew a gasket on the phone accusing me of failing to give him adequate notice because I needed him to review his article quickly.

"What the hell are you doing to me? This is crazy, you are not giving me notice here," he spit into the phone. "I cannot read this and get back to you in 24 hours."

"Look, Clay, I am all alone here. My staff evaporated and I'm doing this all by myself. You were the last article I got. I do not think I am asking a lot of you to read this and get back to me. You are acting like you never read this before," I said.

"Fine, I will get you what I can," he said.

I was not sure what I was interrupting in his life. He was practically a law professor now, a man of leisure. My last-minute work probably forced him to miss his tee time at a new country club or the seminar on how-to sexually harass female law students that all new law professors must attend.

The next morning, the fax in the mailbox was completely covered with handwritten notes in the margins and across the text. Clay was less than satisfied with the editing job on his article. In fact, he said that someone inserted an erroneous citation. His note in the margin was pretty rude: "THIS *SHOULD NEVER* HAVE BEEN INSERTED HERE. THIS IS A MISTAKE AND IT MAKES ME LOOK LIKE A DAMN FOOL."

Some of his margin notes were off base. He did not have proper short citations throughout his article and failed to properly cite several things. He did not know the difference between the form for a string citation, a list of cases or statutes one after another as compared to a textual footnote, which is treated like regular text. Also, every citation to McKinney, the publisher of the New York statutes was cited in the possessive to read "McKinney's," which is how it is referred to colloquially but not proper Bluebook form.

He called this afternoon and yelled at me, complaining that someone inserted errors. We went through his margin notes, mostly because I could not read his handwriting.

"I cannot believe the job you guys did. I have never had this happen to me," he said.

I was no more pleased with the mistakes than he was, but there was only so much of his abuse I could take. I told him that I do not know who made these mistakes and again explained to him that I was practically on my own at this point because my staff is gone.

"I don't care. I don't want to hear you complain about this," he yelled at me.

That was the last straw. I quickly retorted, "First of all, we would not be having this argument today, Clay, if you submitted your article nine months ago when it was originally due."

There was complete silence. The author, a model of professionalism, could not respond to that. Then, sensing the wound open up, I hit him again, "Furthermore, you submitted this article without proper short cites for cases or statutes." BAM! "You did not put parallel cites in many of your cases." BAM! "You submitted the article in WordPerfect, not MS Word which required writing a computer macro program to fix it, which took a week." BAM. "And, by the way, McKinney's is not possessive according to the Bluebook except when you are dealing with session laws. You cited it possessive throughout the article." BAM-BAM.

Clay failed to realize how bad his piece really was. I explained to him that this was precisely why I sent him a draft of his article for review. There was no excuse for someone inserting something erroneous. I can almost understand how someone could insert the Model Rules of Professional Responsibility citation into the article based on his original draft.

He seriously overreacted and had no right to react the way he did, especially to me. He was a bit more humble the next time we spoke a couple of days later to deal with the final draft and his final recommendations. I could barely contain the laughter when the last thing he said to me was, "So, what are you guys doing about this article for next year? Have you farmed it out to someone else or can I write it again?"

"I have no idea what the editors are planning for next year," I told him, adding, that the two articles editors were not around: "one just got married and the other was at yoga camp eating sprouts with her legs wrapped around her head."

"Could you leave a message for them about this?" he asked. I was more than happy to oblige. I left the articles editors a clear, unmistakable message about Clay: get a new legal ethics author.

If dealing with Clay was not enough frustration for one day, I still needed to talk with Professor Woodson about the torts article. When I spoke with her two weeks earlier, she told me that I would have the article "by early next week." That "early next week" should have been on Monday, August 14, for an article that should have been submitted in January. This was Friday, August 11.

I caught her in her office, not a place where she spent a lot of time. She told me she was working on the article as we spoke and I would have it next week.

"I hope I get it next week because all the other articles are done and the only article I am waiting for is yours. I needed this article seven months ago," I said.

"I know when you needed this article. I'm tired of hearing your CRAP!" she yelled.. "I don't' know why I agreed with you to write this article."

"You agreed with my articles editor, not me. If I knew you would be like this, I would have gotten someone else to write this article. I don't know why you agreed to write this article in the first place. It seems like you did not care about it at all."

Due Point
Monday, August 21 2000

Everything for the Survey is ready at this point. I just needed to fill in a couple of questions on the legal ethics article and fill two holes in the employment law article. All that's left was the torts article.

On Thursday, I called the employment law author, an attorney at another Syracuse law firm. There were two footnotes citing sections of the New York Labor Law that were incomplete: a typo, an extra number in the section and a blank space where the section number needed to go. I spent about 40 minutes in the library flipping through the New York Labor Law attempting to figure out which sections he was citing, but could not.

By Monday, I was at the end of my rope and called him again. Only now, Fred was out of the office and not returning until Wednesday. His secretary, with whom I had spoken numerous times in the last few months, ran the usual interference. Fred missed his deadline by about four months. I booked him late because we lost the previous year's employment law author and then lost the person I contracted with in November. So, I booked Fred in mid-November and settled on January 17 as the deadline day. January, February, March and most of April passed without the employment law article.

Sara and I did all the editing on it during our week off between graduation and bar review. There was plenty of editing done on it. I was less than pleased when these two holes persisted, even after Fred marked up and returned the edited version.

When I failed to get an answer from him by mid-morning, my tone with his secretary was less than cordial. I was fed up with her, too. She, like many of the authors' clerical support people I spoke with on the phone, had always been rude to me.

"I want you to give this message to him verbatim: I realize I am not a paying client, but I need these two questions answered. I might not be paying billable hours and calling the shots but he has a responsibility to the law review to answer these questions. These are the last two things I need before I can send the entire book to Nebraska. I need an answer by the end of the day," I said.

At 5 p.m. a female associate called and gave me the information that I needed. I was very appreciative.

Back to the torts debacle. I was bracing for the article. I was prepared to handle all the editing on it myself. I was ready to pull an all-nighter if I had to.

Mike was ready to bag it two weeks earlier. "I say screw her and we put it in the editor's note with her name in it. We need to get the Survey out," Mike said. I agreed, but was still hopeful. I was still hopeful for consistency. The Survey is intended to be a comprehensive record of developments in the law. The topics were supposed to be well-rounded and consistent year-in, year-out. Many topics can be traced back for more than 50 years in our Survey.

I wanted the Survey to be complete. I was already sore from the construction law void and did not want to publish the book with two holes, especially one as big as torts.

I called professor Woodson after lunch. She sounded calm when I asked where the article was. "You didn't get it, I put it in priority mail last night," she said. I told her that was the best news I heard all month.

The article was not in the day's mail. I asked her to send it to me as an email file to my AOL address. She was ready for that request because I had barely finished my sentence when she said, "Oh, they're doing work on the computer system's file server here before classes start, I don't think I'll be able to email it to you. I will try."

I thanked her and for the rest of the afternoon I checked my AOL every 20 minutes. I went down to the mail room and conversed with Robert about priority mail. He assured me that priority mail from Buffalo would take one or two days, tops. At the very least, he assured me, the article would be in my hands by Tuesday or Wednesday.

So, I waited.

Surprise, surprise. The torts article was not in the mail on Tuesday, Wednesday, Thursday or even well into the next week. It did not come as email either.

I just could not understand why someone would agree to write an article and then lie about finishing it for months. If professor Woodson did not intend to write the article I do not understand why she refused to tell me months earlier. If she was a practicing attorney and unilaterally decided not to file a brief or an answer to a motion, she would default. If she failed to perform part of a contract, she would be in breach. Here, she obviously felt as though she was under no duty or obligation to perform. It now became even clearer why Clay was becoming a law professor.

This mendacity and duplicity riled me up. She obviously had no conscience or honor. But why string me along? Why lie about it? I held up production on this book because I earnestly believed that we would eventually receive the torts article. All I got was hostility and lies.

Leaving Town
Thursday, August 24, 2000

When I woke up this morning I had 10 keys on my key ring, by the middle of the afternoon there was one, at this point, the only one I needed—my car key.

Today, after three years of law school and a wonderful summer of studying for the bar and attempting to complete the Law Review, I packed up my truck with two dozen boxes and bags to the point where I could only see straight ahead of me and out my driver's side window and moved home. My landlady, Mrs. C., who rented me her rec. room for three years gave me a hug, told me it was nice having another son for three years, urged me to come back soon and wished me luck. I gave her back her four keys and garage door opener. Then, I stopped in the office one last time.

Getting through campus was a nightmare. Today was the first day for freshmen at Syracuse. This meant long lines of traffic. I remember my first day on campus as a freshman 11 years earlier and remember the chaos and the lines. Anytime a campus is invaded by thousands of stressed-out newcomers and their parents, chaos ensued. I turned my over-stuffed truck onto the access street to the parking garage. Normally, two or three cars on this street at once would be considered heavy traffic. Today, the cars were lined up two-across all the way down the street to access two freshmen dorms. One lane remained open for through-traffic and the metro bus.

As I made the right turn, a police officer directing traffic stopped me and told me to get in the line. I rolled down my window, held out my parking pass and yelled at him, "I'm going to the parking deck. What, do I look like an idiot?" He seemed like a nice guy, he must have been a nice guy because he smiled and said soothingly, "Calm down. I thought you were moving in."

"Why, does it look like I'm moving?" I said nonchalantly as my garment back slid over the seat to whack the back of my head.

I guess I was prone to snap at people every now and then. I could clearly see the lines and the traffic. Only an imbecile would not realize what was going on. There must have been a bunch of idiots around this morning who could not figure out how to drop off their kids.

Like I had done so many times over the past three years, I parked in the Irving garage, and made my way upstairs for the last few thank-yous and good-byes.

I stopped off in the alumni and development office to see how I could get involved in the school's alumni groups. I figured if I could not get a job, I might as well be a pain in the ass of the law school. I probably knew more about Syracuse than half the council members combined. The dean of development told me that he would like to see me involved, the only problem was geography. They already had people in northern and central New Jersey. I thanked him for all the help this year. He was instrumental in many of our alumni-related needs for the 50th anniversary book and banquet.

Over at the Dean's office, I stopped by and gave Elaine, one last goodbye. "It was always nice coming in here since you started. You are one of the few people who you can talk to around here," I said. She gave me a big hug and thanked me.

When I got into the office, Mike was sitting at the computer terminal where he sat for the past three weeks. He told me that the Van Nostron article had major problems because there were no pin cites. One more headache. But that was for book 4.

Betty, my successor, and her managing editor were in their office with the door closed. Already a week of inhabiting the office and they had exceeded the number of closed-door meetings that Mike and I had throughout our entire year. The new staff was in place, and had rearranged the office furniture. They were in the midst of orientation and were eager to have the editors from volume 50 out of their hair. Mike and I were just as eager to get out of their hair.

Professor Woodson's torts article did not arrive in the morning mail, not really much of a surprise. The only thing to do now was to sign the two-dozen forms, double check the page numbers and seal the envelope. It was a tight fit. The 600-page Survey barely squeezed into the overnight envelope.

Shortly after Betty and her managing editor, Ted, emerged from behind the closed door, another new editor, Hank, strolled in, two pizzas in hand that he absconded with from the Lexis training lunch.

Art, who was often a foil and a prod during his office hours, walked in, saw me standing there and grinned, "If I knew you were coming in today, I would have brought you a going away present." His idea of a present was a bottle of Captain Morgan Rum. It was his favorite drink and he really wanted to see me drink a bottle of it. I had a sip at the election back in April, but he wanted to see me get blitzed on it. My friends always wanted to see me get drunk. I'm not sure why. I thanked him.

As I tied up loose ends and shared the pizza, the conversation was light. Betty asked me if there were any last words I wanted to impart. I declined. I put all my last words into a three-page memo detailing everything I needed from her ranging from the plaque for the wall to assistance with the publisher. I gave her the memo the day before. There was really nothing left to say. They were goading me for stories about law review or law school.

They wanted to hear about the Syracuse law professor who submitted the same substandard article to me that he had to the previous staff. It was a sloppy 12 pages about how to write a law review note. We rejected it, and the professor complained to Betty about it. He never mentioned it to me, though. They wanted me to recount my icy conversation with Professor Woodson, the yelling match I had with that law school administrator and the verbal assault Mike and I endured at the hands of the Prince.

Art asked for my email address, which I gave him and spelled out, which brought a huge laugh to everyone in the room. I cannot understand why they thought it was so funny, a slight play on my last name. Ted said it sounded like a Yellow Pages advertisement for gutter repair. Art, whose last name was the same as an insect, said that he could not laugh at my email address, "too much."

Then, Hank observed that everyone in the room but he was a non-traditional student. "Roy, you worked as a reporter. Ted, you were in the military. Betty, you worked. Art, you are older. Mike and me are the only traditional ones."

"I hate the label non-traditional law student," I said .

"If anyone is non-traditional, it's you, Roy. There is nothing traditional about you," Art said.

I thanked him. And Betty and Ted immediately probed me about my distaste for the non-traditional label. I explained that most of the people in my class who wore the non traditional student label were whiners and complainers and felt like they needed some kind of special treatment because they are older than other students. "I may think things suck around here and complain, but I am not a whiner," I defiantly said.

Nowadays, a significant portion of those in law school have some work experience, and are non-traditional. This meant that they took more than a year or two off between their undergraduate graduation and law school. A fair number the so-called non-traditional students did not forego a real career to come to law school. Some were aimless or part-time workers. Some were teachers for a couple of years. I really left a career, a job at a top newspaper, and somewhat resented being lumped in with people who really did not leave anything behind to come to law school. I left journalism because I had a plan, albeit, a plan that may or may not ever be realized. My law review experience, I hoped, would facilitate things.

Then, Art, half-tongue in cheek, like most things he said to me over the course of the year said, "Roy, man, you need to start your own publication so people can read what you write."

"I don't know if people really want to read my cynical rants. Anyway, I don't have the capital," I answered.

"No, what you need to write is an article on the politics of law review. If anyone could write that, Roy, you could," Hank cheerfully interjected.

"Yeah, a book, that would be interesting. You should write a book," Betty added.

I just smiled and said, "Maybe I should."

I slowly loosened my key ring and eased the office keys off—the outer door, the inner door, the mailbox, the desk, the file cabinet. I put them together and handed them over to Betty.

"When I woke up this morning, I had 10 keys on my key chain. I sounded like a jailer. Now, I only have my car key," I said. "Call me if you get the Woodson article."

I wished them luck and made a round of handshakes. Art gave me a sincere two-handed shake, grabbing my right arm all the way near my elbow, and said, "I hope you find the path you're looking for man."

I thanked Mike and told him that I owe him a couple of beers when he moved down to the city at the end of the month.

I waved goodbye and headed out.

Rearview Mirror—Epilogue

Snow flurries fell from the gray sky. It was the first week in November, and it was Syracuse. After 19 months, it was finally time to put Volume 50 of the Syracuse Law Review to bed. The Survey had been in Nebraska for months and was nearly printed. Books 3 and 4, the special 50th Anniversary book were finally ready to go.

From my remote location at home in New Jersey, I had leaned heavily on a few key volunteers to close out the book. Cole, one of the best editors on staff, who was still in Syracuse finishing up his master's degree requirements handled some editing on book three. He was a research assistant for a professor who wrote a products liability article for the third book, and was responsible throughout the year for one of the notes published in the book, as well.

For the 50th anniversary book, we were just waiting on one last article, which Hank, now a 3L and a senior board member, worked on as the professor's research assistant. The 70-page tome on federal criminal law was massive, and Hank had devoted nearly a year to working on it. The 600 footnotes were practically perfect in both form and accuracy. Geneva, my summertime volunteer editor from Ashtabula, Ohio, who did not seek an editorial position, also pitched in. Ted, now a senior editor, helped with some of the formatting, too.

Betty, my successor, was also a source for reliable assistance. On top of all the work she had for her books and staff, she was always willing to make a final check here and there. But despite all the technology—telephones, faxes and email—it would be close to impossible for me to adequately complete the editing on my own without the assistance of these three pillars. I still needed assistance with editing, formatting and printing. As it was, from New Jersey, I spent a several hours a day working on the last of the books.

But now, with the final article ready, it was now time to cut the cord. I came up Friday afternoon and met with a number of my former staff members who now occupied the senior staff. It was nice to see all the familiar faces and many wanted to stop and talk. It was quite refreshing to see everyone. I went to visit Elaine, in the dean's office, to thank her for arranging a VIP parking pass for the weekend, but she was out sick. Parking on a college campus was always fraught with tension.

With the open invitation from Mrs. C., I also had a warm place to stay. It was kind of like a homecoming. The football team was on the road, though, and there was a whole lot of work to do.

Betty and Cole had printed off the entire two books before my arrival, which made it easier. Then, I began reading it all again. Friday night dinner was with Betty at the Panda West, my favorite restaurant on campus. "I don't know how you did it all without pulling your hair out," she confessed over the warm tea and crunchy noodles. "I'm only a couple months into this and it's non-stop, problem after problem."

Betty registered many of the same complaints I had, and encountered many of the same difficulties: apathetic staff; difficult authors; and not enough hours in the day. No matter how much planning editors did, few things could or would run smoothly.

"Half the time I just want to go home and cry," she said.

"Don't worry, you're on top of things, you'll make it," I said.

Saturday was a marathon day in the office. Betty gave me a key so I could come and go as I pleased. Cody drove out from Rochester to meet me for lunch. He also came to see his girlfriend who lived in Syracuse.

As we descended the huge cement staircase from the campus toward Marshall Street, and the Panda West, Cody unleashed the same philosophical rhetoric I had become accustomed to, and frequently appreciated.

"As the People's Editor, would you do it all again?" he asked.

After a long dramatic pause, I answered, "Probably."

"The law review has become your Winchester House," he said.

"What the hell is the Winchester House?"

"It's out in California, some eccentric millionaire built a mansion and believed that once he stopped adding to it or building, he would die," Cody reported. "So he kept putting on rooms, staircases that led to nowhere, windows, doors, walls. He thought once the house was completed, he would cease to exist. See, the law review is your Winchester House."

"Well, I guess I can just die now," I said.

"Yeah, right. But what are you going to do now that it's all done?"

"I'll find another project. I'll come up with something," I said.

A couple of projects surfaced, mainly getting a legitimate job. A couple months later, I landed a clerkship with a wonderful newly-appointed judge in New Jersey Superior Court. Within months of our publication several articles in 50 Syracuse L. Rev. were cited in other publications, including my own article.

Email and alumni functions allowed me to maintain relations with many staff members and friends. I was even able to reciprocate and proofread a couple articles for Betty when it was time for her to send the one of her books to the printer. Over time, however, some of the relationships I cultivated with classmates and staff-mates eventually fizzled out.

After a five-week investigation, the dry cleaner was systematically unable to recover my favorite light blue Brooks Brothers shirt. They found two similar blue shirts, but both were two sizes too big and one was a Polo, not even a Brooks Brothers.

I refused the offer for a store credit. "You lost one shirt already, do you expect me to turn over all my shirts at once? I'm not that much of an imbecile," I told the same cashier who jeered at me for spending $50 on a shirt. The store was honorable, however, and generously paid replacement costs of $45.

Law Review and the Temple of *Boom*

The American law review properly has been called the most remarkable institution of the law school world. To a lawyer, its articles and comments may be indispensable professional tools. To a judge, whose decisions provide grist for the law review mill, the review may be both a severe critic and a helpful guide. But perhaps most important, the review affords invaluable training to the students who participate in its writing and editing.

—Chief Justice Earl Warren[1]

The law review is perhaps the most unique institution throughout the academic world. Law review is an honor society, scholarly journal and social club wrapped into one entity. Law students vie for the coveted membership that opens doors to the upper echelons of the legal community while instilling valuable lessons that few law school classrooms provide.

Law review as an institution, however, is shrouded in mystery.[2] The experience is unparalleled in other academic settings.[3] There are hundreds of scholarly journals in every field. But in the legal community, the law reviews hold a special and important place. To those outside the confines of the legal community, the idea of students choosing, editing and critiquing academic papers, seems foreign, if not ludicrous.[4] These articles, in turn, are written with the intent of not only being published, but of influencing the law by articulating new ideas,

---

[1] Earl Warren, *Messages of Greeting to the U.C.L.A. Law Review*, 1 UCLA L. Rev. 1, 1 (1953).

[2] *See* Roger C. Cramton, *"The Most Remarkable Institution": The American Law Review*, 36 J. LEGAL EDUC. 1 (1986) [hereinafter Cramton]; Michael I. Swygert & Jon W. Bruce, *The Historical Origins, Founding, and Early Development of Student-Edited Law Reviews*, 36 HASTINGS L.J. 739 (1985) [hereinafter Swygert & Bruce].

[3] Michael L. Closen & Robert J. Dzielak, *The History and Influence of the Law Review Institution*, 30 AKRON L. REV. 15, 38 (1996).[hereinafter Closen & Dzielak].

[4] Reinhard Zimmermann, *Law Reviews: A Foray Through A Strange World*, 47 EMORY L.J. 659 (1998).

chronicling developments and providing a point of reference in the constantly changing body of law that runs the American judicial system and society.[5]

Within the insular walls of America's law schools, "making law review" often dominates the conversations and anxieties of many first year law students.[6] The law review mystique and allure permeates most books on the law: academic;[7] anecdotal and biographical[8] and popular fiction.[9] Legal academics, mostly writing in law reviews have also

---

[5] Jordan H. Leibman & James P. White, *How the Student-Edited Law Journals Make Their Publication Decisions*, 39 J. LEGAL EDUC. 387 (1989) [hereinafter Leibman & White].

[6] SCOTT TUROW, ONE L. 160 (Warner Books 1977) ("The initial review sessions were fruitful. We worked together until six or so, probing at each other, trying to clarify, then we'd often sit and gossip for another half an hour, usually about who was going to make Law Review. As exams neared, Law Review somehow seemed to dominate our conversations. Regularly we'd exchange speculations about who the top candidates were ... someone accused me of being a possibility.").

[7] *See e.g.* HELENE S. SHAPO, MARILYN R. WALKER & ELIZABETH FAJANS, WRITING & ANALYSIS IN THE LAW (3rd ed. 1995); DONALD B. KING (Editor), LEGAL EDUCATION FOR THE 21ST CENTURY (1999); RICHARD H. WEISBERG, WHEN LAWYERS WRITE (1987); MARY ANN GLENDON, A NATION UNDER LAWYERS (1994); RICHARD K. NEUMANN, JR., LEGAL REASONING AND LEGAL WRITING (2d ed. 1994).

[8] *See e.g.* CAMERON STRACHER, DOUBLE BILLING (1998);WILLIAM R. KEATES, PROCEED WITH CAUTION: A DIARY OF THE FIRST YEAR AT ONE OF AMERICA'S LARGEST, MOST PRESTIGIOUS LAW FIRMS (1997); RICHARD D. KAHLENBERG, BROKEN CONTRACT (1996); GERALD GUNTHER, LEARNED HAND: THE MAN AND THE JUDGE (1994); ELEANOR KERLOW, POISONED IVY: HOW EGOS, IDEOLOGY, AND POWER POLITICS ALMOST RUINED HARVARD LAW SCHOOL (1994); ALAN M. DERSHOWITZ, CHUTZPAH (1991); JOEL SELIGMAN, THE HIGH CITADEL: THE INFLUENCE OF HARVARD LAW SCHOOL (1978).

[9] *See e.g.* JOHN JAY OSBORN, JR., THE ASSOCIATES (1979); JOHN JAY OSBORN, JR., THE PAPER CHASE (1971). In THE PAPER CHASE, the characters repeatedly wonder whether they will have the grades to make the law review. *Id.* at 20, 28, 81, 150. One character, Kevin, is in awe of being tutored by a member of the *Harvard Law Review*:

> On the wall a picture of round faces, smiling in contentment, hung over golden letters that said HARVARD LAW REVIEW. Kevin couldn't keep his eyes off the letters.

contributed to the mystique, year after year. From law school memoirs such as *One L*, Scott Turow's widely-read memoir about his first-year at Harvard Law School to popular legal thrillers by John Grisham, law review references abound. Whether it is a discussion at Harvard in the student lounge as in *One L* to a discontented junior associate at a major law firm complaining that his boss only hires law review staff members.[10]

Modern legal thrillers, too, are peppered with law review references.[11] In the opening pages of Brad Meltzer's thriller, *The Tenth Justice*, the central character, Ben Addison, a clerk for a United States Supreme Court Justice surveys the room, taking note of his new colleagues, who were editors of their respective law reviews.[12] A number of John Grisham's heroes have law review on their resumes. Darby Shaw in *The Pelican Brief* remembers that in the midst of derailing an international conspiracy she had to meet a deadline for her law review comment.[13] Mitch, the hero in *The Firm*, was an articles editor at the *Harvard Law Review*[14] while Adam Hall in *The Chamber*, was an editor at the *Michigan Law Review*.[15] In an amusing exchange between Adam's grandfather and another deathrow inmate, the grandfather brags about his grandson's law review credential as a badge of honor:

He'd seen them coming out of their white frame house [Gannett House], joking and talking with each other. He'd seen the way ordinary law students walked around the house looking in, wondering, wishing they had the courage to go right up to the window. The way ordinary law students tried to look like they weren't looking at all, and how that made them seem all the more intent.

"Are you really on the Law Review?" It spurted out of Kevin.

Moss's pencil hung between his thin fingers. "Not really, anymore. I don't actively participate. A pompous organization. You might say, I never really *belonged*. But don't study because of the Law Review. It'll make you too tense."

Id. at 85-86.

[10] *See* KEATES at 77-80; 97, 101.

[11] SCOTT TUROW, PERSONAL INJURIES 300 (Warner Books 1999).

[12] BRAD MELTZER, THE 10ᵀᴴ JUSTICE 2 (1997).

[13] JOHN GRISHAM, THE PELICAN BRIEF 121 (1992).

[14] JOHN GRISHAM, THE FIRM 17 (1991).

[15] JOHN GRISHAM, THE CHAMBER 24-25 (1994).

"He's a smart kid. Great education. Number two in his law class at Michigan, you know. Editor of the law review."
"What does that mean?"
"Means he's brilliant. He'll think of something ."[16]

But what does it all mean? This essay lends a degree of perspective to the institution of law review. Because of the extensive academic and historical scholarship already in print, this essay gives credit where credit is due.[17]   Section I of this essay begins with a brief history of the development of the law review as an institution. Section II discusses the purpose and role of the law review in the legal community. Section III discusses the growth of specialty journals. Section IV discusses why law schools and law students publish law reviews. Section V concludes with thoughts on the future of law reviews.

I. The Rise of the Law Review

To understand the world of the law review, the term must first be defined. *Black's Law Dictionary* defines law review as: "a journal containing scholarly articles, essays, and other commentary on legal topics by professors, judges, law students and practitioners. Law reviews are usually published at law schools and edited by law students."[18]   One of the leading articles on the development of law review as an institution succinctly expands the definition: "Thus today, a law review is more properly defined as a periodic publication which may be general in scope or may focus on a particular area of law, edited by students, and which may contain lead articles, essays, and book reviews as well as student-written articles and case summaries." [19]

---

[16] *Id.* at 277.

[17] Extensive and excessive footnoting has long been one of the major criticisms of law review writing. *See* TOM GOLDSTEIN & JETHRO K. LIEBERMAN, LAWYER'S GUIDE TO WRITING WELL 30-31 (1989). *See also* Abner J. Mikva , *Law Reviews, Judicial Opinions, and Their Relationship to Writing*, 30 STETSON L. REV. 521 (2000); Abner J. Mikva, *Goodbye to Footnotes*, 56 U. COLO. L. REV. 647, 647 (1985).

[18] BLACK'S LAW DICTIONARY 894 (7th ed. 1999).

[19] Closen & Dzielak at 17.

Law reviews are published at law schools and edited by law students.[20]   The terms law review and law journal are synonymous.[21] The product is heavily footnoted scholarly articles, essays, commentaries, book reviews and student notes.[22]

The development of the law review as an institution mirrored the development of the modern legal education and the development of the American common law[23] judicial system.[24]   As lawyering grew into a profession and the American judicial system expanded with the growth and expansion and development of the nation, lawyers needed resources to keep up with this growth.[25]   Through the mid-to-late 19th Century, American lawyers, scholars and judges relied on classic, mostly English, legal treatises, a small body reported judicial opinions and a one-volume collection of governing statutes.[26]

The American judicial system with its concentric circles of federal and state jurisdictions and the common law or judge-made law cried for legal periodicals.[27]   There was a giant void for legal reference materials in the growing country.[28]   Judges, lawyers and citizens relying on

---

[20] Leibman & White at 387-88.

[21] J. MYRON JACOBSTEIN, LEGAL RESEARCH ILLUSTRATED   334-37 (6th ed. 1994).

[22] *See* Leibman & White at 394-97; *see also* Closen & Dzielak at 16.

[23] *See*, SHAPO, ET AL at 2, 3,7 ("The United States is a common law country, in that rules of law come from written decisions of judges who hear and decide litigation. The common law is judge-made law. Judges are empowered by statute or by constitutional provision in every state and in our federal system to decide controversies between litigants. When a judge decides a case, the decision attains the status of law, and it becomes a precedent for future legal controversies that are similar.").

[24] *Id.* at 3-7 (describing the vertical structure of the court system through which trial courts rely on decisions from higher courts); *See also* Cramton at 2.

[25] Cramton at 2 ("The emergence of the student-edited law review coincides with the rise of the modern American law school about one-hundred years ago. Both were responses to the need of the legal profession for a more practical exegesis of the rules, precedents, and policy applicable to particular situations.")

[26] Swygert & Bruce at 741-56.

[27] Cramton at 2 ("During the nineteenth century the American lawyer relied primarily on a handful of classic treatises, a small shelf of reported judicial decisions and a one-volume collection of governing statutes.").

[28] *Id; see also* Swygert & Bruce at 741-56.

precedent needed to be kept abreast of developments.[29] A handful of regional and professional journals began to fill this void as did the development of American legal scholars.[30] The birth of the student-edited law review also appears to coincide with the academic growth of the American law school.[31]

Officially, the first student-edited law review was born in, of all places, Albany, New York. In 1875, students at Albany Law School first published the *Albany Law School Journal*.[32]   Although widely-recognized as the first of its kind, today, the emergence and failure of the *Albany Law School Journal* has been silenced by time, intellectual neglect and the absence of any surviving volumes.[33]

Robert Emery, the reference librarian at Albany Law School Library, went on a legal archeological mission to track down copies of the first of-its-kind journal.[34] Scouring the best law libraries on the East Coast along with several national catalogues, Professor Emery was unable to track down a single copy of the *Albany Law School Journal*.[35] The only copy he was able to locate was a glass-framed edition dated April 13, 1876, hanging in the current office of its successor publication, the *Albany Law Review*.[36]

Professor Emery's description of that remaining copy from the 1875-76 academic year makes the journal sound more like a student newspaper than a modern law review:

> It is an eight-page tabloid newspaper in format, printed on cheap newsprint. As in ordinary newspapers of the time, the front and back pages are covered with advertisements, particularly for establishments appealing to law student tastes: "Effler and Hanner's Billiard Parlors, 69 North Pearl Street; Cosmopolitan Saloon ... the Best and Coolest Lager in the City; Broom and

---

[29] *Id.*
[30] *See* Swygert & Bruce at 741-56.
[31] Cramton at 2.
[32] Robert A. Emery, *The Albany Law School Journal: The Only Surviving Copy,* 89 LAW LIBR. J. 463, 463 (1997).
[33] *Id.*
[34] *Id.* at 463-64.
[35] *Id.*
[36] *Id.* at 464.

Hadley's Commentaries on the English Law, or Blackstone's Commentaries Rewritten ... Price $13.00."[37]

The journal published student announcements, law school information and general legal news.[38] However, some substantive content abounded, including the synopses of recent judicial opinions, an editorial on "munificent" salaries paid to high court judges in England compared to the compensation of New York State judges and a discussion of the 14th and 15th amendments.[39]

Even though the *Albany Law School Journal* was thin on substance, compared to today's law reviews with extensively-footnoted articles, that first journal allowed law students to write and publish articles on the same materials they studied in class.[40] Professor Emery concludes by noting that the *Albany Law School Journal* may be regarded as the "forerunner of the modern law review."[41]

Baby Blue – *The Columbia Jurist*

As much of a first step those students in Albany took, Professor Emery points out that the *Columbia Jurist* at Columbia Law School had a divine spark, too.[42] In 1885, a group of six Columbia law students began publishing the *Columbia Jurist*, which also resembled a traditional legal periodical.[43] The Group of Six was unaware that 10 years earlier law students several hours north of Morningside Heights had briefly pioneered in the nascent field of student-legal publishing.[44] The *Jurist*,

---

[37] *Id.* Published every Thursday morning, the journal advertised a circulation of 500 copies. A subscription cost of $1 for six months or 50 cents for three months. Single issues cost five cents at local newsstands.
[38] *Id.* at 465.
[39] *Id.*
[40] *Id.*
[41] *Id.* at 465-66.
[42] *Id.* at 466. *See also* Cramton at 3; Barbara Aronstein Black, *From the Archives (Such As They Are)*, 100 COLUM. L. REV. 1, 2 n. 6 (2000): while recounting the venerable history of the *Columbia Law Review* in its Centennial Anniversary Edition, Professor Aronstein Black referred to the founders of the *Harvard Law Review* and dispatched with the short-lived *Columbia Jurist* in a footnote.
[43] Swygert & Bruce at 764-67.
[44] *Id.* at 766.

in its four-page format, published a smattering of law school news along with substantive articles, similar to professional law journals.[45]   An editor's note in that first edition boldly proclaimed that the new publication "will be of the greatest value to students as a work of reference."[46]

Vowing weekly publication, the editors wrote: "We shall make it a point to publish all news that can interest Law Men. Important cases recently adjudicated will find a place in our journal, and persons of acknowledged merit, in and out of the College, will be regular contributors."[47]

Despite the students' ambition, the *Columbia Jurist* could not sustain itself, and published weekly for three volumes until its demise in 1887.[48]

Crimson Tide

Just as the *Columbia Jurist* closed up shop, the modern American law review emerged in Cambridge at Harvard.[49]

In 1887, Harvard picked up the smoldering torch and ran with it, publishing the *Harvard Law Review*.[50]   The *Harvard Law Review* quickly stood out and would become the prototype for not only contemporaries at other law schools in the late 1800s and early 1900s, but for modern law journals.[51]   The model set by the early editions of the *Harvard Law Review* is still alive today.

---

[45] *Id.* at 767 ("They also took note of developments in the law and, in imitation of the successful commercial law journals, published casenotes of recent decisions and lead articles by 'persons of acknowledged merit.' By calling on contributors from both inside and outside the college, the student editors of the Columbia Jurist 'made their magazine the forerunner of the modern university law review.'")

[46] 1 COLUMBIA JURIST 1, 2, (1885).

[47] *Id.* This first issue included reports on the Moot Court, a recent New York Supreme Court decision ruling that a wife may form a co-partnership regarding a separate estate, citations for cases the professors felt students should read for class, study gossip and other brief notes.

[48] *See* Swygert & Bruce at 766-67.

[49] *See* Cramton at 3; Swygert & Bruce at 769; Aronstein Black at 2-3.

[50] 1 HARV. L. REV. 35 (1887).

[51] Swygert & Bruce at 769-79.

Volume 1 declared its purpose.[52] The articles served not only to inform and educate, but to be authoritative.[53]

In the late 1880s, Harvard Law School was experiencing what former Dean and Solicitor General Erwin N. Griswold described as a rebirth.[54] A unique potion of ingredients, mixed at the right time by the right people combined to produce the *Harvard Law Review*: the 250th anniversary of the founding of Harvard College; a handful of ambitious law students; a supportive and visionary law school administration; and a group of highly-placed, enthusiastic alumni, including 1877 alumnus and future Supreme Court Justice Louis D. Brandeis.[55] Dean Griswold wrote that the founders noted the influences of the two previous student-run journals at Albany and Columbia.[56]

In their historical article, Professors Swygert & Bruce credit law student and founding editor in chief, John Jay McKelvey, for developing the law review at Harvard.[57] Many scholars agree that the birth of the law review at Harvard was yet another outgrowth of the pioneering legal educator Christopher Columbus Langdell.[58] Thus, much like the Socratic and case methods, two law school institutions loved and reviled by generations of law students, the law review can trace its origins to Dean Langdell.[59]

---

[52] 1 HARV. L. REV. at 35.

[53] *Id.*

[54] ERWIN N. GRISWOLD, THE HARVARD LAW REVIEW – GLIMPSES OF ITS HISTORY AS SEEN BY AN AFICIONADO, IN HARVARD LAW REVIEW: CENTENNIAL ALBUM (1987) (also posted at the HLR website: www.harvardlawreview.org.). As a student, the future dean served as President of volume 41 of the *Harvard Law Review. See also* Erwin N. Griswold, *Essays Commemorating the One Hundredth Anniversary of the Harvard Law Review*, 100 HARV. L. REV. 728 (1987).

[55] *Id.* ("[A] group of eight third year students formed a new law club, known as the Langdell Society, and out of this club the *Harvard Law Review* quickly developed ... But this was a remarkable group of students, and they felt moved to act because they would soon be leaving Law School."

[56] *Id.*

[57] Swygert & Bruce at 769-70.

[58] *See* Cramton at 3. ("It was in this setting in 1887 that eight Harvard Law students, moved by the intellectual excitement of Langdell's new type of law school, converted an informal student discussion group into the first surviving student-edited law review, the *Harvard Law Review*.")

[59] *Id.*

In the first edition of the *Harvard Law Review*, dated April 15, 1887, an editor's note declared:

> In publishing the first number of the *Harvard Law Review* the editors feel it necessary to offer a few words of explanation. The Review is not intended to enter into competition with established law journals, which are managed by lawyers of experience, and have already a firm footing in the profession. Our object, primarily, is to set forth the work done in the school with which we are connected, to furnish news of interest to those who have studied law in Cambridge, and to give, if possible, to all who are interested in the subject of legal education some idea of what is done under the Harvard system of instruction. Yet we are not without hopes that the Review may be serviceable to the profession at large. From the kind offers of assistance on the part of the professors in the Law School, and from the list of the alumni who have consented to write for the Review, we feel sure that the contributed articles will prove of permanent value.
>
> It will be our aim to develop the Review on the lines we have indicated, in the hope of deserving the support which we have already received. If we succeed, we shall endeavor to enlarge our field as much as is consistent with our plan. If we fail, we shall at least have the satisfaction of believing that our work has been honestly done in the interests of the Law School and of its alumni.[60]

Almost instantly, the *Harvard Law Review* not only became an authoritative resource, but it became the standard-bearer for all law reviews.[61] The *Harvard Law Review* influence spans many fronts: the apex of legal scholarship by the biggest legal scholars;[62] an influential

---

[60] 1 HARV. L. REV. at 35.

[61] *See* SELIGMAN at 182 ("Within twenty years of its formation in 1886, the Law Review evolved into the most prestigious legal journal in the country. It endures as virtually the only journal that is financially self-sufficient among the better than 180 university law reviews.").

[62] Harvard has the widest circulation of any law review with about 8,000 subscribers and is the most-cited law review. *See About the Harvard Law Review*, www.harvardlawreview.org.

authority for its readers and a model for other law schools to emulate with their own law reviews.[63] And, for more than a century, the Harvard Law Review alumni list has been like a Who's Who of the legal world.[64]

Since 1925, the *Harvard Law Review* has been housed in the now-famous Gannett House.[65] The three-story white-wood-frame Greek Revival house has not only become synonymous with the *Harvard Law Review*, but is known on campus as "a home away from home" as well as a "pressure cooker" for its editors.[66]

Yale,[67] University of Pennsylvania,[68] Columbia,[69] Michigan[70] and Northwestern[71] soon followed. When Columbia law students took a

---

[63] In his famous diatribe against law reviews, Professor Rodell compared the way law reviews emulate Harvard to the way newspapers have "stepped all over themselves in an effort to imitate" *The New York Times.* Fred Rodell, *Goodbye to Law Reviews*, 23 VA. L. REV. 38, 44 (1936).

[64] For example, in a letter by Justice Oliver Wendell Holmes to Justice Felix Frankfurter, April 13, 1916, Holmes wrote: "The Law Review has come, and I can't tell you how touched and charmed I am. Very few things in my life have given me so much pleasure. I well know that I owe it to your constant kindness that I reach such a crowning reward, and I think you from my heart."

The April 1916 issue of the *Harvard Law Review*, volume 29, was dedicated to Holmes on his 75th birthday. ROBERT M. MENNEL & CHRISTINE L. COMPSTON (Editors), HOLMES & FRANKFURTER: THE CORRESPONDENCE, 1912-1934, 51 (1996). *See generally*, Mark Tushnet & Timothy Lynch, *The Project of the Harvard Forewords: A Social and Intellectual Inquiry*, 11 CONST. COMMENT 463 (1995); Learned Hand, *Foreword*, 50 HARV. L. REV. 1 (1936).

[65] *See* Griswold.

[66] KERLOW at 14-15.

[67] *See* Charles E. Hughes, *Foreword*, 50 YALE L. J. 737 (1941). *See also* Fred R. Shapiro, *The Most-Cited Articles from the Yale Law Journal*, 100 YALE L. J. 1449, 1451 (1991) (*"The Yale Law Journal* has been a central component of legal literature, and its centennial is an appropriate occasion for identifying the 'citation superstars' it has published in the course of its century of existence."); Arthur L. Corbin, *The First Half-Century,* 50 YALE L. J. 740 (1941).

[68] The University of Pennsylvania Law Review began publishing in 1896, but traces its roots to one of the country's first law reviews, the American Law Register, which began in 1852. *See* Joseph P. Flanagan, Jr. 100 U. PA. L. REV. 69 (1951); Swygert & Bruce at 755-58.

[69] 1 COLUMBIA L. REV. 50 (1901) .

[70] *See* E. Blythe Stason, *The Law Review—Its First Fifty Years*, 50 MICH. L. REV. 1134 (1952).

second shot with the publication of the *Columbia Law Review* in 1901, the Editor's Note credited past and present members of the *Harvard Law Review* for "kindly suggestions" and "setting before us a standard to which we some day hope to attain."[72]

Within years, many law schools thereafter, as Professor Lawrence M. Friedman, put it "no matter how marginal," established its own law review.[73] Another scholar wrote that many law schools published their own law reviews simply "because that is what Harvard did." [74] This growth was more than merely emulating the elite.[75]

Within decades, every law school published their own law review or journal.[76] By the midpoint of the 20th century, there were more than one hundred law journals. While some faculty argued that the law review field had become "overcrowded,"[77] law schools and law students felt that having a law review was a necessary component of legal education as well as the law school's reputation and standing in the legal community.[78] If a law school wanted credibility, it needed a student-

---

[71] *See* John Paul Stevens, *Introductory Comment*, 75 Nw. U. L. Rev. 977 (1981).

[72] 1 Colum. L. Rev. 1 ("In particular, we wish to thank the editors, past and present of the *Harvard Law Review*, not only for setting before us a standard to which we some day hope to attain, but also for their kindly suggestions."); *see also* William O. Douglas, *Foreword*, 50 Colum. L. Rev (1950).

[73] Lawrence M. Friedman, The History of American Law 693 (2d ed. 1985).

[74] *See* Afton Dekanal, *Faculty-Edited Law Reviews: Should the Law Schools Join the Rest of Academe?*, 57 UMKC L. Rev. 233, 235 (1989).

[75] Closen & Dzielak at 15 ("Almost immediately upon their establishment, the student-edited law reviews became a significant and lasting feature of legal education in the United States.").

[76] *Id.*

[77] *See Editorial Notes*, 1 Ill. L. Rev. 39 (1906); *see also* Paul Shipman Andrews, *Foreword*, 1 Syracuse L. Rev. 1, 1 (1949).

[78] Law review has been recognized as a uniquely American institution "There is not so far as I know in the world an academic faculty which pins its reputation before the public upon the work of undergraduate students – there is none, that is, except in the American law reviews." K.N. Llewellyn, The Bramble Bush 105 (Oceana Publications 1951); *See also* Gerhard Casper, *Foreword*, 50 U. Chi. L. Rev. 405, 405-06 (1983).

edited law journal.[79] One scholar wrote, "The quality of a law school is best judged by the quality of its student-written and –edited law review."[80] Another wrote that law reviews are symbolic representatives of the legal profession.[81] Yet another analogized the law review to a law school's "cathedral" – possibly a temple, too.[82]

As the law review movement spread west, the journals took pride in adopting a regional outlook and influence.[83] In an essay marking the 75th anniversary of the *Indiana Law Journal*, Professor Colleen Kristl Pauwels, recounted the history of the *Indiana Law Journal* and its role in the development of the law in this country from the colonial era to the modern era, noting:

> Also of concern to state law schools in general was the issue of their law review's place in this new enterprise. Harvard, Yale, and Columbia had established themselves as the authoritative reviews of Anglo-American law. Other schools realized the

---

[79] Closen & Dzielak at 35-36 ("These schools created law reviews not only to keep up with Harvard but also for the educational benefit they provided to student editors. Furthermore, it was believed that a law review at a law school was a sign of a 'mature educational institution,' because law reviews demonstrated a school's commitment to legal scholarship." *See also* Swygert & Bruce at 779.

[80] Willard L. Boyd, *Judging the Iowa Law School*, 75 IOWA L. REV. 819, 819 (1990).

[81] Robert Weisberg, *Some Ways to Think About Law Reviews*, 47 STAN. L. REV. 1147, 1149 (1995) ("[L]aw reviews are often the symbolic representatives of the legal profession – they are there to be attacked, revered, rendered egalitarian, or conserved in the ambivalent ways that ambivalent law students treat, or would like to treat, the profession more generally.").

[82] John T. Noonan Jr., *Law Reviews*, 47 STAN. L. REV. 1117, 1117 (1995) ("As cathedrals to every good-sized medieval French town, and as universities to every twentieth century state of the United States, so law reviews are a necessary element of every respectable law school.").

[83] *See* Colleen Kristl Pauwels, *Hepburn's Dream: The History of the Indiana Law Journal*, 75 IND. L. J. i, ix (2000) (citing 1 IOWA L. BULL. 29 (1915); 1 MICH. L. REV. 58 (1902)). See also N. William Hines, *The Iowa Law Review: A Tradition of Excellence*, 75 IOWA L. REV. 821 (1990) (initially the Iowa Law Review focused on cases published in the Northwestern Reporter); John W. Fisher, II, *Introduction to Volume 100 of the West Virginia Law Review*, 100 W. VA. L. REV. 1 (1997).

importance of having a law review, but felt that they must find a unique niche to justify the endeavor. Most state schools found their justification by specializing in the law of their home state, some even initially confining their scope to a review of their state's laws.[84]

The rapid growth and expansion of law reviews mirrored the growth of legal education throughout the country as well as the recognition of the role and value of law review as an institution.[85] In 1930, 43 law schools had law reviews.[86] By 1942, there were 55.[87] By 1955, there were 78.[88] Between 1946 and 1961, numbers increased from 188 to more than 300.[89]

Today, an accurate count is nearly impossible, but many agree that there are more than 400 student-edited law reviews and journals published each year.[90] These journals consume the lives of their student-editors while churning out more than 150,000 printed pages of legal scholarship every year.[91]

---

[84] *Id.*

[85] *Id.* at 15; Closen & Dzielak credit the first reference to law review as an institution to John J. McKelvey, *The Law School Review: 1887-1937*, 50 HARV. L. REV. 868, 873, 880 (1937).

[86] Closen & Dzielak at 38.

[87] *Id.* Closen & Dzielak at 38.

[88] Closen & Dzielak at 38.

[89] *Id.* at 16 (citing Jean Stefanic, *Community of Meaning or Reinscription of Hierarchy?* 63 U.COLO. L. REV. 651, 655-56 (1992)). ("One dynamic variation ... is that law reviews now exist at virtually all American Bar Association accredited law schools, not merely at most of them. Furthermore, many law schools have more than one law review, consisting of one generalist journal and one or more specialty journals.").

[90] Closen & Dzielak at 38.

[91] *See* Judith S. Kaye, *One Judge's View of Academic Law Review Writing*, 39 J. LEGAL EDUC. 313, 316 (1989).

II. Special Purpose

For decades scholars have pointed to one particularly influential law review article as a model for scholarship, creativity and influence.[92] In 1890, Louis D. Brandeis and Samuel D. Warren, wrote "The Right to Privacy" in the *Harvard Law Review*.[93] While law reviews and legal scholarship were still in their nascent stages, the future justice and his law partner, published this article calling for a legal remedy through personal privacy to counterbalance Boston's aggressive and salacious newspapers.[94] The authors argued for a new area of tort law, and thus the right of privacy was born.[95] Prosser & Keeton, in their leading treatise on Torts, trace the judicial acceptance of this new area of law by other writers and courts.[96]

Few legal doctrines can trace their origins to such a seminal moment, which is why this example is often invoked as the model for a law review's role in the legal community. While many elements of modern law still trace their roots back thousands of years to the scholarship of the ancient Romans and Greeks, the Warren & Brandeis article stands not only as a seminal moment for privacy law, but in many ways for law reviews as an institution themselves.[97]

Seven years after the privacy article began to transform defamation and tort law, the United States Supreme Court made its first citation to a law review article in 1897. A dissenting opinion by Justice Edward White in *United States v. Trans-Missouri Freight Assoc*[98] cited to a *Harvard Law* Review article on contracts and restraint of trade[99] Two

---

[92] Kenneth F. Ripple, *The Role of the Law Review in the Tradition of Judicial Scholarship*, 57 N.Y.U. ANN. SURV. AM L. 429, 435 (2000). Kaye, at 316.

[93] Samuel D. Warren & Louis D. Brandeis, *The Right to Privacy*, 4 HARV. L. REV. 193 (1890).

[94] *Id.* at 196.

[95] *Id.*

[96] PROSSER & KEETON ON TORTS 849-51 (5th ed. 1984) (noting that New York was the first state to recognize the right to privacy in *Manola v. Stevens*, N.Y. Sup. Ct. 1890)).

[97] *See* Richard A. Posner, *Legal Scholarship Today*, 115 HARV. L. REV. 1314, 1314-18 (2002).

[98] 166 U.S. 290, 350, n. 1 (1897) (White, J. dissenting) (citing Amasa M. Eaton, *On Contracts In Restraint of Trade*, 4 HARV. L. REV. 128 (1890)).

[99] Amasa M. Eaton, *On Contracts In Restraint of Trade*, 4 HARV. L. REV. 128 (1890)).

years later, the Supreme Court, in a majority opinion in 1899, cited an article.[100] Chief Justice Melville Fuller cited to the *Harvard Law Review* in the majority opinion to *Chicago, Milwaukee and St. Paul Railway Co. v. Clark.*[101]

The rulings on these two cases did not hinge on the articles they cited.[102] However, these initial citations gave the fledgling institution a degree of respectability and provided the justices with useful references and credibility.[103] Professors Closen & Dzielak wrote: "In the years ahead, judges at all levels began to pay greater heed to the views expressed in law review articles."[104]

Recognizing the value of law review articles, Justice Benjamin Cardozo, revered as one of the most prolific judicial writers of the 20th century, wrote: "Judges have at last awakened, or at all events a number of them not wholly negligible, to the treasures buried in the law reviews."[105] At the other end of the spectrum, scholars have enjoyed repeating an exchange between Justice Oliver Wendell Holmes, another of the Court's most prolific writers, who once lambasted an attorney who cited a law review article as authority before the Court, calling the citation and law review articles in general "the work of boys."[106]

In one of the few published empirical studies on who reads law reviews, and why, the authors surveyed lawyers, professors and judges who reported they used law reviews for everything from developing a new framework for a legal issue to reading articles by acquaintances.[107]

---

[100] Discussed in Closen & Dzielak at 26-27. However, Jacobstein writes that the Supreme Court did not begin citing to law reviews until about 1917. JACOBSTEIN at 336 (citing Chester A. Newland, Comment, *The Supreme Court and Legal Writing: Learned Journals as Vehicles of an Anti-Antitrust Lobby*, 58 GEO. L. J. 105, 127 (1959)).

[101] *Id.* (discussing 178 U.S. 353, 365 (1899) (citing James Ames, *Two Theories of Consideration*, 12 HARV. L. REV. 515 (1899))).

[102] *Id.* at 26

[103] *Id.*

[104] *Id.*

[105] BENJAMIN N. CARDOZO, THE GROWTH OF THE LAW 14 (1924).

[106] Hughes, 50 YALE L. J. at 737; *See also* Kaye, 39 J. LEGAL EDUC. at 316.

[107] Max Stier, et al, *Law Review Usage and Suggestions for Improvement: A Survey of Attorneys, Professors, and Judges*, 44 STAN. L. REV. 1467, 1483 (1992). The authors sent the survey to 1,162 lawyers, professors and judges, and 380 or 32.7 percent responded. *Id.* at 1479.

Law reviews aim to provide the legal community with "usable" and "informative" articles.[108] As a scholarly periodical, a law review informs and educates the reader.[109] As an annotation, the law review, with its dense footnotes citing to judicial opinions and case law, it provides a reference and resource to its reader who can be a law student on an intellectual quest to learn or a lawyer looking for a novel argument or support for a novel argument or a judge looking to see how other courts handled similar issues or a law professor writing to test a new idea.[110]

Law reviews record and critique the judicial opinions, statutes and other articles while seeking to propose changes.[111] The role of law reviews in critiquing the highest levels of the judiciary is founded on the same First Amendment values applied to newspapers and other media, in a role of the Fourth Estate.[112] Law review articles are lauded as records

---

[108] Sandra Day O'Connor, *Fiftieth Anniversary Remarks*, 50 STAN. L. REV. 1, 5 (1997).

[109] Richard A. Posner, *The Future of the Student-Edited Law Review*, 47 STAN. L. REV. 1131, 1137 (1995) ("Scholarly journals are not meant to be read the way the daily newspaper is read. No one has time to read 500, or for that matter, twenty-five, law reviews, each published four to eight times a year. The vast majority of the articles in scholarly journals are destined to go directly from the subscriber to the library shelf, there to be available for future reference as the need arises.").

[110] Ronald J. Krotoszynski, Jr., *Legal Scholarship at the Crossroads: On Farce, Tragedy, and Redemption*, 77 TEX. L. REV. 321, 327 (1998). ("At the risk of appearing terminally naïve, I have always assumed that legal scholarship, in whatever form, had as its object influencing the direction of the law—ideally by moving judges, lawyers, legislators, and bureaucrats to rethink or reconsider a particular problem. Whether the argument uses doctrinal analysis, tells a story, or musters empirical social science data, the author's objective is to alter the existing legal landscape—to push or pull the law in a particular direction. Most law review articles will fail in this effort and most law professors expect that their work will go unnoticed. But the improbability of success does not make the effort a waste of time and energy.").

[111] *See* David L. Shapiro, *In Defense of Judicial Candor*, 100 HARV. L. REV. 731 (1987); see also A. Leon Higginbotham, Jr., *The Life of the Law: Values, Commitment, and Craftsmanship*, 100 HARV. L. REV. 795 (1987).

[112] Hughes, 50 YALE L. J. at 737-38 ("If some members of this 'fourth estate' of the law, conscious of their prestige and influence, may seem at times to assume an attitude approaching arrogance, they are at once subject to counter-attack and a balance of sound criticism is attained, with advantage to all concerned. It is idle to expect in legal discussion and judicial opinion, in relation to close

and chronicles for development of law,[113] a contextual reference,[114] references[115] and even "report cards"[116] As a resource that can bring a reader up-to-speed on an unfamiliar topic, law review articles can influence the law even without being cited in a judicial opinion.[117]

As a result, even the highest levels of the judiciary acknowledge and extol the values and benefits of law review membership and the products they publish.[118] Justice Sandra Day O'Connor wrote, "Indeed, when confronted with a novel question, I frequently survey the law reviews for a well-researched doctrinal piece that provides a shortcut into the existing precedents and analysis."[119]

Consumption and praise by the judiciary also translates into another widely-discussed benchmark for law reviews: citations.[120] This noted goal of being cited has also spawned something of a cottage industry among legal scholars who track and attempt to analyze law review

---

questions of high importance, any greater unanimity of view than we find in other domains of human thought – art, science, or theology. And I think we may assume that a bench composed of law school professors or law review editors, impartially chosen, would exhibit views as varying as those of judges whose works they appraise.").

[113] Ripple, 57 N.Y.U. ANN. SURV. AM L. at 436 ("A judge's main interest in the law reviews, however, remains in the traditional areas of legal scholarship. Here, judges read not simply to 'keep current,' but as part of the task of doing our primary work of deciding cases.").

[114] O'Connor. 50 STAN. L. REV. at 3.

[115] Earl Warren, *Introduction*, 1 CREIGHTON L. REV. 7 (1968).

[116] Sol Wachtler, *Foreword, 1991 Survey of New York Law*, 43 SYRACUSE L. REV. 1, 1 (1992) (quoted in *Fifty Years and Beyond*, 50 SYRACUSE L. REV. 1191, 1195 (2000)).

[117] Posner, 47 STAN. L. REV. at 1137-38 ("Law reviews are indispensable resources for judges and their clerks, whether or not the judge's opinion actually cites the article or student note that proved helpful in preparation of the opinion.").

[118] Earl Warren, *Forword*, 51 N.W. U.L. Rev. 1 (1956); Earl Warren, 1 STAN. L. REV. v, v (Nov. 1948).

[119] O'Connor, 50 STAN. L. REV. at 6.

[120] Gregory Scott Crespi, *Ranking Specialized Law Reviews: A Methodological Critique*, 26 FLA. ST. U. L. REV. 837 (1999); Arthur Austin, *The Reliability of Citation Counts in Judgments on Promotion, Tenure, and Status*, 35 ARIZ. L. REV. 829 (1993); Bart Sloan, *What We Writing For? Student Works As Authority and Their Citation By the Federal Bench*, 61 GEO. WASH. L. REV. 221 (1992).

citations.[121] Some of these scholars judge the quality of law reviews based upon those citations.[122] It is debatable whether stating the obvious – that the journals published by elite law schools are most frequently cited by courts and thus achieve a higher ranking and more prestige – adds anything credible to the academic field remains an open question.[123]

III. Specialization

Once every law school developed its own law journal, the expansion continued with specialization. While New York University published the ambitious the annual Survey of American Law, in 1944, Dean Arthur Vanderbilt also established perhaps the first specialized law journal, the Tax Law Review.[124]

Just as every law school publishes its own "generalist" law review, just about every law school publishes at least one secondary or specialized journal or law review.[125] The subject matter for specialized

---

[121] Closen & Dzielak at 26; William H. Manz, *Floating "Free" In Cyberspace: Law Reviews in the Internet Era*, 74 ST. JOHN'S L. REV. 1069, 1075-76 nn. 27-30 (2000); The Editors, *Seventy-fifth Anniversary Retrospective: Most Influential Articles*, 75 N.Y.U. L. Rev. 1517 (2000); Tracey E. George & Chris Guthrie, *An Empirical Evaluation of Specialized Law Reviews*, 26 FLA. ST. L. REV. 813 (1999) [hereinafter George & Guthrie]; Russell Korobkin, *Ranking Journals: Some Thoughts on Theory and Methodology*, 26 FLA. ST. L. REV. 852 (1999); James Lindgren & Daniel Seltzer, *The Most Prolific Law Professors and Faculty*, 71 CHI-KENT L. REV. 781 (1996); Colleen M. Cullen & S. Randall Kalberg, *Chicago-Kent Law Review Faculty Scholarship Survey*, 70 CHI-KENT L. REV. 1445 (1995).
[122] *See id.*; *see also* George & Guthrie, 824-31.
[123] Korobkin, 26 FLA. ST. L. REV. at 865 ("There are a number of reasons, however, why citation frequency is not a perfect proxy for scholarly value and, consequently, is far from perfect basis for ranking journals. While a citation to an article can signify that the article was particularly insightful or original, it might just as easily signify ... [other] characteristics.").
[124] ARTHUR T. VANDERBILT II, CHANGING LAW: A BIOGRAPHY OF ARTHUR T. VANDERBILT 135 (1976) ("As a modern law school was known by its publications, Vanderbilt began to expand the School of Law's publication program. Perhaps the most ambitious undertaking of any law school faculty was the Annual Survey of American Law he originated in 1943, a yearly volume of 750 to 1,000 pages to set forth succinctly the significant changes in the important fields of law.")
[125] See Closen & Dzielak at 16.

journals is as varied as the law itself. Just about every special interest, area of law or public issue has its own.[126] This growth has added to the wealth of scholarship and opened the law journal experience to thousands of additional law students every year.

Some scholars credit this expansion as another example of the democratization of the modern law school experience.[127] Students interested in developing their legal writing, editing and research skills who once would have been excluded from more elitist law journals, are finding new homes in specialized journals. The specialized journals also offer an additional avenue for law students interested in a particular area of the law.[128]

The specialized journal explosion was fueled by three major factors: expansion of law schools[129]; law professors eager for tenure; seeking additional outlets to stave off the "publish or perish" beast;[130] and law students interested in acquiring law journal experience that was once held only by the elite.[131] Some have likened this growth and opening up to democratization of the law review experience.[132] Others call it an

---

[126] George & Guthrie at 823 ("Law schools publish journals in a wide variety of specialty areas, including agricultural law, education law, immigration law, insurance law, maritime law, poverty law, Native-American law, sports law, and torts law. Certain areas, however, have received much more attention than others, namely international law, environmental law, and intellectual property and technology law.").

[127] Robert Weisberg, *Some Ways to Think About Law Reviews*, 47 STAN. L. REV. 1147, 1155 (1995).

[128] George & Guthrie, at 820.

[129] *Id.* at 818.

[130] *Id.* at 819 ("The increase in the number and size of law schools has been accompanied by a tremendous expansion of the legal academy. Law faculty members have played an instrumental role in the boom of specialized law reviews over the past decades."). See also Rodell, 23 VA. L. REV. at 44 ("[I]t is not surprising that the law reviews are as bad as they are. The leading articles, and book reviews too, are for the most part written by professors and would-be professors of law whose chief interest is in getting something published so they can wave it in the faces of their deans when they ask for a raise, because the accepted way of getting ahead in law teaching is to break constantly into print in a dignified way.") .

[131] *Id.* at 820-21. See also Korobkin,, 26 FLA. ST. U. L. REV. at 853.

[132] GLENDON, at 227. Here, the author points out that in the 1970s and 1980s, the system was "radically revised." "During the 18 years I taught at Boston

attempt by specialty journals and law schools to capture readership in a "glutted market."[133] It has also facilitated the growth of interdisciplinary study while giving law professors who have sub-specialties additional avenues for publication.[134]

The rapid proliferation and continued expansion has earned law reviews the label of a "growth industry." [135] This phenomenal boom makes an accurate accounting of the actual number of such journals a difficult task.[136] The debate on the actual count has numbers between 400 to 500 law journals, the majority of them student-edited, published by law schools in the United States.[137] George & Guthrie counted 330 specialized reviews published by law schools.[138] Another scholar estimates that there are as many as 800.[139]

This growth has not come without criticism. Among the regular cacophony of complaints about law reviews is that their student-editors are considered intellectually ill-equipped, even "handicapped,"[140] to select and edit articles,[141] lack editorial or publishing experience.[142] Some

---

College, I witnesses the birth of an environmental law journal, an international and comparative law journal and a Third World law journal." Now "any law student could put law review on his or her resume and any professor's scholarly effects could be crowned with publication." *Id.*

[133] James W. Harper, *Why Student-Run Law Reviews?*, 82 MINN. L. REV. 1261, 1266 (1998).

[134] Richard A. Posner, *Legal Scholarship Today*, 115 HARV. L. REV. 1314, 1323-24 (2002) ("The number of dual-degree (Ph.D.-J.D.) law professors is increasing, and specialized journals, many of them faculty-edited (primarily in economic analysis of law), and a number of the faculty-edited ones refereed, are a publication outlet of growing importance. But interdisciplinary legal scholarship is still far from converging with the standard academic model, and the progress toward that convergence is slow.")

[135] Harper, 82 MINN. L. REV. at 1265.

[136] George & Guthrie at 821-22, counted 875 law journals in the United States, Canada, the United Kingdom, New Zealand and Australia, according to the Current Law Index.

[137] Closen & Dzielak at 15-16.

[138] George & Guthrie at 824.

[139] Kenneth Lasson, *Scholarship Amok: Excesses in Pursuit of Truth and Tenure*, 103 HARV. L. REV. 926, 928 (1990)).

[140] Posner, 47 STAN. L. REV. at 1132.

[141] Rodell, 23 VA. L. REV. at 38 Richard A. Epstein, *Facutly-Edited Law Journals*, 70 CHI-KENT L. REV. 87, 88 (1994); Leo P. Martinez, *Babies, Bathwater, and Law Reviews*, 47 STAN. L. REV. 1139, 1143 (1995); James

scholars have derided the journal expansion's democratization while others jeer that with all the additional journals, legal scholarship has become diluted.[143]   Others have questioned the quality and practicality of the mushrooming interdisciplinary articles in law reviews and specialized journals.[144]

The first salvo was both a complaint and a call to arms.[145]   Writing in 1926, Albert Kocourek, the faculty editor for the *Illinois Law Review*, complained that even in the early 1900s, the field for law reviews had become crowded and in order to better serve the legal communities, journals needed to specialize.[146]   Decades later, Justice William O. Douglas went as far as to refer to some of the new specialized journals as less than objective: "Some law journals may be so biased as to present only one side of controversial issues."[147]

Lindgren, *Reforming the American Law Review*, 47 STAN. L. REV. 1123 (1995); James Lindgren, *An Author's Manifesto*, 61 U. CHI. L. REV. 527 (1994).

[142] Terri LeClercq, *The Nuts and Bolts of Article Criteria and Selection*, 30 STETSON L. REV. 437 (2000); Anne Enquist, *Substantive Editing Versus Technical Editing: How Law Review Editors Do Their Job*, 30 STETSON L. REV. 451 (2000); Darby Dickerson, *Citation Frustrations – And Solutions*, 30 STETSON L. REV. 477 (2000); C. Steven Bradford, *As I Lay Writing: How to Write Law Review Articles for Fun and Profit*, 44 J. LEGAL EDUC. 13 (1994); Alfred F. Conard, *A Lovable Law Review*, 44 J. LEGAL EDUC. 1 (1994).

[143] FRIEDMAN at 693..

[144] Harry T. Edwards, *The Growing Disjunction Between Legal Education and the Legal Profession*, 91 MICH. L. REV. 34, 36, 38-39 (1992). Judge Edwards complains that law reviews are full of mediocre interdisciplinary articles written by law professors. Judge Edwards referred to many interdisciplinary legal academics as "ivory tower dilettantes." Judge Edwards is also critical of legal education, complaining that law schools have abandoned their proper place by emphasizing abstract theory "at the expense of practical scholarship and pedagogy."

[145] *See* Albert Kocourek, *Editorial Notes, The Law Reviews*, 21 ILL. L. REV. 147, 151-52 (1926).

[146] *Id.* at 151-52.

[147] William O. Douglas, *Law Reviews and Full Disclosure*, 40 WASH. L. REV. 227, 228 (1965) (Nevertheless, Justice Douglas added, "Law journals and business journals – freed from any undisclosed partisan bias—furnish helpful guides to the profession. They can be provocative and stimulating by showing the dimensions of a problem. They often reveal complexities and dangers where the frame of reference of a single controversy makes the case seem simple.").

IV. What Is It All For

An article about the law review experience asked what is it all about and why, year-after-year thousands of law students spend hours-upon-hours working on law reviews, publishing hundreds of thousands of pages of material?[148]

As discussed above, law reviews serve the legal community as a reference and source for information.[149] Law review editors choose articles, edit, cite-check and research these articles while undertaking their own legal scholarship inquiry with their own notes, comments or recent decisions.[150] Unlike academic, scholarly and trade journals in other fields and areas, decisions are made by the students, from top to bottom.[151]

In legal education, law review serves an important role in the development of the skills vital to the legal profession.[152]

A wave of criticism from law professors annually addresses the role law students play in legal scholarship.[153] Numerous law review articles take aim at law reviews; one law review published an entire symposium critical of law students editing law journals.[154] Professors seem to enjoy questioning whether law students are intellectually equipped to make

---

[148] Scott J. Atlas, *Why Did We Do It?*, 75 TEX. L. REV. 9 (1996); Erik M. Jensen, *The Law Review Manuscript Glut: The Need for Guidelines*, 39 J. LEGAL EDUC. 383 (1989).

[149] *See* Richard S. Harnsberger, *Reflections About Law Reviews and American Legal Scholarship*, 76 NEB. L. REV. 681, 682-84 (1997).

[150] Leibman & White at.398-401.

[151] Arthur D. Austin, *The "Custom of Vetting" as a Substitute for Peer Review*, 32 ARIZ. L. REV. 1, 4 (1989) ("The use of student edited journals as the main outlet for legal writing is an embarrassing situation deserving the smirks of disdain it gets from colleagues in the sciences and humanities.").

[152] *See* Eugene Volokh, *Writing a Student Article*, 48 J. LEGAL EDUC. 247 (1998); *see also* Mary Kay Kane, *Introductory Remarks*, 50 HASTINGS L. J. (1999).

[153] Ripple, 57 N.Y.U. ANN. SURV. AM L. at 434; David M. Richardson, *Improving the Law Review Model: A Case in Point*, 44 J. LEGAL ED. 6 (1994) (law review editors are "gate-keepers").

[154] *Symposium on Law Review Editing: The Struggle Between Author and Editor Over Control of the Text*, 70 CHI-KENT L. REV. 71 (1994).

selection and editing judgments on their precious articles.[155] Some of the esteemed members of legal academia who seek to have their tenure and reputations judged by what they publish in law reviews also take aim at law review editors.[156] Law review editors, frequently considered inexperienced, obsessive and even passive aggressive, some authors complain lack the experience and intellect to make substantive critiques and editing comments on articles.[157]

Nevertheless, even the most caustic scholars acknowledge that law review membership provides experience and hones skills necessary to the legal practice[158] while law review membership is often regarded as a mark of excellence.[159] Law review credentials are prized by law students for the experience that opens doors to the upper echelons of the legal community.[160] Law review membership is a "certification stamp" or exclusive honor society.[161]

---

[155] Ann Althouse, *Who's to Blame for Law Reviews?* 70 CHI-KENT L. REV. 81, 82 (1994) ("Law review bashing is an easy enough sport to play."); James Lindgren, *Student Editing: Using Education to Move Beyond Struggle*, 70 CHI-KENT L. REV. 95, 95 (1994) ("Student editors are grossly unsuited for the jobs they are faced with."); Gregory E. Maggs, *Just Say No?*, 70 CHI-KENT L. REV. 101, 109 (1994) ("Scorched-earth editing provides one example. Student editors may improve a few pieces by editing every sentence. Over time, however, they may scare away good authors who do not want to subject themselves to the process.").

[156] Epstein, 70 CHI-KENT L. REV. at 87 (lauding the advantages of faculty-edited journals).

[157] Id. at 88.

[158] Ronald D. Rotunda, *Law Reviews—The Extreme Centrist Position*, 62 IND. L.J. 1 (1987). Rotunda points out, "If the goal of law reviews is to change society, then we must acknowledge that they have failed." *Id.* at 2-3. He illustrates from his own experience as a member of the *Harvard Law Review* in the late 1960s, when the editorial staff debated for months whether or not to include an anti-Vietnam War statement. The staff settled on a statement, but the war continued. *Id.*

[159] Martinez, 47 STAN. L. REV at 1141 ("Today, law reviews are seen as a training ground for nascent lawyers, a requisite law student ticket to punch on the route to legal stardom, a primary vehicle for the professoriate to attain tenure if not academic stardom, and, oh yes, a service to the profession.").

[160] STRACHER, at 86; WEISBERG, at 5.

[161] Stier et all, 44 STAN. L. REV. at 1473. ("The consensus, therefore, is that (1) the law review process adds to the quality of a student's legal education, and (2) although the law review membership process exacts important costs both from

Likewise, law firms and judges seek out law students because of what law review membership means.[162] Judges seek law review editors almost exclusively for the most prestigious clerkships while the most prestigious law firms demand law review members.[163]

Law students receive no actual compensation for their work on law reviews.[164] Most receive academic credit. A small handful provide senior editors with stipends. Within months of "making" law review, the tangible benefits accrue: interviews during the second year of law school with top law firms for summer associates positions.[165]

The long-term benefits begin to accrue when the work starts.[166] It is all about the work: detail-oriented citation editing; research; article selection and writing. The law review experience exposes law students to a world of legal research and writing that is notably absent from legal

---

the fabric of the educational institution and from the participating students, external forces – mainly in the form of employment opportunities – provide benefits that encourage maintaining the status quo. As with the evaluations of the quality of the law review product, these assessments are based largely on the observations and intuitions of the commentators. Statistical data are not provided to back up the validity of these claims.").

[162] *Id.* at 1487 ("Even those who do not read law reviews frequently 'use' them by considering law review membership in their hiring decisions.").

[163] Lewis F. Powell, Jr., *Congratulatory Note*, 50 WASH. & LEE L. REV. 3 (1993) ("I cannot claim to have been a member of my alma mater's Law Review. In this way I distinguish myself from many of my colleagues on the Court, and indeed, from all of the law clerks I have hired over the years."); EDWARD LAZARUS, CLOSED CHAMBERS: THE RISE, FALL AND FUTURE OF THE MODERN SUPREME COURT 19 (1999); MARTIN MAYER, THE LAWYERS 110 (1967).

[164] James D. Gordon III, *Law Review and the Modern Mind*, 33 ARIZ. L. REV. 265, 266 (1991) ("Through a brilliant use of reverse psychology, Tom Sawyer was able to hoodwink his gullible friends into thinking that it was actually a *privilege* to whitewash the fence. They did all the work for nothing; in fact, they even paid him for the privilege. The modern analogue to Tom's whitewash is, of course, law review. Law schools want to have law reviews.").

[165] *See* Philip S. Anderson, Speech, *The Legal Profession: Independence and Scholarship*, 28 STETSON L. REV. 411 (1998); Roger C. Henderson, *A Tribute To Student-Edited Law Reviews*, 25 ARIZ. L. REV. 1, 1-2 (1983).

[166] Rotunda, 62 IND. L.J. at 4-5 ("Law review editing and writing provide valuable experience for law students. This training alone justifies the reviews' existence ... The prospect of publication forces the student to engage in a little extra effort, to be a little more careful.").

education after the first year research and writing classes offered by most law schools.[167] Writing is the lawyer's tool.[168] Law students, in order to be effective lawyers, must not only develop proficiency as writers, but must learn to research and effectively and properly use judicial opinions, statutes and case law.[169] Practice and repetition is the best way to develop skills as a writer,[170] and absent law review membership, there are few opportunities to continue researching and writing after the first year of law school.

The much-vaunted MacCrate report on legal education identified 10 skills fundamental to the practice of law that law students must acquire: problem solving, legal analysis and reasoning; legal research; factual investigation, communication; counseling; negotiating; alternative dispute resolution; organization and management; and resolving ethical dilemmas.[171] Any law review editor will testify that the law review experience not only exposes members to these areas but for many it is total immersion.[172]

Lauded as a merit-based institution, where its members earn their way on for grades or writing skill or a combination of both, law review membership has been held in high esteem by many.[173] Justice

---

[167] THANE JOSEF MESSINGER, THE YOUNG LAWYER'S JUNGLE BOOK 9-11 (2nd ed 2000) ("I'll go on record: were I Emperor, law review would be mandatory for all students, for, you see, law review presents an interesting chicken-and-egg question. Whether it is: 1) mere recognition of latent genius, or 2) an incubator of legal skill is unexamined and, more practically is a rare concern among hiring seniors [law firm partners], they simply favor the halos. Its not really their place to care.").

[168] RICK L. MORGAN & KURT SNYDER (editors) THE ABA OFFICIAL AMERICAN BAR ASSOCIATION GUIDE TO APPROVED LAW SCHOOLS 13 (2000).

[169] SHAPO at 1.

[170] TERRI LECLERCQ, EXPERT LEGAL WRITING 4-13 (1995) (Professor LeClercq compared legal writing to physical exercise); LLEWELLYN, at 112.

[171] ROBERT MACCRATE (chairman), TASK FORCE ON LAW SCHOOLS AND THE PROFESSION: NARROWING THE GAP 1992 (ABA 1992); see also JAY G. FOONBERG, HOW TO START AND BUILD A LAW PRACTICE 352-53 (4th ed. 1999).

[172] Harper, 82 MINN. L. REV. at 1273.

[173] Cramton at 5; DERSHOWITZ at 49-50 (Professor Dershowitz noted that at Yale Law School in the 1960s, he was a classmate of the children of presidents, Supreme Court justices, multimillionaire industrialists, but "the only hierarchy I ever saw at Yale Law School was based on grades, Law Journal writing, moot court competition and classroom performance.").

Frankfurter, who was editor of the Harvard Law Review, wrote of his own law review membership as a model example of American social equality: "There was never a problem whether a Jew or a Negro should get on the Law Review," he wrote. "If they excelled academically, they would just go on automatically." [174]   Years after graduating, Justice Frankfurter was quoted about his experience on the Harvard Law Review as "the divine feeling of being one of the potentates of the profession ... for it was our frequent and joyous duty to reverse even [the United States Supreme Court] in an infallible judgment of one hundred and sixty-five words."[175]

The notion of law review as an honor society has not been without critique,[176] as well, especially in discussions about the racial composition of law review staffs.[177] Another critique compared the law review experience to an aristocracy, preserving the best legal experience law schools had to offer to a select few.[178] Thus, many law reviews opened their membership to students who sought to participate in writing

---

[174] *See* LEONARD BAKER, BRANDEIS AND FRANKFURTER: A DUAL BIOGRAPHY 44-45 (1984); *see also* FELIX FRANKFURTER, REMINISCES, 26-27 (New York 1960).
[175] *See id.*
[176] *See* E. Joshua Rosenkranz, *Law Review's Empire*, 39 HASTINGS L. J. 859, 873-75 (1988) (questioning the validity of the law review experience and law review membership as legitimate credential to gauge law students).
[177] Mark A. Godsey, *Educational Inequalities, the Myth of Meritocracy, and the Silencing of Minority Voices: the Need for Diversity on America's Law Reviews*, 12 HARV. BLACKLETTER J. 59, 62 (1995) ("The first flaw in these arguments is that they inaccurately characterize law reviews as 'honor societies.' In doing so, they ignore the intended functions and purposes of law reviews: (1) to act as an intense research and writing course for students, and (2) to provide the legal community with a vehicle for scholarly and political expression that is capable of transmitting many different views and perspectives.
Furthermore, the 'honor society' mentality makes two erroneous assumptions: (1) that 'grade-on' and 'write-on' selection methods identify the students who are able to do the best job as law review members, and (2) that anonymous 'merit'-based selection policies are inherently fair and impartial simply because they are blindly graded.").
[178] Cramton at 6.

competitions.[179] This opening up also influenced the expansion of the specialized journals in the 1960s.[180]

Justice O'Connor wrote one of the most authoritative and thoughtful reflections on her own law review experience at Stanford, comparing the research, writing and editing to wrestling with ideas.[181]

Writing on the 50th anniversary of the Stanford Law Review, Justice O'Connor, reflecting on her experience the law review decades earlier, described how the editors wrestled with "substantial ideas" as they dedicated themselves to the law.[182] The editors of volume one, who created the Stanford Law Review during a wave of post-war optimism with "impartiality, to place special emphasis on 'the economic, political, and social forces which mold the law,' and to investigate 'developing legal problems in advance of their widespread litigation.'"[183]

Acknowledging the criticism law reviews face, Justice O'Connor wrote:

> In my time on the Review, we tried to publish "usable" and "informative" pieces. In subsequent years, a number of articles offered broad treatment of developing areas of the law. Law reviews have met with a certain amount of criticism for their devotion to abstract concepts. It is true that the subject matter of many pieces has grown further and further removed from the work of practitioners. But at Stanford, the theoretical approaches have not crowded out valuable doctrinal scholarship.[184]

Similarly, writing for the 75th anniversary of the Northwestern Law Review, Justice John Paul Stevens, who served as co-editor in chief for the law review, wrote of the value of the law review experience.[185]

---

[179] *Id.* at 6-7.
[180] *Id.*
[181] O'Connor, 50 STAN. L. REV. at 6-7 ("A position as an editor teaches a young lawyer to organize research, locate precedent, acknowledge authorities, sharpen expression, and make and meet arguments.").
[182] O'Connor at 1.
[183] *Id.* at 2 (quoting *President's Page*, 1 STAN. L. REV. vii, vii (Nov. 1948)).
[184] O'Connor at 5.
[185] Stevens, 75 NW. U. L. REV. at 977.

Justice Stevens's father was a student at Northwestern law school in 1906. Northwestern and two other law schools collaborated to publish the *Illinois Law Review*.[186] Forty years later, Justice Stevens wrote his first law review comment on the Sherman Act. Of the law review experience, he wrote:

> Familiarity with the educational function that is performed by work on the Review is an important reason why I regard law review experience as significant evidence of professional qualification. Memories of the independent attitude that was associated with law review research and writing enhances my confidence as a reader of today's scholarly output. The Review – and I refer not only to Northwestern's but also to the select few of comparable quality – plays an essential role in the legal process, not merely as a training ground for future professionals but as a critic of the lawmaking process and as a source of ideas and inspiration as well. Indeed, in a true sense it is a source of law.[187]

Many jurists found an audience for their writing in law reviews years before rising to the bench.[188]

V. Conclusion

For decades, scholars have been complaining about market saturation with law reviews more than 100 years ago.[189] Today, even with more than 400 law journals and the technological ease with which

---

[186] *Id.*

[187] *Id.*

[188] ALPHEUS THOMAS MASON, HARLAN FISKE STONE: PILLAR OF THE LAW 85 (1956): "Even before he went on the bench, lawyers and judges alike found authoritative support for their conclusions in his essays written exclusively for the Columbia Law Review. At times, his analyses were cited by the United States Supreme Court, several lower federal courts, and appellate courts of at least eight states. Bone-dry, humorless and technical, these articles were so well received by law students, teachers, practitioners and judges that eight of them were collected in 1922 and published under the title Articles by Harlan Fiske Stone."

[189] *Editorial Notes*, 1 ILL. L. REV. at 39.

researchers can obtain articles that suit their most specific needs, demand remains. The push to convert student-edited journals into faculty-edited may continue to echo in the halls of academia, but the student-run institution is too powerful and too important to convert.[190]

Law reviews are a link between academia and the practical adjudication of the law by judges.[191] Despite market saturation and the vocal disdain heaped on the institution by their own writers, Professors Closen & Dzielak touched on law reviews' survival instinct: "The law review has successfully withstood the test of time. It can be expected that the law review institution will survive and will continue to provide significant benefits to legal education, to the legal profession, and to society at large."[192]

Law reviews faced a second explosion in the 1990s with the Internet boom.[193] Practically every law review maintains its own website, and many provide everything from listings of their articles to full text articles to archives of recent editions. The Internet threatens to revolutionize the way law reviews are published[194] and used.[195] The chief eulogizer of a predicted demise of the law review is Professor Bernard Hibbitts who gleefully announced that the Internet would put law reviews "out of

---

[190] Martinez, 47 STAN. L. REV. at 1145.

[191] Ripple, 57 N.Y.U. ANN. SURV. AM L. at 430, 432.

[192] Closen & Dzielak at 53.

[193] *See* David A. Rier, *The Future of Legal Scholarship and Scholarly Communication: Publication in the Age of Cyberspace*, 30 AKRON. L. REV. 183 (1996); Howard A. Denemark, *How Valid is the Often-Repeated Accusation That There Are Too Many Legal Articles and Too Many Law Reviews*, 30 AKRON L. REV. 215 (1996); Gregory E. Maggs, *Self-Publication on the Internet and the Future of Law Reviews*, 30 AKRON L. REV. 237 (1996); Bernard J. Hibbitts, *Yesterday Once More: Skeptics, Scribes and the Demise of Law Reviews*, 30 AKRON L. REV. 267 (1996); Howard A. Denemark, *The Death of Law Reviews Has Been Predicted: What Might Be Lost When the Last Law Review Shuts Down?*, 27 SETON HALL L. REV. 1 (1996); Nabil Adam, et al, *The Development and Practice of Law in the Age of the Internet*, 46 AM. L. REV. 327 (1996).

[194] *See* Bernard J. Hibbitts, *Last Writes? Reassessing the Law Review in the Age of Cyberspace*, 71 N.Y.U. L. REV. 615, 664 (1996) ("[P]urely electronic law reviews provide the ultimate alternative for law professors (and others) suffering under the limitations of the present law review system.").

[195] Manz at 1071-74.

business."[196] The Internet would allow law professors to circumvent the law students they so revile and resent, creating a direct link from the law professor's brilliance to the reader's mind.[197] At the same time, posting law review articles on the world wide web, free of charge[198], could make them more accessible and widen the readership, scholars predict.

Financially, the ripples may be seen in law school budgets, law review budgets and subscription lists. Nevertheless, Professor Manz questions whether free access to law review content will have a detrimental impact on law review finances: "The print versions of the reviews, like books and newspapers, have demonstrated the ability to survive alongside their electronic counterparts. It is also unlikely that Internet access to these publications by the legal community will result in significant increase in the use of law reviews within the legal community."[199]

Despite the criticism and the hours upon hours of time and dedication law review service demands, there is no question that the institution has become too vital to legal education and legal research to abandon. Again, Closen & Dzielak wrote: "Thus the purposes of law reviews are great and their influence encompasses students, practitioners, judges, the law, and society."[200] Professor Manz was more pragmatic, "By now, law reviews have a long history and are a thoroughly entrenched feature of law school culture."[201]

The secretive aura surrounding law reviews, fiction again reveals an interesting perception about the role of law reviews in the legal world. Again, reference may be made to John Jay Osborn, Jr., who penned the noted *Paper Chase*. But this reference is found in his lesser-known work, *The Associates*, where one of the main characters, a young Ivy-

---

[196] Manz at 1070 (quoting Cynthia Cotts, *Will Law Reviews' Editors Go the Way of Medieval Scribes*, NAT'L L. J., May 4, 1998, at A16).
[197] *Id.* at 667 ("In the age of cyberspace, law professors can finally escape the straitjacket of the law reviews by publishing their own scholarship directly on the World Wide Web.").
[198] *Id.* at 1072.
[199] *Id.* at 1086.
[200] Closen & Dzielak at 22.
[201] Manz at 1070.

educated lawyer escapes from the stifling world of a New York City white-shoe law firm.[202]

One young associate, Weston, dined in a fancy restaurant with the firm's venerable senior partner who lavished stories on him about his editorship of the *Harvard Law Review* and subsequent clerkship with Justice Oliver Wendell Holmes.[203] Meanwhile, the other young associate, Littlefield, discards the law firm, escaping to the faculty at the polished Ivory Tower of Yale Law School, after the *Yale Law Journal* agreed to publish his writing tracing the origins of the federal tax code to the writings of ancient philosophers.[204]

"May I congratulate myself? ... I am proofreading the galleys of my masterpiece, the interconnected chain of Cicero memoranda, which are the featured articles in this month's *Yale Law Journal*. May I add that the especially fine piece I did for Lynch will be on view in the following issue? I do, sincerely, believe it was my masterpiece. At least it was the only memorandum I have ever written under conditions of complete abstinence...Cases, research. The law is too complicated. That is why I took it upon myself to uncomplicate the Internal Revenue Code. The taxpayers and the nation will be grateful. Once you return to fundamental principles, the entire code can be simplified. I believe that after publication of my papers, the code may be reduced in some bulk."[205]

This "Great Escape" anecdote may be tongue-in-cheek, yet it speaks volumes to the perception and idyllic place for the law review institution in the legal community and legal education.

---

[202] OSBORN at 196-97.

[203] *Id.*.

[204] *Id.* at 246-49.

[205] *Id.* at 249.

Glossary*

Article I.

Advance sheet—pamphlets containing the most recently reported opinions of a court or the courts of a specific jurisdiction. The volume and page numbers will comport with the later bound reporters.

Announced topic—a single issue of a journal addressing a specific issue or area of the law. See also symposium.

Article—a heavily-documented scholarly piece written by a lawyer, professor or legal professional published in a law review or journal. Articles frequently contain substantial footnotes and discuss historical developments, changes and proposals for legal issues and problems.

Association of Legal Writing Directors (ALWD)—organization of program directors for legal research, writing, analysis and advocacy programs from law schools in the United States and other English-speaking countries; publishes the *ALWD Citation Manual*, an alternative to the Bluebook intended to be less burdensome and easier to use than the long-established Bluebook. See also Bluebook.

Auto-cite—a computerized citation verification service that provides subsequent citations, parallel citations and case history. Conceptually similar to Shepards.

Block or blocked quote—a quote of 50 or more words that is offset by narrower margins.

Bluebook—the uniform system of citation compiled and published by the editors of the Columbia, Harvard, Penn and Yale law reviews, now in its 17th edition.. The vast majority of law reviews follow the rules of the Bluebook for citations and footnotes.

Bluebooking—the act of checking footnote citations to make sure they comply with the rules set forth in the Bluebook. See also Cite-Checking, Subciting, Form & Accuracy.

Bluebook exercise—portion of a write-on competition or staff selection procedure in which prospective members are graded and judged based on proficiency with Bluebook rules and editing skills.

Blueline—editing and marking up a final version of an article or volume after it has been typeset by the printer.

Board of Editors—the top or senior editors on staff charged with setting law review policy and managing the staff and publication schedule.

Book review—a special article that summarizes, analyzes and critiques a new book, frequently a legal topic or by a legal professional or law professor.

Bound volume—the final product in which the single issues are bound by a printer, book binder or library into a single volume. See also single issue.

Bylaws—the rules governing law review or journal membership, duties, obligations, responsibilities, job descriptions for editors and staff members and disciplinary procedures. Also known as a constitution or handbook.

Buckley Amendment—Federal Act that guarantees that no personally identifiable information from a student's educational record may be disclosed to a third party by any official of an institution without the student's written consent. Family Educational Rights and Privacy Act 20 U.S.C. 1232g (2000).

Burton Foundation for Legal Achievement—foundation that honors legal writing with awards for student-written law review articles from the 181 accredited law schools. The Foundation also bestows awards for articles written by lawyers from the top 250 law firms.

Call for papers—an open invitation for submissions to a law review or journal for publication. These calls are often mailed to law school faculty or specialized legal organizations or groups of lawyers or law students.

Camera-ready proof—a final version of an article or all the articles in a specific issue in its final form ready to be printed; sometimes referred to as a contract proof.

Joe Christensen, Inc.—the largest printer of student-edited law reviews and journals in the country. Based in Lincoln, Nebraska, the company has been printing journals since 1932.

Citation—a footnote documenting a proposition or statement in the text. Citations can include anything from a judicial opinion to a newspaper article to an interview or empirical studies to a food recipe. A well-documented citation lends credibility to the article, reflects the amount and type of research performed by the author and allows the reader to know exactly where the author obtained the information.

Citation sentence—the actual text of a footnote.

Cite-check—to review citations for Bluebook conformance, style and accuracy. See also Bluebooking, Form & Accuracy or subciting.

Comment—a student-written article that surveys or critiques specific subjects of legal significance. See also note or case note.

Commentary—see Essay.

Copyflow—the progression and pace at which articles are edited.

Copyright—ownership of literary material; governed by federal law.

Dedication—the act of honoring a figure, mostly a prominent figure in the legal community, an alumnus, law school faculty member or judge by dedicating an issue or volume of the journal to that person. This is frequently marked in the preliminary or first pages in the volume, frequently with a photograph, sometimes with an essay or biography about the honoree. Sometimes an entire issue of a journal will be devoted to the figure, with essays, anecdotes and analyses of the figure's body or work.

Essay—similar to an article, written by a legal professional or law professor, but is not as dense as an article and requires less student editing. An essay tends to be more of a position paper. Also known as commentary.

Faculty advisor—a designated member of the law school faculty who assists the law review editors. The intensity of a faculty advisor's interaction or involvement with the student-editors varies from publication-to-publication. Advisors who assume a more proactive role assist student editors with reviewing submissions and drafts of articles and staff motivation and discipline.

Faculty-edited journal—journal published through an academic institution or legal organization with faculty members sitting in the senior management or senior editing position and students performing basic editing and production tasks. These journals offer more "peer review" than student-edited journals.

Form & Accuracy editing—the process by which an article's footnotes and citations are checked for compliance with the Bluebook rules while the accuracy of the statement asserted is verified. Every journal has its own nomenclature but it is also known as Bluebooking, cite-checking, proofing, spading, subciting.

Grade-on—a law student member who is automatically invited to the law review based on first-year grades. Also the act of earning law review membership based on first-year grades. Typically, those students who rank in the top 10 percent of the class are automatically invited to participate in the law review at a particular law school.

Headnote—a brief summary of the legal rules, facts and holdings of a case that precede the written opinion in reporters and some computerized legal databases. They are useful summaries of the case but offer no value for citation or precedent purposes.

William S. Hein Co. —largest depository of back issues or single issues of law reviews and journals, located in Buffalo, New York. The company holds complete sets of journals in single issue copies and microform.

Information for Authors—statement in the preliminary pages of a single issue or on a journal's website describing guidelines for unsolicited manuscripts. Law reviews accept unsolicited manuscripts from prospective authors but frequently demand the submissions conform to Bluebook rules and the general tenets of grammar. Additional information needed may include an abstract or summary of the article, biographical information or the author's curriculum vitae. Also known as authors' guidelines

Id.—ibid, used to signify citation to the material that was cited in the immediately preceding footnote.

Infra—Latin meaning below, under or beneath. Used in footnotes it is the opposite of supra, referring to citations or discussions detailed later in the work. See also supra.

Internal citation—(also cross-references) citations within the text referring to other footnotes or sections of the text. Internal citations make use of the Latin terms supra and infra.

Law review—a student-run and student-edited scholarly journal comprised of the top students at the law school based on grades and those who rank in a writing competition. Most law reviews are published quarterly during the academic year. Some of the top-ranked law schools publish as many as eight editions throughout the academic year. Also known as a law journal.

Lead article—the first article to be published in a volume or single issue. Status as lead article is also an honor or a position reserved for a special or prominent author. The lead article will be the first article in the volume. This term is also frequently used to refer to any article written by a legal professional published in the front or the "lead" of the book.

Lead note—the first note to be published in a volume or single issue. The lead note is typically the note garnering the top score or highest ranking in a law review's note-writing competition.

Lexis-Nexis—a large electronic database of judicial opinions, statutes, cases, law review articles, news and other public records. The service is made available to every law student at every law school free of charge. For non-students or lawyers, the service charges subscribers for searches or access.

Lexis Eclipse ™ -- a trademarked service provided by Lexis-Nexis that automatically searches databases for requested information. The search commands will cull the database and deliver the documents to the researcher automatically. This is a useful tool to monitor developments in a case or an area of the law .

Masthead—informational table listing the editorial and staff positions. The masthead frequently appears as one of the first pages in the book.

National Conference of Law Reviews—organization of student-edited law journals that holds an annual convention with seminars and discussions about prevalent issues facing law review editors.

Note—a student-written article. The student note is part of the academic component of law review membership and accounts for academic credit. At most law reviews, the top student notes are chosen for publication. Also known as a casenote, a critical analysis of recent court cases or legislation.

Note competition—the internal competition among the law review staff in which student-written notes are written and judged with the top-ranked notes being published. Frequently done in anonymity.

Offprint -- bound single copy of an article, essay or note complete with an individual cover and the actual pages as it appears in the journal. See also **reprint**.

Parallel citation—citation of a judicial opinion as it appears in two or more official reports.

Parenthetical—a) an explanation in the citation of a judicial opinion that states the court, year of the opinion and the weight of the authority, such as en banc, dissenting or concurring opinion. b) information that the author compresses into a footnote, rather than the text of the article. This is detailed information from the source, usually a direct quote, a holding or supporting information citing to an additional source. The parenthetical frequently expresses what the author gleaned from the source or in a judicial opinion the finding or holding of the court.

Peer review—in most scholarly publications authors have articles or studies reviewed, evaluated and tested by peers before publication. This system, which is notoriously absent from most student-edited publications, is intended to lend credibility and stature to scholarly articles.

Pin cite—a citation to a specific page in the work Also known as a pinpoint citation.

Plagiarism—passing off of work that is not the author's. Appropriating literary composition of another, or parts or passages of another's writings, ideas or language and passing them off as original work. Plagiarism does not require exact duplication or intent.

Pocket part—a paperback supplement to a book, collection or statutes that is inserted in the back of the book through a slit in the back cover. It is usually an annual update and the most recent authority. Also known as pocket supplement.

Primary source –statutes, constitutions, administrative regulations and case law. Primary authorities may be mandatory or persuasive. All other legal writings, including law review articles, are secondary authority and not binding on courts. Also known as primary authority.

Proof—to proofread or the final version of a text that has been proofread and is ready for printing.

Recent decision—a short article summarizing and analyzing a judicial opinion from a high court.

Reprint—bound single copy of an article, essay or note complete with an individual cover and the actual pages as it appears in the journal. Reprints have achieved the status of currency among authors because of their fancy, official appearance. See also **offprint**.

Research assistant—a law student who works for or in close proximity with a professor, either for academic credit, work study payment or actual salary who provides extensive research for the professor. On occasion, a research assistant will even draft portions or sections of articles for the law professor.

Roadmap—this is the paragraph that lays out the structure and topics addressed in the article. The typical roadmap paragraph appears within the first pages of the article and gives the reader a brief picture of the topics addressed in the article.

Sanctions committee—the board of editors who enforce the journal's rules and issue sanctions or punishments for staff members who fail to comply with law review duties. Also referred to as Disciplinary Board.

Scribes—organization known as the American Society of Writers on Legal Subjects. Membership is open to law journal editors, authors of one law book or two law review articles or a judge with at least one published opinion. The society publishes the Scribes Journal of Legal Writing, which seeks to promote better legal writing. Scribes also bestows an annual award for law review articles written by law students.

Secondary source—the term given to non-empirical document, typically another law review article or treatise. See also **primary source**.

Self-plagiarism—when an author quotes or excessively uses previous works and fails to cite that work. Scholars debate the notion of self-plagiarism. Sometimes it is simply recycling.

Signal—in a footnote or citation, using a signal helps the author further communicate how the source is used. For example, *see* means the cited authority directly states or clearly supports the proposition; *Cf.*

Means that the cited authority supports a proposition different from the main proposition. Other signals include: *Accord, See also; Compare; But see.* Also known as Introductory Signal.

Single edition—the single edition of the law review or journal. Since many are published quarterly, each volume consists of four single issues that are later bound. See also bound volume. Also known as single issue.

Shepardize—to check subsequent citations of a case or judicial opinion to investigate how the case has been cited or discussed by subsequent cases or to see if a case has been overruled or modified. Shepard's Citation books, a trademarked product of Shepard's Citations, Inc., are published several times a year in pamphlet book-form and later bound form. The act of shepardizing, or determining a case's subsequent history, can also be done with certain online databases.

Short citation—a subsequent citation of a work or document that employ different Bluebook rules.

Sic—editing abbreviation inserted in brackets within a quoted passage to note an error but to ensure that the quote is precisely reproduced. Ex. [sic].

Specialized journal—a law review or scholarly journal that publishes articles on a single subject or area of the law. Specialized journals frequently constitute the law school's secondary journals comprised of those who missed the cutoff for law review or hold an interest in the specific topic. Specialized journals are sometimes published by legal organizations with practitioners or professors directing or overseeing law student editorial staffs.

Statement of ownership—form required by the U.S. Postal Service detailing the publication's management, usually the Editor-in-Chief, Managing Editor and Business Manager. This also states the frequency of publication and the projected date of publication.

String citation—a citation listing numerous cases or articles for support.

Substantive edit—editing an article for content and substance of the text, arguments, authority, line of reasoning, organization, use of footnotes and the overall thesis. This is concerned with "what" the article says. See also Technical edit.

Supra—Latin meaning above; upon. Used in footnotes, sometimes text, to refer the reader to a previous citation of the source.

Survey—an objective article documenting the latest developments on a specific topic in a specific jurisdiction. Also referred to as an entire single issue devoted to developments in a jurisdiction or area of law.

Symposium—a convention or special meeting held or sponsored by a law school or law journal with speeches, essays and articles published in a single edition or special issue of a journal. Symposia are held to commemorate the anniversary or a specific case or development in the law or a distinguished jurist. Also known as colloquium or Announced Topic.

Technical edit—editing the focuses on grammar, sentences, Bluebook conformance and other minor and technical details. See also Substantive edit.

Textual citation—a long, detail-oriented footnote citation that is treated as text under Bluebook rules.

Westlaw—a larrge electronic database of judicial opinions, statutes, cases, news and other public records. The service is made available to every law student at every law school free of charge. For non-students or lawyers, the service charges subscribers for searches or access.

Write-on—a law review or journal members who is invited to join the staff based on performance in a writing or write-on competition. Also the act of making law review through the writing competition.

Write-on competition—the competition held at the end of the first year of law school that opens law review or journal membership to law students based on writing skill or performance on the competition. Typically, the competition will include a closed-universe problem and require prospective members to write a memo or article based on the materials provided. The competition will usually include an editing test. Also known as writing competition.

Law Review Bylaws

STATEMENT OF PURPOSE

(a) The purpose of this organization is to publish the Law Review.

(b) The Law Review is a scholarly journal published quarterly during the academic year.

(c) The Law Review shall provide a forum for high-quality, timely, relevant and accurate articles about prevalent legal issues and issues of concern to the legal community, the school of law, and society, written by legal practitioners, jurists, scholars and students.

(d) The Law Review shall provide its members with intensive experience in legal writing, research, editing and analysis. One volume of the Law Review shall be published each academic year by the members of the Law Review, the distinguished students of the school of law

Article I.

§101 SENIOR BOARD OF EDITORS-Shall consist of the Editor-in-Chief, Managing Editor, Notes and Comments Editor, Form and Accuracy Editor, Lead Articles Editors, Executive Editors, Business Editor, Survey Editor, Special Projects Editor and the Computer Editor.

§102 ASSOCIATE BOARD OF EDITORS- Shall consist of the four Associate Notes and Comments Editors and six Associate Editors.

§103 MANAGING BOARD OF EDITORS- Shall consist of the members of the Senior Board of Editors and the Associate Board of Editors.

§104 ASSOCIATE MEMBERS- Shall consist of those third year members of the Law Review in good standing not elected to either the Senior Board of Editors or the Associate Board of Editors or the Associate Board of Editors.

§105 EDITORIAL BOARD-Shall consist of those Law Review members who have met the requirements of §202(a).

§106 EDITORIAL STAFF-Shall consist of those Law Review members who have not met the requirements of §202(a).

§107 GENERAL MEETINGS- Those meetings that all Editorial Board and Editorial Staff members are expected to attend.

§108 STANDING COMMITTEE- A committee formed by the Editor-in-Chief, and chaired by the Special Projects Editor, which performs as a committee for the entire academic year.

§109 SPECIAL COMMITTEE-A committee formed by the Editor-in-Chief, and chaired by the Editor-in-Chief's designee, to examine a certain policy matter and is dissolved after final recommendations are made to the Editor-in-Chief.

ARTICLE II
MEMBERSHIP DETERMINATION

§201 The Law Review shall consist of:

(a) Students selected for the Editorial Board under §202 herein; and
(b) Students selected for the Editorial Staff under procedures set forth in §203 herein.

§202

(a) No member of the Editorial Staff will be elevated without fulfilling all of the following:
   (1) completion of satisfactory editorial work as per §712 (a).
   (2) writing a Note of publishable quality as per §712 (a).
   (3) completion of all assigned office hours as per §712 (a).
   (4) participating and complying as a member of the Law Review under each and every article of these Bylaws; and
   (5) being a member in good standing of the Law Review.

(b) The Editor-in-Chief, in consultation with other members of the Senior Board of   Editors, will determine which members of the Editorial Staff will be elevated to the Editorial Board through evaluation of the criteria of §202 (a). Those members who have not been elevated will not receive any academic credit and their names shall be immediately removed from the masthead.

§203 Once elected, the Editor-in-Chief, in consultation with the new Senior Board of Editors, shall do all of the following:

(a) determine the approximate number of Editorial Staff positions available:
(b) plan one anonymous spring and one anonymous supplemental writing competition to be implemented by the Notes and Comments Editor;
(c) set forth the procedures and criteria for selecting new Editorial Staff members taking into consideration only the results of the anonymous writing competition and first year grade percentages.

§204 Full time students at this law school shall be eligible to participate in the spring writing competition during the spring semester of their first full year of law school.

§205 Upon completion of twenty-four(24) hours of academic credit (based on the records maintained in the registrar's office) part-time students shall be eligible to participate in the first writing competition for which they are eligible. Part-time students are eligible for membership based solely on their performance in the writing competition; their grades shall not be considered.

§206 The Editor-in-Chief shall seek to inform students who have transferred into this law school of membership opportunities on the Law Review. The Editor-in-Chief shall determine their eligibility for participation in the supplemental writing competition; their grades shall not be considered.

§207 All members of the student body who wish to participate in the Law Review Writing competition must participate in the first writing competition scheduled after they become eligible for possible membership. All members of the student body are limited to participation in only one writing competition.

§208 Membership decisions under this Article are made at the discretion of the Editor-in-Chief in consultation with the Senior Board of Editors.

ARTICLE III
MEETINGS

§301   General Meetings

(a) General meetings must take place at least once a month during the fall and spring semesters.
(b) Notice of all general meetings must be posted on all Law Review bulletin boards at least three (3) business days (excluding Saturday, Sunday and holidays) before a meeting is to occur.
(c) Notice shall comprise of a statement of the time, date and location of the meeting.
(d) The Editor-in-Chief shall preside over all general meetings and determine the agenda for each general meeting.
(e) If the Editor-in-Chief is either unable to attend a meeting or temporarily gives up the chair, the Managing Editor shall assume all responsibilities of the Editor-in-Chief.
(f) The presence of more than one-half of all Law Review members is required at a general meeting to constitute a quorum.

(g) Quorum requirements may not be waived. No official action may be taken in any general meeting in the absence of a quorum.

(h) Attendance by members of the Law Review at general meetings is mandatory.

   (1) The Editor-in-Chief or the Managing Editor may excuse a Law Review member from attendance at a general meeting if the member provide a reasonable excuse to the Managing Editor, in writing at least twenty-four(24) hours prior to the meeting.

   (2) Members absent from a general meeting without excuses are subject to sanctions in accordance with Article IV.

(i) Should a debatable issue arise, the Editor-in-Chief may implement Roberts Rules of Order, which include the following:

   (1) No member may hold the floor more than five (5) minutes at a time;

   (2) A simple majority vote of all members present is required to approve a motion;

   (3) The Editor-in-Chief shall vote only to break any tie that exists.

   (4) Each member of the Law Review will have a single vote to cast on each motion considered in a meeting.

   (5) Votes are to be taken by hand unless otherwise stated in these Bylaws or, if not so stated, a simple majority of those present at the meeting may approve an alternate procedure;

   (6) The following motions shall require a two-thirds vote of those present and voting:

   (A) motion to amend a motion currently on the floor;

   (B) motion to adjourn; and

   (C) motion to amend the Bylaws;

   (7) The Editor-in-Chief shall be the final arbiter of these Bylaws for resolution of procedural questions; and

   (8) The Managing Editor shall maintain a record of the minutes of the meetings.

§302 Special Meetings may be called by the Editor-in-Chief throughout the academic year. Attendance at these meetings shall comport with §301 (h) above.

§303 Meetings of the Senior Board of Editors
The Senior Board of Editors shall meet weekly. This requirement may not be waived. All other aspects of the Senior Board Meetings are at the discretion of the Editor-in-Chief.

§304   Committee Meetings
Except as otherwise stated in these Bylaws, all aspects of the committee meetings are at the discretion of the committee chairperson in consultation with the Editor-in-Chief.

ARTICLE IV
SANCTIONS

§401   Sanctions Committee

(a) The committee will be a Standing Committee
(b) The committee will consist of the following:
    (1) the members of the Senior Board of Editors
    (2) one member of the Associate Board of Editors
    (3) one Associate Member; and
    (4) one Editorial Staff member.
(c) The Executive Editor and the Associate Member positions on the committee shall be elected by the Editorial Board of the Law Review within three weeks of the beginning of the fall semester. These elections shall be held during a general meeting.
(d) The Editorial Staff member position on the committee shall be elected by the Editorial Staff of the Law Review within three weeks of the beginning of the fall semester at a general meeting.
(e) If a member of the Sanctions Committee is the subject of a complaint, that member, for the purpose of that complaint only, shall be removed from the committee.
(f) If a member of the Sanctions Committee has a conflict of interest concerning the subject of a complaint, that member may recuse himself or herself for the purpose of that complaint only.
(g) The chairperson of the Sanctions Committee shall be elected by simple majority at the first meeting of the committee. The chairperson may not be the Editor-in-Chief.

§402 Sanctionable Conduct

(a) member of the Law Review may be subject to sanctions if the member has:
  (1) failed to strictly comply with these Bylaws;
  (2) failed to attend mandatory meetings without excuses as per §301 (h) (1);
  (3) failed to meet any deadlines set by any member of the Senior Board of Editors; including deadlines on all editorial work, all Note writing deadlines and first page assignments;
  (4) failed to submit Note drafts and/or a final Note to the satisfaction of the Notes and Comments Editor;
  (5) failed to complete form and accuracy work to the satisfaction of the Form and Accuracy Editor or the Survey of New York Law Form and Accuracy Editor;
  (6) failed to complete office hours to the satisfaction of the Managing Editor; or
  (7) been found by the appropriate adjudicative body (i.e. a Hearing panel as defined n Part D of the Code of Student Conduct (1992-93) to have violated the Code of Student Conduct in force at the time of the alleged violation.
(b) The above sanctionable conduct is not an exhaustive list.

§403 Disciplinary Procedure

(a) Written complaints referencing sanctionable conduct shall be submitted by a ember of the Law Review to a member of the Sanctions Committee. All complaints must be legibly signed by the accuser. The member receiving the complaint shall notify the chairperson of the Sanctions Committee who shall convene a Sanctions Committee meeting within a reasonable time so as to consider the complaint.
(b) The accused shall be given notice of the complaint at least three (3) business days prior to the initial meeting of the Sanctions Committee regarding the complaint. The notice shall consist of the identity of the accuser and the reasons for the complaint. At the initial meeting of the Sanctions Committee, the accused shall be given an opportunity to be heard regarding the complaint, should the accused so request.

(c) Any official action taken by the Sanctions Committee (except election of a chairperson and a vote for expulsion) shall require a two-thirds vote of the full committee, by secret ballot, and shall be accompanied by a written justification for such action signed by the chairperson of the committee.

(d) A vote for expulsion must be by unanimous vote of the Sanctions Committee and must also be accompanied by a written justification for such action signed by the chairperson of the committee.

(e) Each written justification and complaint shall be kept in a Sanctions Committee file in the Law Review office.

(f) The file of any member of the Law Review against whom a complaint was filed under this Article shall be destroyed upon the graduation of the subject of the complaint.

§404 Sanctions Available for Non-Senior Board of Editors Members

(a) Oral Warning
(b) Written Warning
(c) Law Review Service
(d) Suspension from the Law Review
(e) Loss of either one or two hours of academic credit
(f) Demotion of position
(g) Removal from consideration for Note publication
(h) Removal from the masthead
(i) Expulsion

§405 The following sanctions are not appealable

(a) Oral Warning,
(b) Written Warning, or
(c) Law Review Service.

§406   Exception from Sanctions for Senior Board of Editors Members

(a) A Senior Board of Editors member is not subject to sanctions by the Sanctions Committee. The committee may, however, impeach such a member.

(b) Impeachment may only occur if the senior board member has:

(1) been found by the appropriate adjudicative body (i.e., a Hearing panel as defined in Part D of the Code of Student Conduct (1992-93) to have violated the Code of Student Conduct in force at the time of the alleged violation; or

(2) committed a gross dereliction of duty.

(c) Written complaints referencing impeachable conduct shall be submitted by a member of the Law Review to a member of the Sanctions Committee. All complaints must be legibly signed by the accuser. The member who receives the complaint shall notify the chairperson of the Sanctions Committee who shall convene a Sanctions Committee meeting within a reasonable time to consider the complaint.

(d) The accused shall be given notice of the complaint at least three (3) business days prior to the initial meeting of the Sanctions Committee regarding the complaint. The notice shall consist of the identity of the accuser and the reasons for the complaint. At the initial meeting of the Sanctions Committee, the accused shall be given an opportunity to be heard as to why impeachment is not in order.

(e) Following the hearing, the Sanctions Committee shall vote on whether the impeachment is warranted. Impeachment requires a two-thirds vote of the Sanctions Committee.

(f) Should the Sanctions Committee vote to impeach the Senior Board of Editors member, the chairperson shall immediately notify the Managing Board of Editors of the impeachment proceedings.

(g) Upon notification by the Sanctions Committee chairperson, the Managing Board of Editors shall meet to consider removal of the Senior Board of Editors member from office. The Managing Board of Editors shall notify the impeached at least three (3) business days prior to their meeting. At the meeting, the impeached shall be given an opportunity to be heard as to why removal is not in order.

(h) Upon completion of the review, the Managing Board of Editors shall vote on whether to remove the impeached member from office. Removal of a Senior Board of Editors member from office requires a three-fourths vote of the full Managing Board of Editors. This decision is appealable pursuant to §407 of this article.

(i) A Senior Board of Editors member removed from office will be demoted to Associate Member. No other sanctions will be imposed on such member unless the Sanctions Committee elects to reconsider the actions of the member. Should that election take place, the

Sanctions Committee may avail itself of the sanctions pursuant to §404 of this Article.

(j)   Upon removal of the Senior Board of Editors member from office, a special election shall be called for the purpose of filling the vacant office. This procedure shall also be followed if a Senior Board of Editors member resigns from office.

§407   Appeals Procedure;

(a)   A member of the Law Review who is subject to an appealable sanction may appeal that decision in writing to the chairperson of the Sanctions Committee within three (3) business days of the Sanction Committee's determination.

(b)   Such appeal shall contain the grounds for the appeal and a request for a special meeting of the full Law Review membership within five(5) business days of the date of the filing of the written appeal. An appeal filed less than five (5) business days from the end of the semester shall be deemed to have been filed on the first class day of the next semester.

(c)   An appeal shall be forwarded to the Editor-in-Chief who shall preside over the special meeting. In the event the Editor-in-Chief is the subject of impeachment proceedings, the appeal shall be forwarded to the Managing Editor, who shall preside over the special meeting.

(d)   At the special meeting, the member who is subject to the sanction may present reasons why the discipline should not be imposed. The chairperson of the Sanctions Committee shall present the case against the accused.

(e)   Any sanction imposed by the Sanctions Committee may be lessened or reversed by a majority vote of the membership attending the special meeting. This vote shall be by secret ballot and is final. Upon reversal, any reference to the claimed violation shall be removed from the Sanctions Committee file.

ARTICLE V
NOTE PUBLICATION DECISIONS
§501

(a) At the end of the student Note writing process a number of student Notes will be selected for publication. The number to be selected will be determined by the Editor-in-Chief according to the number of pages available to the next year's Editorial Board.

(b) The "Committee on Note Publication" shall be chaired by the Notes and Comments Editor. As chairperson, the Notes and Comments Editor's duties are ministerial; the Notes and Comments Editor is not to have a vote as to publication.

(c) The Committee on Note Publication shall consist of the Notes and Comments Editor and five (5) Associate Editors.

    (1) The five (5) Associate Editors who serve as members of the Committee shall be appointed by the Editor-in-Chief from among the six (6) associate Editors on a volunteer basis.

    (2) Absent a sufficient number of volunteers from among the six (6) Associate Editors eligible for membership on the Committee, in consultation with the Senior Board of Editors the Editor-in-Chief shall select and appoint the remaining members exclusively from the remaining pool of non-volunteer Associate Editors.

(d) The Associate Editors shall read the Notes and vote on those for publication according to criteria determined by the Notes and Comments Editor in consultation with the Senior Board of Editors.

(e) The Notes and Comments Editor shall refer the suggestions made by the Committee on Note Publication to the Editor-in-Chief.

(f) All publication decisions shall be posted on all Law Review bulletin boards.

ARTICLE VI
ELECTION PROCEDURES FOR MANAGING BOARD OF EDITORS POSITIONS
§601

(a) Nomination to the Managing Board of Editors

(1) Any member of the Law Review may nominate any Editorial Staff member to any Managing Board of Editors position or positions.
(2) The opening of nominations shall be determined by the Managing Editor and shall be posted.
(3) Nominations shall end two calendar days before elections.
(4) Upon being nominated and prior to the close of the nomination process a candidate shall submit a written statement accepting the nomination and setting forth the nominee's qualifications and reasons for seeking the position, along with a current resume. Any reference to law school grades or honors shall be redacted from the nominee's resume.
(b) The Election Hierarchy
  (1) Interviews and Elections for the Managing Board of Editors shall proceed in the following order:
    (A) Editor-in-Chief
    (B) Managing Editor
    (C) Form & Accuracy Editor
    (D) Lead Articles Editors (2)
    (E) Notes and Comments Editor
    (F) Business Editor
    (G) Computer Editor
    (H) Executive Editors (5)
    (I) Associate Notes and Comments Editors (5-7)
  (2) Each election shall be mutually exclusive, having no bearing upon subsequent elections.
  (3) Nominees may run for more than one position, but may be elected to only one position.
(c) The Interview Process
  (1) Immediately prior to the election of Editor-in-Chief each candidate, in order determined by random draw, shall address the electorate for a period not to exceed five (5) minutes.
  (2) The electorate shall, upon conclusion of the Editor-in-Chief nominee's opening address, interview nominees for the position for a period not to exceed thirty minutes.
  (3) Immediately prior to the election of all other Senior Board of Editors positions each candidate, in order determined by

random draw, shall address the electorate for a period not to exceed three (3) minutes.

(4) The electorate shall, upon conclusion of the successive Senior Board of Editors nominees' opening addresses, interview nominees for each office for a period not to exceed fifteen minutes.

(5) There shall be no opening addresses prior to Associate Board of Editors elections.

(d) The Voting Process in General

(1) The Managing Editor shall be in charge of the voting process and shall solicit such help as necessary.

(2) As each position is presented to the electorate for voting, the candidates for that position shall leave the room and ballots shall be distributed to those members who are eligible to vote for that position. Only those members deemed in good standing by the Editor-in-Chief shall be allowed to vote during the election. There will be neither proxy nor absentee voting.

(3) Voting shall proceed by secret ballot, and the Managing Editor or such designee shall collect and count ballots.

(e) Voting for Editor-in-Chief

(1) After the ballots are counted, the candidate with the fewest votes shall be eliminated from the next round of voting.

(2) Voting for the position in question shall proceed with successive ballots until two candidates remain.

(3) Once two candidates remain, one candidate must carry a simple majority of the votes in order to be elected.

(f) Voting for other Senior Board of Editors Positions

(1) After the ballots are counted, if no candidate receives a simple majority of the votes, the candidate with the fewest votes shall be eliminated from the next round of voting.

(2) Voting for the position in question shall proceed with successive ballots until a candidate receives a simple majority of the votes.

(g) Voting for All Other Positions

(1) All candidates for a particular position shall be made known to the electorate.

(2) Considering the number of positions available, the positions shall be filled by those candidates with the most votes.

(3)   In the event of a tie between two or more candidates for the last available position, a second ballot shall be cast for the tied candidates only. The candidate with the most votes shall be elected to that position.

(h) Appointment in lieu of Election
    (1) In the event of resignation or removal of a member of the Managing Board of Editors, the Senior Board may, at is discretion, appoint an associate member of the Law Review to assume the position vacated, without recourse to the election process.

ARTICLE VII
DUTIES OF LAW REVIEW MEMBERS

§701   Editor-in Chief

(a) The Editor-in-Chief is the Law Review's chief executive. It is the Editor-in-Chief's duty to provide the necessary leadership and coordination of the Law Review.
(b) The Editor-in-Chief shall ensure professional operation of the Law Review and timely publication of the Law Review in the level of quality becoming a prestigious law periodical.
(c) The Editor-in-Chief shall make all executive decisions regarding the management of the Law Review.
(d) The duties of the Editor-in-Chief include, but are not limited to the following:
    (1) Chair all meetings of the General Membership and of the Senior Board of Editors.
    (2) Define and assign, in conjunction with the Senior Board of Editors, the duties of the members of the Law Review in accordance with these Bylaws and the needs of the Law Review as a whole.
    (3) Make all final editorial decisions regarding published articles.
    (4) Establish, in conjunction with the Senior Board of Editors, all publication schedules.
    (5) Make all final decisions regarding author contracts;

(6) Represent the Law Review in all matters within and without the school;

(7) Oversee the administration of the Law Review Standing and Special Committees in conjunction with the Senior Board of Editors;

(8) Make all final decisions, in conjunction with the Senior Board of Editors, regarding:

   (A) the administration of the budget;

   (B) elevation to the Editorial Board;

   (C) publication of student Notes;

   (D) Law Review membership;

(9) Assume responsibility for the administration of the Survey, including responsibility to:

   (A) Develop Survey topics and select Survey authors in consultation with the Senior Board of Editor; and

   (B) Coordinate and supervise case law research for all Survey authors;

(10) Appoint a parliamentarian; and

(11) Perform all duties of the Editor-in-Chief enumerated elsewhere in these Bylaws.

§702   Managing Editor

(a) The Managing Editor, in conjunction with the Editor-in-Chief, shall ensure the professional operation and timely publication of the Law Review at a level of quality becoming a prestigious law periodical.

(b) The duties of the Managing Editor include, but are not limited to the following:

   (1) Assist the Editor-in-Chief in managing the Law Review and preparation of the budget;

   (2) Supervise the Executive Editors, Computer Editor, and the Editorial Staff in their duties;

   (3) Establish, in conjunction with the Editor-in-Chief, production and publication schedules for all issues of the Law Review;

   (4) Distribute articles to the Executive Editors for editing according to their duties and the production schedule and assign deadlines for the completion of the Executive Editors' work;

(5) Assign articles for form and accuracy to Associate Editors, create form and accuracy teams from the Editorial Staff, and monitor the performance of those teams;

(6) Distribute all articles in a timely, efficient fashion according to the production and publication schedules;

(7) Maintain contact with the publisher regarding scheduling, production, contracts, and corrections;

(8) Assume responsibility for the staffing of the Standing Committees enumerated in Article IX of these Bylaws in accordance with the requirements of Article IX; and

(9) Assist in other Law Review matters as determined by these Bylaws or by the Editor-in-Chief.

§703   Notes and Comments Editor

The duties of the Notes and Comments Editor include, but are not limited, to the following:

(a) Administer the Spring and Supplemental Writing Competitions;

(b) Assign Associate Notes and Comments Editors to work with Editorial Staff on the preparation of student Notes;

(c) Supervise the Note writing process; and

(d) Chair the Committee on Note Publication.

§704   Form and Accuracy Editor

The duties of the Form & Accuracy Editor include, but are not limited to, the following:

(a) Assume primary responsibility for the form and accuracy of the final work product of the Law Review;

(b) Administrate the activities of the Associate Editors in the fulfillment of their duties;

(c) Work with the Managing Editor to insure proper Bluebook form of the Law Review; and

(d) Instruct the Executive Editors, the Associate Editors and the Editorial Staff as to proper form and accuracy of the final work product of the Law Review.

§705   Lead Articles Editors

The duties of the Lead Articles Editors include, but are not limited to, the following:

(a)   Work with authors who submit articles for publication;
(b)   Work with the Editor-in-Chief to establish the criteria for article selection including but not limited to reputation and publication history of the author, and timeliness, originality, and potential significance of the work, clarity and skill of writing, whether or not the Law Review has published similar material in the recent past;
(c)   Review and recommend works for publication to the Editor-in-Chief;
(d)   Draft contracts with authors (including copyright, reprint and web-posting provisions);
(e)   Serve as liaison between the Law Review and authors during selection and publication process; and
(f)   Additional editorial duties as assigned by the Editor-in-Chief.

§706   Executive Editors

The duties of the Executive Editors include, but are not limited to, the following:

(a)   Assume primary responsibility for editing the style, form and accuracy of each article published by the Law Review during advanced stages of the publications process as determined by the Managing Editor in consultation with the Senior Board of Editors; and

(b)   Work with the Computer Editor and members of the Editorial Staff to compose, mark, compile, and edit Appendices to the Law Review including, but not limited to, the Survey Table of Authorities and the Law Review Index at the end of each Volume of the Law Review.

§707   Business Editor
The duties of the Business Editor include, but are not limited to, the following:

(a) Oversee the business aspects of publishing the Law Review including subscriptions, circulation, advertising, financing and the budget;
(b) Handle purchasing of Law Review merchandise by Law Review members; and
(c) Assume responsibility for responding to and billing for all subscriber and outside requests for copies of the Law Review.

§708   Computer Editor
The duties of the Computer Editor include, but are not limited to, the following:

(a) Assist the Managing Editor with preparation of documents for distribution to editorial teams; work to meet all production and publication schedules in a timely manner; provide other assistance to the Managing Editor as may be necessary or requested in the conduct of his or her duties.
(b) Work with the Executive Editors and members of the Editorial Staff to compose, mark, compile, and edit Appendices to the Law Review including, but not limited to, the Survey Table of Authorities and the Law Review Index at the end of each Volume of the Law Review.
(c) Assume primary responsibility for in-house desktop publishing of the Law Review in conjunction with the Managing Editor and the Editor-in-Chief.
(d) Conduct routine tasks on the Law Review Computers as necessary, including, but not limited to: file management, backups, software installation/modifications, troubleshooting, disk translations, and equipment maintenance.
(e) Assume primary responsibility for maintaining, monitoring and running the Law Review's website and email system, including but not limited to website design, content, publicity.

§709   Special Projects Editor
The Special Projects Editor shall:
(a) Assume primary responsibility for Special Projects including but not limited to Law Review symposia, special issues or dedications.
(b) The Special Projects Editor will work closely with the Editor-in-Chief, Managing Editor, Articles Editor and Form & Accuracy

Editors to plan, execute and manage any special projects to be published in the Law Review.
(c) The Special Projects Editor may be assigned to direct and manage the Standing Committee designated under §901.

§710   Survey Editor
The duties of the Survey includes, but are not limited to, the following:

(a) Plan, execute and manage author selection and articles for the annual Survey of Law and work with authors who submit articles for publication;
(b) Work with the Editor-in-Chief to establish the criteria for article selection including but not limited to reputation and publication history of the Survey authors, and timeliness, originality, comprehensiveness and potential significance of the work, clarity and skill of writing;
(d) Solicit, review and recommend works for publication to the Editor-in-Chief;
(e) Work with the Lead Articles Editors to draft contracts with authors (including copyright, reprint and web-posting provisions);

(f) Serve as liaison between the Law Review and the Survey authors during the publication process; and
(g) Additional editorial duties as assigned by the Editor-in-Chief.

§711   Associate Notes and Comments Editors

The Associate Notes and Comments Editors shall assist the Notes and Comments Editor in all duties, including but not limited to:

(a) Administering the writing competitions; and
(b) Working with the Editorial Staff to review and advise on the progress of student Notes.

§712   Associate Editors

The Associate Editors shall serve at the direction of the Managing Editor with duties including, but not limited to:

(a) Assume responsibility for seeing particular articles through the form and accuracy editorial process by leading the Editorial Staff form and accuracy teams to ensure that the necessary editorial work is completed;

(b) Assume primary responsibility for the continuing education of the Editorial Staff concerning the style, form, and accuracy rules of the Law Review. This duty should include regular meetings with the members of the Editorial Staff whom they supervise to instruct them on these subjects with respect to their form and accuracy work;

(c) Assume primary responsibility for ensuring that the contents, conclusions, and quotations in articles published by the Law Review, as edited by the Editorial Staff, are accurate; and

(d) Serve as members of the Committee on Note Publication in accordance with Article V of these Bylaws.

§713   Associate Members

(a) Each Associate Member of the Law Review shall be a member of at least one of the Standing Committees whose composition and duties are enumerated in Article IX.

(b) Associate Members may select the Standing Committee in which they would like to participate on a first-come, first-served basis, subject only to the requirement that each Standing Committee must be staffed with at least four Associate Members as enumerated in §903 (c) of these Bylaws.

§714   Editorial Staff

Editorial Staff duties include, but are not limited to, the following:

(a) Complete all form and accuracy assignments to the satisfaction of the Managing Editor and the Editor-in-Chief;

(b) Conduct research and writing of an original scholarly paper of publishable quality to be completed within the timetable created by the Notes and Comments Editor and the Editor-in-Chief; and

(c) Complete two office hours every week in the Law Review office under the direction of the Managing Editor or the Managing Editor's designee and serve two (2) office hours for every unexcused absence from a scheduled office hour.

§715 Parliamentarian

The Parliamentarian serves at the direction of the Editor-in-Chief with duties including, but not limited to:

(a) Assist the Editor-in-Chief in Bylaws interpretation;
(b) Insure that these Bylaws are kept up to date as per current practices of the Law Review; and
(c) Chair a special Bylaws amendment committee if one is formed by the Editor-in-Chief.

§716 Advisor
A member of the law school faculty shall sit as advisor to the Law Review.

ARTICLE VIII
LAW REVIEW CREDIT

§801 A member of the Law Review shall be eligible for two credit hours upon:

(a) satisfactory completion of all requirements contained in these Bylaws;
(b) signature of the Law Review's faculty advisor;
(c) signature of the Editor-in-Chief; and
(d) determination by the law school that Law Review members will be entitled to academic credit.

§802 A member of the Senior Board of Editors shall be eligible for one credit hour in addition to the two given to all Law Review Members upon:

(a) satisfactory completion of one year of service as an elected member of the Senior Board of Editors;
(b) signature of the Law Review's faculty advisor;

(c) signature of the Editor-in -Chief (applies to all positions except the Editor-in-Chief);
(d) signature of the Managing Editor in the case of the Editor-in-Chief; and
(e) determination by the law school's administration that Law Review Senior Board Members will be entitled to academic credit in addition to that given to Law Review Members.

ARTICLE IX
COMMITTEES

§901   Special Committees

(a) The Editor-in-Chief may form a Special Committee to examine a particular policy or administrative issue.
(b) Any Special Committee is dissolved following communication of the Committee's final recommendations to the Editor-in-Chief..
(c) The Special Committees shall work under the direction of an editor designated by the Editor-in-Chief.

§902   Standing Committees

(a) The Standing Committees of the Law Review are the Sanctions Committee, the Social Committee, Survey/Symposia Committee, the Outreach Committee, and the Ad Hoc Committee.
(b) The Standing Committees of the Law Review shall report periodically to the Senior Board of Editors.

§903   Standing Committees--Membership

(a) The membership of the Standing Committees of the Law Review shall comprise the Associate Members in accordance with their duties enumerated in §714 of these Bylaws and any other Law Review member in good standing who wishes to participate.
(b) Associate Members shall be given the opportunity to join a Standing Committee of their choice on a first-come, first-served basis, at the first General Meeting of the Law Review held during the fall semester subject only to the limitations of this section.

(c) Each Standing Committee of the Law Review must be staffed by at least four Associate Members except as provided in §904 of these Bylaws.

(d) At a Committee's first meeting of the academic year, the members of each Standing Committee must elect a chairperson who shall chair the meetings of that Committee and serve as liaison with the Senior Board of Editors. The chairperson of each Committee must be an Associate Member.

§904   The Sanctions Committee

The composition, responsibilities, and operation of the Sanctions Committee are controlled by Article IV of these Bylaws notwithstanding the requirements of §§903, 905, 906, and 907.

§905   The Social Committee

(a) The Social Committee shall plan and execute the Law Review Annual Banquet, Law Review Bar Nights, athletic competitions and various other social and fundraising events (e.g. the sale of Law Review paraphernalia), and other Law Review events and programs developed by the Social Committee or by the Senior Board of Editors in consultation with the Committee chairperson.

(b) Additional goals and objectives of the Social Committee may be developed by the Committee or by the Senior Board of Editors in consultation with the Committee chairperson.

(c) The Social Committee is encouraged to cooperate with other groups and associations in this school's community in planning and implementing its programs.

§906   The Outreach Committee

(a) The Outreach Committee shall plan and execute periodic outreach events designed to enhance the reputation of the Law Review in the school's community, to increase the role and exposure of Law Review in school life, enhance relations with the Alumni Association and Board of Visitors, and to educate members of the school's community in ways that promote the interests of the Law Review and the community.

(b) Examples of possible programs to be offered by the Outreach Committee include potential lecture series, and exam-taking workshop, course selection, research and Bluebook workshops.

(c) Additional goals and objectives of the Outreach Committee may be developed by the Committee or by the Senior Board of Editors in consultation with the Committee chairperson.

(d) The Outreach Committee is encouraged to cooperate with other groups and associations in the school's community in planning and implementing its programs.

§907   The Ad Hoc Committee

(a) The Ad Hoc Committee shall plan and execute programs designed primarily though not necessarily exclusively, for the internal benefit of the Law Review and its members.

(b) Examples of possible programs to be executed by the Ad Hoc Committee include developing a test and outline collection for the use of Law Review members (and appropriate policies), and an annual Law Review Retreat for interested members of Law Review to promote continuity of leadership and dedication.

(c) Additional goals and objectives of the Ad Hoc Committee may be developed by the Committee or by the Senior Board of Editors in consultation with the Committee chairperson.

(d) The Outreach Committee is encouraged to cooperate with other groups and associations in the school's community in planning and implementing its programs.

ARTICLE X
ANTI-DISCRIMINATION POLICY

The Law Review supports equal opportunity. No persons shall be denied membership on the Law Review or participation in any Law Review activities on the basis of any legally-prohibited discrimination involving, but not limited to such factors as race, color, creed, religion, national or ethnic origin, sex, sexual orientation, age, or handicap.

Sexual harassment is an act of discrimination and, as such, will not be tolerated.

ARTICLE XI
AMENDMENTS

§1001 These Bylaws maybe amended at any General Meeting of the Law Review by a two-thirds vote of those present and voting provided that the proposed amendment has been distributed to each member of the Law Review at least five business days prior to the General Meeting at which the amendment is considered.

Selected Bibliography

Selected Books

(The) Bluebook: A Uniform System of Citation (17th ed. 1999).

Black, Henry Campbell, *Black's Law Dictionary* (6th Ed. 1990).

Burton, William C., *Burton's Legal Thesaurus* 3rd ed. (1999).

Dershowitz, Alan M., *Chutzpah* (Touchstone Books 1991).

Friedman, Lawrence M., *A History of American Law* (2nd ed. 1985).

Glendon, Mary Ann, *A Nation Under Lawyers* (1994).

Goldstein, Tom & Lieberman, Jethro K., *Lawyer's Guide to Writing Well* (1989).

Gunther, Gerald, *Learned Hand: The Man and the Judge* (1994).

Jacobstein, J. Myron, *Legal Research Illustrated* (6th ed. 1994).

Kahlenberg, Richard D., *Broken Contract* (1996).

Keates, William R., *Proceed with Caution: A Diary of the First Year at One of America's Largest, Most Prestigious Law Firms* (1997).

Kerlow, Eleanor, *Poisoned Ivy: How Egos, Ideology, and Power Politics Almost Ruined Harvard Law School* (1994).

King, Donald B., ed., *Legal Education for the 21st Century* (1999).

Lazarus, Edward, *Closed Chambers: The Rise, Fall and Future of the Modern Supreme Court* (1999).

Mayer, Martin, *The Lawyers* (1967).

Neumann, Richard K. Jr., *Legal Reasoning and Legal Writing* (2d ed. 1994).

Powe, Lucas A., Jr., *The Warren Court and American Politics* (2000).

Ray, Mary Barnard & Ramsfield, Jill J., *Legal Writing: Getting It Right and Getting It Written* (1993).

Seligman, Joel, *The High Citadel: The Influence of Harvard Law School* (1978).

Shapo, Helene S., et al, *Writing & Analysis in the Law* (3rd ed. 1995).

Stracher, Cameron, *Double Billing* (1998).

Turow, Scott, *One L.* (Warner Books 1977).

Weisberg, Richard H., *When Lawyers Write* (1987).

Wolfram, Charles W., *Modern Legal Ethics* (1986).

Popular Legal Fiction

Grisham, John , *The Chamber* (1994).
Grisham, John, *The Firm* (1991).
Grisham, John, *The Pelican Brief* (1992).
Grisham, John, *The Rainmaker* (Double Day, New York, 1995).
Meltzer, Brad, *The 10th Justice* (1997).
Osborn, John Jay, Jr., *The Associates* (1979).
Osborn, John Jay, Jr., *The Paper Chase* (1971).

Selected Articles

Balkin, J.M. & Levinson, Sanford, "How to Win Cites and Influence People," 71 Chi-Kent L. Rev. 843 (1996).
Berreby, David , "Student Withdraws in Plagiarism Uproar, The National Law Journal," May 9, 1983, at 4.
Bills, Robert D., "Plagiarism in Law School: Close Resemblance of the Worst Kind?" 31 Santa Clara L. Rev. 103 (1990).
Bingler, Richard , "Now Comes the Unbending Boss," 7 Scribes J. of Legal Writing 37 (1998-2000).
Bresler, Ken , "Pursuant to Partners' Directive, I Learned to Obfuscate," 7 Scribes J. of Legal Writing 29 (1998-2000).
Closen, Michael L. & Dzielak, Robert J., "The History and Influence of the Law Review Institution," 30 Akron L. Rev. 15 (1996).
Cramton, Roger C., "'The Most Remarkable Institution': The American Law Review," 36 J. Legal Educ. 1 (1986).
Doherty, Frederick, "The Headless Snake of Law-Firm Editing," 7 Scribes J. of Legal Writing 43 (1998-2000).
Emery, Robert A., "The Albany Law School: the Only Surviving Copy," 89 Law Libr. J. 463 (1997).
Fleischer, Matt, "Herein the Said Answer," The National Law Journal, July 17, 2000, at A1.
Friedman, Lawrence M., "Law Reviews and Legal Scholarship: Some Comments," 75 Denv. U. L. Rev. 661 (1998).
Godsey, Mark A., "Educational Inequalities, the Myth of Meritocracy, and the Silencing of Minority Voices: the Need for Diversity on America's Law Reviews," 12 Harv. BlackLetter J. 59 (1995).

Griswold, Erwin N., "The Harvard Law Review – Glimpses of Its History as Seen by an Aficionado, in Harvard Law Review:" Centennial Album (1987).

Harper, James W., "Why Student-Run Law Reviews?," 82 Minn. L. Rev. 1261 (1998). Leibman, Jordan H. & White, James P., "How Student-Edited Law Journals Make Their Publication Decisions," 39 J. Legal Educ. 387 (1989).

Korobkin, Russell, "Symposium: Ranking Journals: Some Thoughts on Theory and Methodology," 26 Fla. St. U. L.Rev. 851 (1999).

Landes, William M., & Posner, Richard A., "Citations, Age, Fame and the Web," 29 J. Legal Stud. 319 (2000).

LeClercq, Terri, "Failure to Teach: Due Process and Law School Plagiarism," 49 J.Legal Educ. 236 (1999).

Levine, Jan M., "Symposium on Legal Education: Response: "You Can't Please Everyone, So You'd Better Please Yourself: Directing (or Teachin In) A First-Year Legal Writing Program," 29 Val. U. L. Rev. 611 (1995).

Lindgren, James & Seltzer, Daniel, "The Most Prolific Law Professors and Faculty," 71 Chi-Kent L. Rev. 781 (1996).

Mikva, Abner J., "Law Reviews, Judicial Opinions, and Their Relationship to Writing," 30 Stetson L. Rev. 521 (2000).

Mirow, M.C., "Confronting Inadvertent Plagiarism," Perspectives: Teaching Legal Research and Writing (Winter 1998).

Schneider, Alison, "Why Professors Don't Do More to Stop Students Who Cheat," The Chronicle of Higher Education, January 22, 1999 at A8.

Sloan, Bart, "What Are We Writing For? Student Works As Authority and Their Citation by the Federal Bench, 1986-1990," 61 Geo. Wash. L. Rev. 221 (1992).

Swygert, Michael I. & Bruce, Jon W., "The Historical Origins, Founding, and Early Development of Student-Edited Law Reviews," 36 Hastings L.J. 739 (1985).

Yarbrough, Marilyn V., "A Nation Under Lost Lawyers: The Legal Profession at the Close of the Twentieth Century: Do As I Say, Not As I Do: Mixed Messages for Law Students," 100 Dick. L. Rev. 677 (1996).

Zimmermann, Reinhard, "Law Reviews: A Foray Through A Strange World," 47 Emory L.J. 659 (1998).

Index

A

Academic credit, 19, 42, 75, 291, 304, 306, 313, 318, 331, 332
Academic fraud, 75, 93
Academic honors, 145
Academic privacy, 109, 145
Albany Law School Journal, 272, 273
Allen, Woody, 124
Alumni, 7, 18, 42, 59, 62, 68, 77, 98, 116, 117, 122, 123, 155, 171, 177, 198, 199, 200, 201, 208, 210, 213, 215, 218, 219, 221, 223, 227, 240, 241, 242, 243, 244, 261, 266, 275, 276, 277
American Lawyer Top 100, 232
Anniversary Edition, 273
Article selection, 129, 203, 291, 327, 329
Authors, 1, 2, 12, 13, 20, 54, 55, 65, 68, 69, 70, 71, 81, 82, 84, 93, 102, 113, 117, 124, 130, 131, 137, 139, 155, 160, 161, 167, 180, 187, 188, 190, 206, 216, 219, 220, 226, 241, 242, 243, 246, 249, 251, 254, 258, 265, 281, 282, 290, 303, 305, 306, 325, 327, 329
Avoiding plagiarism, 99
Awards, 10, 15, 98, 209, 221, 224, 231, 234, 235, 236, 300

B

Back issue, 118
Bar Bri, 131
Bar exam, 2, 4, 29, 127, 155, 183, 221, 223, 224, 225, 226, 227, 228, 238, 248, 249
Bar review, 131, 258
Beer, 9, 24, 25, 40, 100, 101, 113, 202, 203, 205, 211, 215
Bieber's Dictionary of Legal Citations, 77
Big East basketball, 148
Black's Law Dictionary, 68, 74, 77, 122, 228, 229, 270
Bluebook, 6, 7, 20, 22, 23, 28, 29, 30, 40, 43, 52, 63, 84, 85, 135, 151, 178, 191, 249, 256, 299, 300, 301, 302, 303, 307, 308, 326, 334
Bluebooking, 3, 299, 301, 302
Bound volume, 307
Bowers v. Hardwick, 142
Brandeis, Louis D., Justice, 202, 275, 281, 293
Brooks v. United States, 244
Buckley Amendment, 145, 300
Burton Foundation, 224, 228, 234, 300
Burton, William C., 224, 225, 226, 228, 230, 231, 232, 234, 235, 236, 300
Burton's Legal Thesaurus, 232
Bylaws, 300, 311, 313, 315, 316, 317, 324, 325, 326, 330, 331, 332, 333, 335